PRINT, PUBLICITY, AND RADICALISM IN THE

Jon Mee explores the popular democratic movement that emerged in the London of the 1790s in response to the French Revolution. Central to the movement's achievement was the creation of an idea of 'the people' brought into being through print and publicity. Radical clubs rose and fell in the face of the hostile attentions of government. They were sustained by a faith in the press as a form of 'print magic', but confidence in the liberating potential of the printing press was interwoven with hard-headed deliberations over how best to animate and represent the people. Ideas of disinterested rational debate were thrown into the mix with coruscating satire, rousing songs, and republican toasts. Print personality became a vital interface between readers and text exploited by the cast of radicals returned to history in vivid detail by *Print, Publicity, and Popular Radicalism*. This title is available as Open Access at 10.1017/9781316459935.

JON MEE is Professor of Eighteenth-Century Studies at the University of York and Director of the Centre for Eighteenth-Century Studies. He has published many essays and books on the literature, culture, and politics of the age of revolutions in the late eighteenth and early nineteenth centuries. He is also author of *The Cambridge Introduction to Charles Dickens* (Cambridge, 2010).

CAMBRIDGE STUDIES IN ROMANTICISM

This series aims to foster the best new work in one of the most challenging fields within English literary studies. From the early 1780s to the early 1830s a formidable array of talented men and women took to literary composition, not just in poetry, which some of them famously transformed, but in many modes of writing. The expansion of publishing created new opportunities for writers, and the political stakes of what they wrote were raised again by what Wordsworth called those 'great national events' that were 'almost daily taking place': the French Revolution, the Napoleonic and American wars, urbanisation, industrialisation, religious revival, an expanded empire abroad, and the reform movement at home. This was an enormous ambition, even when it pretended otherwise. The relations between science, philosophy, religion, and literature were reworked in texts such as *Frankenstein* and *Biographia Literaria*; gender relations in *A Vindication of the Rights of Woman* and *Don Juan*; journalism by Cobbett and Hazlitt; poetic form, content and style by the Lake School and the Cockney School. Outside Shakespeare studies, probably no body of writing has produced such a wealth of comment or done so much to shape the responses of modern criticism. This indeed is the period that saw the emergence of those notions of 'literature' and of literary history, especially national literary history, on which modern scholarship in English has been founded.

The categories produced by Romanticism have also been challenged by recent historicist arguments. The task of the series is to engage both with a challenging corpus of Romantic writings and with the changing field of criticism they have helped to shape. As with other literary series published by Cambridge, this one will represent the work of both younger and more established scholars, on either side of the Atlantic and elsewhere.

For a complete list of titles published see end of book.

PRINT, PUBLICITY, AND POPULAR RADICALISM IN THE 1790S

The Laurel of Liberty

JON MEE

CAMBRIDGE
UNIVERSITY PRESS

CAMBRIDGE
UNIVERSITY PRESS

University Printing House, Cambridge CB2 8BS, United Kingdom

One Liberty Plaza, 20th Floor, New York, NY 10006, USA

477 Williamstown Road, Port Melbourne, VIC 3207, Australia

314-321, 3rd Floor, Plot 3, Splendor Forum, Jasola District Centre, New Delhi - 110025, India

79 Anson Road, #06-04/06, Singapore 079906

Cambridge University Press is part of the University of Cambridge.

It furthers the University's mission by disseminating knowledge in the pursuit of education, learning and research at the highest international levels of excellence.

www.cambridge.org
Information on this title: www.cambridge.org/9781107590083

When citing this work, please include a reference to the DOI [10.1017/9781316459935].

First published 2016
First paperback edition 2018

A catalogue record for this publication is available from the British Library

Library of Congress Cataloging in Publication data
Names: Mee, Jon, author.
Title: Print, publicity, and popular radicalism in the 1790s : the laurel of liberty / Jon Mee.
Description: Cambridge ; New York : Cambridge University Press, 2016. | Series: Cambridge Studies in Romanticism ; 112 | Includes bibliographical references and index.
Identifiers: LCCN 2016006099 | ISBN 9781107133617 (Hardback : alk. paper)
Subjects: LCSH: Mass media and public opinion–Great Britain–History–18th century. | Mass media and publicity–Great Britain–History–18th century. | Radicalism–England–History–18th century. | Politics and literature–England–History–18th century. | Popular culture–Great Britain–History–18th century.
Classification: LCC P96.P832 G736 2016 | DDC 302.23/2094109033–dc23
LC record available at https://lccn.loc.gov/2016006099

ISBN 978-1-107-13361-7 Hardback
ISBN 978-1-107-59008-3 Paperback

For
Marilyn Butler

Contents

Illustrations

Acknowledgements

> And nothing starts in the archive, nothing, ever at all, though things certainly end up there. You find nothing in the Archive but stories caught half way through: the middle of things; discontinuities
>
> (Carolyn Steedman, *Dust*)

My own strain of archive fever has driven this project forward for nearly three decades. The final periods of intensive research were made possible by an AHRC Fellowship that gave me invaluable time at the British Library, the National Archives, Kew, and in the Seligman Collection at Columbia University. I'd like to thank the archivists and librarians at these institutions and also the Bodleian Library, the Henry E. Huntington Library, the John Rylands Library, the Lewis Walpole Library, Nuffield College, Oxford, and Worcester College, Oxford. I am also grateful to the Leverhulme Trust for funding the 'Networks of Improvement' project. My work on associations in the late eighteenth century for the project has fed directly into this book.

I can easily recover the book's moment of inception. It came when reading E. P. Thompson's *The Making of the English Working Class* as an undergraduate in 1981, but my fascination with the subject matter was sealed when Marilyn Butler very kindly lent me the manuscript of Iain McCalman's *Radical Underworld* to read as a Ph.D. student. My debts to Marilyn, who is deeply missed by everyone, are many and varied, but few compare to this introduction to a lasting and inspiring friend. Soon afterwards, Marilyn also introduced me to Mark Philp whose encouragement and inspiration also pervade these pages. Near the end of the research, he and I spent some happy days in the Treasury Solicitor's papers hunting down radicals. I was lucky to have the fruit of his research, in the shape of *Reforming Ideas in Britain*, to see me through the final year of writing this book.

Final preparation of the manuscript was completed at the Centre for Eighteenth-Century Studies at the University of York, where I followed in the footsteps of John Barrell and Harriet Guest. The staff have been highly supportive in all kinds of ways, not least in providing continual food for thought in relation to the material in this book. The centre has been an immensely stimulating environment to work in and I'd like to thank Mary Fairclough, Mark Jenner, Catriona Kennedy, Emma Major, Alison O'Byrne, Jane Rendall, Jim Walvin, and Jim Watt for directly contributing advice and ideas. Clare Bond has been a particular point of sanity. I look forward to drawing on their time and patience for years to come. I'd also like to thank the English Department at York, especially David Attwell, and the F. R. Leavis Fund for its help with illustrations.

Gillian Russell has been crucial to this book as a friend and colleague. I'd like to thank her for including me on her Australian Research Council grant. Gillian and Kate Horgan generously shared their discoveries from the archives of the London Corresponding Society (LCS). The grant allowed me to visit Australia more than once and I am grateful to John and Mary Ann Hughes for their hospitality in Sydney. Deirdre Coleman, Susan Conley, and Clara Tuite always make Melbourne a wonderful place to visit. Michael T. Davis's work on the LCS has been an important source for this book. I am grateful to him for all the help he has given. I look forward to his forthcoming study of Daniel Isaac Eaton. John Seed gave me lots of useful tips, not least in relation to Lord Gordon and the Protestant Association. He alerted me to the name 'Thomas Hardy' on the petition of the Protestant Association. David Worrall's work on radical culture and more recently on the theatre has always been illuminating. Most recently, Susan Snell, Archivist at the Library and Museum of Freemasonry, gave me some fascinating pointers to relations between the LCS and the masons. The topic deserves further study than was possible in this book. Working on the 1790s has produced a lot of happy collaborations and a genuine sense that the material discussed in this book will be developed and taken forward by a number of younger scholars who have already been gracious in discussing their research with me. David Fallon, James Grande, Georgina Green, Ian Newman, David O'Shaughnessy, and Yasmin Solomonescu have been especially helpful. No one can work in the archive of the Royal Literary Fund without benefiting from Matthew Sangster's help. Penelope Corfield and Amanda Goodrich have given me thoughtful advice on the material in this book more than once. Colin Jones and Simon MacDonald generously shared some of their discoveries relating to Robert Thomson in Paris. Joanna Innes has often said things that made me think twice. Rachel Rogers was very helpful on the British in Paris more generally, not least in relation to Robert Merry's writing about the French constitution. Pamela Clemit has always been helpful, especially with Godwin's letters. Amy Garnai has regularly shared her version of the Merry bug with me in conversation. Thanks also to Robert Jones and David Taylor for finally explaining the 'arrows' in Merry's hat.

I am also grateful to Tom Mole and the other participants in the 'Interpersonal Print' conference at McGill in 2013 who helped clarify some of my ideas around 'print magic'. See http://interactingwithprint.org/ for an account of the full breadth of the ongoing 'Interacting with Print' project. Various trips to California have also allowed me to present papers and discuss ideas over the past two decades. Usually these have been hosted either by Kevin Gilmartin or Saree Makdisi. I'm grateful to both for providing such enlivening contexts for me to discuss and present my work. Returning to Kevin's writing on popular radicalism after 1815 in the later stages of preparing this book provided a great stimulus for my thinking about radical culture in the 1790s. Helen Deutsch has always been hospitable and encouraging. Michael Meranze was always just about tolerant of the detail. Roxanne Eberle generously shared her knowledge of Amelia Alderson with me. Sarah Knott alerted me to Pigott's involvement in Coghlan's memoirs, and gave me the chance to read a draft of her article on 'female liberty'.

Some of the material, especially in Part II, has been discussed in essays and articles published over the past twenty years or so. I am grateful to the editors in each case for their advice and support; details can be found in the bibliography. Thanks also to James Chandler, Linda Bree, and Anna Bond for shepherding me through the press. I'm also grateful to the readers who provided the reports that enabled me to focus my argument more clearly through the last stage of writing. Most of all I am grateful to Jane, Sharmila, and the rest of my family, not least for putting up with my mind being on the Treasury Solicitor's papers, when it should more often have been on them.

Note on references

Where manuscripts are reproduced in Mary Thale's *Selections from the Papers of the London Corresponding Society*, then I have used it as a reference to make access easier for the reader. Otherwise I have referred to the original manuscripts in either the British Library or National Archives. See notes and bibliography for details of the individual manuscripts.

Bibliographical references to printed materials are given in short form in the notes with full details in the bibliography, newspapers and periodicals excepted, where details are provided in the relevant note, or sometimes simply by date in the main text in the case of eighteenth-century newspapers.

Abbreviations

AUM	*American Universal Magazine*
Barrell and Mee	*Trials for Treason and Sedition, 1792–1794*, ed. John Barrell and Jon Mee. 8 vols. London: Pickering & Chatto, 2006–7
IKD	John Barrell, *Imagining the King's Death: Figurative Treason, Fantasies of Regicide 1793–1796*. Oxford University Press, 2000
LCS	London Corresponding Society
LT	Thelwall, Mrs [Henrietta Cecil], *The Life of John Thelwall, by his Widow*. Vol. 1, *London: 1837*
MPM	*Moral and Political Magazine of the LCS*. 2 vols. London, 1796–7
SCI	Society for Constitutional Information
Selections	*Selections from the Papers of the London Corresponding Society 1792–1799*, ed Mary Thale. Cambridge University Press, 1983

Introduction: the open theatre of the world?

The French Revolution was widely regarded at the time as an unprecedented event. One unexpected consequence in London was the emergence of a remarkably rich and vibrant popular radical culture. Enthusiasm for this phenomenon may often steer my tone towards the celebratory, but this book aims to give a sense of the aspirations, complexities, and contradictions involved in the creation of a broad-based movement for radical change in Britain. The story of the radical societies has been told before, primarily by political historians, usually in relation to the unfolding of larger narratives of the struggle for parliamentary reform or the creation of working-class consciousness. Those narratives are important here, but my approach is particularly concerned with the emergence of popular radicalism through experiment, contestation, and performance, especially in its relations to the medium of print and the associational world that surrounded it. Print is taken in this book to have been a condition of possibility for a popular radical platform, creating the circumstances for London to act as the major clearing house of ideas and as the organisational centre of a movement spread across the four nations of Britain. Print made it possible to think of consulting and mediating what Thelwall called 'the whole will of the nation'.[1] Beyond their practical engagement with the medium, the participants themselves shared important assumptions and ideas about print, not least the deep faith they frequently showed in its efficacy as an agent of emancipation. This faith tended towards a form of magical thinking when it assumed a power in the medium regardless of causative relations.[2]

The passing of the Two Acts in 1795 severely curtailed the activities of the popular societies and provides a partial endpoint to this study. The Acts made it impossible for meetings of more than fifty people to gather without the explicit permission of a magistrate and increased the punishments for what were deemed seditious activities. Leaving aside the implications for the law of treason, so eloquently discussed by John Barrell, the

Seditious Meetings Bill had grave repercussions for the kinds of events the LCS could undertake and the kinds of spaces it could operate in.[3] There was a sense in the country at large that the guiding spirit of reform was being threatened with extinction, even though the LCS was not actually banned until 1799. In the build up to the 1795 legislation, Robert Sands wrote from Perth about the difficult part London had been given to play in what he called 'the Comedy of Regeneration':

> We look up to the London Corresponding Society, and the Others who have affiliated with them. We know the whole depends on their exertions and that without them nothing can be done. It is an old doctrine of mine that the Metropolis is the same to a Nation as the heart is to the body: it is the seat of life. If it is pure the whole body must be so, and vice versa. If the Chanel [sic] of corruption is not stopt [sic] in London, you cannot expect it to be so in Perth or anywhere else.[4]

Relations between regional societies and those in London were not as straightforward or as deferential as this may sound. More than once even provincial English societies refused to comply fully with the protocols that the LCS sent them, as was the case with the Tewkesbury Society discussed in Chapter 2. The LCS itself was sometimes subject to internal conflict, for instance, when it came to relations between the executive and its divisions. Nevertheless these tensions themselves speak to the key role London played in the creation of a popular radical platform out of material practices embedded in complex social relations.

Placing this study within the series 'Cambridge Studies in Romanticism' implies an understanding of popular radicalism as a kind of 'literary' culture. At least, it argues for the centrality of the writing, production, and circulation of printed texts that took up so much of the time of the radical societies. If aspects of this approach are 'literary' in general terms, the book is not intended to provide a backdrop to Romanticism and its major poets, novelists, and playwrights.[5] In certain respects, this formation and the associated identification of the literary with what John Thelwall called 'sallies of the imagination' were the product of a crisis brought on by the emergence of the popular radical culture opened up in this book, but the story is not a straightforward one. Thelwall himself could identify 'literature' both with a domain of imagination separable from politics and with print as the principal engine of emancipatory change.[6] My aim has been to pay attention to the everyday labours of the radical societies in creating a public sphere through print and associated practices, from poring over the proper forms of addresses to be issued in their names to penning songs and toasts for tavern meetings.[7] Robert Thomson's efforts writing and collecting for the LCS songs – discussed in Chapter 2 – may represent an uncanny parallel to his brother George's work with Robert Burns, but for all the reorientation to popular melodies in polite taste at this time political songs were rarely allowed into the realm of the 'literary'.[8] The lyrical or literary ballad, as Ian Newman has shown, was increasingly severed from the convivial space of the alehouse in the emergent cultural field scholars now identify with Romanticism.[9] Ironically, for some members of the LCS, Francis Place among them, such activities were too raucous to be regarded as properly within the republic of letters. On these terms, the identification of 'literature' with improvement could separate it from Thomson's songs and toasts just as effectively as the idea that it belonged primarily to an interiorised realm of the imagination.

In terms of those who frequented and created this culture, the picture that emerges is not one peopled solely by 'the radical artisan' often associated with E. P. Thompson's *Making of the English Working Class*.[10] This divergence may be accentuated by my focus on print and its associated practices, but it also speaks to a period when radical discourse was largely concerned with a split between the represented and the unrepresented, between a narrow identification of the political nation with the elite and a broader idea of 'the people'.[11] Many of the subaltern classes who involved themselves in the popular societies did not have easy access to the medium of print because they could not write or sometimes even read. Nevertheless, they frequently interacted with print by hearing pamphlets and newspaper paragraphs read aloud at meetings or joining in with songs that were circulated on printed sheets. The popular societies were made up of a broad social range from what Thomas Hardy called 'the lower and middling class of society called the people'.[12] The LCS's collaboration for most of the period 1792–5 with the more polite Society for Constitutional Information (SCI) only further complicates these social issues.

Within this broad formation there were a number of 'gentleman' radicals, such as Joseph Gerrald, who were members of both societies. Gerrald became a flamboyant hero of the struggle in 1793; his fate – transportation to Botany Bay and an early death – made him a print celebrity to the radical societies in 1794–5 and beyond. Gerrald seems to have been associated with another gentleman, Robert Merry, an SCI member active in the collaborations with the LCS in 1792, even if he never joined the more popular society. Gerrald and Merry had both been students of Samuel Parr, 'the Whig Dr. Johnson', attended SCI meetings together in 1792, and came to know and be influenced by Parr's friend

Godwin. The progressive education both received from Parr seems to have taken fire at the French Revolution and driven them into contact with men from very different social backgrounds.[13] Friends of Merry saw in this process – discussed in detail in Chapter 3 – a fundamental loss of social identity:

> The change in his political opinions gave a sullen gloom to his character which made him relinquish all his former connexions, and unite with people far beneath his talents, and quite unsuitable to his habits.[14]

A more precipitous descent can be traced in Charles Pigott – tracked in Chapter 4 – with whom Gerrald and Merry both associated. By February 1794, isolated after being discharged from prison, Pigott was a member of the LCS, but also touting for as much hackwork as he could get, producing a spurious volume of scandalous memoirs and the scabrous attacks on aristocratic women in the *Female Jockey Club*, before his death from prison fever. His personal circumstances in 1794 may have driven Pigott further in this direction, but in terms of their later populist orientation it is worth noting that both he and Merry were using the newspapers to communicate their opinions from at least as early as the 1780s. They were well aware – as Merry put it to Samuel Rogers – of the effects of a 'daily insinuation' in the press.[15]

The popular radical movement often owned these elite activists with pride, not without serious reservations in Pigott's case, but respect for literary talents with the pen did not simply translate into social deference. The shoemaker Thomas Hardy was the key figure of the 1792–4 period, prior to the treason trials. Highly literate, purposeful, and well read in the canon of English liberty, he learned from Scottish Presbyterian traditions that placed a high premium on modest confidence in one's own abilities.[16] Hardy doesn't seem to have felt any desire to be known as an author or even the founder of the society. Thelwall, on the other hand, claimed for himself a genteel ancestry, and had already struggled to make a way for himself as a writer and editor after abortive careers as a silk mercer, a tailor, and a lawyer. Thelwall never abandoned his literary aspirations, even if at different times in his life they seemed to lie in a far from simple relation to his politics.

Others who merit more extended treatment than constraints of space will allow in this book include William Hamilton Reid. In the 1780s, Reid – 'the son of persons occupying no higher status than that of domestic servants' – had been puffed as the English Burns by the newspaper editor James Perry.[17] He was soon supplying copy at a penny a line for the *Gazetteer*, especially translations of continental news, along with poetry and songs. For the LCS, where he was active from at least June 1792, he knocked out productions like 'Hum! Hum! A New Song' shown here (Figure 1). Reid seems to have seceded from the LCS in 1795 for religious reasons, joining the shadowy group sometimes known as the Society for Moral and Political Knowledge. Driven underground after the Two Acts, he was arrested at one of their meetings in February 1798. Even then he continued to pursue an aspiration to write, bringing out *The rise and dissolution of the infidel societies in this metropolis* (1800), with the support of the bishops of Durham and London, before turning his coat once again to publish a biography of the SCI leader John Horne Tooke.[18]

Religion remained an important aspect of print culture for W. H. Reid throughout his literary career, as it did for the clerk Richard 'Citizen' Lee, who first appeared in print as the religious poet 'Ebenezer', before the period of a few months transformed him into Citizen Lee, a journey traced more fully in Chapter 5. Thelwall, Reid, and Lee all aspired to authorship before they joined the popular societies. Others seem to have first found their voice via their involvement. John Baxter, for instance, followed up the pamphlet *Resistance to Oppression* (1795), discussed in Chapter 2, with *A new and impartial history of England* (1796) dedicated to the efforts of the LCS. Numerous others unknown must have written songs, helped frame addresses, and so on. Not all aspired to become authors; a few sustained a position as writers, several (or their widows) later applied to the Literary Fund for relief, including Reid and his fellow LCS songwriter Robert Thomson. Literary aspirations were not necessarily the equivalent of a desire for self-expression that placed a premium on the individual over the struggle. Men like Reid and Thelwall may have been first drawn to a career in print on the assumption that the republic of letters in its proper form was a sphere open to talents underwritten by the freedom of the press, but they soon discovered that this was far from the case and pressed for a more genuinely accessible domain.

In so far as they can be reconstructed from the archive, these backstories also indicate that the popular radicalism of the 1790s was the product of forces that reached back before 1789, even as they were crucially influenced by the sense of the French Revolution as an unprecedented event. The Revolution was both a sign such men had been expecting, a fulfilment of a spirit of progress they believed they were sustaining, and something that required them to rethink their relations to power. Synchronically, radicalism in the 1790s was not the expression of a coherent ideological code or language, but the product of the social practices of the surrounding culture

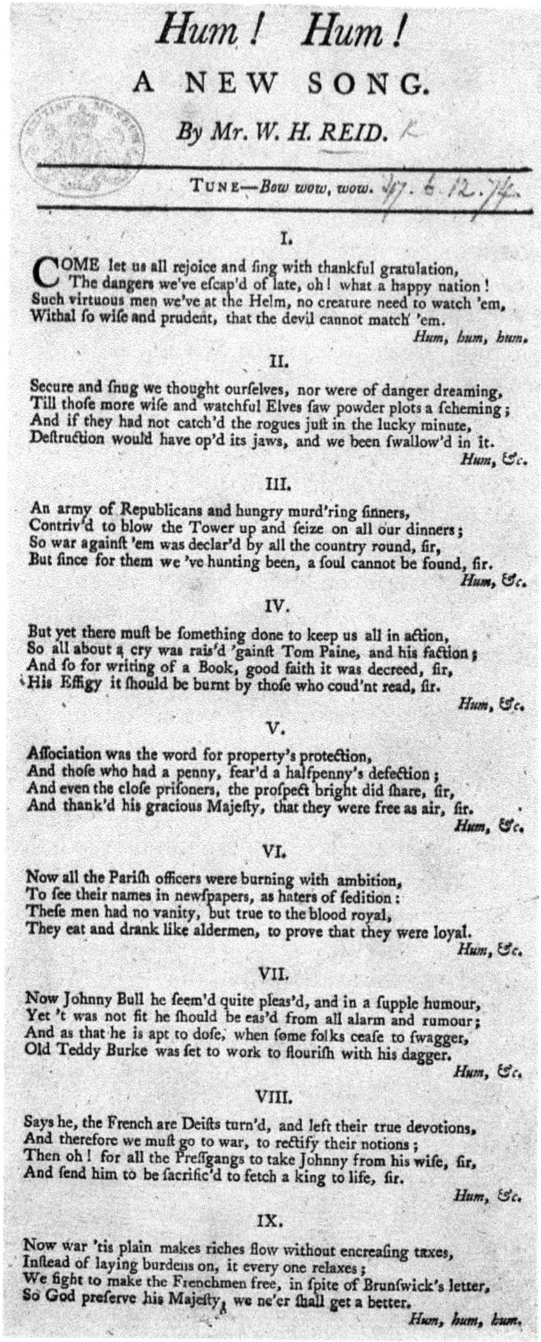

Hum! Hum!

A NEW SONG.

By Mr. W. H. REID.

TUNE—*Bow wow, wow.*

I.

COME let us all rejoice and ſing with thankful gratulation,
The dangers we've eſcap'd of late, oh! what a happy nation!
Such virtuous men we've at the Helm, no creature need to watch 'em,
Withal ſo wiſe and prudent, that the devil cannot match 'em.
Hum, hum, hum.

II.

Secure and ſnug we thought ourſelves, nor were of danger dreaming,
Till thoſe more wiſe and watchful Elves ſaw powder plots a ſcheming;
And if they had not catch'd the rogues juſt in the lucky minute,
Deſtruction would have op'd its jaws, and we been ſwallow'd in it.
Hum, &c.

III.

An army of Republicans and hungry murd'ring ſinners,
Contriv'd to blow the Tower up and ſeize on all our dinners;
So war againſt 'em was declar'd by all the country round, ſir,
But ſince for them we 've hunting been, a ſoul cannot be found, ſir.
Hum, &c.

IV.

But yet there muſt be ſomething done to keep us all in action,
So all about a cry was rais'd 'gainſt Tom Paine, and his faction;
And ſo for writing of a Book, good faith it was decreed, ſir,
His Effigy it ſhould be burnt by thoſe who coud'nt read, ſir.
Hum, &c.

V.

Aſſociation was the word for property's protection,
And thoſe who had a penny, fear'd a halfpenny's defection;
And even the cloſe priſoners, the proſpect bright did ſhare, ſir,
And thank'd his gracious Majeſty, that they were free as air, ſir.
Hum, &c.

VI.

Now all the Pariſh officers were burning with ambition,
To ſee their names in newſpapers, as haters of ſedition:
Theſe men had no vanity, but true to the blood royal,
They eat and drank like aldermen, to prove that they were loyal.
Hum, &c.

VII.

Now Johnny Bull he ſeem'd quite pleas'd, and in a ſupple humour,
Yet 't was not fit he ſhould be eas'd from all alarm and rumour;
And as that he is apt to doſe, when ſome folks ceaſe to ſwagger,
Old Teddy Burke was ſet to work to flouriſh with his dagger.
Hum, &c.

VIII.

Says he, the French are Deiſts turn'd, and left their true devotions,
And therefore we muſt go to war, to rectify their notions;
Then oh! for all the Preſſgangs to take Johnny from his wife, ſir,
And ſend him to be ſacrific'd to fetch a king to life, ſir.
Hum, &c.

IX.

Now war 'tis plain makes riches flow without encreaſing taxes,
Inſtead of laying burdens on, it every one relaxes;
We fight to make the Frenchmen free, in ſpite of Brunſwick's letter,
So God preſerve his Majeſty, we ne'er ſhall get a better.
Hum, hum, hum.

Fig 1 W. H. Reid, 'Hum! Hum! A New Song' [1793].

reacting to events and ideas. This book understands radical culture as a complex and unstable field of forces, 'fragmented' as Mark Philp has it, reacting to events in France, and indeed to global forces and events; seeking to influence change in Britain and aspiring to influence change in a wider world.[19]

For many of those involved, books were regarded as a principal agent of political change, sharing Louis Mercier's belief that Thomas Paine's *Common Sense* (1776) had not only roused the American colonists but also provided 'a general shock to the political world, which has given birth to a great empire, and a new order of things'.[20] This idea was reinforced by the general explosion of print in the final decades of the eighteenth century and the rapid development of an infrastructure that enabled the transmission of knowledge.[21] Most historians of print identify a takeoff in the number of imprints from as early as the 1760s.[22] Nevertheless the trade was far from industrialised, print runs were relatively small, and booksellers and printers – many of whom joined the radical societies – often provided a close-knit form of interaction with writers and readers of a sort noted many times in these pages. The idea of a political society as the hub for the creation, collection, and dissemination of political information in print was a defining feature of both the SCI and the LCS. Both societies also eagerly exploited formats that had been extending the reach of the press, especially newspapers and periodicals, acting upon a widespread belief that they had become integral to the political process. 'But, gradually, they have assumed a more extensive office', wrote the *New Annual Register* in 1782, 'they have become the vehicles of political discussion in a far higher degree than they formerly were, and, in this respect, they have acquired a national importance.'[23] Some members of the radical societies, as we have already seen, had already exploited these media in the 1780s and were to continue to exploit them in the 1790s. The LCS used newspapers to advertise its meetings and was very close to Sampson Perry's newspaper the *Argus*, at least in 1792, and then the *Courier* and the *Telegraph* in 1794–5. In terms of periodicals, the LCS twice attempted to compete in the market for information with its own: the short-lived *Politician* that struggled into life at the end of 1794, and the marginally more successful *Moral and Political Magazine* (1796–7).

Various associational practices had become interwoven with such formats over the course of the eighteenth century. Periodicals frequently reported the activities of clubs and societies, which often formed themselves around subscriptions. Books clubs and reading societies circulated their rules and regulations, sometimes printed in periodicals, producing a high degree of uniformity across their activities.[24] Many of the protocols of the SCI and the LCS were governed by these emergent general conditions for interacting with print. Except for the fact that many reading societies banned the discussion of politics and controversial religion in their rules, the first gathering of Thomas Hardy and his friends in the Bell in January 1792 looks like just such a group. Hardy's decision in 1806 to donate his political pamphlets to the Mitcham Book Society seems to acknowledge the continuities. Songs and toasts were an important aspect of the structured conviviality of the associational world more generally. The vigour supplied by Robert Thomson's songs and toasts seems to have saved LCS divisions threatening to fold in 1792. Although oral performance was central to the vivifying effects they had on dwindling divisions, bringing those who could not read into the associational world, circulation of songs and toasts around the society often depended on print. The medium also allowed Thomson and others to reproduce songs for LCS meetings that had previously been used in very different social milieux.

Print was often taken to be the precondition for discussion and debate. In his account of the enlightening effects of the printing press, Thelwall concurred with his lawyer John Gurney that 'the invention of printing had introduced political discussion'.[25] Although written correspondence between societies across the postal network was a key form of circulation, handled by Hardy in the important position of secretary until 1794, he understood the printing of the LCS's first *Address* in 1792 as the moment when it became public. Both the SCI and the LCS self-consciously presented themselves as nodes via which radical opinion in the country could enter into dialogue, creating a space in which the popular will could come to know itself. More than once, as with the Tewkesbury Society, the LCS invited groups to adapt their forms and practices and even change their names to become corresponding societies after the image of the parent society. Resistance to such proposals sprang from an anxiety about forms of organisation that might slide into another version of the 'virtual representation' that its members associated with aristocratic despotism.[26]

At certain points the societies seem to operate under the spell of 'print magic', that is, a faith that print could liberate mankind simply by bringing ideas into printed circulation. In terms of a distinction made by William Warner, this could appear to be a dream of 'communication' over 'transmission', whereby differences of time and place are overcome in a republic of letters imagined as a transparent and unified domain of the circulation of ideas.[27] Frequently, 'print magic' provided the societies with a sustaining myth, a confidence in a deep logic that bonded print to progress and positioned any political defeat as a merely local matter. Several autobiographies from the period attest to the transformative effects of the encounter with print in the 1790s, and situate individual narratives of improvement within a larger narrative of liberty. Nevertheless faith in print magic coexisted with a serious attention to the everyday labours of composition, production, and circulation. This attentiveness to transmission was reinforced by the legal architecture governing the circulation of knowledge and opinion. In the form of the various laws governing opinion, especially seditious libel and, ultimately as it turned out, the law of treason, these legal constraints, for all their inefficiency, had serious effects on the forms that radical print culture could take. Prosecutions soon forced the LCS and SCI to be bitterly aware, if they were not already, of the difficulties of transmission, the intricacies of mediation that needed detailed work on forms and modes, whether to avoid prosecution or, more positively, to find the most appropriate forms of representation for the popular will. Their members often exploited these formal possibilities brilliantly, not least in their development of the rich tradition of satire and pasquinade they had inherited from the earlier eighteenth century.

Part I of this book explores these conditions of mediation. Chapter 1 is concerned with the key concepts of print and publicity and their relation to complicating issues of space and gender. The spatial politics of London placed its own constraints on the LCS.[28] The basic need to find venues where it could meet in the face of pressure from local authorities was one important factor. After the Royal Proclamation of May 1792 landlords were increasingly threatened with the loss of their licences (and their livelihoods) if they provided a home for the radical societies. The LCS fought to find a place for itself in the diversified social geography of eighteenth-century London. Beyond the practical exigencies of finding somewhere to meet, it was insisting on its place before the public, refusing to fulfil the account of its activities as inherently underground and conspiratorial. This response need not be understood only as a reaction to external pressures that invested in 'respectability'. Thomas Hardy had some sharp things to say about conventional understandings of that word in his memoirs. There is no reason to think that the LCS did not understand itself to belong properly within the public sphere. It regularly demonstrated that it was open to inspection, not simply to defend itself from slurs that it was conspiratorial, but because it was committed to what Thomas Paine called 'the open theatre of the world'.[29] Among those public spaces was the theatre itself, where members protested from within the audience and leafleted in the foyers as well as writing plays.

As with much of the broader associational world of clubs and societies, women seem to have played little official part in the popular radical societies, despite Robert Thomson's toast to 'patriotic females' in his *Tribute to Liberty* (1792).[30] Nevertheless, this study aims to restore a sense of the female presence in popular radical culture, even if individual women are mainly glimpsed only in the interstices of LCS activity. Susan Thelwall attended debates with her husband and provided commentary to her family on the development of radical opinion in London. Eliza Frost publicly denied the government's claims about her husband. Susannah Eaton ran her husband's shop when he was in prison or in hiding. John Reeves complained of her 'particular parade' in selling libels for which her husband was in prison.[31] In 1793 the LCS encouraged a 'female Society of Patriots', noted in Chapter 1, but no record of it ever meeting survives. 'Female citizens' did attend the general meetings of 1795 and anonymously addressed the publications of the societies. More generally, though, the LCS seems to have conformed to masculine definitions of citizenship and related practices, not least in the homosocial environment of singing and toasting at dinners. Predictably perhaps given these perspectives, the part played in Lydia Hardy's death by events surrounding her husband's arrest was presented as a deep intrusion into the domestic realm. Such intrusions provided a trope that had an important role to play in Thelwall's writing, where the domestic sphere was often represented as the moral ground of his political character.

Chapter 2 takes a chronological route through 1792–5, tracing the way in which print formats and practices were elaborated and tested across different popular radical groups, especially in relation to the experience of the LCS and its members as they responded to events in Britain, France, and the wider world. At the heart of these responses a fundamental question of representation and mediation faced the popular societies. How were they to identify and give form to the 'general will' of the people? Rousseau had understood the 'general will' to be unrepresentable in theory. The British system of representation, he avowed, reverted to a form of slavery after each election: 'Every law that is not confirmed by the people in person is null and void.'[32] Despite their commitment to a programme of universal suffrage within the British system, the popular radical societies did not necessarily accept Parliament as the final horizon of their endeavours. The commitment to the circulation of political information in the societies accepted Rousseau's assumption that 'the general will is always right, but the judgment by which it is directed is not always sufficiently informed'.[33] Thelwall for one was aware of a tension between the idea of 'the scattered million' and 'the people' the societies wished to represent.[34] In 1795, the bookseller and LCS member Daniel Isaac Eaton brought out an edition of Rousseau's *Social Compact* in his Political Classics series, but there is no reason to assume it provided the theoretical basis for the approach to these questions in the British popular societies.[35] In terms of their everyday practice, the primary focus of this book, the radical societies encouraged an ongoing process of debate indebted to Paine's idea that 'discussion and the general will, arbitrates the question, and to this private opinion yields with a good grace, and order is preserved uninterrupted'.[36] They self-consciously tasked themselves with what Seth Cotlar calls 'the difficult process of constructing and sustaining an incessantly deliberative, politically efficacious and professedly inclusive mechanism for forming and discerning the general will'.[37]

Plenty of those in and around the popular radical movements were aware both of the theoretical arguments of Rousseau and of their influence on the French Revolution. Robert Merry and David Williams were directly involved in framing constitutions in the context of the French National Convention in 1792. Debates between the LCS and SCI early in 1794 about consulting more broadly with other radical societies reached deadlock over the word 'convention'. To some, it simply implied a canvassing of opinion, but to others it represented a more significant step towards new forms of mediation for the will of the people. Pitt's government chose to see their meetings in the worst possible light, identifying their goal as an anti-parliament. If the delegates from the two societies do not seem to have been very close to making any such claim themselves, wrangling within the LCS continued through 1794 and 1795 about its own constitution, especially the relation of the divisions to the executive. Some members – Thelwall included – argued that any form of constitution represented a usurpation of the rights of the divisions. Possibly informed by Godwin's thinking in Thelwall's case, there seems to have been a line of thought within the LCS that continuously aimed at the devolution of power. One might see in these various debates 'the rudiments of a deliberative theory of publicity' that Gilmartin discusses in relation to British radicalism after 1815. Ernesto Laclau's idea of 'populist reason' and its permanent negotiation of heteronomy and autonomy might even be glimpsed in the LCS decision ultimately not to impose its forms and methods on the wider movement, but one should also bear in mind Gilmartin's acknowledgement of an alternative tendency 'to treat internal conflict as the consequence of error or government interference, something to be corrected rather than negotiated'. 'Print magic', understood, as it rarely was, in its purest form, often represented differences only as the 'prelude to some final reconciliation or union, not a permanent condition to be addressed through ongoing procedures of public arbitration.'[38] The idea of an endpoint when all debate and discussion would cease often featured as part of the rhetoric of popular radicalism in the 1790s, often shaped by a Christian sense of millenarian revelation as much as by anything like Rousseau's notion of the ultimately transparent authority of the 'general will'.[39]

In terms of the trajectory of my own thinking about this culture, it goes back over thirty years to reading E. P. Thompson's *The Making of the English Working Class* as an undergraduate in the politically unpromising era of the early 1980s. Thompson understood the LCS primarily in terms of a class coming to consciousness. Since then literary scholars and historians have offered a diversity of accounts that have moved on from the Thompsonian model in their accounts of the radical societies. In the early 1980s, scholars sometimes suggested that radicalism failed because of the lack of coherence in its arguments for reform. Such a perspective tends towards a view of the domain of politics as a rational debate governed by the force of the better argument familiar from Habermas's work, whether directly indebted to him or not. Such an approach can fail to register asymmetries of power and resources in economic and cultural senses and the limits to the Enlightenment faith in the reach of the republic of letters.[40] This book attempts more fully to situate the complexities of popular radicalism in its everyday business, including at least some account of the domestic world on which it frequently drew and/or intruded. Recent scholars of radicalism have done much to explore the ways that ideology emerges in performance. Building on their work, I examine public lectures, toasting, tavern debates, and song, but also more mundane and less colourful associational practices, such as day-to-day editorial discussion about what to publish under the LCS's name.

Scholars following Iain McCalman's work have been particularly interested in the radical 'underworld' that emerged after 1795, once the popular radical societies were forced underground. This book is very much indebted to those enquiries, but is more concerned with the attempts of the societies to create a role within a broader public sphere prior to the narrowing of opportunity after the Two Acts passed into law. Of the studies brought out in the wake of McCalman, it perhaps most closely resembles the account of popular radicalism after 1815 given in Kevin Gilmartin's *Print Politics* (1996). Particularly concerned with the nexus of publicity and print, Gilmartin's approach focused 'on the print resources developed in relation to the other aspects of radical culture (meetings, clubs, debating societies, petition campaigns, boycotts)'.[41] This approach takes print as the key term in a cluster of issues relating to mediation, including association and performance. Consequently, the book is primarily concerned with the attempts of the popular societies to affiliate themselves to and in the process transform the enlightened public sphere, and with the various rebuffs they received.

Part of this process was the role of print personality as a form of mediation, that is, both attacks on personalities by the radical press – Pitt being the most obvious example, Charles Pigott being the most obvious exponent – but also the development of personae by writers and booksellers. Samuel Taylor Coleridge complained in 1809 that he lived in 'this AGE OF PERSONALITY, this age of literary and political *Gossiping*'.[42] Ironically he was writing about the veteran reformer Major John Cartwright, a member of the SCI, whose manner if not his politics he was praising precisely for their 'freedom from *personal* themes'. The radical societies contained enough people familiar with the emergent modes of popular press to know the value of personality in print. Pigott, especially, had no compunction about mixing scandal with republican principles, but as an author he published anonymously for the most part and presented himself as a version of 'the negation of persons in public discourse' that Michael Warner has identified with eighteenth-century republicanism in America.[43] The same holds true for Thomas Hardy in his role as secretary of the LCS. Hardy tended to subsume identity within his office, but for many others 'the bold signature', to use Gilmartin's phrase, was deemed more useful.[44] Many radical authors and booksellers created identities that functioned as nodal points in the flow of political information and could compete for attention in a world where personality was becoming a key aspect of publicity in the theatre and the newspapers.

Individual members of the society soon developed a use for personality in developing their claims to a place within the public sphere. Robert Merry imagined himself disseminating the spirit of liberty from pole to pole. Recitation of his odes added his glamour to political meetings. Radical writers and lecturers were prone to annexing a Whig-Protestant martyrology passing down from Hampden and Sydney, but whose numbers were added to from their own ranks, most conspicuously by Joseph Gerrald. Nor was print personality as it functioned in radical culture just a question of authorship. Daniel Isaac Eaton's shop at the sign of 'the Cock and Swine' developed its personality from his acquittals for selling an allegory of a tyrannical game bird to the swinish multitude. Eaton at 'the Cock and Swine' and Lee at his 'Tree of Liberty' participated in a print marketplace where personality mattered as an interface between print and its readers. For all the universality of the public sphere constructed by radicals, it was still populated by showmanship of the sort that thrived across eighteenth-century print culture. If Pitt's political legerdemain was parodied in the guise of Signor Pittachio after the pattern of an Italian street magician, this did not mean that radicals themselves were averse to the theatre of politics. Thelwall joined the travelling showmen in the newspaper columns around his advertisements by hawking his lectures north and south of the river for 'positively the last time'. As lecturer and orator whose words were circulated in diverse textual forms from song sheets to the pages of the *Tribune*, Thelwall was the most prominent shape shifter among the print magicians of the radical movement by 1795.

Part II of this book attends to the question of personality by looking at Thelwall as one among four different radical careers. Two of my case studies, Robert Merry and Charles Pigott, were radicals *from above*, that is, they were men born into the elite who became detached from a sense of belonging to the dominant culture of eighteenth-century Britain.[45] Citizen Lee and John Thelwall are more obviously representative of the LCS's claim to represent 'the people', although they both harboured aspirations to participate in the republic of letters prior to their political awakenings, as we have already seen. They had also already positioned themselves in print as 'friends to humanity'. It was a soubriquet not unusual with the societies, which often invoked a larger 'moral' vision beyond any narrow programme of parliamentary reform.[46] Gerrald, Henry Redhead Yorke, Merry, and Pigott may be numbered among those who consistently invoked the universal cause of the human race against tyranny from the perspectives of what Amanda Goodrich calls 'Enlightenment cosmopolitanism'.[47] Although Linebaugh and Rediker have suggested that Hardy and his associates soon gave up this platform, there is plenty of evidence that it was never dropped from the purview of the radical societies, whatever the external pressures to justify the Britishness of their interest in reform.[48]

For many, this broader moral programme depended on a religious vision of the 'human', although no less invested in various forms of print mediation, whereas for others religion contradicted what they saw as an Enlightenment imperative towards rational debate. Both secular and religious imperatives could translate into a broader 'moral' concept of reform, if of very different kinds. Religious differences always complicated Thelwall's relations with Coleridge, for instance, and within the LCS, freethinkers objected to 'saints' like John Bone doing missionary work within the divisions. Although these differences produced internal schism in 1795, the different parties felt no compunction about continuing to correspond and collaborate with each other when it came to printing and circulating cheap books. Religious and non-religious, various members believed that knowledge, not just political knowledge, was central to the improvement of the people. Although the English radical movement is often presented as narrowly concentrated on constitutional matters and an English tradition of liberty associated with the names of the Whig pantheon, the contribution of London Scots with a heritage of Presbyterian resistance seems to have played an important part, especially in 1792–3.

More broadly, the radical societies continued to have strong international contacts, not least because a steady stream of their members were forced to flee or migrate to France and the United States from as early as 1792. Events in Ireland and Scotland were constantly in the thoughts of the London societies. Many of those involved had arrived in the metropolis from those countries. London societies corresponded with French *confrères*, especially in 1792, their more elite members often drawing on experiences of Enlightenment cosmopolitanism that preceded the Revolution. Some of these members participated in the British Club at Paris over the winter of 1792–3 and agents like John Frost and Robert Merry travelled back and forth reporting on events. Merry eventually moved to France, was forced to return to Britain after Robespierre moved against foreign fellow residents in Paris, and tried to make for Switzerland in 1793 before finally migrating to the United States three years later. Members like Gerrald and Redhead Yorke heralded from an Atlantic world that seems to have contributed to their outsider perspectives, even though they claimed and were often granted gentry status. Others like Richard Lee and Merry fled to the United States after 1795, where they continued to contribute to a transatlantic radicalism, under the dyspeptic eye of William Cobbett. Despite the pressure to defend their Englishness and state their continuities with homegrown traditions, especially after war began in February 1793, the 'moral geography' of the radical societies was not limited to London or even what is now the United Kingdom.

Popular radical publicity aimed, in Redhead Yorke's words, at a 'complete revolution of sentiment'.[49] The radical societies insisted that they were part of a general process of improvement from which political versions of 'reform' could not be omitted. To do so, they implied, would breach the promise of Enlightenment in so far as it had at least appeared to propose the existence of a republic of letters that knew no boundaries. The establishment of this 'open theatre of the world' was as much the object of the popular radical societies as parliamentary reform. Their faith in the power of print and publicity was bracing in this regard, but also brought with it vulnerabilities, not least a tendency to see an unfolding moral revolution as the necessary result of the story of print. Reading, writing, and discussion were their primary agents for imagined change. When the state closed down these channels of dissemination with the Two Acts, they struggled to imagine other ways of organising to attain the laurel of liberty, although many of them kept their faith alive, even in exile on distant shores. My own larger hopes for my account of their struggles here is that it might fit with Geoff Eley's ambition for scholarship to continue to reveal 'how the changeability of the world might be thought or imagined'.[50]

PART I

Publicity, print, and association

CHAPTER I

Popular radical print culture: 'the more public the better'

Founded in January 1792 by a London shoemaker, Thomas Hardy, and a group of friends, the LCS is commonly seen as the key organisation in the emergence of a new kind of popular radicalism. The 1770s and 1780s had witnessed the appearance of a movement aimed at political education and parliamentary reform, but its participants had been mainly drawn from the landowning classes, associated writers and journalists, lawyers, and other professionals, plenty of nonconformist ministers among them. The LCS came to mediate between these classes and London's artisans and shopkeepers in the name of 'the people' broadly construed. Proposing an unlimited membership and charging a cheap subscription rate of one penny per week, the LCS aimed to broaden the processes of political discussion and the printed circulation of ideas.[1] On the national stage, until it was proscribed in 1799, the LCS also played a major part in organising relations between radical societies across England, Wales, Scotland, and Ireland. Modern historians, especially since the revival of scholarly interest in popular conservatism in the 1980s, have been inclined to celebrate the initiative displayed by the LCS, but disparage a perceived lack of cogency in its political platform. H. T. Dickinson, for instance, described the reform movement in general as 'hopelessly divided on what changes ought to be made' and unable 'to devise any effective means of implementing their policies'.[2] There is more than a little truth in these judgements, but as bald statements they give little sense of the task facing the reform movement as it sought to animate the constitutive power of the people against the congealed authority of the Crown-in-Parliament.[3] The fact of major differences within the reform movement is undeniable, but that is hardly a surprise if we examine any reform or revolutionary movement, successful or otherwise. In the case of the 1790s, this diversity reflects the experimental nature of the movement as it faced a range of new possibilities in the wake of the American and French Revolutions. Almost as soon as a radical reform movement appeared on this new terrain, it also had to contend with all kinds of challenges, not least the government's attempts to use all the resources of the state to extirpate it.

In the face of these pressures, the LCS and its allies engaged in an attempt to create an expanded public sphere out of the widening of popular debate. In a memorable phrase, E. P. Thompson expressed a wish to rescue those involved from the 'enormous condescension of posterity'. Nevertheless, even he saw the besetting sin of English Jacobins as 'self-dramatization'.[4] The judgement may be reasonable enough in relation to several of those discussed in these pages, perhaps most obviously John Thelwall, although it may also underestimate the way in which performance, including the performance of personality, was an important aspect of the theatre of Georgian politics across the board. If the LCS and its members critiqued the theatricality of Pitt and others as an empty show, a shabby trick played to deceive the people, they also insisted on their right to produce a drama of their own, with starring roles for radical celebrities. Negative judgements of the radical societies are often predicated on their failure to adhere to a distinct ideological programme, a judgement implying an idea of practice as a mere *parole* to the *langue* of intellectual history.[5] Sometimes the LCS is represented as disappointingly falling back on conventionally constitutionalist discourse or failing to exploit the political possibilities of the language of natural rights made available by Paine's *Rights of Man*. More sensitive to the difficulties of the task it faced would be an acknowledgement of the variety of ways the radical societies put pressure on the authority of constituted power in order to assert the constituent authority of the people. My approach thinks of the LCS in relation to language as embedded in social practices and understands contests over those practices as essential to the politics of the radical movement. The LCS is read not as some absolutely coherent agent, but as a locus for the circulation of print structured by reading, meetings, lectures, *conversazione*, various encounters in bookshops and many other spaces in the associational world of eighteenth-century London.[6]

From this perspective, to follow Iain Hampsher-Monk, the politics of the radical societies may not lie simply with the speech act in the text, but in 'the very act of publication'. In this regard, Hamphser-Monk contends 'the medium, not the content . . . is the message, the very fact and facility of such "electric" (a favoured metaphor) communication evinced and comprising the political mobilization of hitherto unpoliticized people from different parts of the country'.[7] If this book ends with a defeat of a kind in the passage of the Two Acts through Parliament at the end of 1795, then the triumph of the radicalism of the 1790s was the creation of a popular politics that extended into the nineteenth century. John Bone, Daniel Isaac Eaton, Thomas Hardy, William Hone, Sampson Perry, Francis Place, Thomas Preston, and John Thelwall are only a few of those appearing in these pages, who re-emerged as writers, publishers, booksellers, and activists in the radical cause after 1800. Nineteenth-century commemorations of the Scottish martyrs and those acquitted of treason at the end of 1794, now largely forgotten in British public culture, were only the outward sign of a continuity of popular radicalism that extended into the reform agitation of the 1820s and 1830s and beyond.[8]

Some of the activities of the radical societies have been regarded as an attempt to discipline a plebeian culture of 'riot, revelry, and rough music' into the practices of political citizenship, but there are ample reasons to be wary of assuming that forms of organisation, lectures, and debating societies, for instance, were experienced as a new form of discipline, when they were variations on what were becoming familiar features of the commercial culture of 'the town', increasingly accessible to the social classes who participated in the LCS.[9] The various sociable gatherings Francis Place later described as mere epiphenomena of the serious political business of the LCS were events taking place in a complicated urban terrain where customary practices had been adapting for some time to interlinked worlds of print and leisure. In this regard at least, the LCS was an extension of the phenomenon – identified by John Brewer with the Wilkes agitation in the 1760s – of 'independent men, made free through association and educated through the rules, ritual and constitutions of their own clubs and societies'. These associations partly legitimated their activities through the 'invented' tradition of popular resistance that they claimed had produced the Revolution of 1688.[10] The popular societies laid claim to this tradition – with various redefinitions of 'independence' – and extended it further towards a democratic idea of the sovereignty of the people, sometimes styled 'the general will', as the constituent power. Towards the end of *Rights of Man*, Paine had contrasted the 'savage custom' that solved disputes over government by civil war, with 'the new system' where 'discussion and the general will, arbitrates the question' and 'reference is had to national conventions'.[11] At its most radical, this 'new system' extended to arguing for the right to call a convention to collect the general will, and even, so the government maintained, to represent it. Over 1793–4, as John Barrell has shown, Pitt's ministry began to construe these arguments not only as seditious but also treasonable in so far as they presented the popular societies as more legitimately representing the people than Parliament. For their part, members of the LCS like John

Baxter, as we shall see in Chapter 2, insisted that attempts to stop the popular societies consulting together were a sign of tyranny that triggered a customary and constitutional right of resistance.

There were certainly tensions within the LCS about discipline and organisation, anxieties about presenting a respectable face to the public, but also arguments about what constituted proper forms of public practice in the name of political citizenship. Eley may be right to note that 'the advanced democracy of the LCS *presumed* the very maturity and sophistication it was meant to *create*'. Polemically, the presumption was essential to the case for universal suffrage, but the struggle to create a democratic culture in the popular societies was a sustained and extraordinarily rich response that seriously alarmed the government of the day and prompted it to take measures.[12] Many contemporaries – not only radicals – regarded these measures as both unnecessary and unprecedented. The response to them formed a crucial part of the shaping context of radical print culture. Charles James Fox described Pitt's measures culminating in the Two Acts as a 'Reign of Terror'.[13] If the phrase is characteristically melodramatic, it does at least speak to the emergent sense of a new landscape for political discourse, one radicals like Baxter regarded as a state of exception that might justify calling a convention.[14] In the 1770s, John Jebb, a favourite author of Hardy's, had insisted on 'the acknowledged right of the people to new-model the Constitution, and to punish with exemplary rigour every person, with whom they have entrusted power, provided in their opinion, he shall be found to have betrayed that trust'.[15] Pitt's attempts to close down the avenues open to political opinion suggested to some members of the LCS that the moment had arrived when the compact between the people and the state had to be renegotiated. Censorship and repression, in this regard, could both generate and thwart radicalism.

The LCS was part of a complex and distinctive print culture, not without its internal stresses, far from it, but one that was shaped by the practices of eighteenth-century society more generally and the developing contexts of which it was a part. At its heart is the relationship between the LCS and the SCI, founded in 1780, but revived in the early 1790s under the gentleman radical John Horne Tooke, to disseminate political information. The most obvious fruit of the collaboration between the LCS and the SCI was the circulation of cheap editions of Paine's *Rights of Man*, but their relationship continued in one form or another, and with different degrees of intensity, from 1792 until the treason trials at the end of 1794. There were important tensions between the two societies, not least to do with social status, roughly speaking between the politer constituency of the

SCI and the more popular complexion of the LCS, but these differences were far from absolute. Some key individuals, for instance, Joseph Gerrald, were members of both societies, refusing to observe distinctions between the elite and the lower classes that structured received ideas of who exactly constituted the political nation. Figures like Gerrald and his associates Charles Pigott and Robert Merry, both of whom are discussed more closely in Part II, were regarded as shocking examples to the landowning classes of the personal consequences of dabbling in political alliances with the lower orders.

Part II of this book attends more closely to individuals and texts involved in this broader picture and the complications of their careers. The relation of the conduct of individuals to the societies of which they were members was a crucial one, not least when it came to prosecutions for political opinion. Was a libellous publication the responsibility solely of its author or publisher, or did it represent the official point of view of the LCS or the SCI? This question was asked at more than one trial and also in Parliament. The world of print explored here is not just constituted out of the publications of the SCI and LCS, or of the other political societies associated with them, but also out of the 'unofficial' publications of individual members. Some of those involved in the societies, including, for instance, Merry and Pigott, assumed a right as gentlemen to comment on public affairs in print. They were already authors before 1792, practised at writing for newspapers and pamphlets, and, in Merry's case, associated with Sheridan's management of the press. Their situation was rather different from that of most members of the LCS, but these did include many who were already immersed in print culture as booksellers, avid readers, members of book clubs and Bible societies, like Thomas Hardy and his brother-in-law George Walne. Such men probably understood their involvement in the LCS as part of a more general commitment to moral improvement. John Thelwall certainly harboured and achieved literary ambitions before he became involved in radical politics. Others, like the silversmith John Baxter, became authors and publishers through their participation in radicalism, becoming 'literary men', to use a term that crops up more than once in the archive. Frequently the LCS showed respect for and even deference to the professional skills of writers, not least in late 1794 when it needed copy for *The Politician*. At the end of his trial for treason in 1794, the judge, Chief Justice Eyre, confessed to finding Thelwall's 'character' to be 'one of those extraordinary things that puzzle the mind the more they were examined'. How could 'a man of letters, associating with the company of gentlemen' have conspired with and even encouraged those accused of plotting treason?[16] The judge's question was a specific version of a more general puzzle. The question of how a distinctive republic of letters could have emerged from such places remained an enigma to a ruling elite, rarely willing to grant someone like Thelwall the literary status begrudgingly allowed to him by the Chief Justice.

Radical print culture in the 1790s was structured as much by tensions between its members as their cooperative will to change their world for the better. The disorientating speed of events that the French Revolution unleashed across Europe further complicated things, as participants had to decide upon the significance of those events for their sense of what was possible in the British situation. As France moved from *ancien régime* to constitutional monarchy and then to a republic, so the possibilities of what might be done by reform changed too, a fact reflected even in Thomas Paine's writing. Often described as a republican because of his role in the American struggle against Great Britain, Paine shifted his thinking about Europe as different possibilities emerged in Britain and France. He moved from supporting a constitutional monarchy under Louis XVI to a republic, at least by late 1791, but only announced his support for universal suffrage in Britain in his *Letter Addressed to the Addressers*, published in August 1792. Quite probably, this development was influenced by his experiences with the LCS and SCI over the spring and summer of 1792.[17]

When we examine the archive of the radical movement in London, a picture emerges of less-heralded individual members of the LCS and SCI also revising their sense of the possibilities before them, even if the official line of the societies stuck to the Duke of Richmond's plan of universal suffrage and annual parliaments as their immediate objective. John Horne Tooke famously described his attitude to reform in terms of getting off the Windsor coach at Hounslow, even if his fellow passengers intended to proceed to the terminus. The LCS encouraged all the societies to get on the stage to Richmond and debate the final destination once on board. The radical societies did not simply act out an inherited script of parliamentary reform. They continually recycled resources from the past, often quite literally by republishing the duke's plan from the 1780s, or even earlier texts from the commonwealth canon. The cutting and pasting techniques that were essential to the rapid-fire achievement of periodicals like Thomas Spence's *Pig's Meat* (1793–5) or Eaton's *Politics for the People* (1793–5) did not simply endorse the texts they reproduced, but implicitly transformed them in the interests of raising the political consciousness of their readers. Both Eaton and Spence were LCS members who suffered imprisonment for their commitment to the cause, but by no means all their publications were official LCS materials.[18] They published ideas that went beyond those endorsed by the LCS as a corporate body, as with Spence's appropriation of James Harrington's *Oceania* (1656) in support of his radical land plan.[19] Nevertheless, anxious as the LCS and SCI may sometimes have been to distance themselves from the views of individual members, Spence included, they were committed to putting a diversity of texts into circulation to stimulate widespread discussion of possible political futures. *The Politician* described the aim of the LCS as 'the diffusion of political knowledge by a system of mutual instruction', an ambition interrupted by 'that system of unconstitutional persecution, which was the harbinger of the present most execrable and ruinous war'.[20] Even so, the journal declared itself open to contrary points of view, including those of a veteran reformer, ironically naming himself 'An *Aristocrat*', who contributed an essay to the first issue arguing against the policy of universal suffrage that the LCS officially supported.

Publicity

Making the question of publicity central to the radical societies in the 1790s may smack of anachronism, but it was a conscious part of their thinking and shaped their political practice. Perhaps nothing puts this into starker perspective than the reasons Maurice Margarot gave in 1796 for refusing the chance to escape from Botany Bay on the American ship that spirited his fellow convict Thomas Muir away:

> I came in the Public cause, and here I will wait for my recall by that Public, when the cause shall have prospered as perhaps it will have done before you receive this.[21]

Transported for his participation in the British Convention at Edinburgh of late 1793, Margarot always defined himself as someone acting in a 'Public cause'. To creep away on an American ship, as he saw it, would have been to betray the public function that the LCS placed at the centre of its mission. Looking back from 1799, Hardy claimed that 'the Society was very open in all its measures, indeed their object was publicity, the more public the better'.[22] Publicity was not simply the medium for the message of parliamentary reform; it was part of its object.

The LCS conducted itself in the manner in which it understood public bodies to behave. In the process, it affirmed the right of its members – whatever their social class – to be regarded as an actively constituent power, part of the political nation. In this regard, as John Barrell memorably puts it, the LCS also offered its members not just 'jam tomorrow', but also 'a sense of immediate, present participation, to whoever would join it and engage in [their] activities and debates'. Barrell is surely right to claim that 'for many members of the LCS the prospect of participating in the society's democratic structures may have been as powerful in persuading them to join as the prospect of eventual parliamentary reform'.[23] Ironing over some of the internal controversies about the LCS's constitution, a matter I will return to at the end of the next chapter, Francis Place, writing much later, gave a succinct account of the organisation of the LCS:

> The Society assembled in divisions in various parts of the Metropolis, that to which I belonged was held; as all the others were weekly; at a private house in New Street Covent Garden. Each division elected a delegate and sub delegate, these formed a general committee which also met once a week, in this committee the sub delegate had a seat but could neither speak nor vote whilst the delegate was present.

He also gave a glimpse into the relationship between the official business of the LCS and the penumbra of print sociability that went on around it:

> We had book subscriptions ... the books for which any one subscribed were read by all the members in rotation who chose to read them before they were finally consigned to the subscriber. We had Sunday evening parties at the residences of those who could accommodate a number of persons. At these meetings we had readings, conversations and discussions. There was at this time a great many such parties, they were highly useful and agreeable.[24]

Place's account is more or less corroborated from other sources, including spy reports, which speak of the admixture of official meetings, still often centred on reading, and more informal *conversaziones* or 'parties'. Both the divisional meetings and these parties could be much more convivial than Place makes them sound, but it would be wrong to assume that only the more raucous sorts of sociability were somehow authentically 'popular'. For one thing, toasts and songs, often with copious consumption of alcohol, were ubiquitous across all classes of the associational world. John Horne Tooke, the gentleman radical of the SCI, often got spectacularly drunk at political dinners, as several visitors noted, including those Whigs who regretted attending the infamous anniversary dinner of the SCI on 2 May 1794. The consequences of such conviviality could be grave. On 24 January 1798, at a meeting to celebrate Fox's birthday at the Crown and Anchor, attended both by Whig politicians and members of the LCS, the

Duke of Norfolk toasted '*our Sovereign's health ... the Majesty of the People!*' The toast was seen as a deliberate slight to the king and provoked considerable commentary.[25] The king saw to it that the duke was dismissed from his positions as colonel of the militia and Lord Lieutenant of Yorkshire.

Many of the activities encouraged by the LCS represent what Lottes has called a 'train[ing] in the democracy of the word'.[26] Place's description of a divisional meeting certainly seems to sanction this vocabulary:

> The chairman (each man was chairman in rotation,) read from some book or part of a chapter, which as many as could read the chapter at their homes the book passing from one to the other had done and at the next meeting a portion of the chapter was again read and the persons present were invited to make remarks thereon. As many as chose did so, but without rising. Then another portion was read and a second invitation was given – then the remainder was read and a third invitation was given when they who had not before spoken were expected to say something. Then there was a general discussion. No one was permitted to speak more than once during the reading. The same rule was observed in the general discussion, no one could speak a second time until every one who chose had spoken once, then any one might speak again, and so on till the subject was exhausted – these were very important meetings, and the best results to the parties followed.[27]

These details and other aspects of LCS governance correspond closely to the activities of book clubs and reading societies widespread in the associational world of the eighteenth century, not least in the attempt to create a level plane of discourse to facilitate equitable participation in discussion. Lottes claims that the primary aim of the LCS became a disciplinary concern for each of its members 'to acquire knowledge on his own without intellectual guidance'. The *Report of the Committee of the constitution, of the London Corresponding Society* (1794) insisted that the primary duty of a member was 'to habituate himself both in and out of his Society, to an orderly and amicable manner of reasoning'. Many members were committed to the idea of 'rational debate'. Sometimes this insistence sounds like a reactive proof of their abilities against the insinuations of much conservative propaganda to the contrary, but even 'rational debate' could imply a variety of practices. The report of the committee of constitution was soon mired in arguments about the best form of democratic protocol within the LCS itself, especially the relation of the divisions to the central committee. In the context of these arguments about the report of the committee on the constitution, Hodgson and Thelwall clashed violently about systems of governance early in 1794: 'Hodgson argued in favour of some System being requisite Thelwall against the necessity of any and his opinion was most applauded.'[28]

This account might be tainted by the exaggeration of a spy report eager to identify the LCS with anarchy, but other sources confirm that such differences did cause schism within the LCS in 1795. Discussed at more length in Chapter 2, these disagreements were not simply matters of form in any superficial sense. They were rather part of serious debates about how to mediate the sovereign will of the people. These debates could focus on different aspects of the various media of expression available to the society, taking in questions of how members ought to address each other or the conduct of large political meetings. In his account of these debates, Lottes may be relying too much on Place's perspective when he assumes that 'the divisions were turned into political classrooms from which all plebeian sociability was banned'.[29] I will return to the convivial sociability of songs and toasts later in this chapter, but a major part of the plebeian life world that Lottes ignores is religion. John Bone and Richard Citizen Lee, among others, refused to leave their beliefs at the door of the meeting, even if Thomas Hardy did, despite the strength of his religious convictions. Some LCS divisions defended their right to create their own political space against the centralising drive identified by Lottes. The very idea of the division as a reading group could play into the resistance to political organisation. Furthermore, what was read at the meetings seems to have extended from classics of political philosophy to the squibs and broadsides that could make these gatherings more free and easy than classrooms.[30] From this perspective, again, the Lottes version of political education at the LCS appears too austere. Toasts and songs, squibs and burlesques, were all part and parcel of the theatre of Georgian politics broadly construed, familiar to patrician and plebeian alike. Reading often coexisted with singing. Political education was not confined, in this sense at least, to the kinds of texts that might produce the disciplined citizen of Lottes's account.

These different currents flowing into the LCS meant there were necessarily tensions about the kinds of activities and publications to which the society should lend its name. Clubbing together over books – reading, buying, and printing them – had an obvious economic advantage that John Bone made clear when he proposed a publishing scheme to the LCS in May 1795. He had just seceded in a dispute over constitutional arrangements, probably exacerbated by his religious beliefs, to set up the London Reforming Society, but the schism did not prevent him proposing cooperation for the dissemination of political information. 'Among the embarrassments the Press has laboured under', wrote Bone back to his old allies in the LCS, 'none has had a greater tendency to impede the progress of knowledge, than the difficulty of circulating books.' Bone proposed that the LCS join together with the Reforming Society to print political books in large runs, copies being given to members in return for their membership dues; 'by this means, an uniformity of sentiment would be produced in the whole Nation, in proportion to the diffusion of knowledge'. Print magic, here, it seems, brings with it the idea of an ultimate union as the terminus of discussion and debate. More prosaically, the economic advantages of Bone's plan would also be 'a very powerful stimulus to induce men to associate'.[31] He also addressed a perceived want of matter brought up in the reply to his original proposal. First, he answered, 'there are in the Patriotic Societies splendid talents, that only want the calling forth into use'. Secondly, 'why not publish the works of other authors . . . publishing anything that is calculated to do good'. He mentions Joseph Gerrald's *A Convention the Only Means of Saving us from Ruin* (1793), Redhead Yorke's *Thoughts on Civil Government* (1794), and 'any other useful book, of which you can get the copy-right'. Finally, he suggests, 'there is no necessity to confine ourselves to Politics'; perhaps hinting at his religious interests, 'there is not a species of knowledge from which some good might not be extracted'.[32] The LCS replied positively. Members from the two societies met to discuss the plan, but the collaboration never seems to have got beyond an abridged version of the *State of the Representation of England and Wales*, already published by the societies in 1793.[33]

Choosing which other texts should be put out in the name of the societies would almost certainly have led to wrangling, especially in the light of their recent constitutional schism and Bone's religious opinions. Before he seceded, Bone objected to works like d'Holbach's *The System of Nature* and Paine's *The Age of Reason* being circulated around the divisions.[34] Questions over exactly which texts the LCS should issue in its name caused problems from early on in its history. These problems were exacerbated once it became clear that government surveillance would be quick to identify the LCS with any views that could be construed as seditious. The LCS printed material primarily to encourage public discussion, but also to assert – even to memorialise – its right and the right of the people at large to a place in national debate: addresses to the public, to the king, and accounts of its own constitution and resolutions were the staple of its official output. In 1795 the London Reforming Society adopted the same method: 'Publicity of conduct, discovers purity of motive; it was therefore being just to yourselves when you resolved to publish your proceedings.'[35]

On 11 July 1793, the central committee of the LCS met to discuss events at its general meeting, held three days before, where an address to the nation had been read. Written by Margarot, the address was chosen from three originally submitted to the committee.[36] As was so often the case with the LCS, the July meeting was taken up with matters of publicity and its costs. An error in the printed version of the address was discussed and accounting for ticket receipts took up most of the rest of the meeting. Finally, coming to 'other business', George Walne reported that he had found a pile of pamphlets intended for use as wrapping paper on a counter at a local cheesemonger's. The pamphlet was *The Englishman's Right: A Dialogue* (1793). Walne purchased the whole bundle and offered it to the central committee at cost price (3 farthings each copy). Written by Sir John Hawles and originally published in 1680, Walne had come across the eighth edition of 1771. After some discussion, the LCS central committee accepted Walne's terms, but then entered into several weeks of deliberation over what to do next. At the general committee two weeks later, one delegate brought forward a motion to print a new edition. Eventually, a sub-committee did some light editing, translated all the Latin phrases into English, and added an appendix on the empanelling of juries, a topic of pressing concern for their members facing prosecution; but this summary hardly does justice to the fate of the pamphlet over the next few months.

First, a committee meeting postponed publication until it could be discovered how many copies each division would buy. A meeting on the first day of August reported back that the divisions (somewhat optimistically) had promised to buy 750 copies. The committee decided to charge members 2d, strangers 3d, with 4d marked 'on the book'. Two thousand were to be printed '& the press kept standing'. The country societies were to be informed of it by circular letter. The printer's estimate had said it would not cost more than 2d per copy to reprint with the appendix. These decisions produced only another round of deliberation. The appendix on juries now had to be written. A sub-committee was appointed to write it consisting of Joseph Field, Matthew Moore, Richard Hodgson, John Smith, and George Walne. A week later the central committee met to discuss their work. It approved the edition, but censured the sub-committee for having already submitted it to the press. The print order was stopped. The next meeting delayed it again, although the secretary was given an order to purchase copies of Richard Dinmore Jr's *A Brief account of the Moral and Political Acts of the Kings and Queens of England* for distribution around the society.[37]

Discussion of the appendix was still going on in September when a mistake on a technical question was discovered. John Martin was called in to give his expert legal opinion.[38] Only on 19 September did the LCS finally order *The Englishman's Right* to be printed. Hardy wrote to various other societies encouraging them to take copies. On 17 October, he asked Henry Buckle of Norwich to promote the pamphlet as 'a book that ought to be in the possession of every man'. Eight days later, he wrote to Daniel Adams, secretary to the SCI, offering the pamphlet on the same terms, before proceeding to news of the election of delegates to the Edinburgh Convention.[39] More than the 700 projected were sold, but the receipts were much less than must have been expected if the LCS was calculating a return of 2d a copy or more. Although some of those sold probably ended up as cheese wrapping anyway, at least one survived to be passed on to another generation of radicals. When Hardy wrote to the Mitcham Book Society in August 1806 to donate various pamphlets to them in hopes of keeping the flame of reform alive, *The Englishman's Right* was among them.

This extended account of *The Englishman's Right* serves to illustrate how long and hard the LCS debated what to put out in its name. Beyond its list of official publications, individual members produced a wealth of printed matter in their own names or anonymously; material read, discussed, sung, or otherwise performed at meetings. The question of the extent to which this material was owned by the radical societies was a fraught one, inevitably when the government was aiming to fix responsibility for seditious libel and later treason. After being arrested in May 1794, Hardy was interviewed by the Privy Council. The council asked about Eaton's role as a printer. Hardy acknowledged the bookseller's association with the LCS, but also took the view that Eaton 'prints freely – too freely'.[40] The response is not only, I think, a self-protective reflex at a juncture when the judicial process was putting Hardy's life in hazard, but also indicates some of the tensions within the embryonic democratic culture being fostered by the LCS. Why would Hardy worry about Eaton's freedom? Hardy himself was no narrow reformer focused solely on parliamentary reform. Although he came to the idea of the LCS through reading SCI publications from the 1780s, he also had a background in religious dissent, possibly also in the Protestant Association, but definitely with the campaigns for the repeal of the Test and Corporation Acts and for the abolition of the slave trade.[41] All these contexts would have given him ideas about 'publicity' and the way it worked, not least in relation to the politics of petitioning.[42] Hardy always showed himself anxious about the public face of the LCS, but there was a more general concern to find appropriate forms of intervention. The LCS was confident about the transformative power of print, but also careful about its forms and protocols.

Before turning to discuss some of the general attitudes to print in the radical societies, there is more to be said about the LCS in relation to Jürgen Habermas's idea of the public sphere.[43] Among others critical of Habermas's idealisation of the 'bourgeois public sphere', Eley has insisted on the 'diversity' of the eighteenth-century public sphere, which he defines as always 'constituted by conflict'.[44] Explicitly thinking about groups like the LCS, Eley claims that the French Revolution encouraged various subaltern groups to claim for themselves the emancipatory language of the bourgeois public sphere: 'It's open to question' he continues, 'how far these were simply derivative of the liberal model (as Habermas argues) and how far they possessed their own dynamics of emergence and peculiar forms of internal life.' Among these alternative dynamics, Eley acknowledges the variety of religious traditions that certainly informed the development of men like John Bone, Thomas Hardy, Richard Lee, and George Walne. These and other aspects of urban culture helped to sustain an alternative to Habermas's bourgeois public sphere, says Eley, that was 'combative *and* highly literate'.[45] Anticipating aspects of Eley's critique, Terry Eagleton claimed that the 1790s witnessed the emergence of what he called a 'counter-public sphere': 'a whole oppositional network of journals, clubs, pamphlets, debates and institutions invades the dominant consensus, threatening to fragment it from within'.[46] Key words here relative to the question of dependency raised by Eley are 'invades' and 'within'. There is no doubt that the activities of the LCS and its members disclosed the limits of the inclusive idea of the public that Habermas writes about. Pitt's repression from 1792 showed that those outside the political classes possessed no acknowledged right to free debate, at least not when it came to questions of political representation and reform. Out of this situation, the popular societies managed to create the vibrant print culture that is the focus of this book, but the achievement was not predicated on any autonomously *plebeian* public sphere. Rather the LCS developed various forms available in the 'urban contact zone' where, however unevenly, 'elite' and 'popular' cultures interacted, in terms, that is, of its deployment of already existing platforms such as debating societies, reading groups, the newspapers, and other aspects of print sociability that had developed from at least the time of the Wilkes agitation.[47]

In 1793, having faced a second unsuccessful prosecution for selling Paine's writings, Eaton issued a handbill announcing his disgust at the 'aristocracy of the press' and his determination 'to liberate the REPUBLIC *of*

Letters from the undue influence exerted by those *Tyrants*, Pride and Avarice' (Figure. 2). For some of Eaton's readers, especially any with a complacent faith in print magic, the phrase 'aristocracy of the press' may have been an oxymoron. The press was widely thought to operate with an

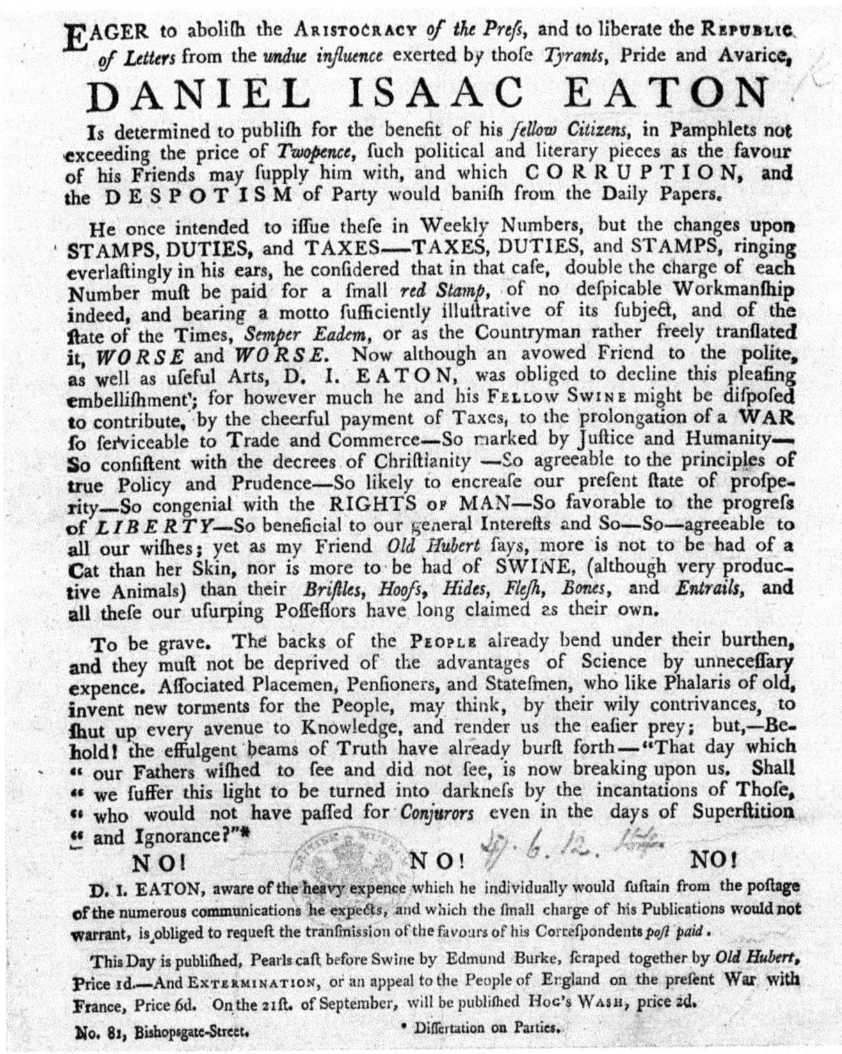

EAGER to aboliſh the ARISTOCRACY *of the Preſs*, and to liberate the REPUBLIC *of Letters* from the *undue influence* exerted by thoſe *Tyrants*, Pride and Avarice,

DANIEL ISAAC EATON

Is determined to publiſh for the benefit of his *fellow Citizens*, in Pamphlets not exceeding the price of *Twopence*, ſuch political and literary pieces as the favour of his Friends may ſupply him with, and which CORRUPTION, and the DESPOTISM of Party would baniſh from the Daily Papers.

He once intended to iſſue theſe in Weekly Numbers, but the changes upon STAMPS, DUTIES, and TAXES—TAXES, DUTIES, and STAMPS, ringing everlaſtingly in his ears, he conſidered that in that caſe, double the charge of each Number muſt be paid for a ſmall *red Stamp*, of no deſpicable Workmanſhip indeed, and bearing a motto ſufficiently illuſtrative of its ſubject, and of the ſtate of the Times, *Semper Eadem*, or as the Countryman rather freely tranſlated it, *WORSE* and *WORSE*. Now although an avowed Friend to the polite, as well as uſeful Arts, D. I. EATON, was obliged to decline this pleaſing embelliſhment; for however much he and his FELLOW SWINE might be diſpoſed to contribute, by the cheerful payment of Taxes, to the prolongation of a WAR ſo ſerviceable to Trade and Commerce—So marked by Juſtice and Humanity—So conſiſtent with the decrees of Chriſtianity —So agreeable to the principles of true Policy and Prudence—So likely to encreaſe our preſent ſtate of proſperity—So congenial with the RIGHTS OF MAN—So favorable to the progreſs of *LIBERTY*—So beneficial to our general Intereſts and So—So—agreeable to all our wiſhes; yet as my Friend *Old Hubert* ſays, more is not to be had of a Cat than her Skin, nor is more to be had of SWINE, (although very productive Animals) than their *Briſtles*, *Hoofs*, *Hides*, *Fleſh*, *Bones*, and *Entrails*, and all theſe our uſurping Poſſeſſors have long claimed as their own.

To be grave. The backs of the PEOPLE already bend under their burthen, and they muſt not be deprived of the advantages of Science by unneceſſary expence. Aſſociated Placemen, Penſioners, and Stateſmen, who like Phalaris of old, invent new torments for the People, may think, by their wily contrivances, to ſhut up every avenue to Knowledge, and render us the eaſier prey; but,—Behold! the effulgent beams of Truth have already burſt forth—"That day which "our Fathers wiſhed to ſee and did not ſee, is now breaking upon us. Shall "we ſuffer this light to be turned into darkneſs by the incantations of Thoſe, "who would not have paſſed for *Conjurors* even in the days of Superſtition "and Ignorance?"*

NO! NO! NO!

D. I. EATON, aware of the heavy expence which he individually would ſuſtain from the poſtage of the numerous communications he expects, and which the ſmall charge of his Publications would not warrant, is obliged to requeſt the tranſmiſſion of the favours of his Correſpondents *poſt paid*.

This Day is publiſhed, Pearls caſt before Swine by Edmund Burke, ſcraped together by *Old Hubert*, Price 1d.—And EXTERMINATION, or an appeal to the People of England on the preſent War with France, Price 6d. On the 21ſt. of September, will be publiſhed HOG's WASH, price 2d.

No. 81, Bishopsgate-Street.

* Diſſertation on Parties.

Fig 2 Daniel Isaac Eaton [A circular, together with a prospectas of a series of political pamphlets.] © The British Library Board.

inherent tendency to undermine aristocracy and open oligarchy up to public scrutiny. Others, on the other hand, already had bitter experience of the point he was making. Eaton was showing up the contradiction between the emancipatory claims of the republic of letters and the practical barriers to participation. For Eaton, the 'REPUBLIC *of Letters*' was not a space where freedom of exchange was guaranteed, but a place in need of liberation. Eaton's response to the situation was to start publishing 'for the benefit of his fellow Citizens, in Pamphlets not exceeding the price of Twopence'. At the foot of his handbill, Eaton advertised the first fruits of this new policy: 'Pearls Cast before Swine by Edmund Burke, scraped together by *Old Hubert*', that is, by the apothecary James Parkinson; 'EXTERMINATION, or an appeal to the People of England on the present War with France, for 6d', and finally, on 21 September, the first part of the periodical *Hog's Wash*, later known as *Politics for the People*.[48] The *Extermination* pamphlet might be called Eaton's first original publication, allowing that it was a typical miscellany that looked towards the more daring mixture of his *Politics for the People*. There Eaton cooked up a rich stew into which were thrown contemporary newspaper squibs, songs, and excerpts from the Whig canon. From August 1794, Eaton also produced a series of Political Classics, including authors such as Thomas More, Algernon Sydney, and, as we have seen, Rousseau. This series has been seen as proof of Eaton's affiliation to a 'Real Whig' tradition, but did these texts somehow retain a stable meaning across multiple platforms?[49] The inclusion of Rousseau suggests that something spicier was going on. Certainly Eaton seems to have believed there was an English tradition of liberty worth knowing, but continually reverenced only in the breach by the nation's elite. To use the title of a miscellany published by the Aldgate Society of the Friends of the People earlier in 1793, it was 'a thing of shreds and patches', but one that might be reworked and put to good use by new readers.[50] Eaton did not imagine any autonomous tradition of plebeian opposition, but tasked his readers with newly determining the shape of the public sphere.

Print magic

Michael Warner begins his study of the role of print culture in the American Revolution with the discussion of an essay by John Adams. Writing in 1765, Adams narrated the progress of print as 'a relation to power' a narrative of an idea of the press as 'indispensible to political life'. Carefully distancing himself from its causative claims, Warner sees this narrative as emerging fully in the Atlantic world of the mid-eighteenth century.[51] This faith was a pervasive part of eighteenth-century discourse, especially in the Anglo-American Protestant imagination, where it functioned in opposition to an idea of feudal and papal tyranny. From perspectives Adams shared with many others in the anglophone world, print had freed the people from a 'religious horror of letters and knowledge'.[52] Print is not simply the medium for new ideas in this kind of narrative, but comes bearing a truth in itself; 'letters have become a technology of publicity whose meaning in the last analysis is civic and emancipatory'.[53] Sharing Warner's scepticism as to the truth of its claims, I understand this narrative – for all its self-identification with Enlightenment – as a faith in print's magic. Traces of it appear in Paine's confidence that 'such is the irresistible nature of truth, that all it asks, and all it wants, is the liberty of appearing. The sun needs no inscription to distinguish him from darkness.'[54] The spread of truth, paradoxically needing 'no inscription', transcends the need for any mediation whatsoever. This magically transformative power stands in a certain tension with the more calibrated emphasis elsewhere in *Rights of Man* on continual debate and discussion.

Recent historians of print have tended to echo Warner's scepticism about taking such attitudes as evidence of the causative power they celebrate. Leah Price, for instance, distances herself from 'the heroic myth – whether Protestant, liberal, New Critical, or New Historicist – that makes textuality the source of interiority, authenticity, and selfhood'.[55] Price is developing James Raven's caution about placing too much trust in eighteenth-century accounts of print and progress, including those that link 'the activity of the press to increased literacy and popular political energies'.[56] Those within the radical movement in the 1790s repeatedly made this link. Place's retrospective accounts of the LCS as a moral force, for instance, depended on its introduction of its members to the virtues of print: 'It induced men to read books, instead of wasting their time in public houses, it taught them to respect themselves, and to desire to educate their children.'[57] Jonathan Rose claims that men like Place and Hardy 'were acutely conscious of the power of print, because they saw it work'.[58] But Raven's caution against extrapolating from individual cases to the larger picture is worth heeding: 'The testimony of the self-improved endorses an undue reverence for the process and volume of learning.'[59] Encounters with print often did have a transformative effect, but it was not always so, and print was not necessarily as magically effective as some accounts represented it. The LCS spent a lot of time working hard to create and calibrate its effects.

Looking back on his experiences in the 1790s, Thomas Preston, who had been a member of the LCS, represented reading as crucial to the political awakening of the people:

> The increase in reading had dissipated the delusion, and people now knew the meaning of words, whether spoken in the Senate, written in lawyer's bills of costs, or printed on an impress warrant. The charm of *ignorance* which had so long lulled my mind into comparative indifference at people's wrongs, was now beginning to disappear. The moral and political sun of TRUTH had now arisen. The arguments, the irresistible arguments, laid down by the 'Corresponding Society' had riveted my heart to the cause of liberty.[60]

Popular radicalism often exploited the idea of the improving power of reading for rhetorical purposes, for instance, against the counter-revolutionary narrative that Paine and his associates were spreading poison through the press. What was poisonous from the loyalist perspective was a panacea against ignorance for radicals. Many of these thought that it had been working its curative effects ever since the invention of the press.

The idea of the emancipatory magic of the printing press appears again and again as a trope in the 1790s. In 1792, for instance, David Steuart Erskine, Earl of Buchan, and elder brother of Thomas Erskine, the chief defence lawyer at Paine's trial, argued that if a free constitution was 'the panacea of moral diseases', then 'the printing press has been the dispensary, and half the world have become the voluntary patients of this healing remedy'.[61] Two years later, in a speech given at the grand celebration of the acquittal of Hardy, Horne Tooke, and Thelwall, the Earl of Stanhope transposed Buchan's medical trope into a more familiar image of enlightenment:

> The invaluable ART OF PRINTING has dispelled that former Darkness; and like a *new Luminary* enlightens the whole Horizon. The *gloomy Night of Ignorance* is past. The pure unsullied *Light of Reason* is NOW much diffused, that it is no longer in the power of *Tyranny* to destroy it. And I believe, and hope, that glorious *intellectual Light* will, shortly, shine forth on Europe, with *meridian* Splendor.

Neither Buchan nor Stanhope, as it happens, subscribed to the strongest version of print magic in these speeches. Their faith was anchored in a constitutionalist perspective wherein the press mediated prior forms of legal and political authority. Stanhope qualified his paean to the press:

> The Art of Printing (that most useful and unparalleled Invention) is however, as nothing, without *that*, which alone can give it energy and effect: you need not to be told, that I mean, the sacred LIBERTY OF THE PRESS, that *Palladium* of the people's Rights.[62]

Stanhope made his own contribution to the art of printing, designing the first iron letterpress in 1800, a development that allowed a greater number of impressions per hour, and speeded up the administration of the panacea of print to the patient. In this case, Stanhope's version of print magic drove technological innovation, not the other way round, but it also drew back from those versions of Paine's faith in the irresistible power of truth that perceived no limits to its horizons.[63]

Where radicalism dreamed of print as 'a medium itself unmediated', then it often used the trope of an electric immediacy of communication.[64] Thelwall, as Mary Fairclough has noted, routinely spoke of 'a glowing energy that may rouse into action every nerve and faculty of the mind, and fly from breast to breast like that electrical principle which is perhaps the true soul of the physical universe'.[65] His was the positive version of the 'electrick communication every where' feared by Edmund Burke, promising or threatening, depending on one's point of view, to jump across all channels of 'transmission'.[66] Elite reformers like Buchan and Stanhope may have had reservations about the democratic implications of this trope. In contrast, Thelwall's political lectures, perhaps the key radical medium of 1794–5, speedily reissued in pamphlet form and widely advertised and reported in the press, often echoed Paine's sense of the potentially limitless effects of the power of truth.[67] In a lecture on the history of prosecutions for political opinion, he projected the idea of an ineluctable progress flowing from the invention of printing. He quoted John Gurney, defence lawyer at Eaton's second trial, discussed below, on the idea that the libel laws had originated in a panicked response to the emergence of the printing press:

> when the invention of printing had introduced political discussion, and when *seditious publications* (that is to say *publications exposing the corruptions and abuses of government and the profligacy of ministers*) made their appearance ... The control of the press was placed in admirable hands, a licenser, the king's Attorney General, and a court of inquisition, called the Star Chamber.

Interestingly, Gurney was representing the art of printing as the antecedent of political discussion. Not simply a medium that reports debate, the press is imagined as its condition of possibility. Typically, Thelwall swelled to the theme in the lecture room:

> Fortunately for mankind the press *cannot* be silenced. Placemen and pensioners may *associate* for ever; inquisitions may be established, and the Nilus of corruption pour forth its broods of spies and informers; but

> wherever the press has once been established on a broad foundation, liberty must ultimately triumph. It is easier to sweep the whole human race from the surface of the earth than to stop the torrent of information and political improvement, when the art of printing has attained its present height.

For Thelwall, so many of these 'engines of truth' were now dispersed around the globe that the progress of liberty was unstoppable. Radical print culture, as John Thelwall told it, was the articulation of a spirit of progress hard-wired into the story of the press.[68]

From this perspective, whatever local setbacks might occur, an inherent logic guaranteed the irreversible spread of knowledge and thence emancipation. There was often a strong polemical motive recommending this technological determinism in difficult times. Stanhope's speech, for instance, was made after the apparent setback of the treason trials, when the radical societies needed to believe that the logic of print was being restored to its true course. Hardy saw it being fulfilled when he wrote to congratulate Lafayette on the July Revolution of 1830:

> Political knowledge is making a great, and rapid progress. It is now diffused among all classes. The printing press is performing wonders. It was a maxim of the great Lord Bacon that *Knowledge is power.*[69]

Such faith was sustaining in the face of repression and after the experience of repeated defeat that Hardy was hoping had finally been overcome. After the passing of the Two Acts at the end of 1795, Thelwall rallied his former colleagues to a belief that reading and discussion, especially his own works, were the way forward. On 15 December 1796, he sent the central committee copies of his recently published *Rights of Nature* with the following letter:

> There is nothing for which I am more anxious than to see the spirit of enquiry revived in our society & prosecuted with all its former ardour. Depend upon it, nothing but information can give us liberty; & however unpromising things may, at this time, to some appear: I cannot but believe that events must be hastning [sic] which will make us wish that the time now lost in wrangling or supineness, had been spent in reading & political discussion, by which our minds might have been prepared for liberty & enabled to obtain it. As a patriotic contribution, towards reviving the discussion so desirable, I present the society with twelve copies [sic] of my first Letter on the Rights of Nature, in answer to Mr. Burke; recommending that twelve readers be appointed by the Committee to read them to the respective divisions, & that the books be of course given to the readers as a trifling compliment for their trouble.[70]

The idea of the LCS as a society of reading circles – each with its own appointed readers – corroborates Place's later account of the Society, but seems almost to become an end in itself here, preparatory to some crisis whose coming it seems to have no very obvious active relation to. Faced by the restrictions brought in by the Two Acts, Thelwall counsels trusting to a deeper narrative of the power of print and discussion, rather than any particular form of political organisation to specific ends. Against that, it must be said, Thelwall does not present reading as a retreat into self-improvement, but as part of an ongoing public commitment, to reading *as* dissemination, even if its relationship to political change seems more occluded than it had in his lectures of 1794 and 1795. He pays an attention typical of the LCS to the disposition of the reading and discussion of his work. This kind of more practical awareness of the need to organise and work with the means of dissemination was not uncommonly intertwined with the technological determinism that I call print magic.

At their most declamatory, radical orators represented resistance to their political cause as an impossible attempt to restrain the inherently progressive drive of print dissemination. From this position, government attempts to control the radical press were foolish attempts to turn back history itself, ripe for satires like Eaton's *The Pernicious Effects of the Art of Printing* (1794). Longing for the return of the dark night of the Stuarts, the authorial persona 'Antitype' rails against the magical power of print:

> BEFORE this diabolical Art was introduced among men, there was social order; and as the great Locke expresses it, some subordination-man placed an implicit confidence in his temporal and spiritual directors – Princes and Priests – entertained no doubts of their infallibility; or ever questioned their unerring wisdom.[71]

On one level, the ironies of the pamphlet may work to suggest that print magic was a mere sham, a Whig myth to be exploded by Eaton's corrosive satirical method. *Pernicious Effects* reveals that the elite had never really believed one of the comforting myths of 'British liberty'. The vaunted freedom of the press, from this perspective, was a smokescreen to distract from the need of the people to assert their rights. On another level, Eaton's pamphlet may seem to confirm implicitly the basic premise of print magic as a force that can no more be turned back than can the tide. From this perspective, the joke on Antitype is that he can't see the ineluctable progress of print. His views, Eaton implies, are destined for the dustbin of history.[72] In its multiple implications for understanding the power of the medium, Eaton's pamphlet highlights some of the tensions between the radical commitment to working in print and the technological determinism identified by Warner.

In practice, Eaton never trusted that freedom would come simply through the circulation of what the SCI and LCS called 'political information' (the primary form of most of their official publications). As someone who was still involved in radical print culture up to his death in 1814, Eaton might be placed among the honourable company who created the disposition of post-1815 radicalism towards press freedom described by Kevin Gilmartin: 'The recognition (and experience) of press corruption went a long way towards discouraging strictly determinist attitudes: attention shifted from the nature of the technology to the conditions under which it developed.'[73] Certainly Eaton showed an unparalleled ability to adapt print to circumstance in order to sustain what Stanhope called its 'energy and effect'. For Stanhope himself, the principle of the liberty of the press, with the constitution behind it, was the legitimate idea that could impart this energy and restore British liberty. Eaton, in contrast, was quick to realise the potential of irony as a resource. Well he might, given that the principles of the free press proved far less protective of him than a noble lord. Eaton's engagement with print often took the form of hand-to-hand combat with the Association for Preserving Liberty and Property against Republicans and Levellers, founded in November 1792. He deployed whatever weapons lay to hand in the armoury of print, often appropriating the satirical methods of earlier participants, including Marvell, Pope, and Swift, regardless of their original political sympathies.

Since the abolition of the Licensing Act at the end of the seventeenth century, the chief means for controlling political opinion had been the law of seditious libel. This legal condition had already shaped the nature of print culture for many decades before the prosecutions of Paine and his publishers in 1792.[74] Many of the techniques developed by Eaton and others drew on this archive of resistance, but they were quick to adapt and disseminate them to a wider audience. Legal procedure meant that the indictment prepared for any sedition trial had to include exact statements of the libel being prosecuted. February 1793 saw Thomas Spence acquitted of selling *Rights of Man* because the book was misquoted in the indictment. The situation was even more complicated in prosecutions that depended on the interpretation of figurative or ironic material. Eaton's trial in February 1794 for publishing the 'King Chaunticlere' allegory became the most celebrated instance. On 16 November 1793, Eaton's *Politics for the People* carried a story based on a Thelwall performance at the Capel Court debating society.[75] Thelwall's allegory told the story of a tyrannical gamecock,

> a haughty sanguinary tyrant, nursed in blood and slaughter from his infancy – fond of foreign wars and domestic rebellions, into which he would sometimes drive his subjects, by his oppressive obstinacy, in hopes that he might increase his power and glory by their suppression.

The government claimed that the allegory as printed by Eaton libelled George III. In such cases, the prosecution had to specify exactly what construction they were putting on the passages named in the indictment. The glosses or 'innuendoes' that appear on the charge were requirements of the legal process: the first reference to the 'gamecock' in the indictment was followed by an innuendo explaining the phrase as being used 'to denote and represent our said lord the king'.

John Gurney's brilliant defence of Eaton secured an acquittal. The prosecution had gone so far in its eagerness to find libels, argued Gurney, that they had 'set themselves to work to make one'. More obvious, he argued, to see the gamecock as Louis XVI, or tyrants in general, than George III, who surely, he added archly, could not be understood as a tyrant.[76] The growing self-consciousness of radicals about the manufacture of libels – as they saw it – can be glimpsed in the fact that just three issues before 'King Chaunticlere', Eaton had already published a sonnet 'What Makes a Libel? A Fable':

> In *AESOP's* new-made World of Wit,
> Where Beasts could talk, and read, and, write,
> And say and do as he thought fit;
> A certain Fellow thought himself abus'd,
> And represented by an *Ass*,
> And *Aesop* to the Judge accus'd
> That he defamed was.
> Friend, quoth the Judge, How do you know,
> Whether you are defam'd or no?
> How can you prove that he must mean
> You, rather than another Man?
> Sir, quoth the Man, it needs must be,
> All Circumstances so agree,
> And all the Neighbours say 'tis Me.
> That's somewhat, quoth the Judge, indeed;
> But let this matter pass.
> Since twas not *AESOP*, 'tis agreed
> But *Application* made the *Ass*.[77]

If Eaton had published Thelwall's allegory in full awareness of the defence that could be provided for it, as the sonnet suggests, others quickly picked up on his example. Soon after Eaton's acquittal, for instance, Thomas

Spence published two pages under the title 'Examples of Safe Printing', framed as a response to 'these prosecuting times'. They included a passage from Spenser's *The Faerie Queene* glossed by bogus innuendoes pretending to distance the poem from any malicious intent:

> That tiger, or that other salvage wight:-
> Is so exceeding furious and fell,
> As WRONG,
>
> [Not meaning our most gracious sovereign Lord the King, or the Government of this country]

Spence is alerting his readers to the possibilities of the medium and what can be said by not saying what one means:

> Let us, O ye humble Britons be careful to shew what we do not mean, that the Attorney General may not, in his Indictments, do it for us.

If there was a kind of print magic being conjured here, it was far from being a simple faith that it was enough to print the truth for it to be victorious.[78]

Spatial politics

Print made it possible for radicals to imagine themselves addressing a potentially limitless category of 'the people' and for their readers to imagine themselves as subjects within this category, but these relationships were not experienced as an impersonal information economy or an anonymous public sphere. Personality was one diversifying element within the radical print economy, tracked in four detailed examples in Part II of this book. So too was the variety of spaces wherein readers encountered print and met to debate and discuss it with each other. The radical societies imagined themselves as disseminating political information through a world where print and improvements in transport and communications made 'the people' a more knowable entity than it had ever previously been. The mail coach system, introduced in 1784 by John Palmer, 'provided unprecedented opportunity for "correspondence" and for the diffusion of radical material beyond its metropolitan strongholds'.[79] This speeding up of communication was a crucial part of the context that recommended the electrical metaphor of political sympathy's rapid movement from breast to breast. Such ideas were reinforced at LCS open meetings, where the radical societies could show themselves to be 'public' institutions, rather than a conspiratorial underground their opponents often claimed, but these were only perhaps the most obvious of a range of locations constructed and inhabited by the SCI and LCS.

Location is an important issue for thinking about radical culture. The venues where things happened or were imagined to be happening changed their meanings, an issue that had legal status when it came to questions of innocence or guilt in trials for sedition and treason, as we shall see. Theories of the role of space in the production of social meaning now abound, but in the 1790s places were inevitably fought over as part of a process of establishing the political geography of London. Spaces were contested most obviously in competitions over occupancy. Debating societies were systematically driven from public houses over 1792–3. More complex to resolve were questions of how spaces were understood and perceived. The LCS's idea of itself as improving, for instance, meant that it also produced various spaces in the image of the associational worlds of the eighteenth century, actively participating, as it saw it, in the wider political nation. In 1797, for instance, the informer (never uncovered by his comrades), clerk, and aspiring playwright James Powell wrote to Richard Ford his paymaster in the Treasury Solicitor's office asking for his promised remuneration.[80] Powell's plaintive letter gives an insight into some of the aspirations of those associated with the LCS, and some of the complexities involved in understanding the spaces of popular radicalism.

Powell records expenses involved in setting up a 'conversatione' that he boasted was more numerously attended than one Thelwall inaugurated after his acquittal. Among those who attended Powell's gathering was Citizen Lee, who became 'a constant attendant on that evening but on every other when I was not at home'. When Lee fled to America at the beginning of 1796, he went with Powell's wife. Perhaps more surprisingly, at the time of the 'conversatione', early in 1795, Godwin seems to have been meeting with LCS members as a group, including Powell, Thelwall, and probably Citizen Lee. The entry in Godwin's diary for 17 January refers to 'tea Powel's, w. Ht, Thelwal, Iliff, Bailey, Walker, Manning, Hubbard, Lee, Johns, Fawcet & Dyer'. A similar cast also assembled on the last day of the month: 'tea Powel's, w. Thelwal, Bailey, Hubbard, Vincent, Hunter, G Richter, Walker, Bone, Manning & Lee'.

Meeting with LCS members may have been an attempt at Godwin's 'collision of mind with mind'.[81] No doubt the members of the LCS who attended these meetings were thrilled at the chance to meet the philosopher, which is not to say that they necessarily agreed with his ideas. Tea with Godwin did at least provide an opportunity for the LCS men to demonstrate that they were quite as capable as he of sustaining intellectual improvement. The question of Godwin's influence in the LCS is a topic for later on, but for now I want to pause over Powell's letter and read it with the brief entry in Godwin's diary. On the face of it, Powell's provision of 'bread & cheese & porter' might seem appropriate for members of an organisation often identified with the culture of the alehouse. 'Tea', the term used in Godwin's diary, on the other hand, suggests something more 'polite', perhaps 'domestic' even, as if Powell had got the best china out to welcome the famous political philosopher, but this juxtaposition would imply too crude an opposition between 'polite' and 'popular'. Powell almost certainly knew Godwin before January 1795. He was from a respectable background; at least his father had been a clerk in the Customs House, 'a man of property', Francis Place claimed.[82] Powell certainly harboured literary ambitions, as did others who attended the meeting with Godwin, including Thelwall and Citizen Lee.[83] Secondly, Powell's 'conversatione' took place not in an alehouse, but in a 'private' or 'domestic' context. Powell's wife was evidently a regular presence. Whether she was a participant or someone whose domestic labour facilitated the event and added to its politeness is not known. Many years later Francis Place – who dismissed Powell as 'honest, but silly', still not knowing him to have been a spy – claimed she was 'a woman of the town'.[84] Regardless of Place's judgement, the Powells quite probably aspired to rational improvement of the sort Godwin wrote about in *Political justice*.

'Tea' is Godwin's description of his meeting at Powell's, but the word needs careful treatment. The evidence of the diary is that it may simply be Godwin's general word for any modest repast served in the home (in late afternoon). In the diary, it is often used for meetings that included the consideration of weighty philosophical questions (often in mixed company), and need not imply politeness in a way that militated against the vigorous discussion of political issues. Take, for instance, the 'tea' at 'Barbauld's w. Belsham, Carr, Shiel, Notcut & Aikin jr', on 29 October 1795, where Godwin and his friends 'talk of self-delusion & gen principles'. The same was true at Helen Maria Williams's salon, which aspired to rather more in terms of intellectual exchange than the word 'politeness' may sometimes seem to imply. All these occasions seem to have allowed for the collision of mind with mind, to some degree at least, within the home, even if not within strictly 'domestic' circumstances. For my purposes, the main point is that the LCS and its members involved themselves in the diffusion of knowledge across a diversified urban terrain, which included their homes. The *conversaziones* held by Powell, Thelwall, and others were intrinsic to their commitment to 'reform'. They were one of many spaces beyond LCS meetings proper, but produced by their activity, where ideas were hammered out and solidarity cemented in a convivial environment. Convivial these spaces may have been, but they were also often contested, usually threatened by surveillance, and sometimes even violently interrupted by law officers and their minions.

Epstein has argued for a better understanding of the relationship 'between the logic of spatial practices and language, or better the production of meanings'. Radical culture in the 1790s provides Epstein's key examples of 'naming, mapping, tracking, settling, imagining and counter-imagining' as it played out in 'taverns, courtrooms and the street'. Following Michel de Certeau's understanding of '*space*' as '*practiced place*', Epstein relates spatial production to 'democratic political practice, possibilities of representation, and visions of possibility'.[85] The ambit of these practices included spaces beyond the tavern and the street, including the bookshop and the theatre, and even, for instance, prisons. No less important were everyday places where the practices of taking 'tea' or 'bread & cheese & porter' might give a cast to understanding the activities of the LCS very different from the hostile representations found, for instance, in Gillray's *The London-Corresponding-Society alarm'd* (Figure 3). Gillray's representation of the spatial practices of the LCS as subhuman and beneath contempt, of course, was easier to sustain after the Two Acts had in one sense driven the LCS underground, although in publications like John Gale Jones's *Sketch of a political tour* (1796) the LCS continued to imagine the development of a public sphere out of the interactions between citizens in a variety of places beyond the alehouse, including a stage coach, a circulating library, and even a dance at a public assembly.[86]

Eighteenth-century spaces such as taverns and coffee houses have been understood in Habermasian terms as arenas of 'conviviality where ideas circulate freely among equals'.[87] London's debating societies may seem to be the apotheosis of this idea, but they were subject to an ongoing commentary about their respectability before the 1790s. After the royal proclamations against seditious writings in May and November 1792, they were very much subject not only to surveillance, but also direct and often violent interventions in their proceedings. The reports the spy Captain George Munro sent into the Home Office in November 1792 often struggle to fit his understanding of popular culture with what he saw at the LCS's own debates. He melodramatically described the meeting he saw at the Cock and Crown tavern as a gathering of the 'lowest tradesmen, all continually smoaking and drinking porter', but then concedes they were 'extremely civil'.[88] Such concessions were rare in spy reports. When he

Fig 3 James Gillray, *London-Corresponding-Society alarm'd: vide guilty consciences* [1798]. Courtesy of the Lewis Walpole Library.

started reporting in February 1794, John Groves insisted that it 'requires some mastery over that innate pride, which every well-educated man must naturally possess, even to sit down in their company'.[89] Perhaps more anxious about his social status than Munro, Groves may have felt a social pressure to confirm to his masters that he was of a different order from the men he was reporting on. How such men managed to organise themselves into their own version of the public sphere continued to puzzle polite commentators and the government alike.

John Barrell has provided a nuanced map of LCS organisation across London boroughs.[90] My concern is less with geography than with the production and contestation of different kinds of space. Michael T. Davis has shown the importance of 'the politics of civility' in the LCS. Thomas Hardy's account of the first 'public' meeting – in the Bell on Exeter Street off the Strand – described the participants as 'plain, homely citizens'.[91] The Bell may very well have been neat and 'homely' compared to some of the alehouses where LCS divisions met. Newman rightly points out that distinctions between alehouses and taverns have often been flattened out in analysis.[92] Davis notes how much of the LCS's official documentation is concerned with the orderliness that Place was keen to stress in his

Autobiography. Davis primarily understands these self-representations as the product of the LCS's need 'to represent itself as inclusive, autonomous, as a rule-regulated organization based upon the principle of equality and rational deliberation in order to invert the political messages of loyalists'.[93] This idea of civility extended even to prison sociability, which included visits from Godwin, Amelia Alderson, and various other literary figures sympathetic to reform.[94]

The LCS frequently did represent its own behaviour as intended to 'defeat the various calumnies with which they have been loaded by the advocates of Tyranny & Oppression'.[95] But this self-representation should not be understood only as a functional need to demonstrate its respectability. There is a danger of constructing the LCS as most authentically itself when involved in 'unrespectable' tavern-based activities, as I have already mentioned, and somehow only deferring to external notions of respectability when it met in more disciplined social forms. Quite apart from the practicalities involved in running business meetings, the LCS carried on the popular aspect of enlightenment that saw 'reform' as an opportunity for participation across a diversity of social worlds from debating societies to other forms of print sociability. Lydia and Thomas Hardy (as abolitionists), Citizen Lee (as an evangelical poet, first published under the sponsorship of the *Evangelical Magazine*), and John Thelwall (as a member of debating and numerous other literary and scientific societies) all participated in such worlds before they joined the radical societies. Each saw the LCS as an extension of their commitment to a spirit of improvement, however variously understood.

Long before the 1790s, the contact zones of urban leisure were already subject to complex pressures of policing, representation, and interpretation. In 1781, David Turner, president of the Westminster Forum, presented its debates as a site for the integration of what he calls 'public conversation', but acknowledged that sometimes they failed to transcend their 'ale-house' (Turner's word) associations. The roughness of the debates, Turner believed, discouraged some of those capable of 'classical erudition' from attending, although he insisted that plenty of the educated classes did go.[96] Several times Turner mentions the presence of women at the debates. On one occasion, in response to a remark on the growth of population, 'the brilliant set of ladies in the gallery, spread their fans before their faces'.[97] The presence of women was always crucial to how meaning was constructed in social space. They could grant an aura of respectability, although for some commentators their presence could itself function as a sign of transgression. Powell's wife may have passed from one to the other pole of this representation during the life of his *conversazione*. Her disappearance with Lee into exile in America may have confirmed her status as a 'woman of the town' from Place's point of view, but to others her presence at Powell's gatherings may have conferred politeness on them.

The spatial definitions of such places could have very real consequences for radical groups, as the case of John Frost shows.[98] Frost was an attorney who had been closely involved with the SCI from its beginnings in the 1780s and played an important role in its revival under Horne Tooke's leadership in 1791. When Paine left for Paris in September 1792, Frost accompanied him, writing back regularly to Horne Tooke to describe their progress. Returning to London in October, Frost sat on the SCI committee chosen to confer with the LCS over addressing the French Convention. Reporting on Frost's speech to an LCS meeting a few weeks later, the spy Munro described him as 'almost the only decent Man I have seen in any of their Divisions'. The SCI chose Frost with Joel Barlow to deliver their address to the Convention (and a consignment of a thousand pairs of shoes for the French army). Munro's report of the event from Paris maliciously described Frost being mistaken for a shoemaker by the Convention's deputies.[99] On 6 November between his two trips to Paris, Frost had attended the dinner of an agricultural society at the Percy, a fashionable London coffee house. On his way out, he was stopped by the apothecary Matthew Yateman and asked about France. The two men already knew each other, but their conversation grew heated after Frost told Yateman 'I am for Equality and no King.' When Yateman asked if he meant 'no King in this country', Frost is said to have bawled out 'no Kings in Englands'. At this point, according to their evidence in court, others became involved in the fracas. Although a complaint against Frost was made immediately, the government did not take any action until it was sure he was back in France. A price was put on his head, but Frost wrote from Paris vehemently denying that he had fled justice, and reminding Pitt that they had at one time attended the same meetings in favour of reform. Almost certainly the government wished to avoid a trial, not least because of Frost's possession of correspondence with Pitt from the 1780s, later reprinted in the proceedings of the trial. Probably to dissuade Frost from returning, the government newspapers began suggesting that he had fled to avoid bankruptcy. His wife Eliza informed the *Morning Chronicle* that he was solvent, which Frost proved on his reappearance. With Frost back in London, stalemate ensued. Sheridan queried the silence on the case in Parliament on 4 March to suggest that the government now wished to drop it.

When the trial did finally commence two months later, Thomas Erskine's defence strategy turned on two issues. The first was whether Frost spoke 'advisedly', that is, whether he could be charged with intentionally aiming to spread disaffection if he had been in drink. The second part of the defence depended upon understanding the space of the coffee house as 'private' and properly beyond the reach of a law on seditious words. Erskine insisted that the 'common and private intercourses of life' were protected from prosecution:

> Does any man put such constraints upon himself in the most private moments of his life, that he would be contented to have his loosest and lightest words recorded, and set in array against him in a Court of Justice?

Informants, who 'dog men into taverns and coffee-houses', as Erskine put it, 'eavesdropping . . . upon loose conversations', were proving themselves no gentlemen in their failure to respect distinctions between private and public life. The prosecution agreed that it was hard to imagine a case in which 'the public necessity and expediency of a prosecution should be so strong as to break in upon the relations of a private life'.[100] It rejected the idea that 'a public coffee house' could be imagined in these terms. The Attorney General insisted there had been no 'breach of the sweet confidences of private life': the word 'sweet', as Barrell has noted, implying something like an understanding of 'private' as 'domestic'.[101] Few instances from the 1790s reveal more clearly how space was central to the production of meaning. The prosecution's mention of 'sweet confidences' at Frost's trial, implicitly using an idea of female spheres of influence to quarantine the domestic from the political, also shows how much questions of gender were continuously involved in the production of those meanings.

Gendering radicalism

Political meetings in the eighteenth century were routinely masculine affairs, dominated by rituals of speech-making, toasts, and serious alcohol consumption, equally routinely reported in the newspapers, and, in this regard at least, open to public scrutiny and censure. So Charles James Fox's speech to the Whig Club in December 1792, a few weeks after the incident with Frost at the Percy coffee house, and a few days prior to Paine's trial, was reported in the newspapers and, not unusually, garnered satirical poems by way of response. One such poem presented the event as a series of empty toasts on the principles of reform:

The zealous Whigs, obedient to command,
Drink till they stare, and call again for more:
Nor does the Bottle quit their ready hand,
Till *Whigs* with *Whigs* lie Tumbling on the floor.[102]

Originally printed in the *Sun* newspaper, the poem also came out in a Ridgway pamphlet accompanied by a satirical account of Frost's trip to Paris. Imprisoned for publishing Paine's *Rights of Man* a few months later, it was Ridgway who had put Fox's speech – or a version of it – into circulation as a two penny pamphlet. Fox's allies in the Whig Club swiftly wrote to the newspapers to distance their leader from the declaration of support for reform. The satirical poet makes great play with the price of Ridgway's pamphlet and implied that Fox was selling himself cheap in drink, but shows no signs of discomfort at or censure of the bibulous behaviour itself. Fox is indulging, as it were, in what men-of-the-world did, without it necessarily compromising his claims to be regarded as a public figure. The satire comes from the idea of an alliance of a statesman like Fox with the principles of Paine in a 2d pamphlet.

Plenty of other satirists in the 1790s exploited the idea of gentlemen drunkenly losing their sense of social hierarchy by consorting with lower-class radicals, or at least seeming to consort with them in sentiment if not in practice. Take, for instance, the satires on the anniversary dinner of the friends of the French Revolution held at the Crown and Anchor on 14 July 1791. After toasting 'The Rights of Man', Merry's *Ode for the fourteenth of July* was recited and then its chorus sung to celebrate the Fall of the Bastille.[103] Although there are conflicting reports of the poet's presence at the meeting, Merry's poem, as Harriet Guest has pointed out, 'delights in communicating a social exuberance that, in male company at least, appears limitless and unconstrained'.[104] The social trajectory of Merry's heady blend of poetry and radical politics is the subject of a later chapter, but its direction was implicit in the familiar electrical metaphor:

Fill high the animating glass,
And let the electric ruby pass
From hand to hand, from soul to soul,
Who shall the energy control,
Exalted, pure, refin'd,
The Health of Humankind.[105]

The response of the Treasury newspapers to these dinners, in Guest's words, 'oscillated rather uneasily between treating the occasion as a serious threat to national stability and security, and dismissively mocking its folly'.[106] 'The Political Mirror' paragraphs that appeared in the *World* (15 July 1791) began by placing the meeting in the context of the political sociability of the time:

> In the circumstance of a set of people assembling for the purposes of conviviality – however numerous the meeting – however mixt – or however riotous and brutal in its conduct and effects, there can be no cause for even momentary alarm.

Having confirmed the idea that British society was tolerant of such meetings – even when they met 'for the avowed purpose of celebrating an important political event' – the paper then suggested that these gentlemen would need to be watched with special vigilance, partly because they were in danger of losing a properly masculine sense of their social and political identities:

> The Englishman who can now avow such rapturous admiration of a Government *unformed* and *inefficient* has lost all due respect for his own – and in a mind thus prone to change, and doating on licentiousness, the transition from thought to action is made with an accommodating facility.

W. T. Fitzgerald satirised 'REVOLUTION DINNERS' in *The Sturdy Reformer* (1792) as scenarios where elite libertinism descended into social confusion:

> In the world no distinction of rank shall be seen,
> But a billingsgate Drab be a Mate for a Queen;
> Dukes, Dustmen, Grooms, Barons, in friendship shall meet
> And with porter and gin hiccup through the street.[107]

The idea that irresponsible members of the elite were encouraging those who had no head for politics to think themselves deprived of their rights was a criticism often made against Merry, especially after May 1792 when he became increasingly active, first in the SCI's negotiations with the LCS, and then later in the British Club at Paris. Ironically, at around the time Fitzgerald was attacking gentleman reformers, he and Merry were also serving together on the committee of the Literary Fund.[108] Re-elected to the Fund's committee *in absentia* in May 1792, Merry never appeared there again. He had fallen out of one form of 'sociability' and towards another that men such as Fitzgerald thought scarcely merited the word.

The relative tolerance shown for the bibulous behaviour of Merry and his friends at the Crown and Anchor dinner was not likely to be extended to the LCS. Sometimes the two worlds mixed, as at the anniversary dinner of the SCI on 2 May 1794 also held at the Crown and Anchor. Horne Tooke invited some few Whig MPs thought to be sympathetic to reform, but also gave away free tickets to LCS members.[109] Among those who attended from more respectable circles was the MP for Beverley, John Wharton. Interviewed by the Privy Council after the arrests for treason had begun, Wharton was embarrassed and perhaps fearful, insisting that he had attended only because Horne Tooke had persuaded him that he would lend the 'convivial' meeting an air of respectability. Pressed about the presence of LCS members and the kinds of toasts Horne Tooke and others gave from the chair, Wharton claimed to have been shocked to see them at the meeting, admitting it dangerous 'to give such Toasts to such persons'. 'So much disgusted with the proceedings of the day', was Wharton, 'that I expressed my resolution to many of my Friends that night to have nothing more to do with such societies.'[110] Others did not see much out of the ordinary run of conduct at political meetings. Thomas Symonds told the Privy Council it 'did not appear to him that the people at the dinner were so very inferior a class'.[111] Horne Tooke was a gentleman in social terms and his conduct was quite as inebriated as that of Fox and his friends had been at the Whig Club. When at their free-and-easies LCS members went through their own boozy rituals and symbolic toasts, they were articulating their own version of eighteenth-century political theatre, but even when they mixed at the politer arena of the Crown and Anchor elite reviewers seldom saw it in these terms.

Some of the LCS's own members also thought drunken levity unworthy of an organisation aiming at political reform. Here the issue was less about social hierarchy than codes of behaviour the members themselves deemed appropriate to the LCS as a political association. These concerns could manifest themselves in terms of broader cultural shifts associated with the improvement of manners and morals. They could also be raised in relation to questions of the political discipline discussed by Lottes. The larger associational world that housed the political theatre of the eighteenth century was growing more inclined to worry at the libertinism of Fox and his ilk by the end of the eighteenth century. Songs and toasts were becoming objects of concern, for instance, when they seemed to license behaviour coming to be seen as unrespectable. *The Toast Master*, for instance, was reissued in 1792, probably to take advantage of the profusion of political dinners 'in this grand aera of contention for political and civil Liberty', but warned that 'the Libertine alone' would be disappointed by its selection. This 'genteel collection' was careful to distance itself from any 'Language that is degrading to human Nature' and any 'evil Tendency arising from improper Sentiments'. A few years later *Pocock's Everlasting Songster* (1800) presented its collection of songs and toasts as avoiding 'those of a political, wicked or vulgar tendency, which have so long been suffered by Chairmen of different Societies to reign predominant'. The 'rules for behaviour' it offered were designed in part at least to make it more possible for women to be part of convivial meetings: 'at this place it will not be amiss to say, that a popular toast which has been the too general rule to give first ("To the Exclusion of every Female," whose company we ought rather to court than discourage) has been a disgrace'.[112]

LCS toast lists seem to respect these rules for the most part. Thomson's list in *Tribute to Liberty*, discussed in the next chapter, included toasts to 'the Rights of Woman' and 'female patriots'. Women were present at LCS-related events, but not at divisional meetings, from what the archive shows, or, probably, at the more boisterous alehouse celebrations. Thelwall's radicalism tended to be strongly freighted towards the idea of an affective domain that distanced itself from the libertinism of men such as Horne Tooke. The memoir published by his second wife acknowledged her husband's political debts to Horne Tooke, accepting he was his 'political father', but printed Thelwall's reservations about his 'deficiencies of heart and morals'. The memoir made it clear that Tooke's politics could not excuse his moral laxity:

> I still indeed respect the politician, but I abhor the man . . . the being who even in his attachments and social intercourse is merely a politician, is without feeling.

These comments were primarily to do with the coldness Horne Tooke showed Thelwall after the treason trials, advising him to quit politics, but they also reveal that Tooke had advised Thelwall that he could have done better than marry his first wife Susan Thelwall, or 'Stella', as he called her in his poetry.[113] From the sentimental perspectives that informed much of Thelwall's writing, Tooke was a representative of an older Whig-aristocratic idea of sociability that was increasingly the object of discourses of moral improvement from across the political spectrum.

Thelwall's moral perspective sometimes translated into an idea of separate spheres that would exclude his wife from involvement in his political life.[114] His poetry 'To Stella' did frequently present hearth and home as a place presided over by his wife's genius from which he was torn by the demands of politics. The lived experience of their political and domestic lives was more complex. Her letters to her family at home reveal Susan Thelwall to have been passionately involved and well informed about her husband's struggle to keep the popular debating societies open. They also suggest that she sometimes attended them with him. Her presence might be understood as similar to Amelia Alderson's experiences of radical London in 1794, as Guest puts it, 'from within a group of kith and kin'.[115] Outside that protection, politically active women, especially from outside the elite, were very vulnerable to the kind of misogynistic assessment Place made of James Powell's wife. Thelwall was certainly in the vanguard of those who defended the domestic virtues of the radical movement. He often spoke from the position outlined by Anna Barbauld's *Civic sermons to the people* (1792):

> Love then this Country; unite its idea with your domestic comforts ... remember that each of you, however inconsiderable, is benefited by your Country; so your Country, however extensive, is benefited by every one of the least of you.[116]

Invasions of the sweetness of domestic life by informers were central to Thelwall's descriptions of his struggles with political authority, as Wagner has shown in her account of his 'exploitation of privacy'. From early on in the 1790s, Thelwall routinely presented his private life as the basis of his political virtue. At the same time, he represented intrusion into his premises in Beaufort Buildings as an unwonted intrusion into private life:

> My hours of conviviality have been attended by spies and sycophants, my doors beset with evedroppers [sic], my private chambers haunted by the familiar spirits of an Infernal Inquisition, and my confidential friends stretched on the rack of interrogatory, in order to extort from them the conversation which in the unsuspecting hours of social hilarity may have been uttered at my own table.[117]

The irony, of course, as Wagner points out, is that Thelwall invited scrutiny of the space that he constructs as vulnerable to invasions by public authorities. 'The very sphere of life [Thelwall] aims to protect from public interference', she writes, 'is the sphere he places squarely before the enquiring eyes of the public.'[118]

In the rejoinder to the attack on his lecturing in Godwin's *Considerations on Lord Grenville's and Mr. Pitt's bills* (1795), Thelwall invoked the philosopher's bachelorhood and his supposed social reclusiveness as evidence of his unfitness to judge of politics as a social domain. Godwin's 'life of domestic solitude' had rendered him unsympathetic to 'every feeling of private, and sometimes public justice'.[119] Here the gendered separate spheres sometimes imagined in Thelwall's poetry are collapsed into a more complicated relationship. The domestic is not opposed to the political, but serves as its condition of possibility. In practice, Thelwall's 'private chambers' in Beaufort Buildings were also places of 'conviviality' and 'social hilarity'. Effectively the headquarters of the LCS in the early months of 1794, Beaufort Buildings provided Thelwall with a lecture hall, a family home (on the top floor), a place for LCS committee meetings (on the ground floor), and, on the same level, a bookshop for distributing radical literature; but even before their removal to Beaufort Buildings Susan Thelwall participated in the political life of the metropolis.

The couple had married in the summer of 1791, when Susan Thelwall was seventeen. Among the papers seized at Thelwall's arrest in 1794 were two letters she wrote back to her family in Oakham. The first is dated 19 December 1792 from the period when Thelwall was struggling to keep open the debating societies:

> I suppose you have heard by the newspapers that politics run very high at present, but as those papers are generally the vehicles of falshood & corruption, you perhaps may receive truer information from a female democrate. The society which was last winter held at Coach Makers Hall & which has this winter been remov'd to the King's Arms Cornhill has been illegally suppressed.

Self-conscious about the novelty of her involvement in politics, it seems, she makes her politicisation the occasion of sending the letter at all: 'I should perhaps not have written (for I believe you are a letter in my debt) if I was not become a great politician.' The letter recalls accompanying Thelwall to a debate at the King's Arms, Cornhill, a few weeks earlier, in an 'exceedingly crowded room', where 'a foolish Aristocrate' loaded him with 'invective and abuse'. The meeting eventually broke up in confusion. The debate was almost certainly the one attended by James Walsh, a Bow Street officer, on 'The Alliance of Kings against the Liberties of France' on 12 November, with around five hundred people present.[120]

Mary Thale and Donna Andrew have shown that women often attended and spoke at debating societies, especially around 1780, a peak, it seems, for such societies in the metropolis, but they continued to be a visible presence into the late 1780s. In 1780 'The Female Congress' met at the King's Arms, presumably in the same great room where Thelwall spoke in 1792. By this time it was no longer a tavern, having been broken up into separate apartments after a fire in 1778, but a large room available for auctions as well as debates. La Belle Assemblée was another female society thriving at this point. In February 1780, meeting in rooms in the

Haymarket, it boasted that its members 'knowing nothing of the affairs of state, do not interfere with them', but by the following month it was asking its members: 'Whether it would not be for the benefit of this Country, if Females had a Voice in the Elections of Representatives, and were eligible to sit in Parliament, as well as the Men?'[121] When La Belle Assemblée was revived for a few weeks in 1788, now in Golden Square, it began by again raising the question of votes for women.[122] The City Debates met at the King's Arms in this period, proud of 'the display of female eloquence from which this society has already received so many obligations', before being replaced by one comprised mainly of law students at the end of 1791. The students were keen to distance themselves from the previous management. Public opinion was far from undivided on debating societies, especially when it came to the involvement of women. *The Times* of 29 October 1788 took the view that 'the debating ladies would be better employed at their needle and thread, a good sempstress being a more amiable character than a female orator'.

There is no evidence that Susan Thelwall directly participated in the debates she attended in 1792, even if we know other women were doing so a few years before. The King's Arms may no longer have been part of a tavern by then, but even so things obviously got boisterous enough for the Lord Mayor to use the riotous behaviour as a pretext to close the debating society down. Susan Thelwall's letter and other sources suggest that the mayor had provoked the disorder with this end in mind. She had obviously been reading newspaper reports of Fox's speech at the Whig Club, and judges it to have been more radical than the radical societies had anticipated:

> Fox's speech, which I suppose you have read, & which is bolder & more explicit, than any body expected of him, has put us poor democrates a little in heart again. If you have read it, you are informed that a proposition was to be made to suspend the Habeas Corpus Act, which will prevent persons who are taken prisoners from receiving bail, which will be a fine oppressive thing; for I am informed that more than a thousand names are down for prosecution, among which, I suppose, is my Thelwalls.[123]

Her next letter, probably from 9 March 1793, the day of a dinner of the Friends of the Press that Thelwall attended, complains at political interference in the publication of *The Peripatetic*, but notes with pride the interest that aristocrats were showing in his work: 'Mr. T has receiv'd information from Horne Took that several Members of Parliament & those sort of folk among the Blues & Buffs that is the opposition party have made great enquiries after him & seem'd inclin'd to assist him.'[124] She revels in informing her brother of her new status as a political woman, announced in her first letter: 'things are gone to such a length that you see it even makes us women politicians'. She even contemplates imprisonment in the cause: 'For my part, Mr T has taken such an active part in them, that I have been in expectation of accompanying him to prison. Well, if it should be so never mind. I think I might accompany him there in a much worse cause.' Taken together, Susan Thelwall's two letters convey not just her sense of pride in her husband, both as a radical and literary man, but also an equally vigorous sense of her own engagement with public affairs.

Nearly three years later, after he had actually been imprisoned, John Thelwall was in dispute with William Godwin about whether the virtues of conversation and debate could be sustained in populous assemblies as in more constrained forms of sociability. Thelwall's construction of a private sphere against the encroachment of state surveillance was not centred solely on the domestic space, but was constituted by a complex sense of the relations between the domestic and other spaces of urban sociability, including the coffee house, lecture theatre, playhouse, and convivial meetings in the tavern where he often cut a memorable figure. Presenting the domestic space as at the heart of what was being attacked by government was not unique to Thelwall. Richard Citizen Lee, for instance, had come to prominence within the radical movement (as Powell noted in his letter) with his efforts on behalf of the imprisoned patriots. These seem to have included a poem he published on the death of Lydia Hardy. Lee's poem was published in a cheap freestanding pamphlet, sold for the benefit of the families of those imprisoned under the suspension of the Habeas Corpus Act.[125] Lydia Hardy is made a martyr to her husband's virtue: '*For thee O husband! 'Tis for thee I die*'. If Lee's poem subsumes her potential for radical agency into wifely duty, not all accounts represent her in quite such passive terms.[126] Soon after Hardy's arrest, the LCS published *An account of the seizure of citizen Thomas Hardy* that presented it as an invasion of private life that Lydia Hardy firmly resisted:

> The house of Citizen Hardy, was assailed about half an hour after six on Monday morning, the 12th May 1794, by a messenger from one of the secretaries of state, accompanied by four or five runners. Mrs Hardy having learned the occasion of the intrusion, requested them to withdraw while she put on some clothes: This they refused, and she anxious of sending for some friends was obliged to dress herself in their presence, one of them walking about all the whole with a pistol in hand.[127]

The scene could be construed as a pointed rewriting of Burke's famous account of Marie Antoinette in his *Reflections*. The object of sensibility is now not limited to the refined sufferings of the queen of France, but extended to the family of the shoemaker secretary of the LCS. In his *Sketch of a political tour*, John Gale Jones proudly records bringing a lecture audience to tears with his account of the death of Mrs Hardy.[128] 'The same unconstitutional means', insisted the LCS pamphlet, had seen 'Citizen Eaton's house plundered', with the illegal confiscation of 'a considerable quantities of printed books'.[129] Home and bookshop are conjoined here as spaces that ought to be beyond the reach of government interference, but not as outside political practice as such.

Women do not seem to have been members of the LCS itself, but they were a presence in the radical movement in a broader sense, and not simply identified with the sanctity of the home as a sphere absolutely separate from politics. Sarah Thomson and Susan Thelwall both petitioned the LCS for family support when their husbands were in prison, on the assumption that the society had a moral obligation in this regard. John Hillier's statement to the Privy Council in the wake of the May arrests for treason claimed to remember Thomas Breillat's wife interrupting a meeting to ask the group when they were going to free the prisoners from Newgate.[130] Here was a case of the domestic exploding into the political. There are other accounts of women being welcomed into the political sociability of the LCS. Amelia Alderson, of higher status than most of the women mentioned so far, recorded a visit to Eaton's shop with her cousin Ives Hurry:

> I then told [Mrs Eaton] that curiosity led me to her shop, and that I came from that city of sedition Norwich . . . at last we became so fraternized, that Mrs. Eaton shut the shop door and gave us chairs. I will not relate the information I heard, but I could have talked with him all night.[131]

Another customer, who turned out to be Charles Sinclair, lately released from gaol in Edinburgh, told Alderson 'that democratic women were rare, and that he heartily wished he could introduce me to two charming patriots at Edinburgh, who were, though women, up to circumstances'.[132] Bookshops were important places of radical sociability, but perhaps represented a more easily insulated space than the King's Arms. Powell's self-pitying letter to his superiors in the Treasury Solicitor's office notes that he had first met Lee in Eaton's shop. When their husbands were in prison or on the run, as Eaton may have at the time of Alderson's visit, women like Susannah Eaton ran their businesses and hosted radical *conversaziones*.[133]

Locking the door and placing the chairs in a circle may have construed the bookshop space into an intimate or domestic configuration, but the conversation follows the latest political news. Alderson certainly ventured into the diversity of social spaces in eighteenth-century London. The same evening that she visited the bookshop, she went on – with Hurry, Sinclair, and a man she calls MacDonald, who was probably the journalist D. E. MacDonnell – to visit Joseph Gerrald in Newgate. Alderson also seems to have been on familiar terms with radicals like Thomas Hardy, passing on his greetings to William Godwin in one of her letters, which also includes a casual mention of visiting political lectures in Norwich.[134] Returning to Norwich from these exciting London scenes was a matter for regret in at least one of her letters to Godwin. Nevertheless, as Guest points out, Alderson's relative licence may have been conditional upon friends and family strongly connected to London's radical networks. The same may hold true, as I have suggested, for Susan Thelwall's visits to hear her husband debate.[135]

Amelia Alderson and Susan Thelwall may have been special cases in their freedom to visit various scenes in the landscape of London radicalism, but radical associations did not necessarily elide women in their world-view. Arianne Chernock has warned against the assumption that available masculine categories of citizenship always operated to the exclusion of women. She notes, for instance, that John Gale Jones defended the idea of a 'female legislature' on his tour of Kent in 1796.[136] Earlier, in the late summer of 1793, the LCS's central committee had recommended 'the establishment of a female Society of Patriots &c'. The minutes confirmed 'this Society will give every assistance to all who work to promote the cause of Reform'.[137] The question of female suffrage had certainly been alive in many of the debating societies that had given LCS members their civic training. In October 1788, 'a Club of female literatae' had proposed a debate at Coachmakers' Hall, the venue where Thelwall made his name. Such groups, as we have already seen, did not confine themselves to what the Coachmakers' Hall society called 'questions as more immediately interest the female heart', but also debated the role of women in politics. Just such a group may have fed into the society of female patriots welcomed by the LCS. The open-air LCS meetings of 1795, addressed by Gale Jones, Thelwall, and others, were reportedly 'crowded with Citizens, both male and female'. In the account of the 26 October meeting published by Citizen Lee, the spatial rhetoric is of a gathering 'met in the open face of day', scorning attempts to drive it underground in retreat from 'the eye of observation'. If the language of invasions of privacy appears in its reference to a victimised cast of 'the helpless widow and wretched orphan', at the open meetings women were implicitly taken to contribute to the 'persevering efforts of reason'.[138] Interestingly, Lee's account ends with an advertisement for a cheap edition of Wollstonecraft's *Rights of Woman*, flanked by others for two scurrilous pamphlets, *A faithful narrative of the last illness, death, and interment of the Rt. Hon. William Pitt* and *A True Copy of an extraordinary Indictment found in a Pocket Book dropped by an Attorney General.*[139] Whether Lee ever brought out the cheap edition of Wollstonecraft seems unlikely, but perhaps only because he was arrested a few weeks after the meeting. He advertised it in more than one place. Similarly William Hodgson produced a proposal for a treatise called *The Female Citizen*. His address 'To the Public' argued that 'in a general Struggle for FREEDOM . . . it would be a scandalous Omission to overlook the Injuries of the FAIRER PART OF THE CREATION'.[140] Like the 1793 proposal for a society of female patriots, Hodgson and Lee's advertisements suggest we should be careful of any assumption that the radical movement operated with an exclusively masculine notion of citizenship. Nevertheless, the proliferation of radical societies after 1792, the focus of the next chapter, did not see this 'scandalous Omission' rectified. Hodgson and Lee's proposals seems to have been lost in the turbulence of 'these prosecuting times' when both men found themselves imprisoned for seditious libel.

CHAPTER 2

The radical associations and 'the general will'

'The general will is always good, and can never deceive. By what sign shall we know it?' This question was asked in an essay published by Citizen Lee in 1797, exiled in Philadelphia.[1] The answer given was: 'By the open call of the general and common interest.' Despite the confidence of this answer, Lee and his former associates in London had been searching for political and cultural forms commensurate with the sovereignty of the people since the foundation of the LCS in 1792. Not just a body focused on the extension of the franchise, the LCS participated in a more general enquiry into how best to collect and represent the opinions of the people. The issue was often 'moral' as well as 'political', to use the terms of the magazine the LCS began to publish in 1796. 'Painite democrats', writes Seth Cotlar,

> devoted so much time and energy to the production and dissemination of print because they regarded it as the best way to create a world where political ideas and decisions would emerge out of conversations among ordinary citizens and not just filter down from their leaders.[2]

Paine's *Rights of Man* had celebrated revolutions as 'the subjects of universal conversation'.[3] How best to sustain this universal conversation, what forms it should take, were questions asked by the radical societies from the very beginning, when Thomas Hardy set out the terms he thought the LCS should proceed upon.

Mr Hardy's correspondents

Thomas Hardy is now routinely acknowledged as the founder of the LCS and most often mentioned as one of the defendants at the treason trials of 1794, with the 'gentleman radical' Horne Tooke and Thelwall. Of late, Thelwall has started to generate a rich secondary literature, focused especially on his poetry, the relationship with Coleridge and Wordsworth, and most recently his novel *The Daughter of Adoption*.[4] These developments followed on from the interest in Thelwall's political ideas and his role as the 'organic' intellectual of the LCS stimulated by E. P. Thompson's essay 'Hunting the Jacobin Fox'.[5] My final chapter engages with the recent academic work on Thelwall, but Hardy has scarcely ever been thought about as a political agent in the same terms. Instead his place has been as a solid figure with 'a demure cast of character', as his friend Francis Place put it.[6] Historians of radicalism usually present him as the representative artisan radical, *the political cobbler*. Thompson excepted him from what he called 'the characteristic vice of the English Jacobins – self-dramatization', but in the process only confirmed the idea of Hardy set out in John Binns's picture of him as a man who 'dressed plainly, talked frankly, never at any time assuming airs or making pretensions'.[7] Binns may be providing an accurate enough description of Hardy, but dressing plainly and talking frankly were themselves forms of self-fashioning that carried with them certain social meanings.

Examining Hardy's role in giving the LCS its early character reveals a more complex figure than accounts of him as a stolid constitutionalist with eyes fixed on the Duke of Richmond's plan allow. Although this is not the place to talk about his later career in any detail, in it he fulfilled a role as the historian and archivist of the LCS; continued to be active in support of the radical MP Sir Francis Burdett; played a key role in setting up a society for London Scots; facilitated the return of several political exiles via the Literary Fund; and wrote regularly to newspapers and magazines under the pseudonym 'Crispin'.[8] Just after his death, *Memoir of Thomas Hardy, Founder of and Secretary to, the London Corresponding Society* (1832) was published.[9] Hardy's *Memoir* originated as an institutional history of the LCS begun no later than 1799, the year the society was outlawed. Only after several failed attempts to get it published, offering it at least twice to the journalist John Dyer Collier, in 1802 and 1807, did he transmute it into the posthumous autobiography.[10] Hardy's *Memoir* stands at the end of a sustained effort on his behalf to keep the possibilities of a democratic politics alive. The bundle of pamphlets he donated to the Mitcham Book Society was part of the same attempt: 'I sincerely wish that it may prosper – societies of that kind are calculated to diffuse much knowledge and information to the members who compose it when judiciously conducted.'[11] Hardy's later accounts of the earliest weeks of the LCS present it as emerging from precisely the kind of popular discussion and debate he imagined the Mitcham society perpetuating.

The LCS fashioned a place within the 'public conversation' that had been emerging out of the uneasy relationships between newspapers, debating societies, and politics throughout the eighteenth century.[12] By 1790 there was 'a cacophony of open debating societies discussing a medley of topics'.[13] John Thelwall found his way into the political arena via the Society for Free Debate at Coachmakers' Hall in the 1780s. The occasion for Thelwall's involvement was probably the surge of public interest surrounding the fall of the Fox–North coalition and the fate of the Pitt ministry over 1783–4.[14] An earlier satirical poem on the Society there, dating from 1780, described it as a place where 'our introductory sixpences, like death and stage-coaches, had levelled all distinctions, and jostled wits, lawyers, politicians, and mechanics, into the confusion of the last day'. The last phrase alludes to the millenarian confusion of the Gordon Riots of 1780, occasioned by Lord George Gordon presenting the petition of the Protestant Association to Parliament. Gordon had announced his plans at a meeting at Coachmakers' Hall attended by two thousand people at the end of May 1780. The ferment surrounding Gordon was an important part of the surge in activity in the debating societies. By 1792, its effects were far from dissipated. A mob was rumoured to have been gathering to break Gordon out of Newgate on the evening of the 14 July dinner of 1791. His influence was a palpable if often unwelcome presence in the early years of the LCS until his death.[15]

Thomas Hardy arrived in London in 1777. At some unknown point, he became an associate of Lord Gordon's and very likely a member of the Protestant Association. Gordon is an important figure in the early pages of Hardy's *Memoir*, although they distance the shoemaker from the nobleman's 'wild schemes'.[16] In its early months, the LCS blocked attempts by Gordon and his associates to gain influence in the society, although his spectre haunted the LCS even after his death in 1793.[17] Hardy's role in these decisions is not clear from the surviving minutes, but in the *Memoir*, where they are not mentioned, he defended Gordon as 'a much injured man'. This opaquely sympathetic passage implies an establishment conspiracy against Gordon, presenting him as a victim to 'the malice of his persecutors', but declines 'to state who they were'.[18] An earlier draft 'History' of the LCS mentions no trace of any connection between Hardy and Gordon; presumably the memory of 1780 was still too close to risk even mentioning the name in a document designed to justify the LCS as a public body. In both the 'History' and the published *Memoir*, Hardy presents the origins of the society as arising from a culture of informal engagement in public affairs by working men in their leisure hours: 'After the business of the day was ended they retired as was customary for tradesmen to do to a public house after supper. . . conversation followed condoling with each other on the miserable and wretched state the people were reduced to.'[19]

Evidence from Hardy's letter book of the period both corroborates and complicates this picture. Written on the back of the first letter in Hardy's surviving correspondence is a draft of LCS rules and resolutions. They register his characteristic sense of the people's ability to shape their own destiny:

> Providence has kindly furnished men in every situation with faculties necessary for judging of what concerns them it is somewhat strange that the multitude should suffer a few with no better natural intellects than their own to usurp the important power of governing them without controul.[20]

Addressed to a cousin back in Scotland, the next letter was written only a few days after the LCS started meeting. Beginning with family matters, including Lydia Hardy's ill health, it uses an everyday metaphor to introduce the politics of the day:

> A dish of Chat about politicks Foreign or domestick I relish very well when I have leisure hour or two & will give you my opinions in few words without being asked of the revolution of France [which] at this present moment engrosses conversation.[21]

The French Revolution Hardy describes as 'one of the greatest events that has taken place in the history of the world' and goes on to explain that there is 'a good deal of talk here of society's forming in different parts of the Nation for a reform of parliament'. Some sense of Hardy standing on the edge of a new way of thinking about and doing politics is hinted at by the fact that 'nation' here was originally written as 'kingdom'. Hardy is beginning to conceive of those linked across the hundreds of miles between England and Scotland as 'the people' of a nation and less as the 'subjects' of a kingdom. More specifically, Hardy seems to be edging towards the sense of 'an emerging nation of reader-citizens' that Seth Cotlar sees as central to Paine's legacy.[22]

The idea of nation scouted in Hardy's letter may also suggest a people inhabiting something like the homogenous empty time of Benedict Anderson's imagined communities. Anderson's communities are synchronised across distance in space by print, including acts of reading the daily newspaper.[23] Whether literally present to each other to discuss the news of the day in London public houses, as were Hardy and his friends, or dispersed members of a familial network linked by correspondence, as Hardy was with his cousin, these networks develop a national imaginary facilitated by emergent systems of public communication. Nevertheless, further examination of Hardy's correspondence reveals his idea of time to have been neither homogenous nor empty in the Andersonian sense. Ultimately, Anderson's thesis assumes the steady onward march of nation predicated on a secular modernity, but a messianic religious perspective, not surprising in an associate of Lord Gordon's, fired Hardy's private worldview. At Hardy's trial in 1794, the prosecution – without much explanation – made a great deal of the 'enthusiasm' of his belief that the rights of man would herald universal peace. At one point, he is even linked with the millenarian 'Fifth Monarchy Men' of the previous century. 'In their case', the judge commented in his summing up, 'their treason grew out of their religion.'[24] Little obvious in the published documents of the LCS or even those seized by the government seems to warrant such a digression. The spy George Lynam had testified to the exclusion of Gordon's associates, seemingly ignorant of Hardy's association with the nobleman.[25] Possibly the link between Hardy and enthusiasm was based on the general assumption that popular opinion operated as a kind of virus, whether religious or not, but the court may also have drawn its own conclusions from the religious complexion of those who testified to Hardy's piety. Most of them were Scots Presbyterians, including the minister James Steven (sometimes Stevens), of the Crown Court chapel, which Hardy attended.[26] No doubt an English judge ready to bring up the Fifth Monarchy men in his summing up already had his own negative view of Scots Presbyterians and the 'auld licht'.

From his arrival in London in the 1770s, Hardy had worshipped at Crown Court, near Covent Garden, initially presided over by Rev. William Cruden, the predecessor of Steven.[27] Something of the flavour of Cruden's own scriptural politics can be gleaned from the volume of sermons he published after his death:

> THERE are no slaves in the house of God. *His yoke is easy; his burden light*; and *his work* truly *honourable and glorious*. Much of the allegiance rendered to earthly Sovereigns, is the effect of dread or compulsion, and dictated by the fears of the subjects; and as extorted from them, in many cases, by the tyrannical engines of arbitrary power, they long for an opportunity of breaking off the yoke.[28]

Brad Jones has recently suggested that this kind of religious questioning of the legitimacy of government formed a trail of gunpowder from the

Protestant Association to the radicalism of the 1790s.[29] The Baptist minister William Winterbotham followed this trail to Newgate in 1793.[30] Hardy may have started in much the same place to end up in the same prison in 1794. The Protestant petition that sparked the riots of 1780 lists 'Thomas Hardy' next to 'William McMaster', the name of another member of the congregation at Crown Court.[31]

Later in the 1780s, Hardy was involved in controversy about the rights of the congregation at Crown Court chapel. Debates over the right of the congregation to select its minister were just the kind of thing that made English judges suspicious of Scots Presbyterians. Hardy seems to have been a ringleader in the resistance to an attempt to impose a minister on Crown Court after Cruden's death. His draft *Memoir* makes the connection between kirk politics and his later radicalism explicit:

> This circumstance is mentioned to show what hand Thomas Hardy had in this, and what a great fire a little spark may kindle: He afterwards was the founder of the London Corresponding Society which threatened destruction to the old & deep rooted corruptions of the Government of the country by a radical reformation of the gross abuses in the government – both these things were begun by him with the purest motives, to do good to his fellow men.[32]

In the version published in 1832, instead of this rapid assertion of the connection between religious politics and the LCS, Hardy inserted an anecdote about an unfortunate visit of Lord Gordon to Crown Court at the shoemaker's invitation. The effect within the text is to break the more direct causal relationship between kirk politics and radicalism that the draft proposes, although Gordon's behaviour as described in the anecdote – he stood up and execrated the minister for giving a pre-prepared sermon – scarcely meliorates Anglican stereotypes of Scots Presbyterians.[33]

One of those involved in the early tavern discussions about founding the LCS was George Walne, Hardy's brother-in-law, who later discovered *The Englishman's Right* in a cheese shop. In 1791, Walne's name appeared at the end of a pamphlet called *Divine Warrants, Ends, Advantages, and Rules, of the Fellowship Society*. Based at Crown Court, this 'Fellowship Society' aimed at promoting 'prayer, spiritual conversation, &c.', with rules about meeting for discussion very like those of the LCS:

> That we shall keep a correspondence with other Christian Societies of the same nature in *England* or *Scotland*, &c. in order that brotherly love may be promoted, and that all may be edified. That we shall endeavor, in our several stations, to have a conversation becoming the *Gospel*; and to use

every mean in our power, to raise up a seed to serve OUR Glorious Lord JESUS CHRIST, THE HEAD AND KING OF HIS CHURCH.[34]

Within months, Walne was putting this experience of print publicity at the service of the LCS. *Divine Warrants* also anticipates the LCS's desire to make its resolutions and rules open to public inspection, using print to advertise its mission and reassure readers of its credentials. Walne and his associates were drawing on a long history of print organisation within Dissent. In the campaign against restrictions on Dissenting ministers in 1772, for instance, a Baptist minister Daniel Turner wrote to Josiah Thompson to call for 'a perpetual standing committee for correspondence or something of that nature'. His correspondent Thompson proposed a permanent standing committee of twelve ministers in London 'under the Style and Title of ye Corresponding Society'.[35]

Perhaps the most obvious ways that Protestant Dissent had organised through print in the years immediately prior to the formation of the LCS was in the various campaigns against the Test and Corporation Acts.[36] Hardy seems to have been immersed in this literature. In an 1803 letter to John Evans of Islington, author of *A Sketch of all the Denominations of the Christian World* (1808), he recommended a tract written by David Bogue, but published anonymously.[37] Scholars now best know Bogue as an evangelical Independent minister, who set up an academy in Gosport, near Portsmouth, in 1777. He played an important part in the formation of the *Evangelical Magazine* in 1793 and the London Missionary Society soon afterwards.[38] James Steven, Hardy's minister at Crown Court, was closely involved with Bogue's ventures.[39] Hardy took another opportunity to remind a historian of Dissent of Bogue's radical past when in 1809 he wrote to Walter Wilson, author of *The History and Antiquities of the Dissenting Churches* (1808–14).[40] Hardy claimed that Wilson had omitted an 'unanswerable' pamphlet published with Charles Dilly from a list of Bogue's publications. Hardy also suspected there was one other, perhaps two, published by Joseph Johnson. He thinks it was called something like 'The French Revolution foreseen in 1639', but then, perhaps rather archly commenting on Bogue's more recent respectability, added, 'that being rather of a political nature perhaps he would not like to own it'.[41]

Hardy was not an obscure reader of Bogue's pamphlets, unknown to their author, but corresponded and met with him in the early 1790s. The two men had even gone on board the transport ship *The Surprise* together in 1794 to convey funds to Maurice Margarot, about to be transported to Botany Bay.[42] According to Hardy's *Memoir*, Bogue was later one of the 'particular friends' – along with James Steven – with whom he spent the evening after his acquittal.[43] The government had been suspicious enough of the relationship with Bogue to raise it at the trial.[44] Although the prosecution do not seem to have had access to their letters, Hardy and Bogue had corresponded in the first few months of the LCS's existence, showing a shared interest in the millenarian understanding of contemporary political history. In a letter from June 1792, Hardy first raised the question of their views on 'civil' government. He sent Bogue a copy of the LCS's resolutions and asked for his opinion.[45] Evidently the response was not hostile. A few weeks later, Hardy wrote to another clergyman in the Portsmouth area and asked him to pass on his regards to Bogue, 'you will find him a true friend in the cause of freedom'.[46] In these letters, Hardy was patching into a network of Dissenting opinion experienced in the ways of organising opinion in print.

He also had his own experience from the campaign for the abolition of the slave trade to draw upon. The Treasury Solicitor's Papers include a moving letter from Lydia Hardy to her husband, written in April 1792, when she was convalescing in the country with her family, which throws some light on their joint commitment to abolition. After mentioning her ill health and the pleasure she takes in reading the Bible, she switches topic to ask: 'What has been donn in the palement house consurning the slave trade[?]'[47] On 8 April, Wilberforce had introduced his latest abolition bill to Parliament. Its fate takes up much more of the letter than the LCS. She asks after 'Vassa' (Gustavus Vassa or Olaudah Equiano, as he is more often known now) and hopes he will be successful on his tour to Scotland. The tour was to promote a new edition of his *The interesting narrative of the life of Olaudah Equiano*. On 8 March 1792, Hardy had written to Rev. Thomas Bryant of Sheffield on Equiano's recommendation as 'a zealous friend for the Abolition of that accurs'd traffick denominated the Slave Trade'. Hardy explained to Bryant that he assumed 'that you was a friend to freedom on the broad basis of the Rights of Man for I am fully persuaded that no man who is an advocate from principle for liberty for a Black Man but will strenuously promote and support the rights of a White Man'.[48] In the *Memoir*, Hardy recalls reading Bryant's reply to the assembled LCS members, who adopted the correspondence as a 'transaction . . . of the whole body'.

Hardy claimed that its effect 'tended very much to animate the Corresponding Society in the great cause of *Parliamentary* Reform'. Connecting the importance of publicity to both causes, Hardy had given Bryant a statement of the principles of the LCS: 'the views and intentions of this

Society are to collect opinions and know the determination (as far as possible) of the unrepresented!' Hardy's association with Equiano would have brought practical knowledge of the role of 'opinion' in an increasingly complex communications system.[49] Equiano wrote to Hardy in May asking him to acquire copies of those newspapers spreading damaging reports that he had not been born in Africa. Switching to wish Hardy success with the LCS, he informs him that he has not come across any reform societies in Scotland. More generally, as several scholars have noted, Equiano provided a bridge between the emergent radical societies and the abolitionist movement.[50] His letter to Hardy ends with an expression of religious faith common in Hardy's own correspondence: 'I am resolved ever to look to Jesus Christ – & submit to his Preordinations.'[51] This faith was underpinned by a sophisticated awareness of the role of print networks in spreading the twinned message of political reform and abolitionism that the two men shared.

This twinned message looked beyond any narrowly constitutionalist concern for the reform of Parliament.[52] Hardy's ardour was powerfully informed by his religious zeal, as Richard Citizen Lee recognised. Another staunch abolitionist, Lee wrote 'Tribute of Civic Gratitude' to commemorate Hardy's acquittal of the charge of treason. Lee provided a note insisting that Hardy was a 'CHRISTIAN HERO':

> Let the infidel candidly investigate (if Infidelity can possibly be candid) let him candidly investigate this illustrious Character, and then lift his audacious Front to the Heavens and tell the ALLMIGHTY, that pure Christianity is inimical to the Cause of Freedom – Rather let him yield to the Power of Conviction, and own with Admiration the Rationality of that sublime System which, while it gives GLORY TO GOD, inculcates PEACE ON EARTH, and GOOD-WILL TOWARDS MEN.[53]

As the defensive tone of his note suggests, Lee's poem appeared at a point when religious differences were causing problems within the LCS, discussed more fully later in this chapter. Suffice to note for now that Lee's collection *Songs from the rock* (1795) was devoted to the idea of the French Revolution as the fulfilment of biblical prophecy, full of the rhetoric that had once been identified with Gordon's Protestant Association. Hardy had his own millenarian perspective on contemporary events. In a letter he wrote to Bogue in 1793, Hardy provided a vision of the resistless spread of political change through the media of print and political discussion:

> Of course the subject of a reform in parliament will be repeatedly agitated in the House of Commons the debates will be published in the newspapers

> then circulated in different parts of the Country. Thousands of people will make it the subject of conversation and enquiry who never thought of it before.[54]

The origins of this kind of thinking in the marrow of Protestant Dissent are revealed when Hardy asks Bogue if he thinks Ezekiel 21: 25–7 refers to France:

> I think there have been two overturns in that country already and a third must take place before the pure gospel of Jesus Christ can prevail in that Nation, although there is a door open for propagating it and I hope it will never be shut till the end of time.

No wonder both men were interested in *The French Revolution foreseen, in 1639*! Hardy's letter to Bogue suggests he understood each wave of the Revolution as part of an unfolding history of Protestant enlightenment. What is equally striking, however, is the *absence* of this aspect of his thinking from his public work for the LCS.

In this regard, Hardy's millenarianism never takes on the public role it does in Citizen Lee's poetry, where it explicitly justifies his politics. Hardy never allowed his own religiosity to play any part in the LCS's attempts to represent the voice of the people. Michael Warner's discussion of the eighteenth-century republic of letters identifies a secularising shift whereby the Protestant idea of print as a medium for the unfolding of God's word gave way to the idea of 'the public' as a more secular entity.[55] Although the displacement of the former by the latter was surely a much more uneven process than Warner allows, as Lee's case shows, it is a distinction relevant to thinking about Hardy's religious beliefs in relation to his 'public' role. If his private correspondence reveals how far his thinking was structured by his religious zeal, he seems to have been very careful not to allow it to enter any of the LCS's official business or documents. His manuscript 'History' is explicit on the fact that the LCS was careful to avoid religious disputes. All kinds of religious believers were represented in the LCS, Hardy claimed, including those who 'cared for none of those things'.[56]

This claim does not necessarily mean that Hardy himself found the prohibition comfortable. Certainly, religious controversy did rear its head in the LCS, especially after Paine's *Age of Reason* (1794) appeared. By 1795, after Hardy had stepped down from his role as secretary, various schisms appeared over religious matters. Perhaps his former comrades missed his careful navigation of this particular ground. The complexity of Hardy's own position resists any straightforward secular teleology. His concern with political reform did not mean he simply abandoned the religious idea of progress found in his letters to Bogue. Indeed, next to his comment about avoiding religious disputes, an annotation gives an extract from what he calls 'an excellent recent publication', James Bennett's *Sacred Politics*, as if he couldn't quite help himself.[57] Published anonymously in 1795, Bennett's pamphlet ends by concluding that 'the Scriptures incline strongly in favour of a well-ordered democracy'.[58] Reviewers quickly condemned the pamphlet as 'sedition, dressed up in scripture, recommended by the name of Jesus'.[59] Whatever his enthusiasm for Bennett's thinking, Hardy did not allow it to play a direct part in his 'public' role with the LCS. Hardy's retrospective accounts of the early years place their emphasis on the abilities of the people at large to organise themselves rather than any sense of divine favour. His *Memoir* reprints Lee's poem on the death of Hardy's wife, records the fact that the poet migrated to American soon afterwards, but suggests no other association between them. Understandably enough, Hardy glosses over the enthusiasm of Lee's religio-political poetry, and says nothing about the tribute he was paid as a specifically 'Christian hero'. Hardy's public vision of the LCS, one might say, simply did not acknowledge this category, at least not in the public sphere.

Hardy's primary public mode was to collect popular opinion, placing questions of religious belief to one side. On 10 April 1792, Hardy wrote to the Borough Society, Thelwall's original base, invoking a universal perspective that may have originated in his religious beliefs, but does not allude to them:

> As we are all engaged in the same grand and important cause there is an absolute necessity for us to unite together and communicate with each other that our sentiments and determinations may center in one point viz to have the rights of man established especially in this island but our views of the rights of man are not solely confined to this small island but are extended to the whole human race black or white, high or low, rich or poor.[60]

Among those to whom he had also written in the early months of the LCS was Lord Daer, another Scotsman, whom he reminded that his subscription was due. Written on the auspicious date of 14 July, the letter celebrated the success of the society against the 'combined influence of Court Minions and those who do the dirty work of a corrupt and despotick and trembling administration'. Hardy was confident of the imminent fall of tyranny:

> The Aristocracy is trembling in every joint for their exclusive privileges. Excuse me for speaking so plainly I am addressing you as a member of the

> same society with me and a fellow labourer in the glorious cause. I am a plain man love honest dealing and hates dissembling. I was happy to see your name at the head of a long list of patriots engaged in a similar cause in another part of the Nation.[61]

Typically Hardy ended the letter on a practical egalitarian note: 'I have taken the liberty of renewing your ticket for this Quarter at the very large sum of one penny it is here enclosed.'

If Hardy disciplined his own religious convictions into a public role that he believed would best advance the cause of reform, this self-discipline did not translate into social deference, a point that should be borne in mind when thinking about his relationship with the elite reformers of the 1780s. Daer was the eldest son of the Earl of Selkirk, a member of the Friends of the People that had been formed in April 1792 by Charles Grey and his Whig associates, but also a rare nobleman willing to participate in the more popular societies. He was present at SCI meetings in April and participated in the shadowy 'London Society of the Friends of the People' that existed briefly in mid 1792.[62] Unlike its Whig namesake, this society was committed to the platform of universal male suffrage. Following the usual practice of finding a nobleman to assume positions of leadership in all kinds of associations, Daer was proposed as chairman of the LCS, but Hardy's manuscript recalls 'it was objected it wd. appear to be a party business and might prevent them exerting themselves in their own cause'. Hardy's manner towards Daer in their correspondence suggests that he shared this opinion. Despite their shared Scottish roots, Daer's social status, and his influential connections within reform more generally, Hardy refused to defer to the nobleman when it came to leadership of the LCS and insisted instead on addressing him as 'a fellow labourer in the glorious cause'.[63]

Nevertheless, Hardy chose not to come forward in 1792 as the 'founder' of the LCS, a matter he also discusses in the manuscript history. He was concerned as to perceptions of 'respectability', although he quickly provides the gloss, 'the common received idea of respectability'. He insisted upon the origin of the LCS, as we have seen, in the discussions of ordinary tradesmen. If he refused to stand forward as the founder of the society, Hardy did agree to sign his name to its first address as secretary (even though its author was Margarot). The explanation given in the 'History' is that Hardy was the most 'independent' of those involved. He felt the need to go on and explain his idea of this word too, perhaps because it was so mired in the Whig idea that only the propertied classes could truly be trusted with the welfare of the state. In contrast, Hardy disputed any idea of 'independent' as 'rich and increased in worldly goods'. Instead, as a self-employed journeyman, he was free from the control of an employer, but also independent because 'conscious that I was doing that which was right – fearless of consequence'.[64]

Authorised by the signature of this independent man, the address and resolutions were sent to the SCI, then the newspapers, before being distributed by the LCS as a handbill.[65] In Hardy's manuscript 'History of the LCS', this event is represented as the crossing of a threshold: 'after that time the London Corresponding Society became public'.[66] For Hardy, it appears, publicity involved certain acts of self-discipline, the regulation of his own religious zeal, and a certain orientation towards the nation in print, including an independence from the authority of the political elite, whatever advice he may have taken from them. In the published *Memoir*, this discipline meant that the personal was defined primarily in terms of the political, even including the brief description of the death of Lydia Hardy ending with Lee's poem.[67] Compared to the way Thelwall was to place his private affections at the centre of his claims to political virtue, Hardy seems to have identified his public self much more completely with the LCS, excluding the personal and the religious, both in his political conduct in the 1790s and in his later writing.

Ferment 1792–3

Publication of the April address and resolutions was the first step towards the LCS taking leadership of the popular societies emerging onto the public stage in London and across Britain in 1792. Although in retrospect this role may seem to have been inevitable, the LCS was initially part of a bubbling ferment of such societies, responding to events in France and to Paine's *Rights of Man*. The most prominent of these societies was the SCI, of which Paine himself was a member, and which had facilitated the publication and dissemination of the first part of his book.[68] Paine's ideas changed in response to this ferment, only explicitly advocating universal suffrage in his *Letter Addressed to the Addressers* after his involvement with the LCS and SCI. Hardy was quick to make contact with John Horne Tooke, the leading figure in the SCI, and the two societies began to collaborate from early on in 1792, sending representatives to each other's meetings. The popular radical movement in London, however, extended further beyond these two key organisations than many accounts notice, even if most of the societies that emerged were short lived and would repay further research.

Hardy's 'History of the LCS' is a useful point of departure for understanding this rapidly developing situation. His sense of the LCS's achievement was predicated on its sustained commitment when other societies rose and fell. He acknowledged the initial importance of elite groups. Grey's Society of the Friends of the People 'carried people to flock in astonishing numbers to the Corresponding Society', but these Whigs were guilty of arrogating to themselves a role as natural leaders that Hardy was unwilling to grant. His moral sense of the importance of 'the people' coming to a sense of itself was always likely to bridle against such assumptions. Those who formed societies in imitation of Grey and his associates – he mentions the Borough and Aldgate societies, as well as others who used some version of the title 'friends of the people' – he dismissed as 'professed friends who are only seen in the sun shine of prosperity'. The readiness of these societies 'to learn from their superiors' he described in a cancelled passage as 'proof of great docility in them':

> when these go beforehand, those follow – when those stop, those stand still – they called themselves friends of the people when in reality they were part of the oppressed people they wished to befriend.[69]

Hardy also carefully distinguished the LCS from those who had promoted parliamentary reform in the previous decade. Hardy saw his colleagues in the LCS as 'another class of reformers – they were of the lower and middling class of society <u>called the people</u>':

> these two classes of reformers being almost total strangers to each other – some of those strenuous for a certain reform in 1782 scarcely knew those who had associated for a reform in 1792.

The 'History' shows a sharp awareness of what was at stake when it came to the question of leadership within the movement: 'the higher class as they are called have at all times made use of the middling and lower classes as a ladder to raise themselves into power then kick it away'.[70]

Nevertheless, the situation on the ground in 1792–3 was more fluid than Hardy's later account suggests. Clubs and individuals charted various courses across a rapidly changing political landscape in this period. The parts played by Grey's Friends of the People and the SCI are fairly well known, but there were many other groups in London closer to the LCS in this period, even if Hardy treats them as transient.[71] For instance, the LCS courted the assistance of the Borough Society (also known as the Southwark Society of the Friends of the People) for much of 1792. Thelwall was heavily involved there. The Aldgate Society, formed out of a disaffected division of the LCS early in 1793, made its own contribution to print radicalism via the satirical miscellany *A Thing of Shreds and Patches* (1793), but association with Gordon tainted them in many eyes. Other groups, like the Holborn Society, self-described as republicans, seem to have merged with the LCS early in 1793.[72] Nor, in this volatile early period, were the class profiles of participants quite as neat as Hardy suggests in his retrospective accounts. Merry was involved in the early stages of Grey's Friends of the People, for instance, but his name disappears from membership lists by the middle of 1792. At meetings of the SCI, which he had joined in 1791, he played a conspicuous role in its collaborations with the LCS. Merry retained a confidence in the 'electric' power of print to spread enlightenment on a global scale. Many 'literary men' who shared Merry's sympathies showed an appetite for association in this period, although far from all of them were willing to condone his sense of its limitless social horizon.

In 1790, Merry was one of several reform-minded writers involved in the inauguration of the Literary Fund. The brainchild of the minister and political theorist David Williams, its primary purpose was to aid authors in distress, but its mission was predicated on a sense of the influence of men of letters on political affairs that drew inspiration from events in France. Many early members of its general committee were political reformers. Aside from Merry, they included John Hurford Stone, Thomas Christie, editor of the *Analytical Review*, Godwin's friend Major Alexander Jardine, and Captain Thomas Morris, brother of the famous political songwriter Captain Charles Morris.[73] These were men, as John Gifford put it later, 'neither remarkable for the purity of their religious tenets, nor for the soundness of their political principles', but they were not necessarily averse to exploiting the protection of an aristocratic patron, and early in 1791 Merry was asked to use his connections to approach the Duke of Leeds, already president of the Philanthropic Society.[74] By 1792, reform sympathies within the Literary Fund manifested themselves in a notable overlap with SCI membership. Merry was unable to attend the Literary Fund's committee meeting of 4 May, because he was at the SCI with Paine in a key period for its discussions of the distribution of cheap editions of *Rights of Man*.[75] Despite his absence from the meeting, it re-elected Merry to the committee, but he never reappeared. Two SCI members who did attend the May meeting of the Literary Fund were John Hurford Stone and George Edwards (both of whom, as it happens, also seem to have been involved in the short-lived London Society of the Friends of the People at around this time). Thereafter, like Merry, they seem to have been busier with the SCI than the Fund. Stone is reputed to have turned down Williams's offer to serve on the Fund's committee. By the end of 1792, Edwards, Merry, and Stone were in Paris with Paine, where they participated in the British Club at White's Hotel frequented by John Oswald, vegetarian theorist and revolutionary soldier, who received financial aid from the Fund.[76]

Williams conveyed the Fund's grant to Oswald in Paris, but seems not to have attended the British Club. He already had a reputation in France as a serious political thinker. J.P. Brissot had invited Williams to consult on the new republican constitution. Manon Roland placed Williams above Paine as a philosopher:

> Paine throws light upon a revolution better than he concurs in the making of a constitution. He takes up, and establishes those great principles, of which the exposition strikes every eye, gains the applause of a club, or excites the enthusiasm of a tavern; but for cool in a committee, or the regular labours of a legislator, I conceive *David Williams* infinitely more proper than he. Williams, made a French citizen also, was not chosen a member of the Convention, in which he would have been of more use; but he was invited by the government to repair to Paris, where he passed several months, and frequently conferred with the most active representatives of the nation.[77]

The terms of her praise hint at a distinctive aspect of Williams's thinking, particularly his deep ambivalence about popular associations, and his preference for committee work or smaller more 'select' gatherings than he found in the raucous activities of the National Convention.[78]

Williams's justification of a charity for authors had been the assumption that their highest calling was as writers of constitutions:

> Princes are influenced, ministers propose measures, and magistrates are instructed by the industry of literature; while the authors of hints, suggestions, and disquisitions, may be languishing in obscurity, or dying in distress.[79]

Both Williams and Merry took up this role in France in the debate on the new republican constitution.[80] Newspaper advertisements from 1791–2 suggest the pressure of events in France on the definition of the 'literary' supported by the Fund. Take this one from the *World* for 16 February 1791:

> At a period when LITERATURE is asserting its just claims, to influence the Councils, and point out the interests of POLITICAL SOCIETIES ...
>
> The COMMITTEE ... solicit, not those only who are friends to LITERATURE, from TASTE and LOVE OF SCIENCE, but all who are interested in the

> most effective and important instruments of public information and public prosperity.

The strong link between constitutions and literary men was later eclipsed by a defence of the general utility of literature in most of the other writing by Williams on the Fund, but in these heady months it was at the heart of his thinking.

Williams always made it clear that the Fund was not intended to encourage people into authorship. He also saw the provision of relief as a means of stopping the rancour that produced 'libel' and 'personal satire' among those disappointed of a literary career, modes that were at the heart of Georgian political theatre.[81] Beyond the Fund, as a political writer, Williams imagined himself occupying a philosophical position above the political societies, giving them direction perhaps, but not joining them, a position not unlike the one Godwin took up after the success of *Political justice*. He spelled out his position in a letter to Brissot from May 1792:

> The Constitutional Societies which have adopted Paine & his Pamphlets . . . are here actuated by bad Men; & their exertions are petulant & intemperate. The Indiscretion of the Government in prosecuting Paine . . . will give these Societies great Advantage. – But I join none of them; because I think they waste the Spirits & excite the Hopes of the People to no Purpose; & they alarm Government just enough to be on it's guard, but not to reform any of it's [sic] Abuses. . . I am for instructing the People only: & having no Contest with Government, until I can give it a mortal Blow.[82]

Williams was a theorist of conventions as the proper medium for the expression of the general will, but far from sanguine about the direct participation of the people out-of-doors.[83] In France at the end of the year, he was shocked by the constant interruptions from the gallery in the Convention. He did make his own contribution to the French constitutional debate in *Observations sur la dernière constitution de la France* (1793), but predictably enough the document seems never to have been printed in England. Despite their ostensible political sympathies, Williams already had doubts about Paine and his associates in the SCI. He had always been a proponent of that species of Enlightenment thinking that looked for unlimited enquiry within regulated conditions. In *Lessons to a young prince* (1790), for instance, he had written 'I never saw an assembly, exceeding twenty, whatever the abilities of the members, that was not more disposed to passion and tumult, than to reason and judgment', a position echoed in Godwin's *Political justice*.[84] For both Godwin and

Williams, the autonomy of private judgement had to be preserved when it came to political justice.

Nevertheless, like Godwin, Williams actively participated in the more selective versions of conviviality in literary London. In his case, these were mainly comprised of likeminded proponents of improvement like 'The Club of Thirteen' from which the idea for the Literary Fund sprang.[85] From 1793, soon after its inception, the Literary Fund began to have an annual dinner. A manuscript list of toasts and songs for the 1793 dinner contains the sentiment 'Government without Oppression, & Liberty without Licentiousness'. A sign of the sensitivity of the political context is that the word 'Tyranny' is struck out and replaced by 'Oppression'. By 1800, there was no equivocation. The toasts included: 'The Constitution of England, untampered, & unimpaired by French Quackery' and 'One Mind, one Heart, one Voice, from the Cottage to the Throne'.[86] No less than the philanthropic gentlemen of the Literary Fund, the LCS confirmed its own sense of identity through toasts and songs, which were later to be scrutinised at the trials of its members, as were the entrance tickets issued in its name. As the membership of the LCS grew, these tickets soon had to be printed rather than handwritten by Hardy, as they initially were. Maurice Margarot had to be persuaded that Hardy's proposed motto 'Unite, persevere, and be free' would not be injurious to the cause. Tickets were also a means of policing entrance to the Society's meetings as it became increasingly conscious of surveillance, by government spies and informers, but issuing them was also an aspect of its conformity to the norms of the associational world more generally. On Thursday 23 August 1792, the LCS's general committee passed a resolution that

> no Delegate, no member of the Society do presume to *publish* or send to any newspaper, any letter or pamphlet or writing connected to the society by any member or society, unless by express order from the Committee under the penalty of exclusion.

The resolution seems to have been prompted by the appearance of a broadside song 'God Save the Rights of Man'. At the 13 September meeting, the delegates of three divisions were severely reprimanded for allowing the song to be published. The author was Robert Thomson (sometimes Thompson) who appeared at the committee meeting of 30 August as 'the pro tempore delegate of Division No. 5'.[87]

By trade, Thomson was an auctioneer, whom the MPM's 'History of the Society' (1796) recalled as one of those early members 'indefatigable in visiting and instructing new divisions'.[88] Perhaps recalling the anxiety about Thomson's song, the 'History' went on to describe his 'lively poetical genius, which did not exactly accord with the calm prudential principles on which the Society was instituted'. Here, Thomson's 'poetical genius' seems to place him beneath what the LCS required of the 'literary men' it at times tried to recruit, but it is the conviviality of song, hinted at in the word 'lively', that seems to be the primary source of anxiety. None the less, the account acknowledged that he was

> extensively admired in the Society, and probably would have experienced a similar degree of approbation from the country at large, had not persecution nearly suppressed his works, and compelled him to seek refuge in France, where, we are happy to learn he has since succeeded as a bookseller.

Thomson was a Scot by birth. He shared ties of religion and a lasting friendship with his countryman Hardy.[89] Thomson returned from Paris some time soon after 1800 to publish a feisty rebuttal of Paine's *The Age of Reason*.[90] After Waterloo, impoverished, he returned again, when Hardy among others helped with an application to the Literary Fund, prudently suppressing his early role in the LCS. Although a very different organisation from what it had been in 1792, the Fund granted him £10 on more than one occasion until his death in 1820.[91]

The brief account of Thomson in MPM is corroborated and extended by the spy reports of Captain George Munro from November 1792.[92] Munro had been having trouble gaining entry to LCS divisions as a 'stranger', but his luck turned when he met Thomson:

> The third [division] I visited was the Marquis of Granby kept by one Pride this is the 5th Division, there were a vast number of Scotchmen in this, it seemed the best attended and best conducted, the Delegates name was Thomson, discovering I was a countryman of his (for he was Scotch) I was admitted a member of this Division with little difficulty, and have the honour of accompanying this with one of their printed papers, which will give you a clear idea of the nature of these Society's who's intentions [are] that of corrupting the minds of the lower orders of the people by inflaming their imaginations with imaginary grievances, and working them up to comit some great excess.

'Papers' suggests a slip or broadside version, possibly one of Thomson's songs, the most influential of which was 'God Save the Rights of Man', the song that had caused ructions at the LCS in late August. The slip version of that song in the British Library shown here (Figure 4) has 'November 1792' written on it, the month of Munro's visit to the Marquis of Granby. The song was later collected in Thomson's *A Tribute to Liberty* (1793)

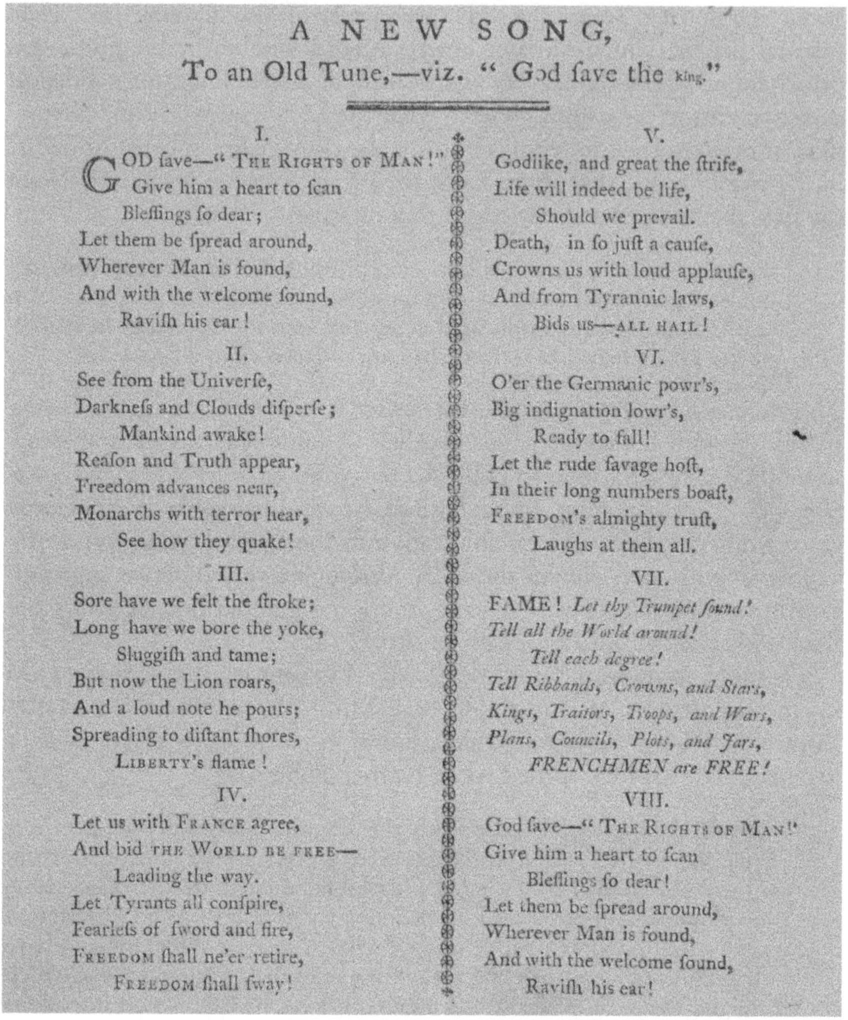

A NEW SONG,

To an Old Tune,—viz. " God ſave the King."

I.

GOD ſave—" THE RIGHTS OF MAN!"
Give him a heart to ſcan
Bleſſings ſo dear;
Let them be ſpread around,
Wherever Man is found,
And with the welcome ſound,
Raviſh his ear!

II.

See from the Univerſe,
Darkneſs and Clouds diſperſe;
Mankind awake!
Reaſon and Truth appear,
Freedom advances near,
Monarchs with terror hear,
See how they quake!

III.

Sore have we felt the ſtroke;
Long have we bore the yoke,
Sluggiſh and tame;
But now the Lion roars,
And a loud note he pours;
Spreading to diſtant ſhores,
LIBERTY's flame!

IV.

Let us with FRANCE agree,
And bid THE WORLD BE FREE—
Leading the way.
Let Tyrants all conſpire,
Fearleſs of ſword and fire,
FREEDOM ſhall ne'er retire,
FREEDOM ſhall ſway!

V.

Godlike, and great the ſtrife,
Life will indeed be life,
Should we prevail.
Death, in ſo juſt a cauſe,
Crowns us with loud applauſe,
And from Tyrannic laws,
Bids us—ALL HAIL!

VI.

O'er the Germanic pow'r's,
Big indignation low'r's,
Ready to fall!
Let the rude ſavage hoſt,
In their long numbers boaſt,
FREEDOM's almighty truſt,
Laughs at them all.

VII.

FAME! *Let thy Trumpet ſound!*
Tell all the World around!
Tell each degree!
Tell Ribbands, Crowns, and Stars,
Kings, Traitors, Troops, and Wars,
Plans, Councils, Plots, and Jars,
FRENCHMEN are FREE!

VIII.

God ſave—" THE RIGHTS OF MAN!"
Give him a heart to ſcan
Bleſſings ſo dear!
Let them be ſpread around,
Wherever Man is found,
And with the welcome ſound,
Raviſh his ear!

Fig 4 [Robert Thomson] *A New song, to an old tune,-viz. "God save the king".*

where it is described as 'composed before the Duke of Brunswick ran away', a reference to the French victory at Valmy on 20 September. This composition date fits in with the chronology of the LCS debates over whether it should be owned by the society. By the time the song appeared in *A Tribute to Liberty*, published from Temple Yard with Robert

Littlejohn, another LCS member, Thomson was a confirmed delegate to the central committee, perhaps in recognition of the 'vigour' MPM later credited him with bringing to the failing spirits of the society. Despite the committee's doubts about identifying his songs as official LCS publications, he had probably been among those dispatched to the Marquis of Granby to revive its fortunes in August. Munro's report from November corroborates his success.

'To the London Corresponding Society', one of Thomson's songs gathered in *Tribute to Liberty,* seems a direct contribution to the process of creating solidarity and imparting spirit to the members:

> See our numbers how they grow!
> Crowding and dividing;
> Eager all their Rights to know,
> Reason still presiding.[93]

A note glosses 'crowding and dividing' as a reference 'to the affiliated divisions which file off every night of meeting to different parts of the town'. For those singing the song at a meeting, it would have provided a sense of unity both 'here' within the particular division and also with those 'dividing' meetings imagined as going on simultaneously:

> Boldly all with heart and hand,
> Meet we here united,
> By each other firmly stand,
> To see our Country righted.[94]

Like 'God Save the Rights of Man', this song probably first existed as a slip that could be passed around at meetings. Others gathered in the collection are still extant as slips, including 'Whitehall Alarmed!' and 'Burke's Address to the Swinish Multitude'.[95] Thomson's book also republished songs that he had not written, including two sung by Charles Dignum at the Revolution Society's anniversary dinner in November 1792. LCS member Robert Hawes of Whitechapel had already printed these as slips.[96] Songs were certainly a very malleable cultural form, easily adapted to circumstances, and capable of being produced as slips, printed in newspapers, or gathered in anthologies. Spence's *Pig's Meat* reprinted 'God Save the Rights of Man' as it did 'Burke's Address to the Swinish Multitude'.[97]

Print allowed songs and toasts to be circulated across different kinds of social space, as with the songs Dignum performed for the Revolution Society, reprinted by Hawes and Thomson for LCS use. The anniversary dinner of the Revolution Society in 1792 took place at the London Tavern, a venue grander than most used by the LCS. Providing LCS members with access to these songs, Hawes and Thomson implied they had as much right to a place in the domain of British politics as the Revolution Society and more exalted associations. The press closely scrutinised the role of songs and toasts at political dinners and meetings, as we have already seen. Reformers and Whigs often began their toasts with 'the majesty of the people' to make their sense of the relative importance of the different arms of the constitution plain. The king appeared only in third place at the Revolution Society's 1789 dinner.[98] Things had changed by 1792. The *Morning Chronicle*'s report of the 1792 dinner of 5 November does not mention the royal family and gives the first four toasts as 'The Rights of Man', 'The Glorious Revolution of 1688', 'May unjust power be opposed by all the friends of just Government', and 'The Sovereignty of the People acting by an equal Representation'. In *A Tribute to Liberty*, Thomson went further in his list of toasts and signalled his affiliations by placing 'Thomas Paine!!!' first, followed by 'The Rights of Man!!!', 'The Rights of Woman!!!', and then 'The Majesty of the People!!!'[99]

Preparing the evidence for the treason trials in 1794, the *Second report from the Committee of Secrecy* noted the use 'even of play bills and songs, seditious toasts; and a studied selection of the tunes which have been in use since the revolution' as a means to 'seduce and corrupt the thoughtless and uninformed': 'The appearance of insignificance and levity, which belongs at first sight to his part of the system, is, in truth, only an additional proof of the art and industry with which it has been pursued.'[100] But the LCS itself, as its magazine 'History' of 1796 implies, was not without qualms about the political theatre of toasts and songs: 'The fervent desire for moral reform, educational improvement, and rational debate', James Epstein and David Karr have suggested, 'was at odds with the norms of plebeian sociability'.[101] One needs to be careful of not oversimplifying the notion of 'plebeian sociability'. Reading, debating, singing, and toasting coexisted as activities within the LCS, even if for some members they might relate to very different forms of print sociability, especially those anxious about descending, as Godwin put it, from 'the conviviality of the feast to the depredations of a riot'.[102] From 1794, for instance, John Thelwall took over something of Thomson's role as LCS songwriter, sometimes printing his songs three to a sheet to ease circulation, but his practice generally made no sharp distinction between the levity of songs, the theatre of toasting, and the gravity of reading groups.[103] The great archivist of the LCS, Francis Place, apparently felt otherwise. He certainly registered the tension between improvement and theatricality described by Epstein and Karr, but then his entire account of the organisation is notoriously marked by his concern with respectability, as he saw it. Place's *Autobiography* strongly favoured the idea that reading and debate were the key activities of the LCS and represented its main achievement as the bringing of sobriety and usefulness to working-class culture. Song's association with conviviality pushed it away from the respectability he accorded other more studious forms of literary endeavour. Songs did appear in his accounts of the older plebeian world that he remembered from his childhood before he joined the LCS in 1794, but primarily as markers of its social degeneracy:

> Some of these songs sung by the respectable tradesmen who spent their evenings in my fathers [sic] parlour, were very gross, yet I have known the parlour door thrown open, that whoever was in the bar and the Tap room might hear every word.[104]

Not that his attitude to this material was simple. He was fascinated enough by it to form a collection and did not note its passing entirely without regret. These songs, he recalled, 'were sung with considerable humour by men who were very much excited'.[105] Place's primary concern is with lewdness rather than politics as such in these passages, but his account of their disappearance is specifically placed in the context of the emergence of the Association for Preserving Liberty and Property:

> John Reeves and his associates together with the magistrates extinguished them. The association printed a large number of what they called loyal songs, and gave them to ballad singers, if any one was found singing any but loyal songs he or she was carried before the magistrate who admonished and dismissed him or her, they were then told they might have loyal songs for nothing and that they would not be molested while singing them. Thus the bawdy songs, and those in praise of thieving and getting drunk were pushed out of existence.[106]

This scenario is precisely the context of Thomson's flight to France under pressure from Reeves, but Place mentions neither the LCS's songwriter in chief nor radical songs more generally. Indeed the category 'political songs' would probably have represented a kind of oxymoron for him. Nowhere does his account of LCS meetings mention the singing of the songs provided by Thomson, Thelwall, or Reid, to name but three of many songwriters in the LCS. Despite their importance in cementing the LCS together and imparting 'vigour' at times of crisis, Place has nothing to say about the role of songs and toasts in its success. They seem to lie outside his idea of what constituted political discourse and beneath what he might have expected of 'literary men'.

'These prosecuting times'

Thomson was one of many victims of the intensification of surveillance after the inception of the Association in November 1792. Although Reeves and his associates operated independently of government, the Treasury was also doing what it could to ensure local authorities all over the country clamped down on sedition, not least by encouraging the harassment of booksellers who stocked Paine's *Rights of Man* and Pigott's *Jockey Club*.[107] The signal event in this new era of repression was the trial of Paine himself *in absentia* on 18 December. The law officers discussed prosecuting publishers of *Rights of Man* from as early as April 1791, but they did not indict J. S. Jordan until 14 May 1792, a week before the first royal proclamation against seditious writings. A summons was served on Paine on the same day as the proclamation was issued, but the government did not act on it, apart from continuing to encourage abuse of the author in the newspapers. In June, the Home Secretary, Henry Dundas, announced the postponement of the trial until December. On 13 September, Paine left for France, where he had been elected deputy for Calais. He was harassed by customs officers at Dover, who seem to have made great show of going through his papers, but no effort was made to prevent him leaving the country at dawn the next day. Now the government could prosecute without the risk that Paine would be there to use the occasion as a political platform.[108]

Paine had placed discussion at the heart of his vision of politics. The commitment to a visible constitution in *Rights of Man* lies not in a desire to set political truth in stone, but to bringing it into print and, thereby, making it available for debate. *Rights of Man* offered an account of political change in the United States as the product of 'public discussion, carried on through the channel of the press, and in conversations', an ongoing process of reader-citizens 'revising, altering, and amending'.[109] 'In this vision of politics', as Cotlar has described it, 'ideas do not emanate from the center, but emerge slowly out of an inclusive and incessant conversation among citizens'.[110] The imagined scenario is something like the discussions between Hardy and his friends held after work surrounded by the newspapers and pamphlets of the day. Paine's presence at SCI meetings in 1792 was another practical manifestation of this cultural imaginary. He both participated in the discussion of political principles, giving advice directly to the LCS, and did what he could – refusing to accept profits from the book – to make sure *Rights of Man* achieved a wide circulation in the popular societies.

Paine's practical involvement with the societies was not something his attorney, Thomas Erskine, emphasised at his trial when it finally came on. He did not wish Paine to be associated with 'tavern' politics. The version of print magic Erskine presented at the trial was distanced from such messy mediations.[111] Erskine's primary strategy was to present Paine as part of a pantheon of political philosophy. Paine undermined this defence when he wrote to the Attorney General from Paris in November 1792 to deride the prosecution. Not only did Paine mock the royal family and taunt the crown officers with the events in Paris of August and September 1792, but he also insisted that 'coffee-houses, and places where I was unknown' were reasonable places for 'collecting the natural currency of opinion'. For the Attorney General, Sir Archibald Macdonald, this idea was laughable as a serious account of the role of 'the people' in the political system, but it was also encouraging sedition. Paine was inflaming 'that part of the public whose minds cannot be supposed to be conversant with subjects of this sort, and who cannot therefore correct as they go along'. The passages chosen on the indictment are there not because of the political ideas they expressed alone, but because of their 'phrase and manner', in Macdonald's words. Here was not 'reasoning and well meant discussion', according to the Attorney General, but 'a deliberate design to calumniate . . . to perform the shorter process of inflammation'. *Rights of Man*, in Macdonald's eyes, was being directed towards readers who could not distinguish scurrility from 'sober discussion'.[112] This part of 'the public', as the Attorney General did at least acknowledge them to be in name at least, was imagined as incapable of any public function.

Erskine objected to Paine's letter from Paris being produced in court, insisting on its irrelevance for the prosecution of a book published months before. His strategy was to abstract Paine's sense of the political nation from any idea of the people at large as directly involved in the political process. The cheapness of *Rights of Man* was simply encouraging 'the most extensive purchase of it' so that 'his work should be generally read'. 'Extensive purchase' allows Erskine to recast the Attorney General's qualitative point about readership into a simple judgement of quantity. Erskine presented *Rights of Man* as addressed 'to the reason of the nation at large, and not to the passions of individuals'. The importance of the French Revolution for Erskine was primarily as a stimulus to the English, 'reminding the people of this country of their own glorious deliverance in former ages'. Paine is to be placed in a long line of British political thinkers, 'persons on whom my friend will find it hard to fasten the character of libellers'. The 'grave speculative opinions' of these political giants cannot be regarded as intended to 'diffuse discontent'. They are examples of 'great authority in all learning'. Each is brought forward by Erskine as 'a distinguished classic in the language' whose address is to 'an impartial public, or to posterity'.[113] He did not present these constitutional master texts as addressed entirely to an abstract idea of the people. He conceded that some were written 'not in the abstract like the author before you, but upon the spur of the occasion'. Political controversy, from this perspective, might provide the winnowing that delivers forth the nation's political classics. Quoting Montesquieu (and anticipating Godwin in doing so), Erskine asserted that 'it matters not whether individuals reason well or ill; it is sufficient that they do reason. Truth arises from the collision, and from thence springs liberty.' Such vigorous collision leads him to a final stirring vision sustained by Milton's 'mighty imagination' of 'a noble and puissant nation rousing itself, like a strong man after sleep'.[114] Erskine was famous for his impassioned performances in the courtroom. Here his speech crackled with tension between the idea of an inter-textual horizon made up of classics and a politically militant nation seeking to turn ideas into action. Not that this tension gave too much pause for thought to the packed jury. Before the Attorney General could rise to reply to Erskine's speech, the foreman declared Paine guilty.

The tension in Erskine's defence did not disappear with the verdict, but lingered on as an issue within the reform movement. On 22 December, four days after the trial, the newly formed Society of Friends to the Liberty of the Press met to congratulate Erskine on his defence. Some of the Friends were very clear that they were not congratulating him on his defence of Paine's book, but only the *principle* of free speech. The Society was an unstable mix of Whig MPs and members of the popular radical movement, including Gerrald and Thelwall. Whatever the Opposition members present thought of those two, they were decidedly uncomfortable with *Rights of Man*. After Thelwall and others spoke in praise of Erskine, an argument broke out centred around a motion of thanks to Erskine. Thomas Maitland, brother of the Earl of Lauderdale, recently returned from France, proposed the motion. Some members questioned 'the propriety, at this time, of making the most distant mention of the work called The Rights of Man'. Maitland's vote of thanks 'might imply their approbation of the whole Doctrines contained in the Book'. Joseph Gerrald immediately rose to assert that 'it was absurd to praise Mr. Erskine's Defence and at the same time to censure his Client's Political Doctrines'.[115]

Gerrald's intervention effectively insisted on the right of the LCS and its members to be understood as an active part of the political nation. Over the course of 1792, the pretensions of the Society of the Friends of the People to shape and control these aspirations had been increasingly under attack in the popular radical press. By November 1792 *The Argus*, the newspaper most sympathetic to the LCS, was unforgiving on the issue:

> We at first observed of this Society, that it appeared to us to be designed as a *conductor* to turn away the lightning accompanying the *thunder* of the Public for a reform of abuses in Government . . . we hope they will [now] lay aside their violent fears, at least those expressed for the several classes of men whose interest they profess to have at heart. There is no occasion for apprehensions from Mr. PAINE's advice on the score of Economy and Reform.[116]

At the Friends to the Liberty of the Press meeting, full of members of the Society of the Friends of the People, these fears were amply on display. The motion of thanks was amended to omit Paine's name and the title of his book. Erskine emerges as the hero of the hour, effectively himself becoming part of a pantheon from which Paine was excluded.

By the beginning of 1793, then, the radical societies were operating in a situation where publishing their opinions and meeting to discuss them were being regarded as seditious. The supposed friends of reform in the political elite were backing away from active collaboration. For the most part it was the booksellers and publishers who became the objects of direct legal sanction. Robert Thomson and Samson Perry were forced out of the country after Paine's departure.[117] Indictments for publishing *Rights of Man*, *Letter Addressed to the Addressers*, and the *Jockey Club* secured the convictions of the booksellers Ridgway and Symonds. Indictments were also sent out to the regions. Several prosecutions misfired because of errors in the paperwork. Different editions of the *Jockey Club*, expanded by the addition of different parts over the course of 1792, caused bibliographical confusion and legal failure because the correct edition of whichever part was improperly named in the indictment.[118] The comedy of legal errors aside, the question of legal forms seems to have intensified an awareness of nuances of mediation in the radical societies. Notions that it was an Englishman's right to discuss politics or that print was inherently disposed towards political progress had to confront a hostile legal context. This situation encouraged flexibility when it came to printed formats, including the exploitation of satire and parody, but it also drew attention to the question of political opinion and its relation to issues of representation. As Thelwall put it in 1795, 'he who devises the method of collecting this opinion with the greatest purity (that is to say with the greatest freedom from influence, fear or corruption) will confer the greatest possible benefit upon the human race'.[119]

Convention politics

Made in 1795, Thelwall's judgement was the result of bitter experience in the struggle to keep open spaces for political discussion. The very language of debate became subject to immense critical pressure. In these conditions, much could depend on a word. John Barrell's *Imagining the King's Death* has delineated the strain put on the key terms of the treason statutes by the government and its supporters. Although at the treason trials the government argued that radicals were arming themselves for a violent insurrection, much of their case turned on the word 'convention' and whether it constituted a forum for the collection of opinion or an anti-parliament, opening up a path, as the prosecution saw it, that must lead to the overthrow of the monarchy. I won't rehearse Barrell's brilliant account of the struggle over use of the word 'imagine' in the statutes on treason, but I do want to pursue the wider question of the battle over words and its relation to other issues of mediation and representation on a larger scale.

Among the very earliest of the publications associated with the LCS, but not actually published in its name, was an attempt at disambiguation in the interest of rational political debate. *An Explanation of the Word Equality* (1793) was a four-page pamphlet probably published in January 1793. In terms of its content, the pamphlet was an explicit rebuttal of the attempts of Reeves and his associates to identify the LCS with the idea that 'the EQUALITY to be contended for, is *an equality of wealth and possessions*'. It goes on to make it clear that equality of rights was the issue, insisting that 'to render property insecure would destroy all motives to exertion, and tear up public happiness by the roots'. Reform, the author went on to insist, was a question of 'great and unchangeable truths' that needed protection 'from the WILFUL PERVERSIONS OF A WORD', but the four-page pamphlet was not quite the straightforward assertion of the plain truth it claimed. The opening paragraph suggested that 'if the "SWINISH MULTITUDE" should take it into their heads that they are justified in *inforcing* such a system, the consequences will rest upon those, who, by a perversion of terms, have wickedly or foolishly propagated such doctrine'. The idea that loyalists were causing or at least imagining the revolution they feared was not an uncommon device of radical rhetoric. It played its part, as we have already seen, in several trials, including Eaton's, and it was to reappear at the treason trials. Possibly *An Explanation of the Word Equality* was an attempt to distance the LCS from Spence's land plan, which did argue for the redistribution of property, but most of the latter part of *Explanation* is an address 'TO THE SWINISH MULTITUDE' in the hope that the definition of the word it provides will encourage them to a careful consideration of the case for reform.[120] Consequently, its primary effect is not to insist on security of property, but to encourage readers of a halfpenny pamphlet into political debate. Indeed, the economic aspects of reform take up the last pages of the pamphlet, which lists a selection of placemen who benefit from taxation and privilege, ending the fourth and final page with a blunt statement of economic constraints: '*The paper will not permit the list to be extended.*'

A motion to have *An Explanation of the Word Equality* published as an official LCS document was put before the general committee of 10 January 1793, but negatived because of the costs. The delegates did agree to subscribe as individuals and 'furnish their Divisions with such as were already printed, at their own Expence'.[121] Quite possibly there was some nervousness in the committee about the pamphlet's equivocations. At this meeting a rule that the committee would only receive manuscripts submitted for publication via delegates was carried. The LCS was worried about the cost of publishing, but also, as with Thomson's 'God Save the Rights of Man', about quite which principles would be affixed to its name. If the LCS did sometimes present itself as the honest repository of grand and inalienable truths, often it seemed more comfortable with presenting itself as a forum for debate and discussion. Even within this scenario, though, issues remained about the exact terms of debate and, not least, the processes by which debate could legitimately be said to represent the popular will. Nowhere were these tensions more acute than in the rolling controversy that surrounded the word 'convention'. Did it simply denote a repository for opinions collected by the LCS from around the country, or was it a medium that might presume to articulate the will of the people?

The account of the American Revolution in Paine's *Rights of Man* had presented a convention as the means of translating the local discussions of smaller clubs and societies into an expression of the popular will. An older tradition went back to at least the 1770s and the writings of James Burgh, an important influence on Spence, and Major Cartwright.[122] In the societies, these ideas were picked up as early as April 1792 in a letter from the Norwich Revolution Society to the SCI. In September, the Friends of Universal Peace and the Rights of Man in Stockport wrote to attack the LCS for its caution and argued all the abuses of the system could be 'done away with at once by the people assembled in Convention'. On 11 November, a 'Society for Political Information' wrote from Norwich to ask 'whether the generality of the societies meant to rest satisfied with the Duke of Richmond's plan only; OR WHETHER IT IS THEIR PRIVATE DESIGN TO RIP UP MONARCHY BY THE ROOTS, AND PLACE DEMOCRACY IN ITS STEAD?' Maurice Margarot was cautious in his reply, but made it clear that the LCS was primarily concerned 'to disseminate political knowledge'. Its immediate object was 'annual parliaments', elected by 'the unbought and even unbiased suffrage of every Citizen in possession of his reason'. 'The trifling difference that may have arisen between the several Societies', he downplayed. The main thing, he argued, was to get 'a majority of the nation to act as they do, the proposed reform will effect itself'. Annual parliaments would be 'the ground-work of every necessary reform', a response that the prosecution at Hardy's trial took to imply that the LCS was open to an ultimate goal of 'a clear and pure democracy'.[123] Margarot's words sound more like a general expression of faith in the power of print to bring about change almost in and of itself.

After consulting with other societies, the LCS decided early in 1793 to unite behind a plan of petitioning Parliament rather than calling a convention. The United Societies at Norwich reluctantly accepted petitioning as the only means available to 'a conquered people', although the same letter also thought that a 'refusal' of the petition would constitute an 'insult' that ought to be registered 'to the remotest part of the kingdom'.[124] The exchange assumed that petitioning was widely recognised as a traditional means of popular participation in the unreformed system. Nevertheless, it had been argued within the living memory of LCS members – at Lord Gordon's trial for treason – that even petitioning could constitute an attempt to overawe Parliament.[125] Parliament itself was often hostile to any pretension to direct representation of the popular will in a petition.[126] In 1793 the LCS was careful to follow what it understood to be the proper forms of addressing Parliament, inviting Fox, as MP for Westminster, to present it to the House. Citing his known opposition to universal suffrage, he refused. Sir Phillip Francis eventually presented it on 6 May. Parliament ordered the petition to lie on the table. Petitions that followed were rejected as disrespectful in their language. Charles Grey's petition fared only a little better, despite representing the opinion of the gentlemen of the Friends of the People.[127]

Given Parliament's perfunctory treatment of what the LCS understood to be a constitutionally ratified form, pressures were bound to mount within the movement to find other ways. Indeed pressures were mounting on many levels to adopt forms free of deference. In his draft reply to Norwich back in November 1792, Margarot had scratched out 'gentlemen' and replaced it with 'fellow-citizens'. At Hardy's trial, the prosecution accepted that the word 'citizen' was in itself inoffensive, but noted the distinction drawn by the LCS committee for revising the constitution between the 'Citizen' of a free state and the 'Subject' of a conquered one.[128] The February 1794 report on the constitution had certainly been scrupulous in its recommendations on the vocabulary to be used within the LCS:

> All political appellations which do not in their immediate interpretation convey an idea of political sentiment or situation, are party names. The following do not fall under this objection as will appear by their explanations.

Republican, -	One who wishes to promote the general welfare of his country.
Democrat, -	A supporter of the rights and power of the people.
Aristocrat, -	One who wishes to promote the interest of a few at the expense of the many.
Royalist, -	Among the ignorant part of mankind signifies, a person attached to regal government: among artful courtiers it is a veil for their own aristocracy.
Loyalist, -	A supporter of the constitution of his country.
Citizen, -	The ancient appellation given to members of free states.
Subject, -	Can only with propriety, be applied to a member of a State, whose government has been instituted by foreign conquest or the prevalence of a domestic faction.[129]

Philp understands this glossary as an attempt 'to stabilize the language in which people expressed their views and disagreements, as well as stabilizing the order and the institutional structure in which they did so'.[130] This process turned out to be much more difficult than Hardy could have imagined when he founded the society back in early 1792.

In the debates about its own constitution, a matter I will return to later, the LCS was very alert to questions of democratic practice more generally. Francis Place, who served on a later committee of revision, claimed it aimed at 'assimilating its organization as much as possible to what we conceived to be the best form for governing the Nation'.[131] Place's comment would seem to run counter to Gunther Lottes's suggestion that questions about internal governance of the LCS rarely translated to its reform programme more generally. Lottes understands the latter as trapped within a tradition wherein 'political representation formed so natural a part of English political culture that the advocates of radical reform had a blunted sensibility to its problems'.[132] Deafness to these questions is not evident in Thelwall's claim that he who devised the best means of collecting 'the aggregate opinion of a nation . . . will confer the greatest possible benefit upon the human race'. Perhaps it is unsurprising that the LCS did not foreground its own constitutional arrangements in its reform programme when they were still a subject of internal wrangling. Lottes is certainly prone to think of the LCS in corporate terms, when it might be better understood as a more provisional entity, both in relation to its own processes and to wider forms of representation, committed to creating spaces for these issues to be debated.

Questions of representation and responsibility also surfaced in the way the LCS imagined its role in relation to other societies. Margarot's answer to Norwich at the end of 1792 seems to prize the unity of the reform movement over any specific political position, possibly implying, as the prosecution at the treason trials claimed, that he was open to further changes to the constitution in the future. Sometimes, however, a desire for unity became a drive towards uniformity. Eighteenth-century book clubs and other literary societies regularly circulated their rules and regulations. The LCS was frequently asked to provide theirs in the name of more effective circulation of political information.[133] A draft letter to Leeds presented at the 1 August committee raised the question of 'uniting their Society to our Own and adopting the title of Corresp. Society'. The committee recommended that a similar offer be made to other societies. This was reinforced the following month when a motion came into the central committee that a circular letter be written to all the 'Country Societies', as those in the regions were called, 'inviting them to adopt our Title & by incorporating themselves, with us form in time a Universal Society'.[134] Before any debate on the issue could commence, the motion was withdrawn, because Hardy had just received a reply from Tewkesbury declining an earlier offer.[135]

John Lloyd had originally written to the LCS from the Tewkesbury Society in July 1793, signing himself your 'fellow citizen & cooperator in the glorious cause of Liberty'. Margarot had replied with copies of the LCS address to the public and a set of rules, 'adviseable for you to abide entirely by'. The draft goes on to inform the Tewkesbury Society that the LCS 'will willingly incorporate your Society with our own under the title of the Corresponding Society in Tewkesbury & if so our Rules will become yours, our Intelligence will be the same & our Correspondence weekly and regularly carried on'. Margarot insisted 'our mode of proceeding must be entirely alike & no reserve must take place between us'. He was confident 'some other societies in other parts of the country will fall into the plan'. The effect he imagined as rendering much more 'forcible ... everything that came from us'. Some societies did adopt a uniform title and rules, including the Manchester Corresponding Society, but one imagines that a society which already existed, like the Tewkesbury Society, with its own rules already adapted to its local circumstances, was less likely simply to dissolve itself into Margarot's plan. Margarot's letter seems tactless to say the least, but it reveals tendencies towards codification and centralisation in the attempt to represent the LCS as the incorporated voice of the people. There seems little doubt that for some at least within the LCS the dream of the flow of knowledge across a commonwealth of reason was part of their idea of improvement. Equally the decision to drop the plan once Tewkesbury and other societies rejected it suggests that the idea of a uniform public sphere was far from being a core principle of the society as a whole. Faced with claims for autonomy from associated societies, the LCS was willing to understand the question of collecting the opinions of the people as a complex matter of representation and self-determination.

On the same day as the LCS approved the letter to Leeds, several divisions recommended that a copyist be hired to transcribe 'all the letters received from the Country'. The purpose was to allow them to be read in each division, so that individual members could have proper access to the activities of the society. The practical question of processing and storing increasing volumes of information for and about the membership was obviously a driving mechanism, but it had political consequences, which the Tewkesbury Society at least resisted, and which the central committee did not necessarily embrace (the debate on the copyist was deferred). Probably as a defence mechanism against prosecution for unguarded comments from correspondents, the committee decided at the next meeting that only 'such parts of the letters received as were proper to be communicated, should be transcribed'. However functionalist one's account of these developments, questions of authorial responsibility and democratic participation were clearly shaping the LCS's decisions at all levels, including the debates, going on at just this time, about whether and in what form the Society should republish *The Englishman's Right* discussed in Chapter 1. They were also debating the writing of a proposed 'Address to the King', not least in relation to the question of the appropriate forms of address that should be used to the monarch.

This last issue was weighty enough to require the setting up of yet another sub-committee, comprising Margarot, Parkinson, Walne, Baxter, and Moore. The plan was for the address to be published, but only after being read at a second general meeting set for 24 October to canvas opinion more widely. Afterwards, Baxter objected that the agreed statement of public grievances had been dropped in favour of a plea for 'speedy termination to the War'. Eaton also signed the protest against this decision as 'unjustified and unconstitutional'. These things may seem mere minutae compared with the larger issues for which the LCS was contending, but such a lofty perspective risks missing Baxter's insistence on respecting democratic forms and on an uncowed disposition towards the king. Gerrald was chosen to read the 'Address to the King' at the general meeting. Not long afterwards he published *A Convention the Only Means of Saving us from Ruin* (1793). Gerrald's pamphlet opened with an account of the disastrous effects of war on the nation in order to argue that conditions in the country were so exceptional as to warrant the calling of a convention of the people. In the wake of the failure of the petitions supporting Grey's half-hearted motion for reform in May, the societies had begun discussing alternatives in earnest, including the possibility of a convention. Gerrald came at the issue in a roundabout way. After spending many pages attacking the war and the corruption of the legal system, he claimed that 'to the want of an adequate representation in parliament may be traced all our sufferings, under whatever aspect they are presented'. Given the refusal of Parliament to reform itself, there was 'no other resource, than the interposition of the great body of the people themselves, electing deputies in whom they can confide, and imparting instructions which they must injoin to be executed'.[136]

Gerrald is typical of what Green calls the 'confrontational exploitation of the ambiguities of constitutional limits'.[137] He was only too well aware that the word 'convention' had a fraught history caught up with questions of whether the people were understood to wield a constituent power. His own uses of the word in the pamphlet's early pages are to do with the National Convention of France's decision to depose Louis XVI, but his argument avoids the word for the most part and concerns itself with British precedents. Gerrald argued that the right 'of assembling to deliberate on the best mode of promoting the public welfare, is no where forbidden by any positive statute'. If the '*right* of assembling then is lawful', he continued, then 'the *power* of exercising that right is a necessary consequence of it'. He finds ample precedent in British constitutional history, but ultimately goes right back to Anglo-Saxon times, at one point providing 'convention' as a gloss for 'folk-mote'.[138] Blackstone's *Commentaries* and the Scottish radical John Millar treated the folk-mote as 'an oligarchic council of wise men', as Barrell phrases it, but Gerrald presented it as 'a democratic assembly'.[139] Burke, Gerrald claimed, had once ranked it 'among public misfortunes, that the House of Commons should be wholly untouched by the opinions and feelings of the people out of doors'. Gerrald dismissed the idea of virtual representation as 'nonsensical jargon' and set about presenting his own plan for a convention, with deputies elected at primary assemblies.[140] An attempt to set up an Irish convention in 1792 had been met with legislation banning just such an association, but Gerrald used this legislation as proof of the legality of such a meeting in England, where no such law existed. He also invoked the authority of the associations of the 1780s, enjoying the fact that ministers like Pitt and the Duke of Richmond had been involved. There are also echoes in the plan of the proposals that Gerrald's friend Robert Merry had put forward to the National Convention in France at the end of 1792. [141] The influences of Paine and David Williams, the latter explicitly acknowledged, are also apparent. Overall, Gerrald made his convention sound much less like a forum for collecting public opinion and more like an alternative to Parliament, but the uncertainty was unresolved. Ambiguity over the implications of calling a convention was soon to land Gerrald in prison.

The LCS never really resolved its attitude to what a convention would be or do, if it ever called one. From early on, various societies had written to the LCS suggesting it as the best way forward. In Scotland, the Scottish Friends of the People – an organisation quite different from Grey's association – had already held conventions in December 1792 and May 1793, without ever resolving the issue. On 17 May, Hardy and Margarot had written to Scotland to ask William Skirving for his view: 'Our Petitions have been all of them unsuccessful; our Attention must now therefore be turned to some more effectual Means – from your Society we would willingly learn them.' In his reply, Skirving recommended what he called 'a general union' of the reform societies as a first step. In July a general meeting of the LCS resolved to promote closer union with all the reform societies, perhaps the origin of the suggestion made to Tewkesbury about names and rules, but also perhaps a step towards Skirving's suggested course. In the correspondence between Skirving and the LCS, a suspicion is registered that Pitt may have been contemplating a version of the anti-convention laws passed in Ireland. Barrell has suggested this fear may account for the hasty meeting of the 'British Convention' in Scotland at the end of 1793.[142] On 24 October, the LCS called a general meeting to elect its delegates for Edinburgh. Helped by the reputation of his pamphlet no doubt, Gerrald was elected. The meeting itself was held on grounds in Spitalfields, owned by a pump-maker Thomas Breillat.[143] The large crowd that attended confirmed to the LCS the potential in large open-air meetings. 'Many who came there to ridicule and abuse', Hardy claimed later, 'went away converted and afterwards joined the society and became zealous promoters of the cause.'[144] Given the scepticism about virtual representation, such meetings came to be understood as an embodied presence of the constituent power of the people daring Parliament to ignore its views.

The government certainly did not ignore events in Edinburgh. The LCS delegates Gerrald and Margarot arrived too late for the General Convention of the Friends of the People, which began on 29 October and ended a few days later with a resolution to petition Parliament for a reform based on the Duke of Richmond's plan. Their advent forced the meeting to reconvene as the British Convention on 19 November. Despite Gerrald's gestures towards the 'folk-mote', it soon began to model itself consciously after the National Convention of France. The implication, as Barrell puts it, was that it understood itself 'as a legislative, not as a petitioning body'.[145] The question of its constitutive power was still being debated when the Scottish authorities dispersed the meeting. The LCS delegates understood a motion to have been passed that justified the calling of a convention if a petition was rejected by Parliament. Skirving and Margarot were brought to trial in January and sentenced to fourteen years transportation. Charles Sinclair, the SCI delegate, was arrested at the same time, but later released. Granted bail, Gerrald appeared as a guest of honour at the SCI meeting on 17 January. Three days later he appeared at the general meeting of the LCS at the Globe Tavern. Friends, including his former teacher Samuel Parr, advised him to flee, but he returned to Scotland for his trial.[146] His decision may have been influenced by a sense of his 'public' role enjoined on him by William Godwin who wrote to congratulate him for being 'Fertile in genius {,} strong in moral feeling {,} prepared with every accomplishment that literature & reflection can give.' Godwin advised him to make use of the trial to tell 'a tale upon which the Happiness of Nations depends'.[147] In one obvious sense the advice failed, as Gerrald received the same sentence as Skirving and Margarot and died in New South Wales in 1796. In another sense, he achieved the immortality that

Godwin promised him. 'Gerrald understood', as James Epstein has put it, 'that he was creating a literary text', one very alert to the mediating contexts of courtroom and print. In order to transmit his words to the reading public as swiftly as possible, the LCS sent a shorthand writer to the court.[148]

Gerrald took up the role of martyr in his defence speech with gusto. Presenting himself, as Epstein shows, as 'a simple individual' upon whom had fallen 'a sacred trust', he placed himself in a long tradition of British liberty.[149] Not presuming to speak for the people, he presented himself as a martyr to their right to be heard. After an opening that set out the case for reform on the grounds of natural rights, he quickly moved to arguing that those grounds were intrinsic to the ancient constitution being eroded by the encroachments of the Crown. He certainly succeeded in entering the pantheon of the radical movement, not as a theorist perhaps, but as an icon of heroic suffering for the people. John Richter wrote an address to Gerrald that he read at the Chalk Farm general meeting on 14 April 1794. Following a string of declarations that presented the nation as declining towards a state where 'BRITONS ARE NO LONGER FREE', Richter addressed Gerrald as 'beloved and respected friend and fellow citizen, a Martyr to the Glorious Cause of Equal Representation'.[150] Here was a reimagining of the 'Glorious Cause' as always tending towards universal suffrage, an idea Thelwall was hammering away at in his lectures at the time, with the crowd at Chalk Farm being implicitly treated as the embodied form of the political nation, 'a literal representation of the virtual collectives enabled by the press'.[151] Richter's address was published in an official LCS account of the meeting. Gerrald's trial had concluded a month earlier, and versions were also quickly published, 'for the BENEFIT of his INFANT DAUGHTER'.[152] Succeeding to Gerrald's role as the LCS's most dashing orator, Thelwall barely gave a lecture without mention of his predecessor, and scarcely ever failed to make use of the seventeenth-century precedents Gerrald used at his trial. A visit to Gerrald on board the *Surprise* before he sailed for Australia added to his stock of emotional scenarios.[153]

By 1795, there was a substantial canon of Gerraldiana. *Joseph Gerrald, A Fragment* published by John Smith, gives a short version of his life, supplemented by another newspaper account, together with 'To Citizen Gerrald' a poem in his praise. Eaton had already published 'Tribute of a Humble Muse to the Memory of Joseph Gerrald' by 'a patriotic female', one of several other poems of this kind, in the pages of *Politics for the People*.[154] *Joseph Gerrald, A Fragment* includes a list of other works by and about Gerrald published by Smith: a new edition of *A Convention* at 2s 6d, *The Trial of Joseph Gerrald . . . with his Portrait*, 4s, *The Defence of Joseph Gerrald*, 1s 6d, *Gerrald's Address of the British Convention*, at 6d. Some of these prices suggest that it was not only members of the LCS who were expected to react to their portraits of the suffering patriot. Eaton brought out two editions of *Authentic biographical anecdotes of Gerrald* in 1795 'written by a friend'. In *Conciones ad Populum* (1795), Coleridge invited his audience to imagine Gerrald:

> Withering in the sickly and tainted gales of a prison, his healthful soul looks down from the citadel of his integrity on his impotent persecution.

Within a year, Coleridge had changed his tune. He tried to persuade Thelwall that Gerrald was one of those 'Atheistic Brethren' who 'square their moral systems exactly according to their inclinations'. The radical movement more generally continued to promote Gerrald as a suffering martyr. Acknowledging that his hero had some faults, Thelwall insisted that Gerrald's life remained largely 'unblemished': 'for what are the little extravagancies of a young man of genius, born, not for the narrow circle of a family, but for the universe – and who, dissipating only what was his own, lays no burthen on society to replace it'.[155]

Constitutional schisms

Gerrald bequeathed to the radical societies a strong idea of the legitimacy of convention politics, but a continued uncertainty as to exactly what they meant. In the early months of 1794, the possibilities of calling one were debated at various meetings and in correspondence between the LCS and the regional societies, but enthusiasm for it seems to have dwindled by May 1794. Nevertheless, the idea that a convention was being planned to overawe Parliament played a crucial role at the treason trials at the end of the year.[156] Rather than retrace Barrell's discussion of the trials, I shall revert to the internal issues of representation within the LCS, especially those surrounding the revision of the constitution. Security matters intensified these debates, especially after the arrests in May 1794, but they were clearly informed by ongoing issues surrounding democratic processes and forms of address. In this regard, the question of the convention was not unrelated, as both turned on how relations between representation and participation were to be conceived. By 1795, these issues had become even more acute within the LCS, as a significant body of members seems to have resisted strengthening the power of an executive committee as a usurpation of the rights of the members gathered in the divisions. Some of the latter left the LCS and formed themselves into separate societies, devoted to reading, discussion, and political lectures as the proper means of political change, sometimes with a distinctively Godwinian inflection.

A strain of thinking in the LCS that tended towards imagining print as telegraphic in the immediacy of its effects, as we have seen, always coexisted with a practical attentiveness to the materiality of its mediations. In this regard, the idea that every document had to be subjected to some form of democratic scrutiny was a foundational if often divisive aspect of the print culture of the LCS. This scrutiny extended to the question of the constitution of the society and ended up opening the larger question of understanding reform in a broader 'moral' sense, where the latter could even include scepticism about the need for government at all. In response to the arrests for treason in May 1794, the central committee hurriedly proposed the adoption of a new constitution without fully consulting the divisions. They were quickly accused of 'an act of great usurpation and aristocracy'.[157] Such accusations had scarred earlier debates on the issue. Reporting on a meeting at division 29 in February, the spy Taylor described the debate between Thelwall and Hodgson on 18 February mentioned in Chapter 1. Despite their agreement on the need for change, Hodgson argued in favour of a proper constitution for the society, but Thelwall thought it unnecessary and gained most applause. Three days later at his lecture, according to Taylor's notes, Thelwall argued that 'Reason truth and justice were at all times better than positive Laws'.[158] His position probably drew on his reading in *Political justice*, where Godwin had declared that 'law is merely relative to the exercise of political force, and must perish when the necessity of that force ceases, if the influence of truth do not sooner extirpate it from the practice of mankind'.[159]

The central committee's proposal for a new constitution was the culmination of the report by different committees that had been sitting since at least March 1793. The *Report of the Committee of the Constitution, of the London Corresponding Society* published in February 1794 was rejected, and a sub-committee to revise it was appointed at the meeting where Hodgson and Thelwall clashed. Hodgson and Richter objected to the new committee and made the issue into one of direct participation: 'any discussion or resolutions of any constituted body relative to this object are Factious & can only tend to *over awe* the opinion of our Constituents'.[160] At around this time, John Pearce, an attorney, seems to have taken to attending meetings with a copy of Blackstone's *Commentaries* under his arm: to 'make a quotation or two for the instruction of the Citizens, respecting the power's [sic] of Bodies who *create* & the Subordination of the *Created*'.[161] The question was of the relative authority of constitutive and constituted power. Blackstone had been a major force in cementing the idea of the sovereignty of Parliament over the people.[162] The LCS's internal struggle over its constitution intersected with its debates about the authority of a convention relative to Parliament. The report of the new committee of revision was ready by April and sent out to be debated by the divisions. The spy Groves claimed that division 2 had to adjourn its debate when it came to the phrase 'all government abstractly considered, being itself an evil'. When the debate restarted at their meeting of 5 May, it was objected that the statement against government 'would give room to the Enemies of the Society & the cause to declaim against their principles'.[163]

While these heated debates were continued, the question of whether a national convention of societies ought to be summoned was also being discussed. Given urgency by the fear that the government was contemplating anti-convention legislation, these were primarily conducted by a secret committee, but complicated by the different opinions on what kind of body constituted a convention. For some, it was the most direct mode of expressing the popular will, and as such potentially a direct challenge to the authority of Parliament. For others, it seems, the gathering was only a means of sounding opinion and deciding on what their next course of action should be. Those who favoured this last understanding, including the SCI's representatives, tended to steer away from the word 'convention' as savouring too much of French practices, notwithstanding the purchase of the word within British constitutionalist discourse. At the beginning of April 1794, a joint conference of the LCS and SCI met to discuss the calling of a convention. Thelwall produced a plan, but the SCI delegates objected to the use of the word 'convention'. Later at his interview before the Privy Council, William Sharp the engraver claimed that most of the meeting was taken up with arguments over forms of words.[164] A few days later, on 14 April, the LCS held a general meeting at Chalk Farm, on the road north out of London. The meeting resolved that the treatment of Gerrald and his fellows was proof that Britons were no longer free. Further, echoing Gerrald, their treatment 'ought to be considered as dissolving entirely the social compact between the English Nation and their Governors; and driving them to an immediate appeal to that incontrovertible maxim of eternal Justice, *that the safety of the People is the* SUPREME, *and in cases of necessity, the* ONLY *Law*'. This opinion could certainly sound like preparation for a convention that would presume to speak for the will of the people to a Parliament that had defaulted on its duty. At the address of thanks to Lord Stanhope, Richter and Hodgson condemned the aristocratic title 'lord' and proposed 'citizen' instead. A similar wrangle followed about the word 'senate', which Thelwall claimed meant 'Respectful & Wise Men'. In all the arguments about words, the question was one of deference to received forms and how much they might be reconstituted in the state of crisis.[165]

The government's decision to arrest the leaders of the societies in May was predicated on the strongest possible understanding of 'convention' politics, that is, in terms of the statute on treason, as an attempt to overawe and ultimately replace Parliament.[166] Although the arrests understandably soon put a stop to the debates in the LCS about internal structures, the hiatus did not last long, despite the absence of key figures in custody. The debate over the authority of the executive rekindled in June 1794, now reinforced by the need to protect meetings from infiltration by spies and informers. Groves explained to his masters that these debates had always had an eye to the question of what was being imagined for the governance of the nation at large:

> The Report of that Commee & the Form of Government recommended gave rise to great Jealousies & Animosities, as founded on principles incompatible with that Liberty which the Society was seeking for in the National System of Governmnt. And as investing Powers & creating Offices & Officers among themselves which would infallibly render the Division a Cypher, and the whole management & Controul be placed in the hands of a few, & thereby their Government will be Monarchical or something worse.

Now it seemed the question of the LCS's constitution might serve to rally the society:

> The increased operations of Government having excited a general panic, and the defection being so great as to threaten the Society with a total annihilation, and it having been adjudged that bringing forward the Constitution again, in any form, rather than being without one at all, would serve to rally the Society, and restore it to its original vigour, the preceding expedient was hit upon & the Motion accordingly submitted.

The central committee recommended that the revised report be adopted, but some of the divisions reiterated the objection of 'usurpation and Aristocracy'. Despite supporting the revised constitution, John Bone rose to observe that 'the French Convention had never dared speak of a Constitution until it had been sanctioned by and had received the compleat approbation of the people'. In the circumstances of needing to prepare for the impending trials, it was decided to put the debate aside and continue using the original constitution, although Hodgson wrote in August from 'on the tramp', having fled to escape arrest, to insist on his old position that the LCS urgently required a new one.[167]

In the light of the government's attempts to prepare for the trials by peppering the press with accounts of the LCS's plans for a convention as a treasonable conspiracy, the committee insisted on its primary role as the dissemination of political information. Accounts of Hardy's arrest and the fate of his wife were published, mainly taken up with rebutting the claims made by the first report of the committee of secrecy that there was any conspiracy afoot.[168] With numbers dwindling in the face of the arrests, attempts were made to revive conviviality. Division 9 devoted an evening to 'pleasure rather than business'. The spy Metcalfe noted 'many Treasonable songs were sung'.[169] Other songs were written by Thomas Upton, an informer, and distributed to the divisions to sell at a half penny. Printing costs were squeezing finances straitened by defections. On 3 July, the printer Citizen Davidson wrote to complain that his bills had not been met, his irritation compounded by the fact the LCS was starting to employ others, presumably to spread its debts. One additional cost was the need to produce new membership tickets to replace those that had fallen into the hands of the government. At first the engraver William Worship was entrusted with the task, but he seems to have been struck by panic at the arrests. A week later Citizen Williams promised a 'voluntary Engraving for the New Tickets' in the form of an old man instructing his three sons that they could only break a bundle of sticks by snapping them one at a time: 'The Allegory is The acquisition of Strength by Unanimity'.[170] The central committee also invested in a series of pamphlets primarily aimed at rebutting the idea that it supported violent revolution, most of them written or revised by Eaton's old collaborator James Parkinson. They were *Revolutions without Bloodshed*, published by Eaton and Smith, with proceeds going to the wives and children of the prisoners; *Reformers no Rioters*, written by Bone, but revised by Burks and Parkinson, published in response to the Crimp riots that shook London a few weeks earlier; and *Vindication of the London Corresponding Society*, largely concerned with defending the LCS from the government press campaign in the weeks leading up to the trials.[171] The final page of Parkinson's *Vindication* carries an advertisement for the others, each sold at a penny, together with one for the LCS's other major print project, a new periodical called *The Politician*.

The idea for *The Politician* had been around in the LCS since July when John Bone raised the issue of a weekly publication 'in the Nature of Paine's Crisis'. No doubt the proposal was partly inspired by the reputation of the *Crisis* as the paper that had stiffened the resolve of the Americans in the War of Independence. Bone's suggestion was agreed and a public receiving box was set up for contributions. Not unusually in the LCS, there then followed weeks of debate about how to go about the business, despite the fact that John Smith reported to the committee of correspondence that 'a New Patriotic Newspaper would shortly be published twice a week'. There was a hint of pride in Smith's confidence that it would be 'a compleat Democratic paper . . . indeed the Society might call it their own Paper'. In this regard, the committee was trying to occupy the ground so successfully worked by Eaton's *Politics for the People* and Spence's *Pig's Meat*, with more control of the content by the LCS itself. The delay may have been exacerbated by the fact most of the members experienced with print were in prison, as was Spence, or on the run, as Eaton seems to have been. A long list of 'literary men' who might be approached was deliberated over. With the pending trials in mind, the committee approached the attorneys Gurney and Vaughan for an essay on 'the Rights of Witnesses'. Hodgson drew up a prospectus for the new paper that provoked furious debate, especially about a passage 'which seem'd to hold out the publication as a medium for discussing other questions than those which immediately related to a Reform in Parliament and universal Suffrage, and partaly [sic] to a part which courted a discussion upon the Merits and advantages of other Governments'. As well as French affairs, Hodgson seems to glance at the broader 'moral' aspects of the LCS's mission of social 'improvement'.

The meeting decided that the document ought to be referred to Parkinson, probably the most experienced LCS writer at liberty. Parkinson decided on a list of 'literary gentlemen' who ought to be approached to revise the prospectus, including James Mackintosh, still regarded as the defender of the French Revolution; the dissenting minister Joseph Towers; Thomas Holcroft, soon to turn himself in on the treason charge; and someone called Beaumont, probably the journalist at the *Telegraph*.[172] Each declined and Parkinson decided Hodgson's prospectus should be sent to a Mr Bayley, who had said he would revise and correct it.[173] At the same meeting, Bone produced the original draft of *Reformers no Rioters*, according to the spy Metcalfe, 'full of the most violent and seditious expressions & calculated to renew the tumults which so lately prevail'd'. Parkinson and Burks were called on to 'revise and modify'. With the treason trials looming, the LCS was being particularly careful about the sentiments associated with its name. Smith was left with the decision as to who should print and edit the *Politician*, 'whose Name is not to be made public'. Contributions were only to be received at Smith's shop. Burks was then given the task of writing to a list of forty-eight 'Literary Men' requesting contributions. Further progress must have been delayed by the fact Smith himself was arrested a few weeks later for his supposed involvement in the pop-gun plot to assassinate the king.[174] In the event, the paper did not appear until 13 December.

Coming only a week or so after the acquittal of Thelwall, the paper was a sign of confidence blossoming again after the victories at the treason trials. The title-page was bold enough to name William Townly as editor, contrary to the earlier decision to withhold such details. Burks and Smith were to receive communications. The paper presented itself as a forum for political discussion, allowing 'rational' attacks against universal suffrage as well as support for the principle. The first number duly contained an essay arguing for reform but against universal suffrage. Another essay, celebrating Margarot, returned to the issue of 'party names'. Signed 'R. H.', the stalwart printer Robert Hawes may have been the author. On a similar theme, an essay in the final issue called for the LCS to rename itself 'Society for Reform', so as to avoid any aspersion that it was in correspondence with the French.[175] Thelwall dominated the third and penultimate number, although he apologised that 'my engagements at this time do not permit me to comply in a more ample manner with your request for literary Communications'. Acknowledging 'the important utility of little publications' as a ready means for the dissemination of political information, Thelwall went on to rebut some of the specific charges made against him at his trial. The next few pages were taken up with a copy of his speech given to the court after the verdict and a poem he had composed in the Tower.[176] Other poems were promised for later numbers, but in the event only one more ever appeared. The fourth number of the *Politician* (3 January 1795) was the last. Contrary to the expectations of the LCS, the stamp commissioners informed the publishers that they were liable for duty. The editors ended with a pledge to return that was never fulfilled.

The LCS made other investments in print over these dark months following the arrests of May 1794. Poems were sent in to the LCS from 'Tommy Pindar junior'. July saw Hodgson receive another 'large parcel of printed verses'. 'Written by a good citizen for the relief of the Wives & Children of the imprisoned Citizens', these were doled out to each delegate to be sold at a halfpenny'.[177] Possibly they were Citizen Lee's poems as

Powell later described him as 'very active in supporting the subscriptions for the persons imprison'd & very liberal himself'. Smith and Burks were selling Lee's poem *On the death of Mrs Hardy, wife of Mr. Thomas Hardy* for 1d each or 7s per hundred in the same cause.[178] The onset of the treason trials also produced some virulent satire against Pitt, including *A warning to judges and jurors on state trials*, which ends with a protracted account of the Grand Vizier hanging himself. Many other imaginings of Pitt's death soon followed, including the wonderful series of mock advertising bills for Signor Pittachio.[179] By mid-1795 satires like *A faithful narrative of the last illness, death, and interment of the Rt. Hon. William Pitt* were flying off the radical presses, not least Citizen Lee's, by this time operating as a bookseller in his own right.

In general terms, the acquittals at the treason trials gave a spur to radical print culture, but the legal process left scars that threatened the unity of the movement. Horne Tooke announced that he was retiring from politics. The SCI effectively ceased to exist. Hardy concentrated on recovering his shoemaking business. Thelwall recommenced lecturing at Beaufort Buildings, but withdrew from the LCS for months. A number of narratives recorded the anger of those who had been arrested, including Thelwall's *Natural and Constitutional Right* (1795), Holcroft's *A narrative of facts* (1795), and Jeremiah Joyce's *Mr. Joyce's arrest* (1795). Not all the prisoners were released quickly. Richter and Baxter remained in prison until mid-December, John Martin until September 1795. *Pig's Meat* published songs from the various celebrations, but Spence also supplied some bitter reflections on the festivities after his release on 22 December:

> If half the wealth, and half the wind,
> That there was spent to no great end,
> Had been employ'd for to relieve
> The wants of patr'ots that now grieve,
> Who blushing for a nation's crimes,
> Dare yield to truth the homage due? [180]

Horne Tooke's conduct at the trials themselves was subjected to scathing attack in the anonymous *John Horne Tooke Stripped Naked and Dissected*:

> After adhering like a buzzing and teizing gnat, for so many years, to the buttocks of the Aristocracy, you now in the period of the grand climacteric, apologise for the annoyance, by the forfeiture of your admitted principle.[181]

If there was personal resentment here, there was also a sense that the movement ought to be orienting itself to its broadest constituency, giving voice to the popular will, rather than deferring to friends of liberty within the elite.

Ill feeling translated itself into rancorous debates in the LCS itself, as the arguments over its constitution flared again between February and May 1795. Several divisions seceded. In an attempt to draw the LCS back together, the committee published an appeal that characterised the contending parties in terms of two extremes. One position questioned the need for any constitution at all. This body of opinion appeared to believe:

> *That the only means of securing social happiness is by the general diffusion of Knowledge, and this being effected, all regard to constitutional and legal rules would become unnecessary.*

From this position, identifiable with Thelwall's in his argument with Hodgson back in 1794, the LCS ought to have been committed to a democratic version of Godwin's faith in the power of discussion alone as a force for political change. The other party in the LCS debate saw such thinking as visionary delusion and insisted that 'constitutional regulations, judiciously formed, are to be considered as beacons rather than as fetters'. This position owed more to Paine's thinking about the importance of constitutions and less to Godwin's ideas of perfectibility. Perhaps unsurprisingly, the leadership showed more sympathy for a position that accepted the impossibility of 'achieving moral perfection'. Instead, it affirmed the need for 'prudent regulations, and the propagation of laudable principles, to guard against those follies and vices which have so frequently disturbed the happiness of Society'. It also confirmed its commitment to 'the Diffusion by means of cheap publications of such Knowledge as may tend to awaken the Public Mind to the necessity of Universal Suffrage & Annual Parliaments'.[182]

The appeal was insufficient to recall the two divisions who had already seceded. At the end of March, division 12 had written to complain of the treatment of its delegate John Bone (who had been accused of spying) and separated itself as the London Reforming Society. At the same time, the main body of his accusers, primarily members of division 16, had left to form 'the Friends of Liberty'. In a letter to the central committee, their secretary Stephen Cooper made clear that the schism had to do with constitutional matters and stated that he had always been against the formation of an executive within the Society. For its part, the London Reforming Society set about proposing a book plan, effectively a restatement of the idea that the divisions represented autonomous cells for the dissemination and debate of political information. It was not averse to cooperation with other societies in this regard, indeed Bone wrote to the LCS in May with his plan.[183] If his idea seems to chime in with an ecumenical vision of little societies bringing about reform via the media of reading and discussion, then Bone's religious views were proving more troublesome to the LCS. He seems to have been a 'saint' who propagated his religious opinions at meetings, probably one of several unhappy with the society's support for Paine and Volney's deism. On 15 October 1795 a letter came from 'the religious Seceders', formerly division 27, saying they had formed a society called 'the Friends of Religious & Civil Liberty'. Despite the rift, they wished to continue to correspond with the LCS, although Hodgson and other LCS members opposed their 'conduct' as enshrined in the first article in their regulations: 'no members should be admitted but who pledged themselves to believe in the Scripturs'.[184] Citizen Lee was probably a casualty of these schisms within the LCS. He may even have joined the Friends of Religious and Civil Liberty. Certainly he and Hawes, another religious man, were the only booksellers of any previous standing with the LCS who sold the new society's tracts.[185]

For the most part, the schismatics continued to coordinate their efforts in one way or another with the LCS, whatever their differences. With food shortages and military setbacks threatening the stability of the government, by early summer 1795 conditions seemed ripe for another concerted push for reform. The situation turned attention away from the question of the LCS's constitution and back to the idea of a larger crisis that threatened a suspension of the compact between the people and their government. The LCS called the first in a series of outdoor meetings for the end of June. The official LCS account described 'a spectacle at once sublime and awful, since it seems as though the whole British Nation had convened itself upon this extraordinary occasion, to witness the propriety of our conduct, and testify for the legality of our proceedings'. This vision of the people gathered in protest, of course, implies that the will of the people was finding an alternative voice in response to Parliament's failure to fulfil its obligations to the nation. At this critical juncture, the 'Address to the Nation' insisted, the slow spread of political information must give way to more urgent councils. 'Calm remonstrances of reason', the introduction continues, must now cede to the 'strong impulse of necessity.' In the face of 'impending danger' it goes on 'YOUR CHIEF, PERHAPS YOUR ONLY HOPE IS IN YOURSELVES'.[186]

Much the same message was hammered out at meetings through the summer and autumn, as it became clear the government intended to introduce legislation against a convention. Threats were made against ministers, especially Pitt, and in one infamous broadside published by Citizen Lee even king killing was imagined. Edward Henry Iliff's *A summary of the duties of citizenship!* on the other hand, cautioned patience. Writing in response to the king's refusal to countenance the addresses of the LCS, Iliff sketches out a situation where the citizenship is surrounded by species of tyranny ranging from the army to the bishops. His pamphlet imagines that the government has broken its compact with the governed, but ultimately advises the LCS to continue its campaign of political education along Godwinian lines: ''Tis not amidst the buzzing tumult of popular assemblies that you will reap the harvest of information.' Instead of listening to 'hot-brained demagogues, that inflame your passions', he urged his readers to seek 'men familiarized to practical, and speculative morality'.[187] Nevertheless, his message was deemed dangerous enough for the pamphlet to be included on the indictment against its publisher Lee.

Apparently much less Godwinian in emphasis, John Baxter delivered a lecture to the Friends of Liberty (9 November) that insisted on the right to resistance. Printed and sold for a penny by his old associate Burks, Baxter insisted that his aim was to preserve the constitution against the incursions of despotism. Resistance, Baxter argued, was not simply a matter of arms, although he produced historical precedents anyway, but also of a right to 'association to obtain a redress of grievances'.[188] Here was an idea of the right of resistance that probed what Jeremy Bentham called the 'juncture for resistance', that is, the point where even Blackstone acknowledged that the people had the right to assert their constituent power. Uncertainty about what Bentham called the '*Common sign*', the signal that this point had been reached, was part of the ambiguity surrounding Baxter's insistence on the right of the people to resist. The same fuzzy logic had informed Gerrald's convention politics. To the government, this way of thinking was simply a new form of treason, asserting a bogus idea of the popular sovereignty against the constituted authority of Parliament.[189]

Despite their differences, Baxter and Iliff both imagined that public opinion would force the government into conceding the argument for reform, as if the manifestation of the constituent power of the people would quite literally overawe Parliament. Exploiting the attack on the king's coach at the end of November, the government chose instead to bring the Two Acts before Parliament, severely restricting rights of association and freedom of expression. London radicalism had built up for itself a complex network of routes for the circulation of political information. Reading, writing, and discussion were the primary media for its imagining of political transformation, in some imaginings even transcending forms of political organisation in favour of a slowly unfolding moral revolution of the kind, for instance, Iliff seems to have derived from Godwin. For a few, especially Citizen Lee, this power of the word was actually a fulfilment of the Word, as the divine right of republics played itself out in human affairs. Thomas Hardy was a religious man, but he did not make the same appeal to divine providence in his shaping of the LCS's public role. Most radicals shared Godwin's secular sense of public opinion shaped by discussion and the dissemination of print, but with Paine showed much more faith than the philosopher in the power of public assembly and constitution making. Despite in some regards being a disciple of Godwin's, John Thelwall argued that these two visions of change were not mutually exclusive. The period had seen a growing confidence in the constituent power of the people as 'stubbornly active and physical'.[190] Many like Thelwall retained the same robust attitude to print as a medium that had to be adapted to circumstance rather than simply left to work its magic. Many authors and publishers came forward in the attempt to shape and give voice to this popular will. Some survived as writers and publishers beyond the heady years of the 1790s. In the process they and their comrades created a new kind of national imaginary that influenced the radicalism of the nineteenth century. Their achievement was in their contentious ideas about what constituted 'the public' and the role of print in forming it for the new century.

PART II

Radical personalities

CHAPTER 3

'Once a squire and now a Man': Robert Merry and the pains of politics

Popular radicalism was the creature of print. It coincided with a period when newspapers, periodicals, and pamphlets, not to mention the theatre, promised to open politics up to the scrutiny of a wider public than had hitherto been known. Print was also literally understood to offer the opportunity to make a name for one's self. The pages of the *World* made Robert Merry a celebrity as the love poet 'Della Crusca'. He put this fame aside in 1790 to write high-flown odes on freedom under his own name, but continued to purvey newspaper satires in the cause of reform, either anonymously or as 'Tom Thorne' in the *Argus*. But he was not simply free to remake himself in any way he chose. 'Robert Merry' was denied the right to the 'freedom of the mind' he asserted in his poetry when he put his name to the service of popular radicalism. To write in this cause was deemed by the conservative press to be resigning the independence only a gentleman could presume to own. 'The poet and the gentleman vanished together' to become a creature of print in a sense his former friends thought entirely servile.[1] Merry did eventually find a realm of comparative freedom in the United States shortly before he died in 1798, aged only forty-three, although even there his name drew opprobrium from loyalists like William Cobbett, who represented him as 'poor Merry', a man whose political enthusiasm had forced him to sacrifice his independence to the theatrical career of his wife.

Odes, dinners, toasts, and plays

On 14 July 1789, ever the cosmopolitan, Robert Merry was in Switzerland, taking a break from the reputation he had created as 'Della Crusca'. Two weeks later, he wrote a melancholy poem 'Inscription written at La Grande Chartreuse'. When it was published the following year, it appeared simply over the name 'R. Merry'.[2] The Della Cruscan craze had been incubated in a period of exile in the early 1780s, when Merry had struck up a friendship with various literary figures, including Hester Lynch Piozzi.[3] Piozzi continued to keep an eye on his career, although she was on the watch for deficiencies of character and increasingly despaired of his radical politics. In January 1788, she had written in her journal:

> Merry is a Scholar, a Soldier, a Wit and a Whig. Beautiful in his Person, gay in his Conversation, scornful of a feeble Soul, but full of Reverence for a good one though it be not great. Were Merry *daringly*, instead of artfully wicked, he would resemble *Pierre*.[4]

The mention of Pierre, the conspirator from Otway's *Venice Preserved*, a play that proved to be controversial in the 1790s, hints at the subversive proclivities of a man who Piozzi understood as unmoored from any stake in his country's established order. Over the winter of 1788–9, Merry dabbled in the print politics of the Regency crisis. His ode on the recovery of the king – co-written with Sheridan and recited by Sarah Siddons for a Subscription Gala at the Opera House on 21 April – was an exercise in opportunism that he tried to disown, at least to Piozzi.[5] The French Revolution gave him a new direction, although the 'Inscription', written in July 1789, only returned to themes that had run through his earlier poetry: the condemnation of the hierarchies of the old order ('the sumptuous Palace, and the banner'd Hall'); the illusions of Christianity ('deluded monks'), and the need for writers to champion the cause of liberty ('But still, *as Man*, assert the *Freedom of the mind*'). Such commonplaces of the European republic of letters were easy to write in 1789, but whether they were to translate into anything more was the challenge of the Fall of the Bastille.

Perhaps the first substantial expression of Merry's intention to take up this challenge was *The Laurel of Liberty* (1790), the poem that appeared under the name 'ROBERT MERRY, A. M. MEMBER OF THE ROYAL ACADEMY OF FLORENCE'. Published by John Bell, 'bookseller to HIS ROYAL HIGHNESS the Prince of Wales', and at this stage at least, owner of the *World*, there was no necessary break here with the world of the Whig and the wit. The elegant format of the slim volume hints at Merry's connections in the *bon ton*, but its dedication is 'to the National Assembly of France the true and zealous representatives of a Free People, with every sentiment of admiration and respect'.[6] Around this time, Merry started to lose interest in his connections with the *World*. Merry and its editor Edward Topham had shared a mutual interest in the Literary Fund in 1790, but Topham was soon begging Becky Wells, the actress who effectively managed the paper for him, to do what she could to keep Merry on board: 'In regard to public business, you must see Merry, for he appears to me now to be doing nothing.'[7] More telling of Merry's direction of travel at this point were those he joined on the board of the Literary Fund, including David Williams and Godwin's friend Alexander Jardine. The change was also registered in the reception of his writing. Despite some reservations about the 'pomp of words' in the *Laurel of Liberty*, the *Monthly* and *Analytical* reviews were becoming enthusiastic supporters of his work. In November 1790, Horace Walpole's traced Merry's political enthusiasm to 'the new Birmingham warehouse of the original maker'. 'Birmingham' here is a metonym for Joseph Priestley and Dissent more generally. By 1793 the author of *Political Correspondence or Letters to a Country Gentleman* – tellingly a Joseph Johnson publication – could feel confident enough to list Merry among the 'ablest pens ... employed, on this occasion', Priestley among them, 'in vindicating the cause of Truth and Liberty'.[8]

Merry's political enthusiasm always had to contend with his need to generate an income sufficient to support a fashionable lifestyle. Although he began to publish over his own name in the early 1790s, his social status and independence were threatened by his precarious financial position. Having squandered his inheritance in the 1770s with profligate habits he never entirely forsook, Merry was necessarily invested in the career open to talents, but underpinned by an assumption that he was in the vanguard of an aristocracy of nature. John Taylor had a straightforwardly economic account of Merry's trajectory in this regard:

> Merry was in France during the most frantic period of the French revolution, and had imbibed all the levelling principles of the most furious democrat; having lost his fortune, and in despair, he would most willingly have promoted the destruction of the British government, if he could have entertained any hopes of profiting in the general scramble for power.

Despite their political differences, Taylor frequented the same circle of wits that scribbled for the press. Given that Merry repudiated him as 'the reptile oculist' in the *Telegraph* in 1795, Taylor's judgements were far from impartial, but he does indicate the way financial need coupled with political belief to force Merry to try a variety of experiments with print politics.[9]

Perhaps the most unlikely of these experiments was *A Picture of Paris*, a pantomime written in collaboration with Charles Bonner and the musician William Shield. Presented at Covent Garden on 20 December 1790, its plot shadowed the events of the French Revolution up to the *Fête de la Federation* of 14 July 1790, promising 'an exact Representation of ... the grand procession to the Champs de Mars ... the whole to conclude with a Representation of The GRAND ILLUMINATED PLATFORM ... on the Ruins of the Bastille'.[10] The climax is the Federation Oath where Louis XVI swore to use the powers delegated to him by the National Assembly to maintain the new constitution. The theatre historian George Taylor sees the production as eager to present the *Fête* as consonant with British liberty. Building on the fact that the Lord Chamberlain licensed the piece, Taylor concludes 'that the authorities in England shared the belief of French moderates that the *Fête* marked the end of the French revolution'.[11] David Worrall rightly suggests that Taylor neglects the fact that the script would not have given Chamberlain too much sense of what happened on stage in the pantomime.[12] Presented only a few weeks after the publication of Burke's *Reflections*, *A Picture of Paris* was entering a rapidly changing scene. *The Argus* (20 December 1790) thought that 'the Managers of the house deserve equally the thanks of the several authors, and of the public at large, for the uncommon liberality displayed in the getting up every scene of this Piece', but then its editor, Sampson Perry, was a sworn enemy of Pitt's. In its review of the pantomime, *The Times* (20 December 1790) questioned 'the propriety of such scenes on British ground'. The theatre, it thought, ought 'to steer clear of politics'. British liberty, it insisted on 30 December, was quite distinct from what had been celebrated on the Champs de Mars:

> We should be glad to be informed what reference the statues of *Truth*, *Mercy*, and *Justice*, exhibited in the new Pantomime of the *Picture of Paris*, has to the subject of it. – Surely the author of this incoherent jumble of ideas does not mean to affirm that the Revolution in France is founded on any of these godlike virtues.

Unquestionably, *The Times* continued, representation of a monarch as merely the delegate of the National Assembly did not pass muster with George III: 'As far as we could collect from looks, the Royal Visitors were certainly not of the opinion with STERNE in the instance of DEBATES at least – that "They manage these things much better in FRANCE".'

Merry was starting to exploit any means he could to disseminate his enthusiasm for the Revolution. The preface to the *Laurel of Liberty* (1790) attacked complacent members of the elite 'so charmed by apparent commercial prosperity, that they could view with happy indifference the encroachments of insidious power, and the gradual decay of the Constitution'. He was confident that the 'progress of Opinion, like a rapid stream, though it may be checked, cannot be controuled'.[13] If Merry represented 'Opinion' as an occluded species of print determinism here, he was also doing everything possible to shape it through the newspapers. He told Samuel Rogers in 1792 that Sheridan had asked him to write for the *Morning Post* during the Regency Crisis: 'No man can conceive says he the effect of a daily insinuation – the mind is passive under a newspaper.'[14] Merry was already aware of print magic as a dark art and not one to which he readily put the name of 'Robert Merry'. In 1794, Godwin recorded that 'Sheridan fills Merry's hat full of arrows', that is, Sheridan was feeding Merry with information to use as anonymous newspaper 'paragraphs'.[15] Usually biographical information of one sort or another, blackmailing or satirical 'paragraphs' were frequently used as political weapons. Writing in 1803, David Williams traced the use of 'fleeting arrows' to Fox's manipulation of the newspapers to bring down the ministry in 1783.[16] Plenty of the insider gossip useful to paragraph writers circulated at theatrical clubs where Merry mixed with Sheridan, Taylor, and others. By early 1792, however, Merry was starting to make radical connections beyond this world and becoming what his friend Samuel Rogers, not altogether approvingly, described as 'a warm admirer of Paine'.[17]

Merry's name added lustre to the political dinners discussed in Chapter 1. His *Ode for the fourteenth of July* – again elegantly published by Bell – was written for performance at the dinner for the friends to the French Revolution held at the Crown and Anchor, as we saw earlier. The festivities were presided over by the Whig MP George Rous. William Godwin seems to have been there, but only as part of the crowd. By this stage, the *World* was no friend to Merry. He was probably intended as a target of its hostile description of the diners as 'men whose profligacy has become proverbial – whose fortunes are desperate, and whose minds are daring and corrupt'.[18] The remark may have been provoked by a provocative jibe at his former colleagues in the opening stanza of the ode:

> FRIENDS OF THE WORLD! This festive day,
> Might sure demand a prouder lay,
> Than ever bursting from the Theban's heart,
> Taught o'er the victor's lids the impassion'd tear to start.[19]

The pun on the name of the newspaper may affirm Merry's new disposition towards an audience beyond the fashionable daily, but more generally the ode retains the high poetic mode of the *Laurel of Liberty*. This was the poetry of liberty to which Merry lent his proper name. The ode, especially the stanzas celebrating the 'animating glass' discussed earlier in the context of the dinner, was reprinted in the newspapers soon after it was performed and later in various anthologies.[20] It provided a vibrantly positive rebuttal of Burke's fear of electric communication everywhere, but sublimates the medium of print it wishes to exploit into an immediacy that moves from 'hand to hand' and then from 'soul to soul'. In its obituary for Merry in 1799, the *Monthly* represented him as 'one of those susceptible minds, to which the genius of liberty instantaneously communicated all its enthusiasm'.[21] In the poetry published in his own name, Merry continually presented himself as the authentic conduit of this genius of communication overleaping the complicated terrain of print transmission.

Neither Merry's reputation for homosocial conviviality, nor the popularity of his ode, protected him from the charge that he was losing his identity as a gentleman in his new political personality.[22] On the contrary, he seemed in some quarters to be daringly dispersing his social identity into the mob through the medium of print. In his satires the *Baviad* (1791) and *Maeviad* (1795), William Gifford spatialised Merry's poetry as a 'Moorfields whine'.[23] The tendency of his journalism, not issued over his own name, was also starting to trouble those who wished for moderate reform under aristocratic leaders. At the end of November 1791, Fox reportedly complained that 'our newspapers . . . seem to try & outdo the Ministerial papers, in abuse of the Princes, the Morning Chronicle is grown a little better lately, but the others are intolerable, the Gazeteer [sic] particularly, Mr Merry has got that I am told'.[24] Merry was certainly still networked into the overlapping worlds of newspapers and theatre. *The Times* noted (10 January) that a new comic opera called *The Magician No Conjuror* was in rehearsal at Covent Garden.[25] The play did not appear until 2 February, but ran for a respectable four nights, garnering Merry a substantial benefit. The songs sold in pamphlet form, and remained popular enough to be republished in periodicals and anthologies over the course of the year.[26] The plot is a standard tale of young love thwarted by old foolishness in the guise of Tobias Talisman, who has retreated to the country to practice the art of necromancy, keeping his daughter Theresa under close confinement. The Gothic possibilities of the female incarceration plot were a favourite of Merry's, one he scouted in his first play the tragedy *Lorenzo* (1791), where the heroine is forced into a loveless marriage by her father, and even earlier in *A Picture of Paris* where it is played for comedy. Much of his writing fantasises about the release of female sexual energies into the arms of a hero somewhat like himself. The hero's victory in the *Magician* – where the incarceration plot is again given a comic twist – is guaranteed when he saves Talisman from a resentful mob. There seems to be a loose commentary here on the role of the government provoking the loyalist mob against Priestley, with Merry projecting an idea of himself as the dashing saviour of the situation for the benefit of all.

Most of the newspapers expressed a dim view of the proceedings in their 3 February editions.[27] Werkmeister believes that Thomas Harris, the manager of Covent Garden, stopped the play because of its 'stinging ridicule of Pitt, who, it was all too evident to the audience, was in fact "The Magician"'.[28] Although she provides little evidence for this assertion, the idea of Pitt as a conjuror was familiar from earlier Opposition satires. *Political Miscellanies* (1787) compared him to the popular Italian conjuror Signor Guiseppi Pinetti who had performed in London from 1785.[29] Contemporary newspaper commentary does not seem to confirm so specific an identification, but it is clear that responses to it were ideological in general terms. The Earl of Lauderdale's support for the play, for instance, was noted in the press. Anne Brunton, married to Merry early in 1792, was not re-engaged at Covent Garden after the 1791–2 season, despite her great success in Holcroft's the *Road to Ruin* in the spring. By this stage, anyway, the couple were being increasingly drawn towards France. Merry was throwing himself into the radical societies and writing for the radical newspaper the *Argus* rather than the fashionable pages of the *World*.

Political societies, 1792–3

'The Argus is the paper in their pay', wrote an informer on an LCS meeting at the end of October 1792, 'and they will have nothing to do with any other.'[30] Although the *Argus* increasingly supported the LCS, its closest relationship was with the SCI. On more than one occasion the Society ordered a copy of the paper to be sent to each of its members. Paine, Horne Tooke, and Merry, who joined the SCI in June 1791, all wrote for it; 'in short', remembered Alexander Stephens, 'it was the rendezvous of all the partizans and literary guerillas then in alliance against the system of government'[31]. Perry had launched the *Argus* in 1789 as editor and proprietor: 'a scandalous paper', reported the *Gentleman's Magazine* in his obituary, 'which, at the commencement of the French revolution, was distinguished for its virulence and industry in the dissemination of republican doctrines'.[32] *The Argus* certainly insisted that the political elite was betraying the people in terms that echoed Merry's *Laurel of Liberty*: 'You have suffered your Constitution to be gradually invaded, till you are now reduced to a state of the most abject slavery.'[33] Pitt was the target of particularly fierce attacks, not least from the satires Merry published in the paper as Tom Thorne:

When PITT was OUT OF PLACE, He thought
It wrong that Boroughs should be BOUGHT;
And SOLEMNLY DECLAR'D, the Nation
MUST HAVE A FAIR REPRESENTATION.
BUT now, become a Courtly Minion,
WE find he alters his opinion;
And shews, in language rather warm,
HE LOVES HIS PLACE, and HATES REFORM.
This proves a difference, no doubt
'Twixt being IN, and being OUT.

On 8 May 1792, the same day it printed this squib, the *Argus* published a paragraph arguing that 'the present House of Commons . . . is not composed of the real representatives of the people'. An ex officio information was served on Perry for libelling the House of Commons within the fortnight.

Perry was still in the King's Bench serving time for previous libels. The date of his release is not clear, but Merry and Perry seem to have collaborated on the paper from at least spring 1792. The poet had successfully proposed Perry's SCI membership in April 1792.[34] 'During the last months of that paper's existence', remembered Merry's obituarist in the *Monthly Magazine*, 'a certain ROSE was never without a THORNE'. The reference was to the controversy surrounding George Rose's management of elections for Pitt, a row that the *Argus* covered closely. Merry's obituary reprinted several of his contributions:

The ROSE is called the first of flow'rs
In all the rural shades and bow'rs;
But O! in London 'tis decreed,
The ROSE is but a DIRTY WEED.

and

From genial hear, the HOT-HOUSE ROSE
Expands and blushes, thrives and blows,
But the poor ROSE will fade and rot
Whene'er the House becomes TOO HOT.

The loyalist press even tried to appropriate the Tom Thorne pseudonym to Merry's evident delight:

The SLAVISH PRINT, that's dead to shame,
In fury for departed fame,
Has even robb'd me of my name:
Alas! My nose is out of joint;
Yet what's a THORNE without a point?[35]

The appropriation of the 'TOM THORNE' pseudonym by loyalist newspapers points to difficulty of controlling such shape-shifting productions. 'His native power', observed Merry's obituary, 'flames out in his odes', assigning his authentic voice to the poetry that came out under his own name.[36] Perry finally fled to Paris before his trial commenced on 6 December to the glee of the *World*:

> The Sampson of the Argus was found too weak to carry off the pillars of the Constitutional Fabric, although he made several ineffectual attempts.[37]

There he rejoined his colleagues from the SCI, Merry and Paine, among the group of expatriate radicals that met at White's Hotel. [38]

Over the course of 1792, Merry had traced his own uneven course from the Society of the Friends of the People to this much more radical set of associates, some of whom had made similar journeys. Merry's name is included in the list of those who signed up at the first meeting of Charles Grey's group of reform Whigs on 11 April, but does not re-appear in later accounts of any of their meetings.[39] By May 1792, Grey's Society had become emphatic in repudiating any association with Paine. On 28 May, Godwin's diary records that his friend Holcroft was dining with Paine and Merry, although he seems not to have met the poet by this stage himself. Merry was at the SCI on 1 June, when the society received a letter from the LCS recording its 'infinite satisfaction to think that mankind will soon reap the advantage ...[of] a new and cheaper edition of the Rights of Man'. SCI minutes show Merry to have been a very visible presence in the intense period of cooperation between the two societies.[40]

Merry was working equally hard to open channels of communication between the British and French societies. *The Oracle* of 15 June reported that 'Mr and Mrs. MERRY have taken the Laurel of Liberty with them to France. – The Poet presents his Ode to the NATIONAL ASSEMBLY.' Sounding a note that was to echo across many hostile accounts of Merry that followed, the paper commented: 'The MERRY POET has now dwindled into a SAD POLITICIAN!'[41] On 28 September, he was present at the SCI meeting when another LCS letter proposed a supportive address to the National Convention. Merry was elected to the committee asked to consult on a joint version. In the same month, he also seems to have begun actively supporting the French move towards a republic in the British press. Advertisements appeared for an apology for the August days and the September Massacres: "A PARTICULAR ACCOUNT of the Rise, and also of the Fall of Despotism in Paris, on the 10th of August, and the Treasons of Royalty, anterior and subsequent to that period. By ROBERT MERRY,

Esq." I have not been able to trace any pamphlet under this exact title, but it may be *A Circumstantial History of the Transactions at Paris on the Tenth of August, plainly showing the Perfidy of Louis XVI.* LCS members Thomson and Littlejohn published it from their Temple Yard press with H. D. Symonds. Symonds was given as the publisher of the Merry pamphlet advertised in the newspapers.[42]

In October, Merry wrote from Calais to his 'friend and fellow labourer' Horne Tooke to tell him that the armies of the Republic needed shoes more than muskets.[43] In Paris, Merry seems to have been part of the most radical faction of the British Club – opposed by John Frost – calling on the Convention to invade Britain and provoke a popular uprising in support. Frost thought it a misjudgement of the political mood in Britain. Merry's universal enthusiasm for a democratic republic extended to making his own proposals for the new constitution of France. His obituary in the *Monthly Magazine* mentions 'a short treatise in English, on the nature of free government . . . translated into French by Mr Madget', almost certainly Merry's *Réflexions politiques sur la nouvelle constitution qui se prépare en France, adressées à la république* (1792).[44] Understandably enough never published in Britain, Merry's pamphlet calls for popular participation at every level of the political process, recommending a role for primary assemblies in confirming laws (an issue debated in France that found an echo in LCS discussions of the relation of the divisions to the central committee). There is also a section on the neglect of literary men under despotism, a personal concern expressed in his work for the Literary Fund. The pamphlet leaves the reader in no doubt that Merry thought Britain just such a despotism. Merry shows little patience for the mixed British constitution. The proposed constitution is based on the classical virtues of an active citizenship. If its foundations were formed by a classical education under Samuel Parr, then the pamphlet was unequivocal about the democratic example of France as the only hope for the regeneration of Britain.

Internal exile, Godwinian, and satirist

At the end of 1793 the *European Magazine* published a pen portrait of Merry:

> Having passed the greater part of his life in what is called high company, and in the *beau monde*, he became disgusted with the follies and vices of the Noblesse, and is now a most strenuous friend to general liberty, and the common rights of mankind.[45]

Compared with most accounts of Merry published by the polite press in 1793, this one is curiously sympathetic. By the time it appeared in print, Merry had been back in Britain for nearly six months. As France under Robespierre became increasingly suspicious of foreigners, the situation had become hostile for cosmopolitan radicals who had made the pilgrimage to the Revolution. His friends Paine and Perry were in prison in Paris. Merry had managed to get back to London in May with the help of Jacques-Louis David.[46] Having kept their readers apprised of Merry's activities in France, the English newspapers took particular delight in retailing the story of his retreat back to Britain, but other circles were making Merry more welcome. Godwin's diary records that he and Holcroft dined with Merry on 11 August, but despite these budding support networks Merry had no obvious source of income and the derision of the press must have made life in Britain insupportable. He borrowed money from Maurice Margarot against a bill for £130.[47] In September, Merry decided to flee for Switzerland with his wife and Charles Pigott, funded by a bank draft for £50 from Samuel Rogers. On 2 September, still keeping their erstwhile star contributor under surveillance, the *World* reported that the trio had crossed to the continent. The information was false. They had turned back at Harwich before even boarding ship.

Merry separated from Pigott and retreated to Scarborough. He wrote to Rogers asking for more money and begged that his presence be kept secret, but by mid-October the newspapers had found him out.[48] Merry outlined his current projects in a series of nervous letters to Rogers and asked for help finding publishers. He seems to have been in a state of shock, not least about the prospects for political change. On 3 November, mentioning fears that his letters were being opened, he was writing an 'Elegy upon the Horrors of War'. A month later, he provided an insight into the mental turmoil caused by the dashing of his political hopes:

> Yet still am I troubled by the Revolutionary Struggle; the great object of human happiness is never long removed from my sight. O that I could sleep for two centuries like the youths of Ephesus and then awake to a new order of things!

Then on 18 December, Merry sends 'a little theatrical Piece, which I mean to conceal being *Mine* not to be exposed Aristocratical Malice'. He described it as 'a free translation of the French Play, of Fenelon, reduced to three Acts', but suspected its subject and his name would prevent it being staged:

> I do not suppose it will be performed, on account of its coming from that democratic country . . . if you think it has any merit – get it published for me I beg of you not to mention my being the Translator in case it should be played – as the name of a Republican would damn any performance at this time.[49]

The Godwin circle provided succour in these difficult months. Merry appears regularly in Godwin's diary from summer 1794, especially in the vicinity of the radical stronghold of Norwich. Anne Brunton had family connections with the area. Her father, John Brunton, managed the theatre. Thomas Amyot reported Merry's presence there in May.[50] By 15 June at least Merry was ranging further afield, dining with Godwin and Holcroft in London. Merry also started to exert a particular fascination on Amelia Alderson, brought up in these Norwich circles. Her 'curiosity' was raised 'to a most painful height' when in 1794 Charles Sinclair revealed that Anne Brunton was a 'firm' democrat and 'a great deal more'. Two years later, in November 1796, she admitted to Godwin

> Poor Merry! – Will you not wish to box my ears when I venture to say, that I do not think his mind at all *matched* in his matrimonial connection? Mrs. Merry appears to me a very charming actress, but, but, but – fill it as you please.

Godwin seems to have been scarcely less fascinated, particularly by Merry's connections with Sheridan and his easy facility as a writer. 'Mr. Merry boasts that he once wrote an epilogue to a play of Miles Peter Andrews, while the servant waited in the hall', he told Wollstonecraft in 1796, 'but that is not my talent.'[51] According to his diary, on 26 June Godwin read an ode by Merry. Two days later, the pair dined at the Alderson home in a company associated with Norwich radicalism. Merry read to Godwin 'specimens of 2 novels' on 30 June. Merry's pressing need to make money from his writing drew scornful commentary in the press. Former friends like Piozzi described him as begging for subscriptions, but Godwin seems to have taken his talk seriously, listening to his opinions of *Political justice* while revising it in July 1796.[52] Quite possibly Godwin also helped Merry place his final major poem, *Pains of Memory* (1796) with his publishers, the Robinsons. During this period, Holcroft wrote a joshing letter to Godwin mentioning 'our good friend Robert Merry, once an [sic] squire and now a man', pointing up the poet's social and political journey from Whig gentleman to radical democrat.[53] If Holcroft was celebrating a political butterfly emerging from the pupae of the fashionable Whig, then the oncoming treason trials were reason for alarm to both men. Merry's name appeared in the SCI minute books used as evidence in the prosecutions of Hardy and Horne Tooke.[54] On 11 October, Merry told Rogers that 'existing circumstances ... appear to me hastily advancing to some great catastrophe'. Only four days earlier, Holcroft had surrendered himself in to the court. 'As things now stand', Merry told Rogers, 'I feel some inclination for going with Mrs. Merry to America, and perhaps if I should do so you would put me in a way how to proceed.'[55]

The acquittals of Hardy and Horne Tooke seem to have given Merry a new lease of life as a satirical journalist, just as they powered a surge of activity in the LCS. Although it is impossible to know exactly what part he played in the cheap productions that poured off the radial presses in 1795, he was remembered long afterwards for the great triumph of *Wonderful Exhibition!!! Signor Gulielmo Pittachio*, the first in a series of pasquinades that followed the acquittal of Horne Tooke on 22 November (Figure 5). 'No minister in any age had been so ridiculed before', Merry's obituary in the *Monthly* remembered. First appearing in the pages of the *Courier* on 28 November, *Pittachio* exploited a trope that went back to the *Political Miscellanies* (1787) and Merry's own *Magician no Conjuror* (1792).[56] Developing the satire on Pitt's 'surprising tricks and deceptions' from *Political Miscellanies*, *Pittachio* presents Parliament in thrall to Pitt's 'magical alarm bell':

> UPWARDS OF TWO HUNDRED AUTOMATA, OR MOVING PUPPETS, Who will rise up, sit down, say Yes, or NO, Receive Money, Rake among the Cinders, or do any Dirty Work he may think proper to put them to.

'Unaccountable MISMANAGEMENT' means Pittachio is unable to bring forward 'several Capital Performers ... for the Purpose of exhibiting various Feats of Activity on the TIGHT ROPE'. Pitt had not been able to manage the guilty verdicts against Hardy and Horne Tooke, but the satire ends by flipping this scenario and imagining that he would instead 'close his Wonderful Performances by exhibiting his own Person on THE TIGHT ROPE FOR THE BENEFIT OF THE SWINISH MULTITUDE'. The Pittachio series was part of a proliferating number imagining the Prime Minister being hanged for his crimes against the people.

The most striking of these were the death and dissection of Pitt satires that appeared first in the *Telegraph* in August 1795. Whether Merry had a hand in these is unknown, but on 27 June 1796 Godwin recorded visiting the offices of the *Telegraph*, where he found 'Merry, Este, Robinson, Chalmers & Beaumont'. Founded in December 1794, the *Telegraph* had succeeded the *Argus* and joined the *Courier* as the most radical of the

WONDERFUL EXHIBITION!!!

SIGNOR

Gulielmo Pittachio

The SUBLIME WONDER of the World!!!

Condeſcends to inform the Public at large, and his Friends in particular, that he has now opened his Grand Hall of Exhibitions at Weſtminſter, with a grand diſplay of his

ASTONISHING AND MAGNIFICENT DECEPTIONS;

Which have been approved by all the Crowned Heads in the Univerſe, and which are unparalleled in the Hiſtory of Mankind.

Firſt—The Signor will bring forward

A Magical *ALARM BELL,*

At the ringing of which, all the Company ſhall become Mad or Fooliſh.

Secondly—He will produce his juſtly celebrated CURIOUS SPY GLASSES, which diſtort and miſrepreſent all Objects that are looked at through them, and occaſion in the Company A SUDDEN AND SOCIAL DISMAY; ſuch as has never before been witneſſed in this Country.

Thirdly—By Means of an ENCHANTED DRUM, he will ſet all the Company a FIGHTING, for the avowed Purpoſe of preſerving

ORDER AND TRANQUILLITY.

During the Battle, Signor Pittachio will convey their MONEY OUT of their POCKETS in a New and Entertaining Manner.

Fourthly—He will produce a moſt extraordinary Effect in the Optics of the Spectators, by means of ſome Gold Duſt, ſo that they ſhall not be able to diſtinguiſh Colors; but ſhall call (at the Signor's command) BLACK, WHITE, and WHITE, BLACK, to the Edification of all Beholders.

Fifthly—He will make ſome Marvellous Experiments upon his own

MEMORY,

By forgetting the moſt Material Incidents of his Life, with an almoſt incredible Preciſion.——N. B. To remove Doubts, theſe Experiments upon MEMORY will be made upon OATH.

Sixthly—By his Oratorical Efforts, he will in the Courſe of a few Minutes perſuade the greater Part of his Audience to ſalute him *à poſteriori*, then to give him three cheers and nominate him

THE HEAVEN-BORN CONJUROR;

With various Slight-of-hand Performances and Whimſical Exuberances too tedious to mention.

In the Courſe of the Entertainments the Sublime Pittachio will exhibit

UPWARDS OF TWO HUNDRED AUTOMATA, OR MOVING PUPPETS,

Who will riſe up, ſit down, ſay Yes, or No, Receive Money, Rake among the Cinders, or do any Dirty Work he may think proper to put them to—N. B. This is a moſt faſcinating Trick.

Afterwards Signor Gulielmo Pittachio will diſcover to the Company the unrivalled Treaſures of his PRIVATE CABINET, formed on a mere Mechanical Principal, without Hinges, Joints, Dove-tail, or Glue.

The Whole to conclude with a Dramatic Piece in One Act, called

The Humbug; or John Bull a Jack Aſs,

In which Signor Pittachio (not having yet engaged any female Performers) will indulge the Company with a Solo on the Viol *d'Amour*,

N. B. The Hall is commodious, but the Company will be kept as much in the DARK as poſſible, to give greater Effect to

The *DECEPTIONS.*

Signor Pittachio is extremely ſorry to inform the Public, that owing to ſome unaccountable Miſmanagement in the Perſons he employed he has been diſappointed of ſeveral capital Performers whom he had hoped to have brought forward, for the Purpoſe of exhibiting various Feats of Activity on the TIGHT ROPE, this Part of the ENTERTAINMENT therefore MUST be Deferred.

To Supply this Deficiency Signor Pittachio will cloſe his Wonderful Performances by exhibiting his own Perſon on

The TIGHT ROPE.

FOR THE BENEFIT OF THE SWINISH MULTITUDE.

VIVANT REX ET REGINA.

[Copied from the COURIER, *Friday, Nov.* 28, 1794.] Sold by all Newſcarriers.

Fig 5 *Wonderful Exhibition!!! Signor Gulielmo Pittachio* (1794). Trustees of the British Museum.

English dailies.[57] Merry's obituary in the *Monthly Magazine* claimed 'some of the best poetry in the *Telegraph* was the production of his pen'.[58] D. E. MacDonnell, the editor, acted as go-between for Merry with John Taylor in the dispute over the satirical paragraph attacking 'the reptile oculist'.[59] If Merry didn't write the *Death and Dissection of Pitt* satires, then he was certainly in the thick of the group of collaborators closely involved in the *Telegraph* where they first appeared.

Fenelon and *The Wounded Soldier* – the play and the poem he had told Rogers about late in 1793 – were also published in 1795. *Fenelon* was never produced, but it was published under Merry's name and dedicated to Rogers. A partial translation of a play by Marie-Joseph Chénier, *Fenelon* saw Merry return to the Gothic incarceration plot. Release for the heroine is obtained by the intervention of Archbishop Fenelon, an interesting switch from the dashing hero of the *Magician*. The choice may indicate the shared interests of the Godwin circle, since Fenelon was one of their acknowledged heroes. In *Political justice*, it is Fenelon who Godwin imagines saving from a fire – in the interests of humanity – in the famous passage that caused a storm over his utilitarian version of universal benevolence. Holcroft's account of Merry's play in the *Monthly Review* began by praising the role of Fenelon's book 'in enlightening mankind'.[60] Merry was writing *The Wounded Soldier* at about the same time Wordsworth was first addressing the same themes in his 'Salisbury Plain' poems. Hargreaves-Mawdsley notes that Merry's language 'is like that of a tract ... intended for the simplest reader'. The effect is surely intentional, even if Merry described his poem to Rogers as 'to avoid offence . . . very tame'.[61]

The Wounded Soldier enjoyed a fairly wide circulation, but first appeared as a penny pamphlet from T. G. Ballard, the author's name appearing only as 'Mr. M–y'. By 1795 Ballard was becoming one of the LCS's regular printers, advertising 'a great Variety of Patriotic Publications'.[62] Ballard also brought out a late version of the *Death and Dissection of Pitt* satire as *Pitt's Ghost* (1795). Citizen Lee also published many of the Pittachio broadsides and various editions of the *Death and Dissection of Pitt.* He attributed one satire – *Pitti-Clout & Dun-Cuddy* (1795) – to 'Mr. M-r-y', but then later acknowledged an error of attribution.[63] Lee's mistaken use of Merry's name may have been an over-eager attempt to exploit what glamour, at least in radical circles, remained of it. These publications were probably as close to the LCS as Merry came after he returned from France in 1793. [64] He never took sanctuary there, unlike his friend Charles Pigott. Merry may have felt safest among journalists like those in the offices of the *Telegraph*, or Dissenting literati like the Aldersons, Godwin, and Holcroft.

Such groups often flowed into each other, as Godwin's visit to the office of the *Telegraph* suggests, but ultimately they could not provide him with a context to continue writing in Britain.

Transatlantic laureate

Merry continued to see Godwin, especially with Holcroft and sometimes with the moneylender John King, financial troubles making Merry's residence in England increasingly untenable. The pattern of sociability intensified in January and February 1796 – Godwin seems to meet Merry at a Philomath supper on 12 January – and they see each other several times in April and in June, leaving together for East Anglia on the Ipswich mail on 1 July. A week later Merry was arrested for debt in Norwich. Godwin and James Alderson helped extricate him, but the episode may have determined Merry to leave for the United States.[65] Although the emigration of the Merrys had been trailed in the press for some time, it still came as a surprise to Godwin and Amelia Alderson when they left in September 1796. Godwin wrote to Merry too late:

> Yesterday evening I heard of your expedition, & heard of it with much pain. I could not forget it all night. I cannot endure to think that a man, whom I regard as an honour & ornament to his country, should thus go into voluntary banishment. If you had thought proper to consult me, I would have endeavoured to dissuade you.

Alderson's letters to Godwin in October and November 1796 advert to the matter more than once. She found it hard to believe that Merry could possibly be happy in the United States:

> I wish much to know how he looked & talk'd when he bade you adieu - whether he was most full of hope, or dejection – My heart felt heavy when I heard he was really gone, & gone too where I fear the charms of his conversation, and his talents will not be relished as they desire to be.

Alderson's estimation of Merry's chances of happiness was not untypical of opinion even in progressive circles.[66] Writing for prospective emigrants in 1794, Thomas Cooper took the view that 'literary men' did not yet exist there as 'what may be called a *class* of society'.[67] The question of whether the new republic could sustain a literary career was an issue Merry had debated for several years before finally deciding to go. He seems to have seriously considered the option at least twice before he set sail: first, in the summer of 1792, according to the actor James Fennell, when Merry expected the forces of counter-revolution to succeed in their invasion of

France; secondly, on the eve of the treason trials, when he asked Rogers for advice about the move.[68] His friend Holcroft's opinion that the United States remained 'unfavourable to genius' and uncongenial to 'energy and improvement' must have weighed on his mind, but his hand was forced by financial necessity compounded by the political context after the Two Acts had passed into law.[69]

As it transpired, there was literary culture enough to greet Merry's arrival with great enthusiasm. Della Cruscanism had been and was to continue to be an important influence on the poetry of the early republic. *Pains of Memory* was to become one of its most reprinted poems and guaranteed that his arrival garnered various poems of acclaim in response:

> With our accord your voices join,
> Let your just rewards be known,
> The laurel'd chaplet for his brows entwine,
> And place him on the LAUREATE's throne.[70]

Fleeing Britain only a few months before Merry, Citizen Lee published these lines in his *American Universal Magazine*. Not everyone was as pleased to see him. Bristling in the American press as Peter Porcupine, William Cobbett attacked both men as part of a conspiracy intent on spreading Jacobinism to the United States:

> *Poor Merry* (whom, however, I do not class with such villains as the above) died about three months ago, just as he was about to finish a treatise on the justice of the *Agrarian system*. He was never noticed in America; he pined away in obscurity.[71]

The last claim is debatable to say the least.

John Bernard knew Merry from his pomp in the convivial clubs of London, but thought he thrived in America, even enjoying the rough and tumble of electoral politics: 'exposed to actual collision with the crowd ... Merry was the only man I knew for whom it had a relish.'[72] A page Merry added to the Philadelphia edition of *Pains of Memory* suggests he saw the possibilities of a democratic literary culture in the new republic:

> With her free sons the social converse share
> See grander scenes and breathe a purer air![73]

Merry seems to have been engaged in thinking about these issues when he died suddenly in 1798, leaving behind him his own dissertation on 'the State of Society and Manners', addressed to 'the curiosity of the European reader, respecting the comparative situation of the United States'.[74] Over the course of the 1790s, Merry's experiences in Britain, France, and the

United States had given him ample material for such a study. In the process, Thomas Holcroft thought, he laid aside his elite identity as a squire and emerged as a properly independent man. His remaking of himself as he engaged with the implications of the French Revolution was somewhat more complex than Holcroft's perspective allowed. If the poet and the gentlemen were not entirely sacrificed to the politician, as his enemies proposed, then they did become part of a complex process of self-fashioning in print that ended only with his death in exile.

CHAPTER 4

'The ablest head, with the blackest heart:' Charles Pigott and the scandal of radicalism

Few people denied Robert Merry's charm. Years after his death, John Bernard still celebrated him from among all those who gathered at the Beefsteak Club, Fox and Sheridan included, as the one with the most 'benevolent mould of mind'.[1] This reputation underwrote Merry's political credentials for many sympathisers, confirming that his character was grounded in right feeling. For others, as we have seen, his political enthusiasm warped and, ultimately, betrayed his sociable nature. Hardly anyone ever made either claim for Charles 'Louse' Pigott, despite the fact that he and Merry were friends from similar backgrounds. Pigott had a lasting image as a man who had 'robbed his friends, cheated his creditors, repudiated his wife, and libelled all his acquaintance'.[2] Nevertheless, he made two of the most influential contributions to the popular radical literature of the 1790s. The anonymous *The Jockey Club* (1792) rivalled *Rights of Man*, at least in the alarm it spread among the government's law officers. His posthumous *Political Dictionary* (1795) was endlessly recycled in the contest over the legitimacy of the traditional language of politics. Both books made great play with the politics of personality without making much of Pigott's own. He did publish some things under his own name, but never created a print personality after the manner of Merry. 'Louse' was the derisive nickname known to the relatively closed circle who shared his elite background. Generally, he proved as adaptive as the insect he was named after, thriving in the crevices of print culture, mixing political theory and French materialism with scandal and blackmail, unevenly espousing a radical politics while continuing to insist on his independence as a gentleman, until the government caught up with him and gaol fever killed him.

Cracking the louse

Pigott was the youngest son of an old Jacobite family whose family seat was the manor of Chetwynd Park, Shropshire.[3] His eldest brother Robert was a member of the exclusive Jockey Club, who became High Sheriff of the county in 1774, but two years later sold the family estates and moved to the continent. Robert played a direct role in the political clubs of Paris during some of the headiest days of the Revolution before settling in Toulouse in 1792 (dying there in 1794). Probably an important conduit of French ideas to Charles, his remittances also bankrolled his younger brother, at least until politics in France blocked this supply line. Charles went to Eton and in 1769 matriculated at Trinity Hall Cambridge. Soon afterwards he lost a fortune on the turf, mixing in high-rolling Foxite circles. His friends, Fox among them, apparently subscribed to help him out of debtor's prison. Nevertheless, Pigott felt free to attack Fox's pose as 'Man of the People'. In the first of two letters that appeared in the *Public Advertiser* in March 1785, he berated Fox for stooping to exploit every ruse available in the unreformed electoral system. Their tone confirmed Pigott's own status as a gentleman of independent mind even as it mourned Fox's manipulation of the mob:

> In committing my thoughts to the public, I am instigated by no other motives, than, I fear, a vain desire of convincing them of their error, and of lamenting those fatal prejudices in many great and exalted characters which have induced them to display such indecent exultation upon a triumph wherein every sensible dispassionate person, who was an ocular witness to the infamous disgraceful proceedings of the Westminster Election, must be affected with the deepest sorrow and indignation.

The second on Fox's position on Irish affairs hints at Pigott's adaptive response to print:

> Newspapers are the great extensive vehicles of general intelligence; and as the Public Advertiser is universally read, I have selected that publication as best adapted to my purpose.[4]

Fox and his friends were ambivalent about newspapers as places to argue out political principles, but they were far from slow to respond to Pigott on the field of satire.[5] Between the two letters, the *Morning Herald* – a vociferous supporter of Fox – published four epigrams, headed '*Reason for Mr. Fox's avowed contempt for one* PIGOT*'s Address to him*', all playing on the idea of the louse as an inhabitant of a vermin-infested (debtor's) prison:

> WHO shall expect the country's friend,
> The darling of the House,
> Should for a moment condescend
> To crack a PRISON LOUSE.[6]

Despite these slap downs, an antipathy to the hypocrisy of Fox's pose as 'Man of the People' was to remain a more or less consistent part of Pigott's rhetoric as he made an uneven and incomplete journey from the elite language of independence to the natural rights arguments associated with Thomas Paine and the French Revolution.

Robert Pigott had published in English on French affairs in the 1780s, including *New Information and Lights, on the Late Commercial Treaty* (1787), which the *Critical Review* dismissed as 'the refuse of political rancour, poured forth with petulance, and in language that violates the plainest rules of English grammar'. In the early stages of the Revolution, he addressed the National Assembly in another pamphlet, also published in English, on the liberty of the press.[7] Charles made his first intervention in the British 'debate' over the French Revolution in *Strictures on the New Political Tenets of the Right Honourable Edmund Burke* (1791). Published by Ridgway, it was designed as an answer to Burke's *Appeal from the New to the Old Whigs* (1791) and *Letter to a Member of the National Assembly* (1791). The pamphlet initially presents itself as an attack on Burke's defection from 'every idea of friendship and party attachment', but shows some sensitivity to Pigott's own vulnerability in this score, given his newspaper letters to Fox. Those attacks, Pigott implied, had been based on policies not persons, but went on to suggest – in relation to the account of Burke – that 'every trader in politics should be scouted'.[8] His most influential contributions to the popular radical cause from 1792 were all to develop just such an unstable mixture of personal muckraking and republican principles for an increasingly popular audience.

Pigott's representation of Burke as a 'deserter from an honourable cause' proposed that 'the principles that provoked and justified American resistance, are exactly similar with those that brought about the French revolution'. Burke was reneging on a conception of inalienable popular sovereignty that he had defended in the case of the American revolutionaries. These differences might be construed as an in-house dispute about the meaning of the Whig tradition, not least because Burke is represented as deserting the social network associated with Fox, except that as *Strictures* progresses a different kind of language emerges. Expanding upon the hints in his earlier letters to the *Public Advertiser*, Pigott dismisses the distinction between Whig and Tory as illusory: 'From the instant either one or other approach the throne in a ministerial capacity, they must, like camelions, change their natural colour.'[9] Even these opinions might be seen as an assertion of pure Whig values, Pigott represents the National Assembly as primarily concerned with the 'correction of abuses', but towards its close *Strictures* starts to invoke Rousseau's notions of the general will.[10] Thomas Paine is lauded as 'the distinguished and successful rival of Mr. Burke'. The language of traditional rights is to be abandoned in favour of 'the lights of reason and truth . . . and . . . that theory, whose basis is fixed on the natural and untransferable rights of Men and Citizens'.[11]

Given the French connections he had through his brother, the appearance of this kind of language in *Strictures* is hardly surprising. Even so, while 'the natural and untransferable rights of man' may dominate the later parts of *Strictures*, it would be misleading to suggest that it entirely effaces the vocabulary of English liberty. Even his later pamphlet *Treachery no Crime* (1793) is still loath to abandon the idea of the excellence of the original constitution despite the 'polypuses and rotten excrescencies that have grown upon it'.[12] What does newly appear there is the influence of *Political Justice*, which it quotes regularly, for instance in representing utility – 'the comparative benefits or injuries which it yields' – as the best gauge of a constitution. Far less reminiscent of Godwin are the personal attacks in *Treachery no Crime* on the 'lazy effeminacy and luxury of courts'.[13] Where for the most part *Strictures* reads as a discussion of political principles, underwritten by the author's name, *Treachery no Crime* (1793) – with 'all the signs of hasty composition', as the *Analytical* complained – is full of scurrilous barbs, but it looks like a pale shadow of the *Jockey Club*, the pamphlet that Pigott had brought out over the course of the previous year. Both were published anonymously, unlike *Strictures*. If 'debate' seems a poor description for the guerilla war being conducted in print over the French Revolution by the end of 1792, then Pigott and the *Jockey Club* played a major part in the transformation from disquisitions on principles to a fight – with the gloves off – over the legitimacy of the ruling classes.

Riding the aristocracy

Pigott had given notice of a willingness to bring the political elite – of whatever party – to the court of the popular press in 1785. The promise was more than made good in the *Jockey Club*, published in three parts as it expanded over the course of 1792. *Strictures* insisted that the author still preserved 'the utmost respect for the personal and political character of Mr. Fox'.[14] The personal affiliations of elite politics survive reasonably intact there, not least because Burke is chastised for reneging on them, but in the *Jockey Club, or A Sketch of the Manners of the Age* (1792) personal knowledge of the Whig oligarchy as well as the Crown and its allies was used with devastating effect to present the ruling elite as morally bankrupt. Taking the form of a series of brief and deeply scurrilous potted biographies, starting with the Prince of Wales, but moving on to his Whig connections, the *Jockey Club* proposed to show 'that a revolution in government, can alone bring about a revolution in morals; while it continues the custom to annex such servile awe and prostituted reverence to those who are virtually the most undeserving of it'.[15]

Unaware of Pigott's identity, John Wilde, Professor of Civil Law at Edinburgh University, saw the pamphlet as following an example learnt from the French:

> The present state of France is, in no small degree, owing to the calumnies circulated against the higher orders, and especially the criminalities forged against the Court. The same game is playing in this country. No instrument employed in it can be contemptible. Vice certainly ought to be justified no where; among the higher ranks perhaps less than anywhere. But he is blind, indeed, who does not see why real vices are exaggerated against them in this age, and others pretended that do not exist. And that man has, in truth, little foresight who does not see the consequence of such publications being much read and believed.[16]

Wilde's assumption was not unreasonable. Pigott had defined his aim as taking 'the dust out of the eyes of the multitude, in lessening that aristocratic influence which so much pains are now taking to perpetuate'.[17] Be that as it may, the patriot idea of a moral crusade in the name of reform in the preface is scarcely preparation for the coruscating and often indecent satire of the sketches themselves. One of the earliest attacks on the *Jockey Club*, the *British Constitution Invulnerable* (1792) identified a division of labour between Paine and Pigott: Paine engaged with principles, the author claimed, where Pigott used his personal knowledge of the political elite to attack their persons. *An Answer to Three Scurrilous Pamphlets* (1792), seemingly written by someone from within or familiar with Pigott's old gambling circles, provided a much fiercer rebuttal. Using Pigott's own satirical tactics, personal knowledge of his past is flourished to claim that he had robbed his friends and repudiated his wife. The author chronicles Pigott's education at Eton, where he was started to be known as 'Louse'; his political disaffection is represented as the result of an unhappy fashionable marriage and gambling debts; his ingratitude to Fox is framed via an anecdote about the subscription to release him from debtor's prison. *An Answer* also claims some paragraphs had first been offered to his victims as blackmail threats: 'Copies of these libels he has occasionally sent to several ladies; some of whom have deprecated his menaces, with presents of Bank paper.'[18]

Certainly Pigott was a master of insinuation and titillation. Many who sympathised with the *Jockey Club*'s politics could not accept its method. Reviewing a fourth edition of Part I in May 1792, the *Analytical Review* could approve of the political sentiments, but judged much of its content 'too *personal* for us to attempt to accompany the author in his biographical sketches'.[19] With no sympathy for Pigott's politics, the author of the *British Constitution Invulnerable* was much blunter: 'gross ideas are concealed under equivocal expressions and indecent subjects amplified'.[20] Colonel George Hanger was already a staple figure of newspaper gossip and satirical prints.[21] The fact that he had been Fox's agent at the Westminster election of 1784 made him irresistible for Pigott's amplifications. The description starts relatively mildly: 'The person in question is admirably calculated to have shone a conspicuous figure in courts, when it was the custom to keep a f—l.' Typically insults turn to accounts of sexual peccadillos in the *Jockey Club*. Hanger was no exception:

> The M-j-r has of late connected himself with a lady of very amiable accomplishments; – none of your flimsy, delicate beauties; she is composed of true substantial English materials, and what there is plenty of her, cut and come again.[22]

Many of the entries show a libertine delight in obscene punning that was a familiar part of the masculine ethos of aristocratic clubs. The description of General William Dalrymple, for instance, notes that he had married 'a young lady who had been much celebrated for the admirable dexterity of certain manual operations, still remembered with a kind of pleasing melancholy by several gentlemen now living'.[23]

Many of the stories had already appeared in newspaper paragraphs. Wilde assumed that the pamphlet had been 'pilfered almost entirely from magazines and former scandalous chronicles of the times'.[24] Pigott was supplying a 'daily insinuation' to the press before he gathered the paragraphs into his book. 'Characters from the Jockey Club' appear in the *Bon Ton Magazine* early in 1792, probably to extort money from their targets. Certainly, Ridgway, one of The *Jockey Club*'s publishers, had been using this kind of technique for a while.[25] Material that later surfaced in the *Jockey Club*'s paragraphs on Charles James Fox appear without acknowledgement in the April issue of the *Bon Ton*, but nothing from the two later parts of the *Jockey Club*, where the affiliation to Painite politics is much clearer. Events in France were regularly featured in the *Bon Ton's* pages, but only as warning tales of the violent excesses of the crowd.[26] Stories of aristocratic debauchery could be a source of amusement in the *Bon Ton Magazine*, but when they were hitched to a republican political programme, then it was another matter.

The first part of the *Jockey Club*, published at the end of February, was relatively mild on Fox and the Whig party. The Prince of Wales is execrated as an example of how 'disgraceful it is to pay homage to a person merely on account of his descent', but the possibility that Fox and, especially, Sheridan might live up to their reputations as friends of liberty is kept alive. At this stage still professing an attachment to 'limited monarchy', Pigott calls upon Fox to rouse himself, live up to his initial welcome for the French Revolution, and exert himself against the encroachments of the Crown. Pigott sees Sheridan as the more principled of the two politicians. If he lives up to his reputation, 'he will be adored while living, and his name enrolled on the register of immortality, amongst the most distinguished patriots and benefactors of mankind'.[27] The superiority of Sheridan over Fox is more pronounced in the second part, published in May, where he appears as the only politician 'whose public principles stand unimpeached'. Fox is castigated for his deference to 'aristocratic connections'.[28] The third part written after the events of 10 August and the September massacres in Paris, published on 15 September, is openly republican, beginning, to the astonishment of the *Analytical Review*, with a deeply unflattering comparison of George III and Louis XVI that implied that the deposition of the latter in August would and ought soon to be the fate of the former. Where Sheridan is the presiding genius of the first two parts, Paine is now praised as 'a real great man'. Fox is dismissed as 'this time-serving leader of a self-interested faction'. The Society of the Friends of the People is attacked for speaking 'the same puny enervating language' and forming a 'barrier between a corrupt government and the real friends of the people'.[29] No doubt Grey's club would have included Pigott among those it believed had 'gone to excess on the subject of universal representation'.[30]

Whereas the first edition had opened its attack on the Duke of York by mocking the English for being 'stupidly rooted in admiration of the glare and parade of royalty', now the very institution of the monarchy is represented as irrelevant.[31] Little deference is given even to the idea of an original unblemished British constitution. After a lengthy quotation from Junius in Part III, Pigott dissents from the earlier satirist's 'hyperbolical eulogium on the English constitution'.[32] The French Convention is presented as the proper model of government:

> Most of our celebrated English laws were framed in times of Gothic barbarism. The regenerated government of France will present itself to our admiration at the end of the 18th century, under the combined auspices of patriotism, experience, and philosophy.

Instead the absolute authority of the will of the people is insisted upon in the third and final part:

> The sovereignty at present resides in the CREATOR, the PEOPLE, who have a natural interest in their own happiness and preservation; where as before it was lodged in the creature, the thing of their own creation, which as we have shown, had an interest directly contrary to, and subversive of them.

Pigott's praise of Robespierre, Marat, and other '*worthy* gentlemen ... members of the Jacobin Club' brings him as close to being an 'English Jacobin' as anyone could be.[33]

Perhaps because it is not framed as a treatise on political principles as such, historians have tended to overlook the *Jockey Club*'s contribution to the Revolution controversy. Even politically sympathetic journals of the time, as we have seen, blanched at the personal content and indecent tone, but neither they nor the government ignored it. On 24 September 1792, the Prince of Wales wrote to Queen Charlotte in a state of high anxiety about the likely effects of Pigott's work. He may have been writing out of a particular fear that the stories told about his circle were likely seriously to compromise his attempt to have his debts paid off by Parliament, but he was right to see that Pigott's pamphlet was not simply a scandal sheet. John Wilde believed it to be dangerously ubiquitous in Edinburgh: 'I know not how it is received in London. Here it is rather a fashionable companion; and even in the lower and middling ranks of life you have as much chance to meet with it, as with a bible or an almanack.'[34] The government took the same view, and may indeed have been keeping a watch on the pamphlet since the publication of Part II. The prince told the queen that it was 'the most infamous & shocking libelous production yt. ever disgraced the pen of man'. She quickly forwarded it to the ministry.[35] Henry Dundas immediately put the copy into the hands of the Attorney General. The Treasury Solicitor instructed magistrates to prosecute its publishers wherever they could, not just in London, but countrywide.[36] Within a few weeks of the prince's letter, prosecutions were underway against Ridgway and Symonds. Both were found guilty of sedition, forced to pay large fines, and confined in Newgate in 1793. Before the year was out, they had been joined there by their author, but not for publishing the *Jockey Club*.[37]

Prison and the LCS

By the time *Treachery no Crime* was published early in August 1793, Pigott was closely involved with London's radical circles. Godwin's diary for 7 August 1793 records dining in John Frost's room in Newgate with Pigott, Holcroft, Gerrald, Thomas Macan, and a 'Macdonald' who was probably D. E. MacDonnell.[38] Pigott found a place in two of Richard Newton's prints of the inmates and their visitors on the state side of the prison (Figures 6 and 7). Published on 20 August, *Soulagement en Prison, or Comfort in Prison* pictures the inmates and their visitors enjoying a convivial meal in Lord George Gordon's rooms with various figures already mentioned several times in this book, including Frost, Gerrald, Ridgway, and Symonds.[39] By the time Newton published *Promenade on the State Side of Newgate* in October 1793, Pigott was a prisoner there himself, awaiting trial. He was probably aware that the government would be watching his movements after the publication of the *Jockey Club*. To mitigate the charges against him, Ridgway had 'authorized and directed his Attorney to give up the name of the Author of the Work'.[40] In September 1793, presumably feeling the net closing in and short of funds, Pigott attempted to flee the country with Robert Merry, but they turned

Fig 6 Richard Newton, *Soulagement en Prison, or Comfort in Prison*. Lewis Walpole Library (1793). Courtesy of the Lewis Walpole Library.

Fig 7 Richard Newton, *Promenade on the State Side of Newgate* (1793). Courtesy of the Huntington Library, San Marino, California.

back at Harwich. Merry went into his exile in Scarborough, but Pigott returned to London, planning to reunite with Merry shortly, not least because his friend was now his main source of money.

On 30 September, Pigott was arrested after an incident at the New London coffee house involving the physician William Hodgson. The official indictment claimed that the two men began proposing republican toasts in their private box after a bout of drinking. The charge revolved around the accusation that Hodgson had denounced George III as a 'German hog butcher'.[41] The proprietor of the coffee house sent for the constables. Hodgson and Pigott were arraigned for uttering seditious words. Unluckily for Pigott, the duty magistrate was Mr Anderson, a target in *Treachery no Crime*.[42] Anderson had Hodgson and Pigott committed to the New Compter gaol. Early in October, Pigott's lawyer, John Martin, discovered mistakes in the warrant. Pigott also complained to the bench that the excessive amount of bail set contravened the Bill of Rights. A jury at the Old Bailey threw out the charges against Pigott on 2 November, but Hodgson was committed to Newgate, and eventually tried and found guilty in December.[43]

While in confinement, Pigott wrote his defence, later published as *Persecution!!!* His account of his evening with Hodgson was of two friends indulging 'in that openness and freedom of discourse natural to persons, who harbour no criminal or secret intentions'. Hinting at an aspect of the defence Erskine had used in John Frost's case, Pigott admitted they were 'affected by liquor, when the temper is consequently more irritable than in moments of cooler reflections'.[44] More generally, he staked his defence on Whig principles: 'FREEDOM OF SPEECH is an ENGLISH MAN'S PREROGATIVE, engrafted on our Constitution, by MAGNA CHARTA and the BILL OF RIGHTS.' When it came to issues of freedom of speech and the liberty of the press, as in the campaign against the Two Acts at the end of 1795, Foxite Whigs and the LCS could work together relatively closely using the same language of liberty. When pleading to a jury, it made sense to appeal to the shades of Russell and Sidney rather than natural rights, but Pigott's defence does not always manage to hold to this line. Although he asserted that his republican principles were derived from perfectly constitutional notions of the 'PUBLIC GOOD', *Persecution!!!* went on to declare 'that my fervent wishes shall be daily offered up for the success and final establishment of the FRENCH REPUBLIC'. These were not words calculated to win an acquittal from an English jury had the case come to trial, but they should not simply be read as Pigott's 'real' opinions emerging from beneath a tactical use of Whig vocabulary. They might better be seen as a snapshot in the process of Pigott rewriting his political lexicon in response to the fast-changing personal and political context, not least the need to save himself from gaol. Even in the 'Preface' to *Persecution!!!*, written after the charge had been thrown out, when he had no need to pander to the prejudices of a jury, Pigott fashions an idea of his sufferings against the backdrop of the pantheon of English liberty:

> During the period of our history, when a Stuart reigned in England; when a Jefferies presided in the court of King's Bench the source of justice was polluted, Judges were venal, and juries corrupt, Virtue and Crime were confounded; or rather Virtue was proscribed and punished; Crime rewarded and triumphant. A pander ennobled by the title of Duke of Buckingham, was the favourite of the prince. Jefferies, whose very name is synonymous with oppression and cruelty, was the protected Judge, under whose sentence and authority, a SIDNEY and a RUSSELL died on the scaffold.[45]

Thelwall's lectures – when they started their new season in February – were full of this sort of appeal, but his relation to this tradition was rather different from Pigott's.[46] As a member of an old family, Pigott was not above asserting his independence as a gentleman over informers he represents as mere men of trade. It was not so easy to jettison patrician values as to take on the language of natural rights. Pigott loftily dismissed his two chief accusers – 'this political pickle merchant' and 'formerly in the linen trade at Bristol' – on the basis of their social inferiority. The language of gentlemanly independence would have been part of Pigott's education at Eton and Cambridge and the common currency of his erstwhile friends in the Jockey Club when the talk turned from the turf to politics. As he insisted in his defence, 'to declare my sentiments without reserve' was 'a habit in which I was bred, and which is rooted in me'. Anything else would be to cover English traditions of liberty with 'our modern servility, transplanted', as he put it with typical sarcasm, 'from the old despotism of France'.[47]

On his release, Pigott appeared at meetings of the Philomath Society attended by William Godwin. Godwin's diary for 14 January reads: 'Tea at Holcroft's: Philomathian supper; visitors Gerald & Pigot'.[48] Gerrald at this stage was on bail. Eaton, who appears with Pigott in the October Newgate print, published *Persecution!!!* in December and announced at the end of March that he had copies of *Strictures* and *Treachery no Crime* available.[49] Pigott became closely enough involved with popular radical circles to join the LCS (a path his friend Merry never took). February 1794 sees his name on a list of the members of division 25 on which Eaton and Thelwall also appear.[50] Exactly when Pigott joined the LCS is not clear. He associated with members like Gerrald and Hodgson from at least mid-1793, but it may be that he only actually joined on his release from Newgate on 2 November. Certainly, there is desperation in the letter he wrote to Samuel Rogers a week later. The letter makes a disingenuous mention of the incident with Hodgson ('the stupid accident with which I presume you have been made acquainted by the papers'). His financial situation had been worsened because events in France had cut him off from the 'remittances' he relied upon from his brother. Merry could not supply the loss:

> It is only <u>real want</u> & a reluctance to apply to the <u>Great World</u> that could prevail on me to request a service of this nature from you, to whom I am unknown, but if you will be kind enough to advance me ten guineas, I think I may venture to aver with confidence that my Friend will make it good or otherwise, if you should have sufficient faith in me I have a French translation of the System of Nature in the Press which on being concluded a Bookseller has agreed to advance me 60L, when I should return the money, should Merry (which I think impossible) not have done so.[51]

The author of the *System of Nature* was the Baron d'Holbach, although editions of the time routinely attributed it to 'Mirabaud'.[52] The promotion of such texts in the LCS infuriated 'saints' like Bone and Lee. W. H. Reid later claimed that the *System of Nature* was 'translated by a person confined in Newgate as a patriot, and published in weekly numbers, its sale was pushed, from the joint motive of serving the Author, and the cause in which the London Corresponding Society was engaged'.[53] Intriguingly, an edition of the *System of Nature* was brought out by Pigott's prison-mate William Hodgson in 1795–6 (embellished with engravings by Henry Richter). Hodgson is the most obvious candidate for Reid's 'person confined in Newgate,' but he and Pigott may have worked together on a translation in prison.[54] Pigott was obviously desperate to make money by selling books on his release. Apart from the mooted translation of Holbach, he seems to have drawn on his gaming past to edit *New Hoyle, or the general repository of games*, eventually published after his death by Ridgway in 1795, with rules for the fashionable card games of faro, cribbage, and rouge et noir added to the traditional compilation.[55] More immediately, though, he seems to have looked to repeat the success of the *Jockey Club*, exploiting the general interest in the scandals of the aristocracy and even, in one instance, posing as a woman in print.

Scandalmonger and lexicographer

Margaret Coghlan had been born into a wealthy military family in 1762. She married the army officer John Coghlan during the American War, but her husband and then her father cast her off.[56] Crossing the Atlantic, she embarked on a career as actress and courtesan, with lovers who included Fox and the Duke of York. She wrote a scandalous memoir naming many names, but reportedly died in London in 1787 before it could be published. The memoir finally appeared in January 1794, published by George Kearsley, 'interspersed', the title page informs us, 'with anecdotes of the American and present French Wars, with remarks moral and political'. There was also a radical preface, extensive remarks on the moral laxity of the elite, and a second volume that celebrated 'the glorious Epoch, the 14 of July, 1789, when Frenchmen threw off for ever, THE YOKE OF SLAVERY'.[57] Throughout Coghlan's *Memoirs* elite marital relations are represented as a form of tyranny in constraint of the natural affections, 'an honourable prostitution', as Coghlan describes it, that introduced her 'to libertines, and to women of doubtful character'.[58] The *British Critic* read the book, not very attentively, simply as a moral critique of 'the licentiousness of elevated life'. Usually among the fiercest critics of radical opinion, the journal assumed Coghlan was still alive, and 'now a prisoner for debt', missing the appropriation of her voice to a radical critique. The author of the interspersions was Charles Pigott.[59] Pigott's amplifications of Coghlan's memoirs returned to some favourite targets of the *Jockey Club*, including, for instance, General Dalrymple. Sarcastically described there as 'equally distinguished for gallantry in love . . . as for bravery in war . . . this son of Mars, this favourite of Venus . . . equal to both and armed for either field', he reappeared in the *Memoirs* as 'this favourite of the fair sex, that renowned Warrior, equal to both and armed for either field'.[60] Pigott often returned to the idea that the officer class was barely more effective – if busier – in the bedroom than on the battlefield. Their commander-in-chief the Duke of York was a favourite target. Pigott had reportedly been discussing the duke's character with Hodgson just prior to their arrest.[61] Coghlan's *Memoirs* drily comments on the duke: 'if this princely *Lothario* shines not with *greater advantage* in the plains of Mars than he excels in the groves of Venus, the combined forces have little to expect from his martial exertions.'[62] On 10 February 1794, *The Times* noted that

> the publication of Mrs. Coghlan's *Memoirs* just on the eve of a Royal Duke [of York]'s return, will not prove very acceptable to him; anecdotes there are of a singular nature; nor should we wonder if on that account they were to be suppressed.

The duke soon had even more to annoy him when Eaton published Pigott's the *Female Jockey Club* on 8 March.[63] In an arch piece of self-promotion, Coghlan appears in its cast on the basis of her 'literary merit'. 'If her soul really breath the sentiments contained in the memoirs,' wrote Pigott praising his own amplifications, then 'she possesses *titles* far superior to any, which all the kings in the world have it in their power to bestow.'[64] 'This author', claimed Erskine,

> libelled all those who were entrusted with the Government of the Country, and all those, whoever they were, who were placed in the most respectable situations [in the *Jockey Club*]; and after having exhausted that sex, he then fastened on the weaker sex, (whom all agreed to protect) beginning with the wife of the Sovereign, [and] the royal princesses.[65]

There are plenty of examples to choose from. Pigott claimed, for instance, that Lady Archer was as '*adept* in certain *manual exercises*', including '*raising a cock* at faro'.[66] Condemning aristocratic women for publicly displaying themselves at routs and gaming tables was becoming a familiar part of the growing moralism of public culture, but Pigott's heady cocktail was far from usual. Throughout the main culprit in terms of public display – the reader is reminded from the *Jockey Club* – are 'the stupid barbarous prejudices of Royalty'.[67]

The *Female Jockey Club* opposes an enlightenment celebration of natural energies to aristocratic artifice in a way that echoes Holbach's materialism. Libertine punning often shares the page with a critique of 'superficial delicacies and luxuries' opposed to 'those heavenly enjoyments, which *Nature* has indulgently yielded, to make the bitter draught of life go down'. The opening entry in the *Female Jockey Club* condemns the enslavement of the royal princesses to 'the sterile solitude of celibacy', reading the royal household in terms of the paternal tyranny regularly attacked in sentimental fiction and the Gothic novel, not to mention much of Robert Merry's writing. '*Nature will prevail*', as Pigott puts it in his discussion of the princesses, becomes an over-determined motto as sentimental moralism meets libertine insinuation.[68] The collection ran into several editions, including a fourth edition of five thousand copies Eaton claimed, but the publisher did not escape trouble.[69] Lady Elizabeth Luttrell brought a libel case against the book for a passage claiming she received '*select* visitors in her private apartments'. There, Pigott claimed, she 'employed to make herself agreeable … forget her age, and act again the joys of voluptuous youth'.[70] A lengthy report of the trial appeared in *The Times* on 31 July. Erskine, appearing for the prosecution, described Pigott's book as a 'supplement to another work of malice [*The Jockey Club*], which had for its object to libel everything that was virtuous, honourable, and respectable in this country'. Erskine's role is an indication, if one is needed, of just how far Pigott had become alienated from his old Whig networks. Eaton was found guilty at the end of July, but settled out of court.[71] Pigott was beyond such mercies, as several newspapers noticed. He had died in his apartments on Tottenham Court Road at the end of June. John Gurney, Eaton's lawyer, described him as 'possessing the ablest head, with the blackest heart … gone to answer for this and all other offences at a higher Tribunal'.[72]

The gaol fever that had killed many others held in Newgate probably killed Pigott. His body was interred in his family vault in Chetwynd, but his legacy was not so easily claimed by the proprieties of the landed gentry. After his death, Eaton brought out a posthumous copy of his *Political Dictionary* (1795).[73] There are fewer better illustrations of John Barrell's claim that political struggle in the 1790s was often about the meaning of words.[74] In the *Political Dictionary*, the vocabulary of customary rights and traditional liberties that conditioned most eighteenth-century political discourse is presented as a smoke screen designed to exclude the people from political participation. The attachment to constitutional monarchy is defined in terms of a Whig preference for closed networks of 'influence' over democratic transparency:

> *Whig*, - a person who prefers the influence of House of Hanover to the prerogative of the Stuarts. I am an enemy to both; but if we must languish under one or the other, I would, without hesitation, prefer the prerogative of the Stuarts, and for this reason – where prerogative is, the defence and justification of an arbitrary act, all the odium which such an act would, is attached to the king himself; whereas, when this same arbitrary act is induced, through the medium of influence, the odium rests on no one in particular.

Every part of the church and state is subjected to pithy evaluation and dismissal.

The Opposition fares little better than the Ministry. The entry under so innocuous seeming a word as 'Fulsome' gives a sense of Pigott's disdain for the manners of the great. The image of Fox as the 'Man of the People,' a target of Pigott's from at least 1785, is reduced to a public show masking private vice:

> Charles Fox eternally passing compliments in his parliamentary speeches on the infamous B-ke. The manner in which members of both Houses of Parliament address each other. Noble Duke, Noble Lord, Right Honorable Gentleman, Learned Friend &c &c &c. This language may very properly be styled fulsome, since it is generally applied to the most unfeeling and corrupt beings of the human race.[75]

Whig principles are implicitly being opposed to the genuine man of feeling who makes an appearance in the 'Preface' provided with some editions. 'Liberty and Property', the twin peaks of Whig ideology, he scornfully defines as 'an indispensable necessity for keeping game for other people to kill, with pains and penalties of the most arbitrary kind, should we think of appropriating the minutest article to the use of our own families'.[76]

From a Burkean point of view, of course, Pigott's defection would have illustrated the dangerous moral relativism unleashed by the enlightenment faith in ideas.[77] From this perspective, he proved himself 'the Louse' who abandoned his class for self-interest masking itself as philosophy. Cut off from the culture to which he was born, Pigott provided a morality tale of the fate of talents and energies unmoored from those English traditions and customs ceaselessly mocked in the *Political Dictionary*. Eaton presented the case rather differently. Some copies under his imprint publish a first-person preface presenting Pigott as a hero of benevolence, who had sacrificed Gothic manners to republican virtue and human natural feeling. The preface comes complete with Richardsonian asterisks, breaking up the text, as if to indicate that sickness is undermining the author's sensitive frame. 'Inequality of style' is excused by 'the capricious and fluctuating temper of mind of the author'.[78] Whether Pigott intended these words for publication cannot be known, although Eaton published the preface with manuscript directions to the editor. Eaton may have been appropriating papers left by his fellow member of division 25, but he was also presenting his late colleague as a man of feeling ruined by a cruel and unjust system. Certainly this kind of self-revelation has more of the libertinism of Rousseau's *Confessions* than Richardson's *Clarissa*. The modesty and polite self-command essential to the Richardsonian ideas of sensibility are flouted in the pages of the dictionary itself. *A Political Dictionary* breathes the spirit of an anti-clerical freethinker, dismissive not only of the moral authority of the elite, but all the institutions of the church and state. The *Dictionary* displays the same disposition that freethinking members of the LCS were pleased to find in the *System of Nature*.

One of the few radical writers who had much to say on Pigott's behalf was Robert Watson, Lord George Gordon's secretary. Watson never shared his employer's religious fervour.[79] He was very much a marginal figure in the LCS, partly because of his association with Gordon, but he praised Pigott as 'a patriotic writer' and his brother Robert as 'a philanthropist'. No doubt Watson considered Pigott, like his former employer, 'a martyr to cruel and sanguinary laws'. Watson showed no compunction about identifying the body of Marie Antoinette with corruption and would scarcely have baulked at the *Female Jockey Club*.[80] Others defended Pigott's principles in the context of reform politics, including George Dyer and Benjamin Flower, but found the personal mode of attack hard to equate with their ideas of benevolence.[81] No doubt their friend Coleridge would have included Pigott among those 'sensualists and gamblers', including Pigott's companion Joseph Gerrald, whom he thought dishonoured the name of 'Modern Patriotism'.[82] Gerrald retained a place among the pantheon of radical martyrs, often identified with the daughters he left behind, thanks to the labours of Thelwall and others to consecrate his name. Pigott's name does not easily fit into any heroic account of the development of popular political consciousness, but after his death his satirical voice became a crucial component in the explosion of radical texts that spewed from radical bookshops in 1795. His name if not his reputation was constantly before the eye of readers on the title pages of one-penny anthologies like the *Voice of the People*, *Warning to Tyrants*, and *The Rights of Man*, published by 'Citizen' Lee at the Tree of Liberty.

CHAPTER 5

Citizen Lee at the 'Tree of Liberty'

The death of Charles Pigott in the early summer of 1794 coincided with the rise of Richard Citizen Lee in the LCS. The numerous 1d tracts Lee published in 1795 gave Pigott's name a short-lived posthumous fame in the radical movement. These publications have also ensured Richard Citizen Lee frequent mention in the scholarship on popular radicalism, despite the brevity of his career. He emerged into radical print culture in May 1794 and less than two years later fled to the United States. Despite his notoriety, exactly who he was and whence he had come puzzled both his allies and enemies alike. He was one of the many who rode the wave of print that rose in the third quarter of the eighteenth century and crashed to the shore in the 1790s. More specifically, he was a product of the explosion of print as a vehicle for religious feeling. In this regard, it is hardly surprising that his fellow abolitionist Thomas Hardy remembered him long afterwards as a 'patriot bard', but others in the movement had no stomach for what they regarded as overzealous religious enthusiasm.[1] He was either excluded or resigned from the LCS because of his warmth on such matters, but the government ensured that his name became emblematic of radicalism in the weeks that ran up to the passing of the Two Acts at the end of 1795. Citizen Lee was named several times in parliamentary debates, particularly over the question of whether he was 'the avowed printer and publisher to the Society'.[2] Members of both Houses of Parliament visited him in his shop, and even pestered his mother in order to find out more about him. If Citizen Lee was in the public eye in these weeks, he never entirely abandoned his 'proper' name. Richard Lee was the author of collections of evangelical, abolitionist, and radical poetry that appeared over 1794–5. Some of the most violent broadsides that issued from his shop at the Tree of Liberty contained lines by 'R. Lee' in them. Even his most satirical output continued to insist on the rights of God against the rights of kings, a position he maintained when he rejoined the fray of print politics in Philadelphia after 1796.

Evangelist of print

A transcription from the Treasury Solicitor's papers of an interrogation which took place on 31 October 1795 illustrates the confusion of the authorities when trying to understand the nature of popular radicalism in the 1790s:

> Q. Are these all the productions of Mr. Lee's pen?
> A. Not all, But those that have his Name to them are.
> Q. You I suppose are Mr. Lee's servant.
> A. No my name is Lee.
> Q. O, then you are Mr. Lee himself?
> A. Yes sir.
> Q. You must be very industrious to produce such a quantity of matter.
> A. There are several persons employed.[3]

The exchange suggests the protean nature of print radicalism in the 1790s, and the government's struggle to comprehend it. E. P. Thompson offered a brief description of Lee as 'one of the few English Jacobins who referred to the guillotine in terms of warm approval', but he has largely remained as much of a mystery in the historiography of radicalism as he was to the government in 1795.[4] Thompson was probably unaware of Lee's appearance in E. F. Hatfield's the *Poets of the Church* (1884). Far from denouncing Lee as a Jacobin, Hatfield commends his 'devout spirit'. Of course, he probably had no idea that his poet had also been the notorious bookseller of the Tree of Liberty. Whether those who included his poem 'Eternal Love' in an American collection under the name of the London Calvinist Maria de Fleury in 1803 and 1804 knew is more debatable.[5] More certain is that Lee's first ventures into print took the path of periodical publication; the route taken by John Thelwall, W. H. Reid, and others who later became involved in the LCS. Both Reid and Lee were products of late eighteenth-century networks where print and religion intertwined.[6] Lee eventually flouted many of the constraints of evangelical piety, but he began writing under the patronage of the *Evangelical Magazine* in 1793–4 with a series of poems over the name 'Ebenezer'.

The *Evangelical Magazine* was founded in 1793 by a group of dissenting and Anglican preachers of Calvinist orientation, among them David Bogue and James Steven, associates at the time of LCS-Secretary Thomas Hardy, as we have seen. The aim of the new magazine was to publish in a style 'level to every one's capacity, and suited to every one's time and circumstances', designed to protect 'true believers, exposed to the wiles of erroneous teachers who endeavour to perplex their minds, and subvert their faith'.[7] At its very inception, the *Magazine* was concerned to channel popular religious feeling by self-consciously exploiting a medium associated with the circulation of ideas to a new reading public: 'on account of their extensive circulation, periodical publications have obtained a high degree of importance in the republic of letters . . . which produced a surprising revolution in sentiments and manners'. Bogue had already, as we have seen, anonymously addressed the court of public opinion on the repeal of the Test and Corporation Act and on the significance of the French Revolution. Like most eighteenth-century periodicals, the *Evangelical* encouraged its readers to become writers, especially those who were drawn from outside the 'literate' classes. Lee was encouraged enough to gather his poems into *Flowers from Sharon*, published at the beginning of 1794, now proudly using his own name as author.

Lee prefaced *Flowers from Sharon* with the kind of apology for its defects typical of those who had newly entered the republic of letters:

> It is not from a vain Supposition of their Poetical Merit, that the ensuing Sheets are offered to the Public; but from a Conviction of the Divine Truths they contain; Truths which, I own, fallen and depraved Reason will always stumble at; and which the unregenerate Heart will never cordially receive; they are too humbling for proud Nature to be in love with; – too dazzling for carnal Eyes to behold. But they are Truths which the CHRISTIAN embraces, and holds fast as his chief treasure. From a real Experience of their divine Power in his Heart, he derives his only Support and Comfort in this wretched Vale of Tears.[8]

Here, the stress on the unmediated experience of grace provides an unstable mix of deference and self-assertion. Compare the preface attached to James Wheeler's posthumous *The Rose of Sharon: A Poem* (1790). The editor makes a great deal of Wheeler 'being with respect to human learning an illiterate (though doubtless sincere) Christian'. The apologia goes on to suggest that the poem 'may very probably receive the censures of the critic. Yet the serious Christian Reader will ... discern so much of real experimental religion as may afford him both pleasure and profit.'[9] In Lee's case, the *Evangelical Magazine* provided a review of *Flowers from Sharon* that praised the genuinely 'experimental' feeling of its former contributor, but simultaneously registered a concern over his presumption that incorrectness would be overlooked in favour of the authenticity of his religious feelings:

> This is perhaps more than a writer is entitled to expect, when he claims the public attention; especially as defects in grammar, accent, rhyme, and metre, might have been removed by the previous correction of some judicious friend. However, these poems, published, apparently, 'with all

> their imperfections on their head', afford the stronger evidence of being genuine; and many of them are superior, even in correctness, to what is naturally looked for in the production of so young a person, who has received little assistance from education, and whose occupation we understand to be that of a laborious mechanic.[10]

Such prefaces and reviews were ways of circumscribing the possibilities available in print for the 'laborious mechanic'. Self-taught poets could be valued for their 'genuine' effusions of the heart, as Reid was when brought forward by James Perry in the *Gazetteer*, but this was not quite the same thing as valuing them as 'poets' in their own right. To do so would have meant encouraging them to abandon what polite commentators perceived as their proper position within the social hierarchy, a fear repeatedly sounded by reviewers. Faced with John Thelwall's poetry in 1801, Francis Jeffrey writing in the *Edinburgh Review* identified the aspirations of such men in print as 'a pleasant a way to distinction, to those who are without the advantages of birth or fortune, that we need not wonder if more are drawn into it, than are qualified to reach the place of their destination'. His review goes on to imply that such cultural pretensions had stoked the fires of the popular radicalism of the previous decade: 'shoemakers and tailors astonish the world with plans for reforming the constitution, and with effusions of relative and social feeling'.[11]

Jeffrey saw Thelwall as someone who mistakenly thought a secular version of enthusiasm could compensate for birth, education, and cultural capital more generally. Lee, for his part, added a conviction of divine inspiration into this mix. Over the course of 1794, he followed precisely the trajectory that commentators like Jeffrey feared, making his conviction the basis of plans for reforming the constitution. In *Flowers from Sharon* that journey is only shadowed in his fierce confidence in the saving power of grace. 'Eternal Love', the first poem in the collection, asserts the unity of the believer with the divine, ('ONE with the FATHER, with the SPIRIT ONE') and looks to a day when the shout 'GRACE! FREE GRACE!' shall 're-echo thro' the Skies!' Lee's collection is pervaded by a faith in the sufficiency of his own spiritual illumination. Later in his own career, Bogue and his pupil James Bennett identified such confidence as the besetting sin of uneducated men who had never actually read Calvin, 'the popular poison, a bastard zeal for the doctrine of salvation by grace'.[12] Ironically, the *Evangelical Magazine* itself was criticised for giving rein to such excesses of popular religious feeling. In 1800, Reid, now writing as a turncoat after his arrest at an LCS meeting, identified 'the Evangelical and other Magazines, still in circulation' for stirring up a popular taste for prophetic illumination and enthusiastic conversion narratives. He would have known as he had travelled this road himself.[13]

The exact details of Lee's religious affiliations in 1793–4 are not easy to trace. One of the poems collected in *Flowers from Sharon* mentions a lecture 'at the Adelphi Chapel, by the Rev Grove'. Thomas Grove had been expelled from Oxford in 1768 for 'Methodism'. He was in London in 1793–4 acting as one of several ministers preaching at the Adelphi, which had no settled preacher at the time. John Feltham's *Picture of London* (1802) mentions Grove disapprovingly as one of a group of Calvinists 'celebrated for their zeal in addressing large auditories'.[14] The list of booksellers on the title page of *Flowers from Sharon* further helps to elucidate his religious context. They include Jordan, Matthews, Parsons, and Terry. Jordan, of course, was the original publisher of Paine's *Rights of Man*. Parsons published Merry's *Fenelon* in 1795, not to mention other works related to reform, but he also sold a great variety of popular religious material. In 1792, Jordan, Matthews, and Terry had also collaborated to republish an 'old ranter' tract from the seventeenth century, Samuel (Cobbler) How's *The Sufficiency of the Spirit's Teaching*. Reid later cited How's book, somewhat improbably, as the source of Tom Paine's idea that 'every man's mind is his own church'.[15] How's tract stresses the sufficiency of the faith of the poor believer over the knowledge of 'the wise, rich, noble, and learned'.[16] For his part, Terry was accused of peddling Paine's *Rights of Man* to the congregation of William Huntington's Providence Chapel. By 1794 he was certainly publishing millenarian tracts feeding off the sense of expectancy generated by the French Revolution.[17] *Flowers from Sharon* participated in and encouraged this expectation, but before 1794 was out Lee had made good on its potential by emerging as a member of the LCS.

The emergence of the citizen

Despite the potential overlaps in their religious affiliations, Thomas Hardy claimed in his *Memoir* not to have known Lee personally, conceivably the case since the poet did not gain any serious profile in the LCS until after Hardy's imprisonment in May 1794.[18] Nevertheless, Hardy's arrest and the subsequent death of his wife clearly fired the uneven and incomplete transformation of the author of *Flowers from Sharon* into Citizen Lee. This development did not entail the abandonment of religion for politics. One version of what happened to Lee is found in James Powell's letter to the Treasury Solicitor discussed in Part 1. Powell claims that Lee had become well known in radical circles for his exertions on behalf of the patriots arrested in May 1794. The chronology hazily sketched in Powell's letter implies he became acquainted with Lee at Eaton's shop.[19] Describing him as principal clerk at Perchard's in Chatham Square, rather than the 'laborious mechanic' assumed by the puff in the *Evangelical Magazine*, Powell says Lee had been 'very active in supporting the subscriptions for the persons imprisoned & very liberal himself. he was very popular in the society'. His most obvious contribution to raising money for the prisoners was the poem on the death of Hardy's wife, discussed earlier. Lydia Hardy had died on 27 August 1794, while her husband was still awaiting trial. Lee had already published poetry under his proper name in *Pig's Meat*, but after the arrests in May he may have thought it prudent to withhold it now. Two of the poems issued in *Pig's Meat* also appeared in a cheaply produced four-page pamphlet under the title the *Death of Despotism and the Doom of Tyrants*, which does bear his name. Probably published much later in the year, after the acquittals, 'The Triumph of Liberty' appears recast as the title poem in the *Death of Despotism*, but 'The Rights of God' keeps its original title, with the addition of a fourth stanza.[20] These poems were also gathered into the collection Lee next published, probably at the very end of 1794, under variants of the title *Songs from the rock*.[21]

Lee issued a handbill calling for subscriptions for *Songs from the rock*. The verso has an advertisement for *Flowers from Sharon* that includes a list of recommendations from clergymen with Hardy's minister James Steven among them. Booksellers accepting subscriptions for the new volume were the radicals Eaton, Smith, and Symonds, along with Jordan and Parsons from among those who had sold *Flowers from Sharon*. The published volumes of *Songs from the rock* carry a note announcing that 'several of the following Poems have suffered much through Omissions and Alterations, which the Fear of Persecution induced the Printer to make, though contrary to the Author's wishes'. Probably for much the same reason the list of subscribers promised on the proposal did not appear. Several names are blanked out in the poems, but this scarcely reduces the seditious nature of the content.[22] Some of these poems were to be reprinted or excerpted in the broadsides and pamphlets of 1795 that bear the imprint of Citizen Lee, but the collection in the form(s) it finally appeared seems to have been shaped by the optimism surrounding the acquittals at the treason trials. The collection opens with 'The Return of the Suffering Patriots' and the title page, which, whatever its final form, always mentions 'a congratulatory address to Thomas Hardy'. There is also a 'Hymn to the God of Freedom for the Fifth of November', the day of Hardy's acquittal. Neither is mentioned in the subscription flyer for the volume. Some versions of the volume describe the address to Hardy as 'added' and lists of publications for sale by Lee from 1795 have it listed as a separate item selling for 1d. The circumstantial evidence is that the volume had been in development before the acquittals, but was published with additional poems after Hardy was freed.

'Tribute to Civic Gratitude' insists on the centrality of Christian belief to radical politics. Hardy was a specifically 'CHRISTIAN HERO' as Lee explained in a note where he confronts 'infidelity', and denies any idea that 'pure Christianity is inimical to the Cause of Freedom'.[23] No doubt the Lord Chief Justice – in the unlikely event he ever read them – would have felt that these words vindicated his summing up at Hardy's trial, but they are directed as much against infidels in the LCS as against the established order. Given this account of Hardy as a specifically Christian hero, the persistence of themes from *Flowers from Sharon* in the volume as a whole is unsurprising. They include the abolitionism of 'On the Emancipation of our Negro Brethren in America' and the millenarianism of 'Babylon's Fall or the Overthrow of Papal Tyranny' and 'A Call to Protestant Patriots'. The last presents plans for British troops to be used to protect the Vatican against French Republican armies as a sign that the British government is in league with the Beast of Revelation. Possibly Lee was among those LCS members sympathetic to Gordon and the Protestant Association. 'Retribution; or the Rewards of Benevolence and of Oppression' is a celebration of the 'rich Glories of FREE GRACE' in a levelling vision of the Judgment Day when 'Monarchs fall beneath thy Frown'.[24] Hatred of monarchy as a human institution set up over against the freedom granted by God's grace is a keynote of Lee's radicalism, pushing beyond the respect for George III usually found – at least ostensibly – in most 'official' LCS publications. The zeal of Lee's radicalism was clearly bound up with the warmth of his religious convictions, a fact that caused problems for him within the LCS. Most of the poems in *Songs from the rock* are characterised by violent language, an unequivocal statement of faith in divine power, and the claim to see and feel that power directly at work in the world.

Nevertheless, it would be quite wrong to suggest that Lee did not have 'literary' aspirations. 'Reform offered a more practical kind of emancipation or empowerment', as Mark Philp has suggested, 'together with a degree of social mobility.'[25] There was a distinctly literary aspect to these ambitions for some members of the radical societies. John Barrell has identified the pastoral bent of much of the poetry found in *Pig's Meat* and *Politics for the People* with the literary and social aspirations of those who joined the societies.[26] Lee's references and allusions to the eighteenth-century poetic canon, including James Thomson and Edward Young, signals a similar desire to join the world of *belles lettres*. Complicating matters, but to similar effect, Lee's religious poetry brought him out of the clerk's office and into the public sphere. *Flowers from Sharon*, at 3s, looks as if it was intended for something like the better-off purchasers of the *Evangelical Magazine*.[27] Devotional poetry offered Lee a form of social mobility and an opportunity for self-definition underwritten by the idea of a grace freely available even to the poorest members of society, but *Songs from the rock* also lays claim to a degree of cultural capital from more literary sources. The volume quotes lines from Joseph Addison, James Thomson, and Young, not to mention the fashionable religious verse of Salomon Gessner's sacred poem *The Death of Abel*, translated by Mary Collyer in 1761, and reissued regularly thereafter.[28] The collection also contains a number of love poems addressed to 'Aminta' (a name taken from a Tasso play). One of the Aminta poems, Lee acknowledged, had already appeared in a magazine. At one point in *Songs from the rock*, he even quotes from Della Crusca.[29] *Songs from the rock* was available at 1s 6d, 'in order to accommodate every Class of Readers', but also in a de luxe edition on fine paper at 2s 6d. Even at his radical zenith, when he traded as the bookseller Citizen Lee, this de luxe edition remained available. Powell's bitter account of Lee's celebrity in radical *conversazione* suggests he also struck a figure as a poet of the people in the debating clubs that flourished in the mid-1790s.

These aspirations do not mean Lee was simply self-interested, but involved in a species of self-fashioning in print. Lee's notion of his right to participate in the public sphere rested not simply on what we might recognise as personal improvement through education, or the universality of private judgement, or even on the power of his imagination as such, but primarily on his confidence in the gift of free grace. Lee himself described *Songs from the rock* as an attempt 'to Promote the united cause of God and Man'.[30] Nearly everything he later published continues to affirm the confidence in the sufficiency of his own spiritual illumination over 'unregenerate reason' set out in *Flowers from Sharon*. Thelwall usually identified such attitudes with the retrograde enthusiasm of the Civil War, but Lee cannot simply be regarded as a throwback to the 1640s. His writing is the product of a complex interaction between such tendencies and emergent aspects of late eighteenth-century print culture. The literary effects of the cult of poetic sensibility, running through his poetic references to Addison,

Thomson, Young, and Della Crusca, who inspired so much magazine verse between them, informs both the love poetry and the more general celebration of benevolence in *Songs from the rock*.

In 1795, Lee even published a translation of an excerpt from Rousseau's *Emile*, under the title *The Gospel of Reason*. Carefully culled and translated from the confession of faith of the Savoyard vicar, it presents Rousseau as an advocate of a religion of free grace rather than an Enlightenment *philosophe*:

> the majesty which reigns in the sacred writing, fills me with a solemn kind of astonishment; and . . . the sanctity of the Gospel speaks in a powerful and commanding language to the feelings of my heart.

The initial reception of Rousseau in England had stressed the 'heat of enthusiasm' in *Emile* and often represented him as a brave defender of Protestant freedom of conscience. *The Gospel of Reason* goes further, presenting Rousseau as a radical apostle of the sufficiency of the spirit's teaching, or regenerate reason.[31] If Merry and Pigott presented their readers with an unstable cocktail of sensibility and French materialism in the cause of reform, Lee's poetry combines sentimentalism with homegrown religious enthusiasm. Merry and Pigott also shared a particular and often personal animus towards Pitt, possibly because they knew and were familiar with the Prime Minister's social world. They were capable of attacking the Crown's encroachment on the authority of Parliament, and sometimes even the institution of monarchy itself, at their most republican, but Lee's radical Protestant imagination provides his writing with a sense of the fundamental wickedness of monarchy. Kingship becomes a form of idolatry. Pitt is its high priest. Lee's confidence in the voice of God speaking directly to his heart enabled him to publish some of the most incendiary material put out by radical presses in the 1790s, underwritten by what the *Monthly Review* called 'the divine right of republics':

> SOLE KING OF NATIONS, rise! assert thy Sway,
> Thou JEALOUS GOD! thy potent arm display;
> Tumble the Blood-built Thrones of *Despots* down!
> Let Dust and Darkness be the *Tyrant's* Crown![32]

Spence printed these lines in *Pig's Meat*, perhaps because he and Lee shared an inheritance in this kind of religious feeling. Both of them saw the compact of church and state as a blasphemous usurpation of the rights of God. This perspective suffused everything Lee published in 1795, including some very black satire.[33]

The Tree of Liberty, 1795

Broadsides and short pamphlets, seldom costing more than a penny, poured from Lee's press over the course of 1795. Although it is not exactly clear when he set up as a bookseller, his shop soon became famous as the Tree of Liberty, or sometimes the British Tree of Liberty. A series of addresses in central London were its home: first, at a shop his mother seems to have owned in St Ann's Street, Soho; then at the Haymarket some time before the end of March 1795, before moving back to Soho in Berwick Street; finally coming to rest in October 1795 on the Strand. Hostile attention from church and king supporters played their part in these shifts. Lee issued a handbill from the Haymarket on 21 March 1795 accusing them of 'maliciously attempt[ing] to deface and obliterate the good name and honourable Title of CITIZEN LEE'. It seems the government's supporters had taken to attacking his shop sign, possibly only recently put up to advertise the new premises in the Haymarket. In one sense, 'the good name and honourable Title' of 'Citizen' distinguished the cheap radical publisher from the literary aspirations of 'Richard Lee', except that his poetry did appear on the playbills and other penny publications, sometimes with his name attached. 'R. Lee' was also used in the colophon of some pamphlets issued from the Tree of Liberty.[34] He did not, then, neatly dissociate his literary ambitions from his radical politics. Instead the cheap publications he issued from the Tree of Liberty combine the violence of the poems of *Songs from the rock*, sometimes explicitly invoking divine aid, with a grotesque sense of carnival, delighting in imagining the death of Pitt, and even – perhaps Lee's trademark – the demise of the king.

In February, Lee reissued a mock playbill 'for the benefit of the Tythe and Tax Club'. (Figure. 8). An earlier version of the bill had been discussed at Thelwall's trial because of its identification of the king with Nebuchadnezzar. Lee now added additional matter: 'For the Amusement of Starving Mechanics'. Possibly Lee was exploiting the buzz surrounding the millenarian prophecies of Richard Brothers.[35] Brothers identified George III with Nebuchadnezzar in a series of prophecies issued in 1794. London's downfall as the modern Babylon was prophesied. While there is nothing to suggest that Lee was a follower of Brothers, his poetry participated in and helped sustain the air of millenarian expectancy the Paddington Prophet had generated at the end of the previous year. Apart from giving the *Tythe and Tax Club* its new title, Lee also added four quatrains of verse above his own name:

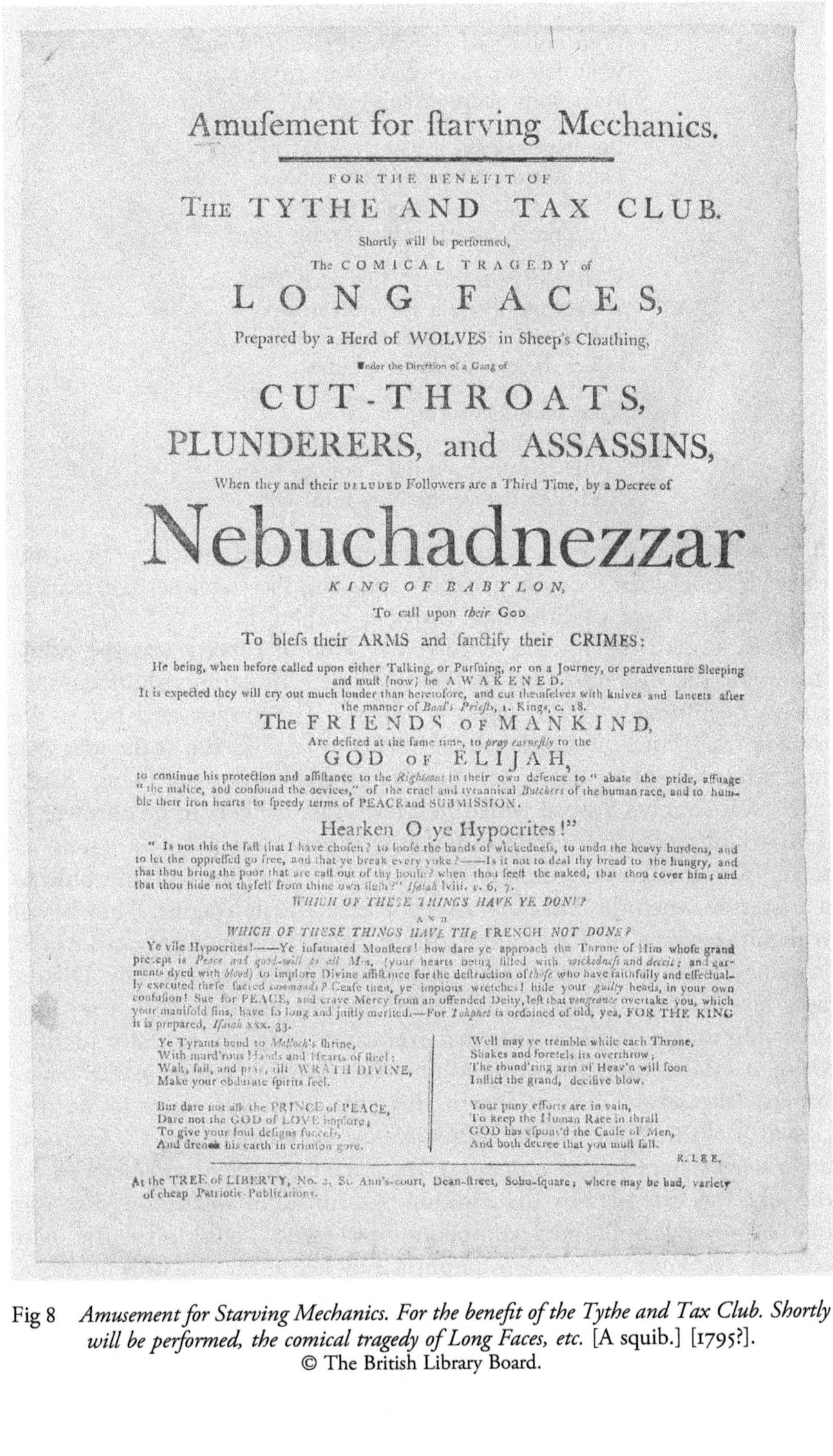

Amuſement for ſtarving Mechanics.

FOR THE BENEFIT OF

THE TYTHE AND TAX CLUB.

Shortly will be performed,

The COMICAL TRAGEDY of

LONG FACES,

Prepared by a Herd of WOLVES in Sheep's Cloathing,

Under the Direction of a Gang of

CUT-THROATS,

PLUNDERERS, and ASSASSINS,

When they and their DELUDED Followers are a Third Time, by a Decree of

Nebuchadnezzar

KING OF BABYLON,

To call upon *their* GOD

To bleſs their ARMS and ſanctify their CRIMES:

He being, when before called upon either Talking, or Purſuing, or on a Journey, or peradventure Sleeping and muſt (now) be AWAKENED.

It is expected they will cry out much louder than heretofore, and cut themſelves with knives and lancets after the manner of *Baal's Prieſts*, 1. Kings, c. 18.

The FRIENDS OF MANKIND,

Are deſired at the ſame time, to *pray earneſtly* to the

GOD OF ELIJAH,

to continue his protection and aſſiſtance to the *Righteous* in their own defence to " abate the pride, aſſuage " the malice, and confound the devices," of the cruel and tyrannical *Butchers* of the human race, and to humble their iron hearts to ſpeedy terms of PEACE and SUBMISSION.

Hearken O ye Hypocrites!"

" Is not this the faſt that I have choſen? to looſe the bands of wickedneſs, to undo the heavy burdens, and to let the oppreſſed go free, and that ye break every yoke?——Is it not to deal thy bread to the hungry, and that thou bring the poor that are caſt out of thy houſe? when thou ſeeſt the naked, that thou cover him; and that thou hide not thyſelf from thine own fleſh?" *Iſaiah* lviii. v. 6, 7.

WHICH OF THESE THINGS HAVE YE DONE?

AND

WHICH OF THESE THINGS HAVE THE FRENCH NOT DONE?

Ye vile Hypocrites!——Ye infatuated Monſters! how dare ye approach the Throne of Him whoſe grand precept is *Peace and good-will to all Men*, (your hearts being filled with *wickedneſs* and *deceit*; and garments dyed with *blood*) to implore Divine aſſiſtance for the deſtruction of *thoſe* who have faithfully and effectually executed theſe ſacred *commands*? Ceaſe then, ye impious wretches! hide your *guilty* heads, in your own confuſion! Sue for PEACE, and crave Mercy from an offended Deity, leſt that *vengeance* overtake you, which your manifold ſins, have ſo long and juſtly merited.—For *Tophet* is ordained of old, yea, FOR THE KING it is prepared, *Iſaiah* xxx. 33.

Ye Tyrants bend to *Molloch's* ſhrine,
With murd'rous Hands and Hearts of ſteel:
Wait, faſt, and pray, till WRATH DIVINE,
Make your obdurate ſpirits feel.

But dare not aſk the PRINCE of PEACE,
Dare not the GOD of LOVE implore;
To give your foul deſigns ſucceſs,
And drench his earth in crimſon gore.

Well may ye tremble while each Throne,
Shakes and foretels its overthrow;
The thund'ring arm of Heav'n will ſoon
Inflict the grand, deciſive blow.

Your puny efforts are in vain,
To keep the Human Race in thrall
GOD has eſpous'd the Cauſe of Men,
And both decree that you muſt fall.

R. LEE.

At the TREE of LIBERTY, No. 2, St. Ann's-court, Dean-ſtreet, Soho-ſquare; where may be had, variety of cheap Patriotic Publications.

Fig 8 *Amusement for Starving Mechanics. For the benefit of the Tythe and Tax Club. Shortly will be performed, the comical tragedy of Long Faces, etc.* [A squib.] [1795?].

Ye tyrants bend to *Molloch's* shrine,
With murd'rous Hands and Hearts of Steel:
Wait, fall and pray till WRATH DIVINE,
Make your obdurate spirits feel.

But dare not ask the PRINCE OF PEACE,
Dare not the GOD of LOVE implore;
To give your foul designs success,
And drench his earth in crimson gore.

Well may ye tremble while each Throne,
Shakes and foretells his overthrow;
The thund'ring arm of Heav'n will soon
Inflict the grand, decisive blow.

Your puny efforts are in vain,
To keep the Human Race in thrall
GOD has espous'd the Cause of Men,
And both decree that you must fall.

If these lines perpetuate the idea of the ungodliness of monarchy that runs through *Songs from the rock*, generally speaking the publisher Citizen Lee was much more of a satirist than the poet Richard Lee.

From around the middle of July, the Tree of Liberty was the prime depot for the dissemination of Pigott's satires in various short compilations, beginning with the *Rights of Kings*.[36] The author died before the treason trials came on, but Lee used his words to poke fun at the idea that imagining the king's death had been construed as treason there. 'Monarch', was simply, 'a word which in a few years is likely to be obsolete.'[37] The lack of prosecutions for sedition in 1795 may have given Lee a sense of safety from the law on sedition. The satires on the Prime Minister built to a crescendo when the *Telegraph* issued a series in late August. They began with an account of Pitt in the throes of 'a violent *diarrhoea*'. He is imagined passing away after two days of humiliating confessions. Dissection reveals Pitt's tongue to be 'quite hollow; and in short, the most deceiving tongue in all respects that ever came under the operator's knife'. Using a joke continually made against the Prime Minister in the newspapers, 'the *sexual* distinctions in this case were not easily to be discerned'.[38] Printed in full as *Admirable Satire on the Death, Dissection, and Funeral Procession, & Epitaph of Mr. Pitt!!!* from the newspaper's office, the joke was extended by the addition of a 'dreadful apparition'. Lee was one of several publishers competing over who could offer the best edition. *The Voice of the People*, published by Lee at the end of September, closes with an advertisement for the '*only genuine Edition, corrected by the Author*'.[39] By late November, Lee had a sixth edition out from the new shop on the Strand, with additional material 'by another hand' purporting to be taken from Pitt's last will and testament. In the will, John Bull is bequeathed Pitt's 'curious Magic Lanthorn, with which he has for many years past amused or alarmed his said honest, simple-minded friend, by showing him conquests abroad, or plots at home'. Advertisements for *Poems on Various Occasions* by Lee and a new edition of Wollstonecraft's *Rights of Woman* appeared on the last page. Neither seems ever to have been published, unless the first was another repackaging of *Songs from the rock*.[40]

John Barrell has suggested that once the Two Acts were introduced into Parliament radical imaginings of the death of those in authority increased in intensity and started to target the king himself.[41] In the radical societies, the Two Acts were widely regarded as a kind of treason against traditional liberties. If Pitt and Grenville defended them as a response to a state of exception, so radicals used them to suggest that the compact between the state and the people was being broken. Addressing the inhabitants of Westminster petitioning against the passage of the bills on 16 November, Sheridan caught the mood in a speech published by Lee: 'the day will come, when the law, weak as it is said to be at present, will be found strong enough to bring to the scaffold your corrupt oppressors'.[42] Fox was reportedly alarmed at the violence of the speech and pulled him back to his seat. The list of items for sale at the Tree of Liberty issued with the account of this meeting, in contrast, was pushing further and further forward with the idea that Pitt's government was destroying the constitution it purported to defend. *The Happy Reign of George the Last*, for instance, addressed to 'the little tradesmen and labouring poor', calls for the people to throw off the monarchy and set up 'parochial and village associations', after the manner of Spence's land plan.[43] Lee did not write most of the pamphlets and broadsides he published. There were too many of them. He told the Privy Council that there were numerous people employed in his shop, but he was also fed material – directly or indirectly – by the circle at the *Telegraph* or those with connections to the Sheridan circle, like Merry and Joseph Jekyll, who provided Pittachio copy.[44] The satires on the death of Pitt suggest a degree of insider knowledge, despite – or perhaps, because of – their evident delight in the evisceration of Pitt. Lee encouraged aspiring satirists, whoever they might be, to send work to him at the Tree of Liberty: 'Communications of Merit, either in Prose or Verse, will be gratefully acknowledged, if directed (post paid) to R. LEE.'

Sheridan later claimed many of them were written and distributed by spies and informers to provide the justification for the Two Acts. No doubt some of them were. Lee may not have enquired too closely into the authorship of what he published, as the misattribution to Merry of the sophisticated pastoral satire *Pitti-Clout & Dun-Cuddy* suggests. Lee's primary concern was to put as much into circulation as possible that undermined respect for things as they were.

His eagerness to challenge the legitimacy of monarchy was to prove his undoing, or, at least, provided the government with an opportunity it had been preparing. The handbill primarily responsible for bringing Lee to the government's attention bore the title *King Killing* (see Figure. 9), but he did not write it on his own. The paragraphs are culled from an essay 'On Tyrannicide' written by John Pitchford, early in 1795, for the first issue of *The Cabinet*.[45] Far from itself advocating king killing, 'On Tyrannicide' is primarily a discussion of the execution of Louis XVI that concludes that most advocates of king killing 'have been dazzled by a few splendid names'. Lee completely distorts his source, omits its view that tyrannicide is 'unlawful, useless, and pernicious', and simply reprints as republican polemic the few paragraphs *The Cabinet* provided, perhaps mischievously, as examples of imprudent 'declamation'. *King Killing* as published by Lee was consonant with the view that monarchy was a form of blasphemy expressed in many of the poems in *Songs from the rock*. The same theme appears as black comedy in the satirical *Rights of the Devil*, available from the Tree of Liberty at the same time, which presents Hell as the 'fountain head' of all terrestrial monarchies and identifies religious establishments as 'the greatest enemies to religion and morality'.[46]

Lee wanted to reach as wide an audience as possible with his cheap publications. He often subdivided his material in order to bring out cheaper versions, as for instance with the separate sale of his poetic address to Hardy or the series derived from Pigott. Charles Sturt claimed that 'Tyrannicide' was dropped as a title in favour of *King Killing*, 'because the people otherwise would not buy it'.[47] Lee seems to have been hawking *King Killing* along with his other wares at the huge LCS rally held in Copenhagen Fields on 26 October, where a hostile crowd shouted anti-Pitt slogans, called for the end of the war, and complained at the economic distress of a virtual famine year. On 29 October, the king's coach was attacked on the way to the opening of Parliament, when a stone was thrown through one of the windows. Someone in the crowd wrenched open a door. Pitt's government used the incident to move against the radical movement and bring the Two Acts before Parliament. Lee

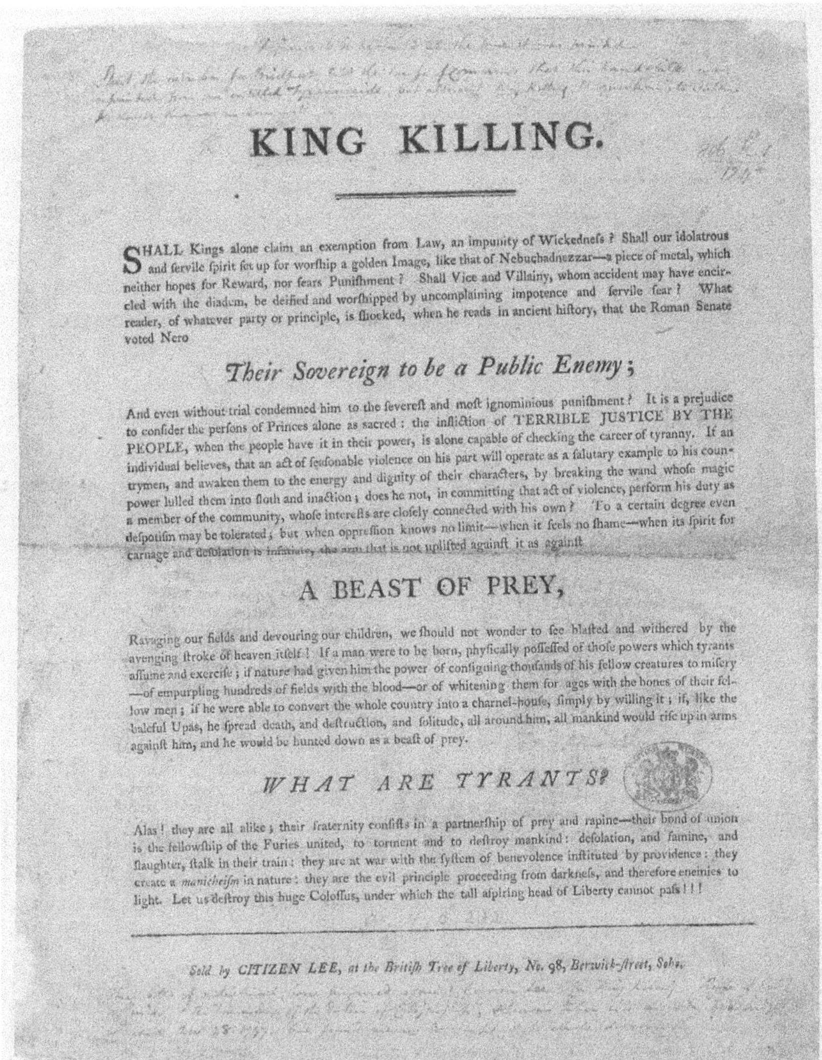

KING KILLING.

SHALL Kings alone claim an exemption from Law, an impunity of Wickedneſs? Shall our idolatrous and ſervile ſpirit ſet up for worſhip a golden Image, like that of Nebuchadnezzar—a piece of metal, which neither hopes for Reward, nor fears Puniſhment? Shall Vice and Villainy, whom accident may have encircled with the diadem, be deified and worſhipped by uncomplaining impotence and ſervile fear? What reader, of whatever party or principle, is ſhocked, when he reads in ancient hiſtory, that the Roman Senate voted Nero

Their Sovereign to be a Public Enemy;

And even without trial condemned him to the ſevereſt and moſt ignominious puniſhment? It is a prejudice to conſider the perſons of Princes alone as sacred: the infliction of TERRIBLE JUSTICE BY THE PEOPLE, when the people have it in their power, is alone capable of checking the career of tyranny. If an individual believes, that an act of ſeaſonable violence on his part will operate as a ſalutary example to his countrymen, and awaken them to the energy and dignity of their characters, by breaking the wand whoſe magic power lulled them into ſloth and inaction; does he not, in committing that act of violence, perform his duty as a member of the community, whoſe intereſts are cloſely connected with his own? To a certain degree even deſpotiſm may be tolerated; but when oppreſſion knows no limit—when it feels no ſhame—when its ſpirit for carnage and deſolation is inſatiate, the arm that is not uplifted againſt it as againſt

A BEAST OF PREY,

Ravaging our fields and devouring our children, we ſhould not wonder to ſee blaſted and withered by the avenging ſtroke of heaven itſelf! If a man were to be born, phyſically poſſeſſed of thoſe powers which tyrants aſſume and exerciſe; if nature had given him the power of conſigning thouſands of his fellow creatures to miſery—of empurpling hundreds of fields with the blood—or of whitening them for ages with the bones of their fellow men; if he were able to convert the whole country into a charnel-houſe, ſimply by willing it; if, like the baleful Upas, he ſpread death, and deſtruction, and ſolitude, all around him, all mankind would riſe up in arms againſt him, and he would be hunted down as a beaſt of prey.

WHAT ARE TYRANTS?

Alas! they are all alike; their fraternity conſiſts in a partnerſhip of prey and rapine—their bond of union is the fellowſhip of the Furies united, to torment and to deſtroy mankind: deſolation, and famine, and ſlaughter, ſtalk in their train: they are at war with the ſyſtem of benevolence inſtituted by providence: they create a *manicheiſm* in nature: they are the evil principle proceeding from darkneſs, and therefore enemies to light. Let us deſtroy this huge Coloſſus, under which the tall aſpiring head of Liberty cannot paſs!!!

Sold by CITIZEN LEE, *at the Britiſh Tree of Liberty, No. 98, Berwick-ſtreet, Soho.*

Fig 9 *King Killing* [A hand bill, reprinted from one entitled 'Tyrannicide'.] [London, 1797 [1795?]].

was the most flagrant example of radical extremism available. On 16 November, the Attorney General, John Scott, came to Parliament to name him as 'printer to the London Corresponding Society'.[48] The aim was to represent *King Killing* and the other pamphlets as official publications of the LCS. Scott read the definition of Royalty from *Rights of Princes*: 'the curse of God in his wrath to man'. He was careful not to read other parts that might have brought guffaws from the benches. The next day Lord Mornington told the House of Peers that he had visited Lee's shop and come away with *The Happy Reign of King George the Last*.[49] Mornington insisted that the various imaginings of the death of the king amounted to 'French treason'. During a brief period of temporary and uneasy cooperation with extra-parliamentary reformers to campaign against the Two Acts, the Opposition tried to defend the LCS by distancing it from Lee.[50] Presenting a petition against the two Bills from Sheffield, Charles Sturt rose in Parliament to confirm that Lee's mother had told him that her son was no longer a member.[51] Several other sources, as we have seen, suggest that Lee had fallen out with the leadership over the spread of infidelity in the movement. Reid later claimed that

> Bone and Lee, two seceding members, and booksellers by profession, were proscribed for refusing to sell Volney's *Ruins of Empire*, and Paine's *Age of Reason*; and that refusal construed into a censure upon the weakness of their intellects.[52]

The LCS issued a statement distancing itself from the bookseller the day after Mornington's speech, but the next day his name still appeared among those booksellers accepting signatures on the LCS petition against the Two Acts.[53]

After a year in which there had been no prosecutions for seditious libel in London, true bills were found against Lee on 28 November.[54] The pamphlets named on the indictments were *King Killing*, the *Rights of Princes* and a *Summary of the Duties of Citizenship*. Lee was arrested the same evening. He did not stay in prison long. By 19 December, the *True Briton* was announcing his escape. *The Times* provided detail:

> The escape of Citizen Lee, from the house of the Officer in Bow Street, was thus effected. Three women, or persons in women's cloaths, went to visit him. Their number having been unnoticed by the attendants, four persons in women's cloaths quitted the house. One of these was the person called Citizen Lee, who has not since been heard of.

Powell later claimed, as we know, that Lee fled with his wife.[55] The government may not have done much to prevent his escape. He had served his purpose in terms of the Two Acts being piloted through Parliament. Lee made for Philadelphia, like many others who fled from Pitt's system of spies and informers. Durey places Lee among those émigrés who contributed to the development of Jeffersonian ideology.[56] Federalists hated their democratic politics, and the Alien and Sedition Acts were in part directed against them. One historian has commented of this period of American politics that 'foreigners seemed to get one sniff of printers' ink and become loyal Jeffersonians', but Lee was not quite so comfortable a fit and continued to insist on the rights of God over the compromises of earthly institutions.[57]

Written on the Atlantic Ocean

Lee arrived in Philadelphia to find himself in the febrile atmosphere building up to the passing of the Alien and Sedition Act. He seems quickly to have been drawn towards the democratic wing of the anti-Federalist movement. He attracted enough notice to win a place in Cobbett's scathing attacks on what he saw as American Jacobinism, unsurprisingly, as Lee was starting his bookshop up right under Cobbett's nose in downtown Philadelphia.[58] Cobbett's vicious attacks on Lee – 'a man who publickly preached *Regicide* and *Rebellion*' – are predicated on his knowledge of the English context, but insist that such men had no place in thinking about politics on either side of the Atlantic. Cobbett places Lee squarely among Philadelphia's crowds of 'raggamuffins, tatterdemalions, and shabby *freemen*, strolling about idle'.[59] Dismissed as one of the 'animals . . . hardly worth naming', Cobbett could not resist mentioning the fact that he 'like a true sans-culotte slipped out of Newgate in petticoats'. In September 1798, Cobbett pithily summarised Lee's American career in a note: 'Citizen Lee first attempted a magazine, then a book, and then he tried what could be got by travelling, and he is at last comfortably lodged in *New-York jail*.' Probably Lee was in debt, but he may also have been picked up under the Alien and Sedition Act of 1798.[60]

Jane Douglas suggested that Lee must have died soon after arriving in the United States, but the broad outline of Cobbett's claim seems to be corroborated by the trail left in print.[61] The 'magazine' was the *American Universal Magazine* (AUM). First published on Monday, 2 January 1797, the AUM is a familiar eighteenth-century blend of original essays, tales, poetry, scientific news, much recycled material, and reports of proceedings in Congress. Running as a weekly over its first four issues, it directly encouraged the debate of democratic forms and principles. The very first issue published an essay insisting on the importance of the periodical press for the diffusion of knowledge. Reiterating in theory Lee's own practice, it insisted 'that much more service is done in the aggregate mass of periodical publications than evil is occasioned by particular parts'.[62] Lee was aligning himself with the democratic idea of the republic as a nation of 'citizen readers' described by Cotlar. Lee's name appeared, for instance, on the subscription list for Thomas Carpenter's *American senator* (1796–7). Stocked in Lee's shop on Chestnut Street, the *American senator* was designed to ensure the population at large had access to the democratic process for purposes of discussion and debate (contradicting the more limited Hamiltonian notion of participatory democracy as properly confined to election day).[63] Certainly the account of presidential inauguration given in the AUM sharply contrasts the visibility of Congress with the pomp and awe of Parliament:

> This ceremony and spectacle must have afforded high satisfaction and delight to every genuine Republican. To behold a fellow citizen, raised by the voice of the People to be the First Magistrate of a free nation, and to see, at the same time, he who lately filled the Presidential Chair, attending the inauguration of his successor in office, as a private citizen, beautifully exemplified the simplicity and excellence of the Republican system, in opposition to hereditary monarchical governments, where all is conducted by a few powerful individuals, amidst all the pomp, splendor and magnificence of courts, independent of the great body of the People.[64]

AUM subscribed to the more radical line sketched out in *Rights of Man* that 'the independence of America, considered merely as a separation from England, would have been matter but of little importance, had it not been accompanied by a revolution in the principles and practice of governments'. Congress is imagined as Paine's 'open theatre of the world'.

Lee maintained a notion of a transatlantic radicalism, a sense of the Revolution controversy as a universal struggle that transcended national boundaries. His religious affiliations, as with Thomas Hardy, helped maintain this internationalist perspective. The providential basis of Lee's thinking gave his publications in Britain and the United States their uncompromising edge, but he had become openminded enough now to advertise forthcoming editions of Volney's *Ruins* and Godwin's *Political justice* in the very first number of AUM, presumably because they provided ammunition for his campaign against the compact of church and state. At least one poem published in AUM, 'Providence, saving the oppressed and working the destruction of Tyrants', contained all the millenarian ire of his own poetry. A subtitle describes it as 'Written on the Atlantic Ocean'.

Given the emphasis on 'deliverance from the tyrant's rage' and the general tenor of its language, it may well have been composed by Lee himself:

> Sav'd from the scourge of Despotism's laws,
> Let all my powers unite with ardent zeal;
> To serve my great preserver's glorious cause,
> The cause of Freedom and of human-weal.
>
> Thou God of love! The cause of Freedom's thine,
> Tyrants turn pale at your approaching fate!
> For injured man, and Providence divine,
> Decree the vengeance that your crime await.
>
> Truth's mighty arm shall lay your honours low,
> War and destruction your delight, shall cease;
> Freedom's young plant in every land shall blow,
> And yield mankind the fairest fruits of peace.[65]

The AUM also maintains the abolitionist principles that permeate Lee's London publications, printing letters on the subject of American slavery from Morgan John Rhees and Edward Rushton: 'Of all the slave holders under heaven those of the United States appear to me the most reprehensible; for man never is so truly odious as when he inflicts on others that which he himself abominates.'[66] Lee joined the Pennsylvania Society for Promoting the Abolition of Slavery in December 1796, only a few months after his arrival. If his religious enthusiasm had caused difficulties for him with the LCS, the same may well have been true for his position within American democratic circles, especially where it sustained his firm abolitionist position.[67] Lee was a print evangelist. His was perhaps the most uncompromising version of the Protestant myth of print magic from the radicalism of the 1790s, but one that resisted any attempt to let the idea of a disinterested public usurp the word of God as the spirit that informed its transformative power. For someone like John Thelwall, the subject of my final chapter, such attitudes represented a disgraceful throwback to 'enthusiasm' that embarrassed his idea of popular radicalism as the expression of a popular enlightenment based on reason and benevolence.

CHAPTER 6

John Thelwall and the 'whole will of the nation'

John Thelwall usually traded under his own name. 'Character' was intrinsic to his claim to act as tribune of the people. By the time of his arrest in May 1794, he had made himself into the most visible member of the LCS through his writing and, particularly, by lecturing at a series of venues around London. In fulfilling the Godwinian criterion of standing 'erect and independent' in his own name, he practised his own version of print magic.[1] For Thelwall, this magic was not the bodying forth of the Word in the French Revolution, as it was for Citizen Lee, but the conjuring of the people as a 'living body' via the power of print.[2] Thelwall's faith was in a secular magic based on materialist notions of sympathy. He was the grateful heir to an eighteenth-century belief in the improving power of magazines and debating clubs. Sympathy for Thelwall was the 'occult' mechanism by which rational debate was extended into a democratic engine of change.[3] His radicalism was staked on his role as a conductor of these energies in two senses of the metaphor, both animating and organising 'the people'. In this regard, he frequently played the showman, confessedly adopting 'the attractive veil of amusement' to arouse the interest of his audience, providing songs for LCS meetings, and even cutting the head off a pot of beer to mime the fate of kings.[4] His part in the struggle against the Two Acts at the end of 1795 was focused above all on the rights of reading and discussion being kept open to the population at large. Their passing into law eventually forced him into internal exile, away from the public spaces of the lecture room, the coffee house, and the theatre. Circumstance reinforced a tendency that had always been a part of his writing. His faith in print transposed into a more intimate medium able to bring a transformation in the individual in a way that the modern reader might recognise as a version of Romanticism. Such an understanding of 'literature' or something like it may emerge in Thelwall's writing after 1795, but it never lost its political ambition, nor imagined its implied audience as isolated readers.

Associated intellect

Thelwall was always ambitious of a literary career. Born into the shopkeeping classes, the biography published by Thelwall's second wife Cecile Thelwall in 1837 noted that from early on 'the prospect of mingling in circles of society, more correspondent to his taste and turn of mind than those to which had hitherto been confined, had altogether formed an association intoxicating'. He was among those many who saw the expansion of the press in the last quarter of the eighteenth century as an invitation. Also like many others, he discovered that freedom of speech and the liberty of the press – keystones of the supposed palladium of British liberties – were not to be taken entirely at face value. Thelwall was involved in debating societies from the early 1780s, eventually managing the debates at Coachmakers' Hall, but early on this interest in the intellectual buzz of London included being 'a professed sermon hunter'.[5] London's chapels and churches were intermingled in the print sociability of magazines and debating societies, but this aspect of Thelwall's intellectual ambition was short lived. He became impatient of religious sentiment in politics and poetry alike, perhaps most famously when in May 1796 he dismissed Coleridge's 'Religious Musings' as 'the licencious (I mean pious) nonsense of the conventicle'.[6] In the 1780s, Thelwall was sending poetry of an entirely secular variety into various periodicals with 'enthusiastic perseverance'.[7] *Poems on Various Subjects* appeared in 1787, eliciting a notice in the *Critical Review* still proudly remembered in his biography.[8] From around 1788 until 1791, Thelwall took over the editorship of the *Biographical and Imperial Magazine*. He also wrote the plays *Incle and Yarico* (1787) and *The Incas* (1792), convinced his work was being plagiarised after he submitted the manuscripts to the theatre managers.[9] His later political practice contested the space of the London theatre for radical culture. He may have described himself as a 'literary adventurer', but the arc of his story in these years is far from unique. Citizen Lee and W. H. Reid are just two others that came to the LCS through an aspiration to join the republic of letters, but neither they nor anyone else associated with the radical societies equalled Thelwall's fame as a performer on the public stage in the 1790s.[10]

Originally, Thelwall was a church and king man with pro-Tory prejudices imbibed from his father. He identified his radical epiphany not with the classic instance of reading *Rights of Man*, but in the attempts to close down the debating societies discussing the Regency controversy in 1789–90, followed by his experiences in the Westminster Election of

1790. From working as a poll clerk, his indignation at abuses seems to have provoked him to campaigning for John Horne Tooke, who remained a central figure in his development. Experience in the debating societies is perhaps the key to his distinctive sense of radicalism as a 'forum', to use Judith Thompson's term, whereby the popular will could make itself known by the active participation of the multitude.[11] Thelwall always prized 'the energy and power of graphic delineation, which, in the enthusiasm of maintaining an argument can be produced, by the excitement of a mixed audience'.[12] The point is not simply that he felt a personal buzz in face-to-face debate, which he clearly did, but that he also saw in such encounters the possibility of discovering principles that none of those involved had previously held, a democratic version of the Godwinian faith in the collision of mind with mind traceable back to Isaac Watts and Milton before him.[13]

Where some in the radical movement predicated their politics primarily on the delineation of clear rational principles, Thelwall saw debate as a *process* wherein such principles were discovered. He gave a speech at Coachmakers' Hall on freedom of discussion worth quoting in full for what it reveals about the nuances of his idea of debate:

> So far is the vulgar objection against discussion from being true – to wit – that after all their wrangling, each party ends just where it began, that I never knew an instance of men of any principle frequently discussing any topic, without mutually correcting some opposite errors, and drawing each other towards some common standard of opinion; different perhaps in some degree from that which either had in the first instance conceived, and apparently more consistent with the truth. It is, I acknowledge, in the silence and solitude of the closet, that long rooted prejudices are *finally renounced*, and *erroneous* opinions changed: but the materials of truth are collected in conversation and debate; and the sentiments at which we most revolt, in the warmth of discussion, is frequently the source of meditations, which terminate in settled conviction. The harvest, it is true, is not instantaneous, and we must expect that the seed should lie raked over for a while, and apparently perish, before the green blade of promise can begin to make its appearance, or the crop be matured. But so sure, though slow, in their operations, are the principles of reason, that if mankind would but be persuaded to be more forward in comparing intellects, instead of measuring swords, I can find no room to doubt, that the result must be such a degree of unanimity as would annihilate all rancour and intolerance, and secure the peace and harmony of society. In short, between all violent difference of opinion, there is generally a medium of truth, to which the contending parties might be mutually reconciled. But how is this to be discovered, unless the parties freely compare their sentiments? – If

> discussion be shackled, how are discordant opinions to be adjusted, but by tumult and violence? If societies of free inquiry are suppressed, what power, what sagacity, in such an age as this, shall preserve a nation from the convulsions that follow the secret leagues and compact of *armed conspiracy*.[14]

If the *Life of John Thelwall*'s account is to be trusted, the speech cannot have been made later than 1792, when the debating society at Coachmakers' Hall was shut down, but there is much in the version printed there that sounds like Godwin's *Political justice*, not published until the beginning of the following year.[15] The stress on the collision of mind with mind balanced against the final authority of the deliberations of the closet is typical of Godwin, as is the idea of the slow harvest of truth, but it was made in the sort of venue where Godwin rarely ventured, if at all. The most likely occasion for the speech would seem to have been the debate of 24 May 1792, just three days after the Royal Proclamation against seditious writings. According to the *Gazetteer*, the question was: 'Are Associations for Political Purposes likely to promote the happiness of the people, by informing their minds, or to make them discontented without redressing their grievances?'[16] For Thelwall, such debates came to be regarded not simply as a forum of exchange but as the alembic of print magic, wherein those involved in reading and discussion might come to know themselves as 'the people' by their interactions with each other. Over 1795–6, this aspect of his development produced a remarkable series of reflections on the formation of a collective consciousness among the labouring classes: 'Hence every large workshop and manufactory', he wrote in his *Rights of Nature*, 'is a sort of political society, which no act of parliament can silence, and no magistrate disperse.'[17]

Thelwall always admitted to being enthusiastic by nature, liable to being swept up by the experience of being part of and speaking to a crowd, but his ideas on sympathetic transmission were underpinned by theoretical reflection on 'certain immutable laws of organic matter'.[18] Thelwall was immersed in debates about materialism and the relations between mind and body from at least as early as his editorship of the *Biographical and Imperial Magazine*.[19] In the early 1790s, he was living in Maze Pond in the Borough, very close to Guy's and St Thomas's hospitals. Always drawn to sites of intellectual exchange, he soon became involved in a weekly medical debating club at Guy's called the Physical Society. The apothecary James Parkinson – Eaton's 'Old Hubert' – was also a member.[20] Thelwall delivered two papers at the society in 1793. The first, on 26 January, vigorously debated over six weeks, was published as *An Essay, Towards a*

Definition of Animal Vitality. Thelwall's essay took the position that organised matter was the foundation of life, but only when united with a vivifying principle he compared to electricity. At the end of the year, another paper seems to have led to him withdrawing or being excluded from the Physical Society, at just the time he was starting to make a name for himself as a lecturer to the LCS. Materialism linked with a democratic politics was too rich a mixture for most of those at the Physical Society. Thelwall later claimed that magazines that had previously been accepting his writing enthusiastically began to reject his work at around this time. The publication of his distinctive prose medley *The Peripatetic* was delayed when the printer who produced the first volume threatened to withhold the manuscript if Thelwall refused to remove the politics. The second and third volumes did appear, but sold by Daniel Isaac Eaton. Four decades later, Thelwall's biography claimed that the episode showed him that 'he must be either a patriot or a man of letters'.[21] The binary in this judgement may reflect a nineteenth-century perspective. In the 1790s, the print networks of the LCS held both paths open to him simultaneously; if, that is, one allowed that a 'man of letters' could thrive in its circuits of print, sociability, and performance.

The Peripatetic is shot through with Thelwall's sentimental materialism, creating a sense of a community interlinked by natural bonds of sympathy, 'a kind of mental attraction', he claimed, 'by which dispositions that assimilate, like the correspondent particles of matter, have a tendency to adhere whenever they are brought within the sphere of mutual attraction'. One of the most arresting features of *The Peripatetic* is the way it builds an auto-critique of the aesthetics of sensibility into its own narrative, acknowledging a debt to Sterne, then distancing itself from the idea of the 'feeling observer' absolved from political responsibility. 'The subject of our political abuses', he wrote in the preface,

> is so interwoven with the scenes of distress so perpetually recurring to the feeling observer, that it were impossible to be silent in this respect, without suppressing almost every reflection that ought to awaken the tender sympathies of the soul.[22]

These were the aspects of the book that caused the printer to interrupt its production. Thelwall's materialist sense of a sympathetic universe shaped not just his poetry and prose, but also his lecturing and debating. Even the King Chanticlere allegory that Eaton published in *Politics for the People* was originally an intervention in a debate on the life principle that clearly owed something to his discussions at the Physical Society.[23]

Thelwall always approached the body politic as animated by 'that sort of combination among the people, that sort of intelligence, communication, and organised harmony among them, by which the whole will of the nation can be immediately collected and communicated'.[24] His writing and lectures he understood as imparting an electrical energy to give life to a 'public', but he also conceived organisation to be part of the process of bringing together into a single body the dispersed members to be animated.[25] An external spark can only work on matter that is internally organised:

> If the people are not permitted to associate and knit themselves together for the vindication of their rights, how shall they frustrate attempts which will inevitably be made against their liberties? The scattered million, however unanimous in feeling, is but chaff in the whirlwind. It must be pressed together to have any weight.[26]

Thelwall later saw the importance of the LCS as its facilitation of this process:

> In fact it cannot be said that up to the time of forming the societies to be mentioned hereafter, there was positively what we now call an 'English public', or in other words an union of opinion of *the majority of all classes* upon one given subject.

In *Life of Thelwall*, these sentiments are surrounded by a discussion of the ease by which 'the mass of the people, could be led into such acts of riot and confusion', a fact imagined as surprising to the nineteenth-century reader. In the 1790s, there was a more radical edge to his idea of 'the mass of the people', not least in his insistence on its role as a constituent power that could presume to challenge the authority of the Crown-in-Parliament. For several months from November 1793 to his arrest on a charge of treason in May 1794, Thelwall devoted himself to exploiting all kinds of media in a variety of spaces to work the magic of conjuring 'the people' from 'the scattered million'.[27]

The political showman

Thelwall's first involvement with the societies seems to have been in April 1792 at the Borough Society of the Friends of the People, not to be confused with Grey's aristocratic group. He was also part of the more elusive London Society of the Friends of the People, which had close relations with the Borough Society. Neither long outlasted the emergence of the SCI and LCS as the coordinated leaders of radicalism in the metropolis.[28] Thelwall devoted much of his energy in 1792 to preserving the debating societies against attempts to harass them out of existence after the Royal Proclamations of May and November. He also joined the Society of the Friends of the Liberty of the Press. The published account of their meeting called to celebrate Erskine's defence of *Rights of Man* describes him as 'A Mr. Thelwall, whose oratory is well known at Coachmakers' Hall, and other places of public debate'. His contribution was to reprobate 'with much vehemence the dangerous conduct of those Associations, who came forward to support the allegations of the existing powers – right or wrong'.[29] Despite the condescension implied in the 'A Mr. Thelwall', his performances at the Society seem to have brought him to the attention of the Opposition. After describing the travails faced by Thelwall in getting *The Peripatetic* published, Susan Thelwall's March 1793 letter to her brother mentions that various Foxites had enquired after him and offered their support, including 'your Mr. Edwards'.[30] Gerard Noel Edwards, MP for Rutland, the county where her family lived, took the chair at the Society of Friends of the Liberty of the Press meeting in December 1792; presumably he subsequently showed an interest in *The Peripatetic*. Edwards did not attend the Society's March meeting because he disapproved of transacting business 'at places for public dinners', but sent a letter professing support for the liberty of the press, on which Sheridan made humorous remarks from the chair. Whether out of principled qualms about such aristocratic connections or for other reasons, Thelwall did not ultimately pursue the path of patronage. Instead, he joined the LCS in October 1793, introduced to the society by Joseph Gerrald, another member of the Friends of the Liberty of the Press.[31]

Thelwall stood for election as a delegate to the Edinburgh Convention soon after joining the LCS, but his candidacy fell on the rule excluding those who had been members for less than three months. Instead in November 1793, the month he made his striking intervention at the debating society at Capel Court, he offered to lecture from Godwin's *Political justice* to raise money for the expenses of the delegates. Given initially at 3 New Compton Street in Soho, these lectures made his name in the LCS.[32] From at least early 1794, he began offering repeat shows of the lectures north and south of the river. The venue north of the river continued to be Compton Street, an address friendly to the LCS because a member – John Barnes – ran a coffee house there.[33] The other was in Thelwall's home ground of the Borough, at the Park Tavern, in Worcester Street, where he also tried to set up a society for 'FREE POLITICAL DEBATE'. The *Morning Post* (10 February) announced a repeat performance of his popular lecture on 'the Moral tendency of a System of Spies and Informers'. There was also to be a debate on the relative harm of the principles and conduct of the American War as opposed to the struggle against France. The advert only alerted his enemies to the event at the Park Tavern and a riot broke out. Thelwall soon gave an account of what happened as a triumph of self-restraint in the face of loyalist attempts to provoke a violent response, but he was driven north of the river to the Three King's Tavern in the Minories. The respite was only brief. The landlord there was threatened with the loss of his licence.[34] On 19 February, Thelwall took out newspaper advertisements announcing that he would now lecture twice a week in Compton Street, until 'a proper Room can be provided and fitted up for the purpose'. His ambition was a venue where 'the best Accommodations will be established for Ladies and Gentlemen', an ambition perhaps only finally met when he took up residence in Beaufort Buildings in April 1794.

During these months of uncertainty, Thelwall received a letter from a former member of the Southwark Friends of the People named Allum, who had migrated to the United States.[35] This letter accused Thelwall of backsliding from the cause of liberty. A wounded Thelwall began drafting a reply on 13 February – never sent – in which he defended himself as 'for the 4 or 5 months past, almost the sole labourer upon whom the fatigue, the danger, & the exertions of the London Corresponding Society (the only avowed sans culottes in the metropolis) have rested'. If this somewhat exaggerated his role, then it did provide a reasonable summary of his activities since the end of 1792:

> I have been frequenting all public meetings, where anything could be done or expected; have been urging & stimulating high & low, & endeavouring to rally & encourage the friends of Freedom. I have been constantly sacrificing interest, & security, offending every personally advantageous connection, till ministerialists, oppositionists & moderées hate me with equal cordiality.

To the charge that he was a 'Brissotist', he gave a more equivocating answer. First, he defended Brissot and his colleagues as true republicans whose virtues and abilities he appreciated. Next, Thelwall argued that 'the prevailing party [in France] are too ferocious, & too little scrupulous about shedding human blood', although like many others, Merry included, he thought allowances should be made 'for the situation in which the despots of Europe had placed them'. He went on to blame Robespierre and his allies for acting with the 'bigoted vices of the Priesthood, they would silence our doubts with their loud & injurious dogmas'. Nevertheless, Thelwall insisted to Allum, 'I am a Republican, a downright sans culotte though I am by no means reconciled to the dagger of the Maratists'.

For Thelwall, typically, it was less important to identify a specific political position in relation to Brissot or Marat, than to argue and fight for 'the right of public investigation upon political subjects'. The newspaper advertisements were a self-conscious strategy in this regard. Thelwall told Allum he understood his lectures to be 'until lately given privately, that is to say without advertisement'. He was identifying the moment when he switched from 'private' lecturing to the membership of the LCS to a broader audience of 'Ladies and Gentlemen'. More mundanely, the letter notes he was forced into the newspapers because the magistrates 'have stripped the town of my posting bill'. (see Figure 10). Then Thelwall gave a full account of the events at the Park Tavern. Having failed to intimidate the landlord, the magistrates sent constables and a motley crowd to interrupt discussion by roaring out 'God Save Great Jolter Head'. The letter ends with a promise to send the latest political pamphlets across the Atlantic, but cannot resist a dig at the state of society and politics in America: 'I fear you are somewhat short of the true sans culotte; that you have too much reverence for property, too much religion, & too much law.' At Thelwall's trial, the letter was produced in court as evidence of his commitment – not in 'abstract speculation', as Serjeant James Adair put it, but as an avowed sans culottes – to a Convention. The prosecution ignored the reservations about Brissot and Marat. The final sentence was used to show that Thelwall's politics had gone even beyond anything espoused in the new republic of the United States: 'Republicans of this country had hitherto viewed America with an eye of complacency, but according to Mr. Thelwall, she had too great a veneration for property, too much religion, and too much law.'[36] Appearing in Thelwall's defence, Erskine insisted that the letter had never been sent because it did not reflect his settled opinions. He put its tone and temper down to Thelwall's habitual enthusiasm, an aspect of his character repeatedly stressed by defence witnesses at the trial.[37] The prosecution presented this enthusiasm as revealing the real intentions behind Thelwall's lecturing.

The government and their supporters piled up the evidence that Thelwall had tried to reach the widest possible audience across a range of media. They produced copies of the songs he had circulated in the LCS (on sale at the doors of the lectures); brought up anecdotes like the decapitation of the pot of beer; and provided detailed accounts of his lectures from the spies. The treason was in the performance, they

Spies and Informers.

On Wednefday, Feb. 5, 1794,

J. THELWALL

WILL BEGIN A

COURSE OF LECTURES

on the moft important Branches of

POLITICAL MORALITY,

to be continued every WEDNESDAY EVENING, at the Long Room, *Three Kings Tavern, Minories*; and every FRIDAY, at No. 3, *New Compton-Street, Soho.*

Subject for Wednefday Night.

Probationary Lecture.----"*The Moral Ten-*
" *dency of a Syftem of SPIES and INFORM-*
" *ERS; and the Line of Conduct to be purfued*
" *by the FRIENDS of LIBERTY during*
" *the Continuance of fuch a Syftem.*"

SUBJECT for FRIDAY NIGHT.

"*The Syftem of LAW, and its Abufes.*"

The Doors to be opened at a Quarter paft Seven, and the Lecture to begin at a Quarter paft Eight o'Clock.

Admittance Sixpence each Perfon.

Tickets to be had at D. I. EATON'S, No. 74, Newgate-ftreet; of T. HARDY, No. 9, Piccadilly; Smith, Portfmouth-Street, Lincoln's Inn Fields, &c.

Fig 10 John Thelwall, *Spies and Informers. On Wednesday, Feb. 5. 1794, J. Thelwall will begin a course of lectures on the most important branches of political morality, etc.* [A posting bill.]

effectively argued, although, of course, this made it difficult to bring as evidence against him. The same difficulty faces anyone writing on any performance history, where what happened has to be pieced together from eyewitness accounts, published scripts, and other sources. The irony of the government's surveillance of Thelwall, as with much of the archive of the LCS, is that it leaves a rich and diverse performance record for 1794–5.

His lecture notes are preserved in the Treasury Solicitor's papers with the letter to Allum and other personal papers seized at his arrest. Thelwall had published some of the lectures in early 1794 and again after his acquittal, but he was left complaining that others – seized by the Bow Street Runners at his arrest – were never returned.[38] The printed versions of Thelwall's lectures need to be treated with an awareness of their distance from what went on in the lecture room. Years later Hazlitt staked his distinction between 'writing and speaking' on recollections of Thelwall's 'very popular and electrical effusions'.[39] In the published versions, Thelwall admitted tidying up for 'stile'; and sometimes backed away from the 'levity' left in some of the printed texts, including his joke about 'those wicked *sans culottes* having taught the new French bow to the *innocent* and *unequivocating* Louis'.[40] Spy reports offer another glimpse into the asides and extempore comments that gave his performances some of their spice, even if their accounts were gingered up for consumption of the law officers. John Taylor's reported that Thelwall's fast-day lecture began with 'a strain of pointed irony'. This included reading from Isaiah 58 on the true spirit of fasting. Apparently Thelwall stopped to ask his audience sarcastically whether one could be charged with sedition for reading from the Bible. Thelwall frequently read from other authors, including Gibbon and Godwin, and commented on what he read as he went along.

Taylor reported in detail on Thelwall's lectures and gave evidence at the treason trials, including a full account of his attempts to exploit a performance of *Venice Preserved* at Covent Garden. At the Compton Street lecture on 31 January, Thelwall apparently feigned surprise at a play being granted a licence when so 'full of patriotic and republican sentiments'. Originally written 'with a view of paying his [Otway's] court to Charles II', as Thelwall recognised, sections had already been appropriated for the radical canon.[41] Thelwall told his audience that he would attend Covent Garden with his friends and then read a conspiratorial dialogue between Pierre and Jaffeir aloud, because he was certain the words of 'some hireling Scribbler' would be interpolated. He promised to stand up in the pit if that were the case and give the dialogue in its proper form. Taylor went to the theatre on

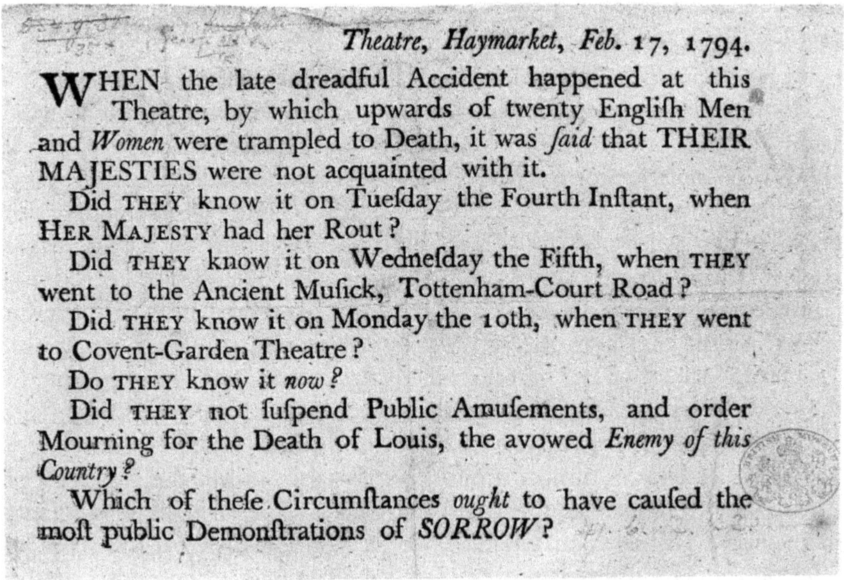

Theatre, Haymarket, Feb. 17, 1794.

WHEN the late dreadful Accident happened at this Theatre, by which upwards of twenty Engliſh Men and *Women* were trampled to Death, it was *ſaid* that THEIR MAJESTIES were not acquainted with it.

Did THEY know it on Tueſday the Fourth Inſtant, when HER MAJESTY had her Rout?

Did THEY know it on Wedneſday the Fifth, when THEY went to the Ancient Muſick, Tottenham-Court Road?

Did THEY know it on Monday the 10th, when THEY went to Covent-Garden Theatre?

Do THEY know it *now?*

Did THEY not ſuſpend Public Amuſements, and order Mourning for the Death of Louis, the avowed *Enemy of this Country?*

Which of theſe Circumſtances *ought* to have cauſed the moſt public Demonſtrations of *SORROW*?

Fig 11 *When the late dreadful accident, etc.* [A handbill charging the king with callousness in regard to the accident at the Haymarket Theatre, 3 February 1794.] [London, 1794]

1 February, where he heard an undoctored version of the dialogue performed. Thelwall and twenty of his friends encored it loudly.[42] Only a few days later, tragic events at the Royal Theatre, Haymarket, gave Thelwall a further opportunity to exploit the theatre for radical publicity. On 3 February, the king and queen and the six princesses all attended the newly reopened Haymarket for the first time. According to *The Times* the next day, such was the rush of the crowd to see the Royal Family that fifteen or more people died in the crush. Taylor reported that Thelwall commented on the tragedy at his next lecture: 'though there was no sorrow expressed for the loss of 20 English subjects, yet there was mourning for Louis, who had been a determined enemy to this country'. He did not stop there, but printed slips and distributed them in the theatre a fortnight later (see Figure 11). Did the Royal Family not know what had happened at the Haymarket, Thelwall's printed sheet asked the theatregoers? Why did they not show the same grief for their own subjects, it continued, they had shown for the death of the king of France? Outraged by Thelwall's effrontery, John Reeves sent to the law officers one of 'a great Number

which were dropped upon the stair case of the first gallery at the Haymarket theatre this evening'.[43]

This was precisely the period that Thelwall started taking out advertisements in the newspapers for his lectures, some of them appearing in the same columns as Monsieur Comus's 'New Philosophical Deceptions', another possible source for Merry's Pittachio pasquinade. Thelwall was a showman himself. A performance of his lecture 'On the Moral tendency of a System of Spies and Informers' used the theatrical device of telling readers it would be 'positively the last time'. He had already been doing repeat performances 'on account of the great overflow', as he put it in an advertisement that also offered *The Peripatetic* and the *Essay on Animal Vitality* for sale at 9s and 2s 6d respectively. Self-consciously appearing in the newspapers, as we know from the Allum letter, Thelwall was reorienting to an audience beyond the LCS, but not simply as self-advertisement. His lectures covered familiar ground comfortably within the pantheon of British liberties, such as the trial of Russell and Sydney, but associated them with Margarot and Gerrald, not to mention his own resistance to state power. He inserted himself in the martyrology along with Gerrald, Muir, and the others prosecuted for their part at the Edinburgh Convention. By going 'public' with his lectures, as he put it, Thelwall was standing forth not as someone involved in the private cabals of conspirators – as the LCS were soon to be presented at the treason trials – but in the open discussion of political principles, defending the liberty of the press, and free to contest spaces of publicity like the theatre and other venues in the contact zone of urban sociability.

Alarm at the success of the lectures grew over the early months of 1794. Their heady mixture of indignation and comedy prospered. At Thelwall's trial, Taylor reported that the *Tythe and Tax Club* handbill had been read out as part of the mockery of the fast day at the lecture of 28 February.[44] An account of his lecture at Compton Street on 21 March noted the presence of Eaton, lately acquitted for the Chanticlere allegory. He and the foreman of his jury were radical celebrities in the audience. The growing sense of the lectures as public events is palpable. An audience, not just radicals, was drawn to see what the fuss was about. A friend of Sir Joseph Banks was induced by the newspaper advertisements to go to Compton Street, close to the scientist's house in Soho Square. He wrote to Banks shocked at what he had heard and seen, torn between contempt and the reluctant admission that he had been impressed by Thelwall's oratory. The expectation had been to hear 'the low jargon of some illiterate scoundrel'. Instead Thelwall delivered 'a most daring & biting Philippic against Kings, Ministers, & in short all the powers that be, deliverd in bold energetic terms, & with a tone and manner that perfectly astonish'd me'. The letter credits Thelwall with deploying a 'force of argument, & an enthusiasm of manner scarcely to be resisted, indeed the effect was but too visible on the audience, many of whom were by no means to be rank'd with the lowest Order of the people'. A genuine fear of Thelwall's communicative power comes off the page. Banks forwarded the letter to the law officers and revealed 'Mr Reeves & myself have Frequently convers'd on the subject of Mr. Thelwall's lectures & we agree wholly in opinion that their Tendency is dangerous in the extreme'. He assumed that Reeves had already discussed the matter with government.[45] In May, Reeves attempted to bring a charge of seditious libel to the court of the Liberty of the Savoy, in whose jurisdiction Beaufort Buildings stood. When the court threw the application out, Reeves tried again with a charge of public nuisance and even arranged for a newly sworn jury to attend Thelwall's next lecture.[46] Aware of what was happening, Thelwall wrote for advice to John Gurney, fresh from his success defending Eaton. 'Avoid any harsh observations upon the King or Monarchy, & Aristocracy', Gurney advised. 'You may say what you please of Reeves's Associations.'[47] Conscious of Thelwall's tendency to extemporise, he also told him to immediately explain away anything he said that might be construed as seditious; to employ a short-hand writer to guard against misrepresentation; and to speak coolly. With the help of Joseph Ritson, who held a legal office in the Liberty of the Savoy, Thelwall escaped this charge, but the reprieve did not last long.[48]

Just five days after the charge of public nuisance was thrown out, Thelwall was arrested. Charged with treason, he now faced the death sentence if found guilty rather than the lighter penalties that came with the earlier charges. Taken into custody at an LCS meeting at Beaufort Buildings called to discuss the arrest of Hardy, the government also seized his papers and books, including Godwin's *Political justice*, Johnson's *Dictionary*, Darwin's *Botanic Garden*, and Blackstone's *Commentaries*.[49] The government's case, as we have seen, was that the convention proposed by the LCS was an attempt to usurp the authority of Parliament by claiming to represent the people directly. Thelwall had publicly alluded to the possibility of such a meeting in his lectures and played a leading part in drawing up plans.[50] He prepared a defence while he was in prison, but Erskine dissuaded him from giving it in court. He published it after his acquittal as *Natural and Constitutional Right of Britons* (1795). Although later in life he claimed to have argued against calling the convention at the

LCS–SCI meetings, his published defence turns more on the meaning of the word and the question of whether calling a 'convention' really constituted an overt act of treason. Characteristically, Thelwall insisted that 'we attempted so to organize the public opinion that it might be made known to the representative, and Ministers, if that opinion really is in favour of Reform, might have no pretence for refusing our just desire'.[51] No wonder his defence team did not want him to make this speech in court, as he was conceding the idea that the LCS saw itself as able to organise the will of the people into an articulate form, precisely the role Parliament supposed itself to fulfil.

Early on in his imprisonment, Thelwall asked the prison authorities to provide him with pen and paper. He used them to prepare a new course of lectures; wrote the defence published as *Natural and Constitutional Right*; and composed a series of poems published in sympathetic newspapers, including the *Politician*.[52] As the *Politician* quickly folded, only two of those Thelwall promised appeared, but he prefaced them with a letter to the editor that denied he ever represented himself as 'without comfort, and *almost without hope*', as some of the newspapers had reported. This issue he saw as 'certainly of considerable consequence to my own reputation, that my conduct and sentiments upon that occasion, should be accurately represented', but also insisted upon 'the importance of character in the present crisis'.[53] Personal moral integrity was to be of increasing importance to Thelwall's identity as an author. He staked much on his 'heart', as Coleridge recognised in 1796, when he told Thelwall he would trust his morals but not those of many other radicals on that basis.[54] Thelwall's self-representations acknowledged – as he had in court – that he was sometimes apt to run away into enthusiasm with the strength of 'social ardor', but frequently used the admission as a vindication of the authenticity of his feelings.[55]

The poems finally gathered together as *Poems written in Close Confinement* (1795) were devoted to the idea of an imaginative sympathy that bound Thelwall to his comrades. Print is the medium of dissemination, but its magic is imagined to transcend media and enter into the immediacy of a connection between persons. 'Stanzas, Written on the Morning of the Trial, and Presented to the Four Prisoners Liberated on the Same Day' celebrates the ability of the individual consciousness to reach beyond its own condition and partake in the benefits of 'social joy' felt by his liberated compatriots:

> For sweeter, from the lonely cell,
> At length to life restor'd,
> Shall every emotion swell
> Around the social board.

From these social considerations, he moves on to imagine the power of his own sufferings 'To benefit mankind'. The expansive movement is implicitly staked on the authority of his own character, understood as a tuning fork that vibrating in harmony with the animated universe. From this period, Thelwall's many invectives against spies and informers intensified in relation to an idea of the integrity of his private character and the authenticity of his domestic relations. Often intrusions into this sphere were represented as form of 'Gothic intrigue and exploitation', as McCann puts it. Merry and Pigott exploited the same trope, but their French materialist ideas of a domain of free nature opposed to aristocratic domination were often represented in terms of erotic release. Thelwall lectures and writing were much more focused on the domestic arrangements of the family unit, 'a model of unmediated communality', as McCann describes it, 'free from the distorting effects of power relations'.[56] Susan Thelwall may have styled herself a 'female democrat', as we saw in Chapter 1, but Thelwall's writing in 1794–5 only occasionally acknowledged the idea of a 'female citizen' in any explicit sense.[57]

Acquitted felon

When he emerged from court Thelwall was understandably exhausted and decided to withdraw from the LCS. Although he claimed to have become a full convert to its goals of universal suffrage and annual Parliaments in the Tower, the early months of 1795 saw him acting on his own behalf. Horne Tooke, whom he considered in the light of his 'political father', advised him to withdraw from politics entirely, but he did not.[58] The poems were gathered together with others under his name and brought out as a single volume with an epigraph from Milton's *Comus*. The paratext might seem to signal a reorientation to an idea of literary culture as a form of leisured reading in private, but the poems scarcely point in that direction, as we have seen. In his first lecture *On the moral tendency of a system of spies and informers*, reprinted early in 1795, he had told his audience that this was 'no season for indulging the idle sallies of the imagination'. He explicitly 'renounced myself those pursuits of taste and literature to which from my boyish days, I have been devoted'.[59] Interestingly, as McCann points out, these renunciations were immediately followed by a poem in the published version of the lecture.[60] Elsewhere in his lectures Thelwall explicitly identified the category of 'literature' with the rise of the printing press as we saw in the first chapter. His sketch of the history of prosecutions for political opinions celebrated 'the morning star of literature, the harbinger of the light of reason'.[61] Implicitly he was opposing the idea that the 'man of letters' could not properly be a politician, just as he had critiqued aesthetic ideas of sensibility that excluded the sufferings of the poor in *The Peripatetic*. In line with this set of assumptions, when Thelwall published his poems from the Tower in 1795, he also recommenced his lectures at Beaufort Buildings, advertised in the volume of poetry.[62] The lectures themselves, published together in the *Tribune* from March, urged his listeners and readers to think of themselves – 'the whole body of the people' – as the constituent power of the nation.[63] Popular discussion, stimulated by the lectures themselves, was the crucible in which the people would make itself known as this 'whole body'.

Thelwall rejoined the LCS in response to the mass meeting it called for 26 October, three days before the opening of Parliament. He spoke at the meeting along with those who had risen to the fore in his absence, like John Gale Jones, and old allies (sometimes adversaries) like Richard Hodgson. It was in the midst of this struggle that he received a blow from an unexpected quarter in the form of Godwin's *Considerations on Lord Grenville's and Mr Pitt's bills* (1795). On the face of it, Godwin wrote as an ally in the struggle against the Two Acts. His strategy was to present the acts as unnecessary measures against philosophical inquiry, but in the process Godwin reiterated the doubts about popular assemblies from *Political justice*. The absence of men of 'eminence' from LCS meetings, according to Godwin, meant that there was no one to 'temper' their excesses. He goes on to imply that Thelwall himself, like an errant magician's nephew, could not direct the spells he was raising. Granting at least that Thelwall always showed 'uncommon purity of intentions', *Considerations* suggests that Thelwall was not able to exercise the control Gurney had recommended to him back in 1794:

> The lecturer ought to have a mind calmed, and, if I may be allowed the expression, consecrated by the mild spirit of philosophy. He ought to come forth with no undisciplined passions, in the first instance; and he ought to have a temper unyielding to the corrupt influence of a noisy and admiring audience.

Once animated, the interest of the crowd – constituted of 'persons not much in the habit of regular thinking' – kindles into enthusiasm, and the infection overwhelms the speaker. Literature requires leisure to consume, and Godwin saw as integral to the reading process a system of regulation lacking from the unreflective sphere of the lecture and other public assemblies:

> Sober inquiry may pass well enough with a man in his closet, or in the domestic tranquility of his own fire-side: but it will not suffice in theatres and halls of assembly. Here men require a due mixture of spices and seasoning. All oratorical seasoning is an appeal to the passions.[64]

There was much here for Thelwall to take offence at, not least because Godwin had attended his lectures at least twice and knew they attracted a mixed audience of curious gentlefolk, Amelia Alderson among them.[65] She shared something of Godwin's view, but better anticipated the response it would meet in radical circles: 'I fear my admiration of them has deprived me in the opinion of many of all claims to the honourable title of Democrat.'[66] Thelwall complained that 'the bitterest of my enemies has never used me so ill as this *friend* has done'.[67]

The sting must have been even sharper because Godwin spoke to a fear Thelwall sometimes acknowledged himself.[68] In his speeches, including the one he made at Copenhagen Fields, Thelwall constantly urged orderliness on his listeners. He conceded in his answer to Godwin that the philosopher-politician had to act with 'a caution bordering on reserve' in case, 'by pouring acceptable truths too suddenly on the popular eye, instead of salutary light he should produce blindness and frenzy'.[69] Thelwall had a complex sense of the irrationality of the mob. Usually, he identified it with popular religious feeling or 'enthusiasm' in the most common eighteenth-century sense of the word. His lectures had pointedly contrasted the principles of the French Revolution with those of seventeenth-century Puritans:

> They had light indeed (inward light) which, though it came not through the optics of reason, produced a considerable ferment in their blood, and made them cry out for that liberty, the very meaning of which they did not comprehend. In fact, the mass of the people were quickened, not by the generous spirit of liberty, but by the active spirit of fanaticism.[70]

No wonder, he was particularly furious that Godwin implicitly compared him with Lord Gordon, whose spectre had haunted the LCS throughout its brief life. Thelwall thought his own materialism was a more rational form of belief, even if he also recognised his own tendency to be overwhelmed by 'social ardor'. Underneath this general anxiety about the mob was also a more particular question about the workings of a democratic culture. Convention politics, as we saw in Part I, necessarily raised the question of how to represent the will of the people, as Thelwall himself put it, 'with the greatest purity'.[71] From at least *Natural and Constitutional Right* onwards, Thelwall showed he understood this issue not just in terms of the articulation of a prior will by the radical orator, but also a necessary process of shaping and mediating the population at large into an understanding of itself as 'the people'. Nevertheless, he remained firm in his belief that the crowd could form itself into a public without the help and assistance of the radical societies and its spokesmen. 'I am a SANS CULOTTE!' he declared,

> one of those who think the happiness of millions of more consequence than the aggrandisement of any party junto! Or, in other words, an advocate for the rights and happiness of those who are languishing in want and nakedness! For this is my interpretation of a sans culotte:- the thing in REALITY which Whigs pretend to be.

The equivocations in this passage are pure Thelwall, shifting between the poles of a British tradition of liberty and the French example, but always insisting that 'the thing in REALITY' would only ever be made manifest by freedom of association and discussion.

Thelwall's faith that this transformation could be managed pushed him to continue his lecturing under various guises until he was beaten into an internal exile.[72] In the letter he wrote to accompany copies of his *Rights of Nature* sent to the divisions at the end of 1796, he had insisted on seeing reading as more than a privatised exercise.[73] His book was to be read *and* discussed within the context of a popular association. Pushed further into exile, when he began an important dialogue with Coleridge and Wordsworth, it would hardly be surprising to see him internalise this pattern, to look within him to a paradise happier far, and abandon the idea of the reader-citizen of the debating societies and lectures. When in February 1801 Thelwall wrote to Thomas Hardy about the imminent publication of his *Poems Chiefly Written in Retirement* (1801), he framed the letter in terms of 'the Age of Paper Circulations'. Developing the pun on the paper currency and print culture, Thelwall told Hardy that he intended to trade 'under the Firm of the Apollo & the Nine Muses' and sought advice 'as to the means of getting as many of notes negociated as possible'. He explained to Hardy that 'having bought a house with my credit', he would 'pay for it with my brain'.

The preface to the published volume presents the poet as the natural man casting the radical aside: 'It is The Man, and not The Politician, that is here presented.' Thelwall seems to accept the very terms used against Merry, associating the man with the poet against the erring radical, explicitly identifying the independent poet and man with the individual property owner. In one sense, the orbit of Thelwall's sympathy had shrunk to an attenuated form of 'paper circulation', cut off from the culture of discussion and debate that he imagined animating the reception of *Rights of Nature*.[74] Within the volume many of the poems also dwell on the sanctity of the family, but not in any simple sense as a domain of authenticity opposed to the political. As Andrew McCann and Judith Thompson have shown, the poems continually advert to the contingencies that have forced Thelwall into retreat. The Two Acts had largely closed down the terrain of reading and debate that framed his most expansive definitions of 'literature'. Moreover, his correspondence with Hardy still implies an active if vestigial network of readers, clustered, perhaps sheltered against the storm, in particular places, certainly, but still imagined as connected to a larger circuit of sympathy.

The networks of readers for the poems were to provide the audiences for the provincial lecture tours Thelwall undertook from 1802, disparaged, with the poetry, by Francis Jeffrey.[75] *Poems written Chiefly in Retirement* may hint at the idea of literature as a distinctive agency of change in itself, bringing about an epiphany of sorts within individual readers familiar from the literature of Romanticism, but this development was never absolute and Thelwall never snapped his baby trumpet of sedition, to use Coleridge's phrase. The first in the series of ten effusions published in *Poems written Chiefly in Retirement* as 'Paternal Tears' was dedicated to Joseph Gerrald, as McCann points out, explicitly linking his private grief to the political relationships of the 1790s. Even when closest to Coleridge, Thelwall seems to have refused the poet's low estimation of Gerrald's moral character.[76] The significance of Thelwall's relationship with Coleridge and Wordsworth has been the subject of much recent debate.[77] It lies beyond the scope of this chapter and of this book, but any account of Thelwall among the poets needs to engage with the complexity of his earlier situation in the LCS. As an orator and writer in the 1790s, Thelwall did not simply act in the name of 'the people', but wrestled with difficult issues of how to create *and* address a 'public' for a democratic culture. Not the least among the issues facing the beleaguered and diverse experiments with democracy undertaken by Thelwall and his colleagues in the radical societies was how to define 'literature' in relation to their aspiration for a culture of reading and debate that would play an active part in defining who 'the people' were.

Notes

Notes to the introduction

1 *Tribune*, 3: 200.

2 The idea of magical thinking is linked to an anthropological tradition that distinguishes 'primitive' from 'rational' thought, for instance, in Lucien Lévy-Bruhls *How Natives Think* (1966). Interestingly in relation to print Bronisław Malinowski's *Magic, Science and Religion* (1954) identified it directly with the idea that words could directly alter the world. My usage acknowledges the persistence of this kind of magical faith at the heart of Enlightenment narratives of progress rather than regarding it as anything to do with 'primitive' societies.

3 See the discussion in IKD, especially 551–603, on the Treasonable Practices Bill, and for a summary of the provisions of the Seditious Meetings Bill, see Goodwin, *The Friends of Liberty*, 887–8.

4 To John Ashley, 19 October 1795, BL, Add MS Place Papers, Papers of the LCS, 27815, ff. 5–6. On connections between the London societies and Scotland, see Harris, 'Scottish-English Connections in British Radicalism'. The letter from Sands is discussed at 203–6.

5 Among canonical literary figures, William Godwin's influence is more to the fore than might be expected, partly because his ideas circulated through Thelwall and his popular lectures.

6 See Chapter 6 for a discussion of these issues in relation to Thelwall.

7 On the 'everyday', see Steedman's *An Everyday Life of the English Working Class*, where the term is used in relation to the stocking-maker Joseph Woolley. Woolley's autobiographical writing pushes against the construction of working-class consciousness in the Thompsonian tradition. In Steedman's eyes, Woolley represents one of those '*who were not as the workers ought to have been*', (7, italics in the original), a reference to Jacques Rancière's *La Nuit des prolétaires* (1981, translated as *Nights of Labour* in 1989). Rancière's workers did not write about their work or class consciousness. They wrote to join the republic of letters via poetry and romantic reveries. My study returns to the familiar Thompsonian ground of London radicalism, but with regard to the way it came to know itself through the everyday practices of print culture.

8 On Robert Thomson's application to the Literary Fund in November 1816, after his return from exile in France, someone has scribbled: 'Son of Robert Thomson, schoolmaster of Banff & Brother of George Thomson Editor of the "Collection of Scotch Songs", the friend & correspondent of Burns.' See BL, Royal Literary Fund, Loan 96 RLF 1/351/1

9 See Newman's 'Moderation in the *Lyrical Ballads*: Wordsworth and the Ballad Debates of the 1790s' forthcoming in *Studies in Romanticism.*

10 See Steedman, *Everyday Life*, especially 7–10.

11 See Wahrman, *Imagining the Middle Class*, especially Part I, and also Penelope Corfield, 'Class by name and number'.

12 See my discussion on page 74.

13 Parr was particularly close to Gerrald. See the detailed account of their relationship in Field, *Memoirs of Parr*, 1: 338–49. In the course of researching his *Parriana*, E. H. Barker wrote to Thelwall, 16 November 1825, asking for details of Gerrald and whether it was true he had written the song 'Remember the Patriots' while awaiting trial. Barker returned the song Thelwall had lent him in a letter to Francis Place, 16 November 1825. See BL, Place Papers, Papers of the LCS, Add MS 27816, ff. 234 and 236. Neither Barker nor Field has anything to say about the relationship with Merry. Hargreaves-Mawdsley, *English Della Cruscans*, 65, notes that Merry 'always spoke of Parr with affection'.

14 *Gentleman's Magazine*, 69 (1799), 54.

15 See the discussion of this phrase page 117.

16 For a very useful recent account of the Scottish context of these traditions, see Honeyman, 'That ye may judge for yourselves'.

17 The description of Reid's origins comes from the obituary in the *Annual Register*, 68 (1826), 253–4. No mention is made of his radicalism there, although his religious leanings – 'he was long bewildered in the labyrinths of mystical divinity' – are raised. His parents were in the employ of the Duke of Hamilton, rumoured to be Reid's father, who had him educated at St James's parochial school. See the letter from 'Crito Sceptic' and James Perry's reply in the *Gazetteer*, 8 January 1787. Haig, *The Gazetteer 1735–1797*, notes that Reid's poetry appeared in the paper regularly for the next six years. Reid had been involved in the Foxite *Rolliad* project before he joined Perry at the *Gazetteer*. After Perry left the paper, Reid provided copy for the new editors William Radcliffe and then D. E. MacDonnell. Various receipts for Reid's work at the *Gazetteer* up to the end of 1794 are at C 104/67 and 104/68 at the National Archive, Kew. On 30 May 1793, the LCS ordered that a thousand copies of a patriotic song composed by Reid should be printed for distribution to the members. See *Selections*, 67. This was probably 'Hum! Hum!' (see figure 1). For further details of his career, see McCalman, 'The Infidel as Prophet' and Haig, *The Gazetteer 1735–1797*, 205–7 and 224–5. 'Anecdotes of W. H. Reid; and his Progress in Poetry', *Gentleman's Magazine*, 58 (1788), 593–4, offers an account of Reid's early life.

18 Reid applied to the Literary Fund for relief in 1802. He confessed in his application that early praise for his poetry misled his 'warm imagination' to

believe he was 'pursuing the track to fame and glory'. In 1806, his name appears in a list of dubious claimants, who 'ought, on any future application, to be referred to a Committee of Enquiry'. Nevertheless he continued to apply to the Fund with success until his death, when his widow also applied. See the full case file at BL, Royal Literary Fund, Loan 96 RLF 1/117.

19 See Mark Philp's chapter, 'The Fragmented Ideology of Reform' in his *Reforming Ideas in Britain.*

20 See Mercier, *Fragments of Politics and History*, 1: 78. Mercier believed: 'The world is governed by books. Why? Because the human race requires knowledge, and because every successful revolution may be ascribed to either letters or philosophy.' See *ibid.*, 1: 126.

21 In this regard, popular radical culture might be regarded as an episode within Siskin and Warner's idea of the Enlightenment as 'an event in mediation'. See Siskin and Warner's 'This is Enlightenment: An Invitation', especially 12–15.

22 See Suarez, 'Towards a Bibliometric Analysis'.

23 'A Short View of the State of Knowledge, Literature, and Taste, in this Country', *New Annual Register for 1781* (1782), xx. Michael Warner quotes from this essay, *Letters of the Republic*, 33, but references it to the American Presbyterian theologian Samuel Miller's *Retrospect of the Eighteenth Century* (1803).

24 See Allan, *A Nation of Readers*, and St Clair, *The Reading Nation*, Chapters 2 and 13 respectively.

25 See the discussion in Chapter 1.

26 On eighteenth-century theories of virtual representation, see Pole, *Political Representation in England* and Cannon, *Parliamentary Reform.*

27 See Warner, 'Transmitting Liberty', 103–4.

28 Theorists who have influenced my thinking on these issues include Lefebvre, *The Production of Space*; de Certeau, *The Practice of Everyday Life*; and Sennet, *The Fall of Public Man.* Epstein, discussed on page 45, has done most to establish the importance of the 'spatial turn' for thinking about popular radicalism. See also Featherstone, 'The Spaces of Politics of the London Corresponding Society', Parolin, *Radical Spaces*, and Newman's excellent articles 'Edmund Burke in the Tavern' and 'Civilizing Taste'.

29 Paine, *Rights of Man*, 182.

30 See Chapter 2.

31 Reeves, 'Report on Sedition, 29 April 1794', National Archive, TSP, TS 11/965, f. 29.

32 Rousseau, *A Treatise of the Social Compact*, 118. See also, *ibid.*, 123: 'The sovereignty, however, cannot be represented, and that for the same reason that it cannot be alienated. It consists essentially of the general will, and the will cannot be represented: it is either identically the same, or some other; there can be no mean term in the case.' I quote from the 1795 translation Eaton published in his Political Classics series.

33 *Ibid.*, 49. The phrase 'general will' was often used by those involved in the radical societies, but rarely with any specific reference to Rousseau's technical sense of the term.

34 See Chapter 6.
35 On the context for Eaton's series, see Chapter 1.
36 Paine, *Rights of Man*, 272. Paine's faith in discussion as the expression of the general will was mocked by loyalists like George Chalmers in his *Life of Thomas Pain*, 91: 'Were the *question* sent to the schoolboys of England, as the *arbitrators*, the *general will* would determine, with much *discussion*, that the foregoing quotations exhibit the most egregious instances of bad grammar and despicable ignorance.' Avoiding any direct address to the question of the sources of the general will, behind this passage is an assumption that only those who had access to good grammar and education could presume to represent it.
37 Cotlar, *Tom Paine's America*, 161. Unusually, using Laclau's ideas, Kevin Inston understands Rousseau's doctrine of unrepresentability as tending towards an open-ended quest for democracy by affirming the impossibility of closure. See Inston, 'Representing the Unrepresentable'.
38 Gilmartin, *Print Politics*, 6–7, and Laclau, *On Populist Reason*, 378.
39 For a valuable account of the influence of Rousseau in the lettered culture of the period, including the issues of transparency and unrepresentability, see Dart, *Rousseau, Robespierre, and English Romanticism.*
40 See Siskin and Warner's discussion of the relationship of their work to Habermas's in this regard, 'This is Enlightenment : An Invitation', 22–3.
41 Gilmartin, *Print Politics*, 3.
42 Coleridge, *The Friend*, no. 10, 19 October 1809; 2: 138.
43 See Warner, *Letters of the Republic*, 42
44 Gilmartin, *Print Politics*, 35.
45 See Goodrich, 'Radical "Citizens of the World"', 613, on radicalism 'from "above" rather than below'.
46 For important contributions to the relations between abolitionism and radicalism, see Walvin's 'The Impact of Slavery on British Radical Politics' and *Making the Black Atlantic.* See also Huzzey, 'Moral Geography', especially, 112–13.
47 Goodrich, 'Radical "Citizens of the World"', 622.
48 P. Linebaugh and M. Rediker, *The Many-Headed Hydra*, 340. Thelwall never let the question of abolition drop in his lectures. Yorke called for the 'total and unqualified emancipation of the Negro slaves'. See Sheffield Society for Constitutional Information, *Meeting, held at Sheffield*, 22.
49 Yorke, *Trial*, 14.
50 Eley, *A Crooked Line*, 10.

Notes to Chapter 1

1 The unenfranchised sections of the population already played a lively and important part in the theatre of politics, but primarily in relation to local issues. Philp notes that claims to innovation in the 1790s rest on the introduction of more abstract and principled forms of political literature to a plebeian audience, but also the development of ways of demythologising aspects of elite

political discourse and the rituals and symbols of inherited authority more generally, *Reforming Ideas*, 31. The LCS offered its members direct involvement as a constituent authority in these processes rather than simply reform in their name.

2 Dickinson, *Liberty and Property*, 271.

3 See Loughlin, 'Constituent Power Subverted', especially, his discussion of 'the invocation of popular sovereignty . . . located only in a parliamentary form', 42. Loughlin understands this as a deliberate strategy to 'conflate the constituent power of the people with that of the constituted authority of the commons'. For a thoughtful exploration of Loughlin's terms in relation to the 1790s, see Green, *The Majesty of the People*.

4 See Thompson, *The Making of the English Working Class*, 12 and 134. Thompson excuses Thomas Hardy from this judgement, 173. See my discussion of Hardy in Chapter 2.

5 See Philp's various comments on assumptions of coherence in *Reforming Ideas*, including, 288, his critique of 'a growing tendency to treat the march of ideas in ways that ascribe an order and coherence to people's thinking and acting that, in my view, does not match what people were saying and doing or how they experienced the world'.

6 Alexander Stephens described meeting David Williams, Major Cartwright, and others at Ridgway's shop after Debrett's closed: 'Such shops in my time have been what certain coffee houses were in the days of the Spectator.' See 'Ridgways' in 'Stephensiana. No. VI', 138. For more on Ridgway, see Manogue, 'The Plight of James Ridgway'. Ridgway's career and its fluctuations, like many other radical booksellers mentioned in this book, would repay a full-length study.

7 Hampsher-Monk, 'On Not Inventing the English Revolution', 148. Hampsher-Monk develops the useful point that radicals often sought 'to operate *on* language' (my emphasis): 'to change that language, either syntactically or in terms of the way it was socially embedded', 149, including the mining of Whig and classical sources by Eaton and others.

8 Among the various commemorations of the Scottish martyrs in the nineteenth century, see *The political martyrs, Thomas Muir, Thomas Fyshe etc* [1837]. Joseph Hume initiated a campaign in 1837 that eventually saw the erection of the monument to the Scottish martyrs that now stands on Carlton Hill. He also campaigned for the second monument in London that stands at Nunhead Cemetery.

9 See Eley, 'Nations, Publics, and Political Cultures', 329. I use 'the town' in line with Habermas's formulation of the 'market of culture products' of the town as one of the constituent elements of the eighteenth-century public sphere. See Jürgen Habermas, *The Structural Transformation of the Public Sphere*, 30. Many of those associated with the LCS had access at least to some aspects of the town via the newspaper, theatres, and print shops (as opposed to the 'ton'). Ian Newman's phrase 'the urban contact zone' usefully describes this sphere. See note 47 below.

10 Brewer, 'Commercialization and Politics', 261, and Wilson, *The Sense of the People*, 212–13.
11 Paine, *Rights of Man*, 272.
12 See Eley, 'Nations, Publics, and Political Cultures', 326. For recent accounts of the pressures exerted on literary culture more generally by Pitt's measures, see Bugg, *Five Long Winters* and Johnston, *Unusual Suspects*.
13 See Goodwin, *Friends of Liberty*, 390.
14 On the state of exception in relation to the situation in the 1790s, see Green, *The Majesty of the People*, especially 175.
15 See Jebb, *An Address to the Freeholders of Middlesex*, 9. A Unitarian minister very active in the reform movement of the 1780s, Jebb seems to have been a particularly important influence on Hardy's thinking. Hardy names Jebb among the authors he had been reading prior to setting up the LCS. See *Selections*, 5. On one of the manuscript versions of Hardy's *Memoir*, given to Sir Francis Burdett, the following epigraph from Jebb appears: 'May ye employ the most active exertions in the service of Man! Human efforts will at best appear feeble; but No Effort is Lost'. See BL, Thomas Hardy, Memoir, Add MS 65153B, f. 3. Thomson's *Tribute to Liberty*, 93, includes a toast to 'the memory of Dr. Jebb and may his maxim *that no effort will be lost*, be the motto of all reformers'.
16 See Barrell and Mee, 8: 105.
17 See the account of these shifts given in Philp in *Reforming Ideas*, 198–206. Paine was also collaborating on the *Argus* at this period. See page 119.
18 On Eaton's career, see Daniel McCue, 'Daniel Isaac Eaton and Politics for the People' and Davis's, 'Behold the Man'.
19 On Spence and Harrington, see Hammersley, 'Spence's *Property in Land*'.
20 *The Politician*, no. 1, 13 December 1794, 1 and 4.
21 Margarot to Thomas Hardy, 1 March 1798, BL, Place Papers, Papers of the LCS, Add MS 27816, f. 112. See also, Roe, 'Maurice Margarot: Radical in Two Hemispheres'.
22 Hardy, 'Introductory letter to a Friend' (1799), BL, Place Papers, Papers of the LCS, Add MS 27817, f. 62.
23 Barrell, *The Spirit of Despotism*, 57.
24 Place, *Autobiography*, 131.
25 The attempts of Whig newspapers like the *Morning Chronicle* to excuse Norfolk's toast were rubbished by *The True Briton* on 1 February: 'In the forty years that this toast is said to have been given, we believe it is the first time it has been given in a studied manner, the object of which evidently was to ridicule our Sovereign.' See also the discussion of the incident in Green, *Majesty of the People*, 17–23. On the SCI dinner of 2 May 1794, see pages 51–2.
26 Lottes, 'Radicalism, Revolution, and Political Culture', 95.
27 Place, *Autobiography*, 131.
28 *Selections*, 114. The incident is discussed in context in Chapter 2. Thelwall and Hodgson seem to have remained on good terms later. At least, Thelwall wrote to ask Hardy to secure a hat from Hodgson in May 1797.

See Thelwall to Hardy, 19 May 1797, University of Notre Dame, Special Collections, MSE/MD 3811/3/ f. 1.

29 Lottes, 'Radicalism, Revolution, and Political Culture', 95.

30 See Davis, 'The Mob Club?' and '"An Evening of Pleasure Rather than Business"'; Epstein, *Radical Expression*; Epstein and Karr, 'Playing at Revolution'; McCalman; *Radical Underworld*, especially, 1–25; Worrall, *Radical Culture*, especially, 9–35.

31 *Report of the Committee to the London Reforming Society*, 16–17.

32 *Ibid.*, 18.

33 See *Selections*, 251, and *Correspondence of the London Corresponding Society*, 24–6.

34 See Chapter 4 on Pigott's planned translation of d'Holbach and other editions in circulation.

35 *Report of the Committee to the London Reforming Society* [3].

36 *Address to the Nation from the London Corresponding Society* (1793). The discussion of the address took place over late June and early July. See *Selections*, 74–5. Thale only provides a brief excerpt from the meeting of 11 July. The minutes are at BL, Place Papers, Papers of the LCS, Add MS 27812, ff. 48–55 (with a later version at 27814, ff. 121–3).

37 A note on the later copy of the minutes identifies Dinmore Junior as the author. See also Hardy's letter to Paine, 15 October 1807, BL, Place Papers Dratt of Letters of Thomas Hardy, Add MS 27818, ff. 72–3. Dinmore was a member of the flourishing radical societies in Norwich, who migrated to the United States later in the 1790s. See Durey, *Transatlantic Radicals*, 212–13. Citizen Lee may have intended to use Dinmore's book for *The Crimes of the Kings and Queens of England* advertised at the end of his American edition of William Winterbotham's *An historical . . . view of the Chinese Empire* (1796). Ridgway and Symonds originally published both Dinmore's and Winterbotham's books in London.

38 Martin was a lawyer and LCS member arraigned for treason in 1794.

39 Both letters are in the National Archive, TSP, TS 11/953.

40 See the Privy Council minutes at the National Archive, Privy Council Papers PC 2/140, f. 58. Hardy's response is discussed in McCue, 'Daniel Isaac Eaton and Politics for the People, 73, and Davis, 'Behold the Man', 173.

41 Philp, *Reforming Ideas*, 294, notes that accounts of Hardy's attachment to the Duke of Richmond's plan tend to underestimate the way 'constitutionalist language was repeatedly accompanied by more universalist claims'. Influenced by his religious beliefs, Hardy assumed, for instance, that anyone interested in abolition must also be concerned in the extension of the franchise. On abolition and the press, see Oldfield, *Popular Politics and British Anti-slavery*, 58–9, 103–4, 131–2, and 137.

42 On abolition and petitioning, see Walvin, 'The Impact of Slavery', 344–5, and Oldfield, *Popular Politics*, 112. Issues about respectability that dogged petitions for reform also caused problems for the abolition petitions of 1788 and 1792.

43 See Habermas, *Structural Transformation of the Public Sphere*, for the classical statement of these ideas.
44 Eley, 'Nations, Publics, and Political Cultures', 306.
45 *Ibid.*, 304 and 305. See his comment on religious traditions, 306.
46 *The Function of Criticism*, 24. The phrase 'counter-public sphere' goes back to Negt and Kluge's *Public Sphere and Experience*, where it is identified with that 'unity of the proletarian context of living', 6, which corresponds in certain regards with my attempt to ground this book in the everyday life of print relations, despite my scepticism about the 'unity' of those relations.
47 I take the phrase 'urban contact zone' from Ian Newman's 'Civilizing Taste', 450. The LCS and its associates can be understood within Michael Warner's broad definition of a counterpublic as 'formed by their conflict with the norms and contexts of their cultural environment, and this context of domination inevitably entails distortion'. See Warner, *Publics and Counterpublics*, 63. My reservations come in relation to definitions that seem to overstate the degree of autonomy of the publics involved. See Nancy Fraser's idea of 'parallel discursive arenas where members of subordinated social groups invent and circulate counterdiscourses to formulate oppositional interpretations of their identities, interests, and needs' in 'Rethinking the Public Sphere', 123. I am indebted to Fraser's thinking about Habermas, but 'parallel discursive arenas' may not be a helpful formulation if strictly taken to imply two lines that do not cross.
48 Parkinson is a fascinating figure who awaits a full discussion in terms of his role in the radical politics of the 1790s. He was close to Eaton and a member of the Physical Society with Thelwall (see Chapter 6). On his medical work, see Critchley, ed., *James Parkinson*.
49 See McCue, 'Daniel Isaac Eaton', 72.
50 See Aldgate Society of the Friends of the People, *A Thing of Shreds and Patches*. This pamphlet, dated March 1793, brings together extracts from various sources, including Burke, Pitt, and others, as resolutions of the society. The notes indicate the ironies in the main text, including the word 'leveller', identified as a principle of despotism. The pamphlet was sold by Parsons and signed S. Godfrey, Lord George Gordon's attorney. The Aldgate Society merged with the LCS soon afterwards, forming division 12, before splitting again to become the British Citizens when the LCS refused to accept Godfrey as their delegate. See Chapter 2, note xx.
51 Warner, *Letters of the Republic*, 3 and 32. Adams originally published his essay in four instalments in the *Boston Gazette*.
52 Quoted, *ibid.*, 1.
53 *Ibid.*, 3.
54 Paine, *Rights of Man*, 159.
55 Price, *How to Do Things with Books in Victorian Britain*, 16.
56 Raven, *The Business of Books*, 132.
57 Place, *Autobiography*, 198.
58 Rose, *The Intellectual Life of the British Working Classes*, 25–6.
59 Raven, *The Business of Books*, 132.

60 Preston, *Life and Opinions*, 35.
61 Buchan, *Essays on the Lives and Writings of Fletcher ... and ... Thomson*, 214–15.
62 *Substance of Earl Stanhope's Speech*, 8.
63 On Stanhope's innovation, which he refused to patent, see Moran, *Printing Presses*, 49–58, and Mosley, 'Technologies of Print', 190. Vincent, *Literacy and Popular Culture*, 201, notes that the low cost of the press meant that it 'extended rather than inhibited the possibilities of small-scale decentralized manufacture', 201. Anyone with around £30 and access to a room could set up a press. Many members of the LCS were printers.
64 Warner, *Letters of the Republic*, 3.
65 Thelwall, *The Tribune*, 3: 265. See the discussion in Fairclough, *Romantic Crowd*, 116.
66 See the discussion of Burke's trope in *ibid.*, 73–4. On 'transmission' as opposed to 'communication', see my introduction,
67 See Chapter 6 for a detailed account.
68 Thelwall, *Political Lectures, (no. II.) Sketches of the history of prosecutions for political opinion*, 10–11 and 29.
69 BL, Thomas Handy, Memoir, Add MS 65153B, f. 28v.
70 BL, Place Papers, Papers of the LCS, Add MS 27815, f. 142.
71 Antitype, *Pernicious Effects of the Art of Printing*, 1.
72 Compare Kevin Gilmartin's account of radicals after 1815: 'confidence in a free press became a frankly polemical position directed against the government's confidence in press restrictions, and its use of print as an instrument for resisting social change', *Print Politics*, 25.
73 Gilmartin, *Print Politics*, 26
74 See, for instance, examples discussed in Kropf, 'Libel and Satire' and Harling, 'The Law of Libel and the Limits of Repression', on the cumbersome and inefficient nature of the libel laws as a means of repression.
75 Eaton published 'King Chaunticlere; or, The Fate of Tyranny' in *Politics for the People*, no. 8, on 16 November 1793, 1: 102–7. The published article traced the allegory to a debate on the question of 'the comparative Influence of the Love of Life, of Liberty, and of the fair Sex'. Compare the later account at LT, 110, where Eaton is said to have 'dress[ed] it up in certainly very strong terms which Thelwall would never have used'.
76 Barrell and Mee, 1: 291–2.
77 The poem was published on the title page of *Politics for the People*, no. 5, 26 October 1793.
78 *Pig's Meat*, 2: 14.
79 Fairclough, *Romantic Crowd*, 191. See also Whyman, *Pen and the People*, 58–61, on the difference made by John Palmer's reforms of the 1780s, not least in creating the idea of a uniform, time-governed system that linked the nation.
80 Powell's letter is at the National Archive, Privy Council Papers, PC 1 23/38a. *Selections*, 256, notes that Powell lived near Godwin in Somers Town. The two

seem to have socialised, perhaps prior to Powell's involvement in radical politics. Powell published *The Narcotic and Private Theatricals* (1793), with H. D. Symonds, a publisher closely associated with the radical movement. For a fuller discussion of Powell's later career in the theatre, see Worrall, *Theatric Revolution*, 280–99. Powell wrote the story 'Such Things Are' for the LCS's MPM.

81 Godwin, *Enquiry concerning political justice*, I: 21.

82 BL, Place Papers, Collections relating to Political Societies, Add MS 27808, f. 93. Place described Powell as 'a man whose relatives were gentlefolks, well informed respectable people, but he was an only son, had been indulged and spoilt', *Autobiography*, 179. Place seems not to have realised Powell was a spy. Nor did Thelwall. He put down the information Powell passed to the Privy Council in 1794 to 'either . . . flurry and agitation, on his own account, or from unguarded simplicity', LT, 248. Thelwall had known Powell from at least 1792.

83 Edward Henry Iliff, also present at the January meeting, was an actor, who in 1796 published *Angelo*, a novel, dedicated to Godwin's sometime sponsor, the notorious financier John 'Jew' King. Godwin and Iliff seem first to have met in September 1794 at a meeting of the Philomath Debating Society. Thelwall and others associated with the LCS were members of the same society. See O'Shaughnessy, '*Caleb Williams* and the Philomaths' on the membership. On Godwin and Iliff, see the online Godwin diary for 30 September. They also met on 3 October. Correspondence between Godwin and Iliff survives from early 1796, when the latter was asking for help with his writing. See *The Letters of William Godwin*, I: 161–3. At the foot of one of his letters to Godwin, 163, Iliff included 'Powel' and 'King' in a string of names whose import the philosopher could not make out. For Godwin and King, see Scrivener, 'The Philosopher and the Moneylender.' King helped finance the *Argus*. See Chapter 2 for further discussion of Iliff.

84 Place, *Autobiography*, 179.

85 Epstein, 'Spatial Practices/Democratic Vistas', 294 and 297.

86 Jones, *Sketch of a political tour*, 5, 26–7, 56–7.

87 Epstein, '"Equality and No King": Sociability and Sedition', 43.

88 See Munro's report, 14 November 1792, in *Selections*, 27.

89 Groves report, 12 June 1794, *Selections*, 184. Groves was a solicitor.

90 Barrell, *Spirit of Despotism*, 16–74.

91 Davis, 'The Mob Club?' For Hardy's account of the Bell, see *Memoir*, 44.

92 See Newman's 'Edmund Burke in the Tavern'.

93 'Davis, 'The Mob Club?', 26–7.

94 See McCalman's 'Newgate in Revolution' for a full account of the prison as a radical hub. Godwin's diary contains numerous references to dinners and meetings in Newgate, especially in 1794. On the longer history of Newgate prison as a radical space, see Parolin, *Radical Spaces*, 17–48.

95 The phrase appears in a message of thanks from division 18 to the central committee, 9 July 1795, *Selections*, 261.

96 [David Turner], *A Short History of the Westminster Forum*. I: 20.

97 *Ibid.*, 2: 90.

98 See Epstein, '"Equality and No King"', and Barrell, *Spirit of Despotism*, 75–9 and 83–6.

99 See National Archive, TSP, TS 11/959 for Munro's report. The day before Frost's trial, the government decided not to use his testimony in court to protect the identity of their spy. See the National Archive, Home Office Papers, HO 48/3.

100 Barrell and Mee, 1: 236–7, 239, and 246.

101 Barrell, *Spirit of Despotism*, 85.

102 *A Speech at the Whig Club*, 7–8. Ridgway published it as *The speech of the Right Hon. Charles James Fox* (1792). Fox's allies denied that he had given the sentiments ascribed to him in the Ridgway version. *A Speech at the Whig Club* reproduces the correspondence and another poem – 'An Answer to the Above Letters' – mocking Fox's defenders Andrew St John and Robert Adair. Ridgway's third edition of the speech contained an address insisting on the veracity of the text. The back page advertised *The Last Declaration of the London Corresponding Society of the Friends of the People in Answer to the Place and Pension Society* (1792). This would seem to be the *Address of the London Corresponding Society to the other societies of Great Britain, united for obtaining a reform in Parliament* (1792).

103 In its hostile report, *The Times*, 15 July, complained that the chairman did not give 'the King', but 'The Nation, the Law, and the King'. The same report describes Merry 'obliged to sit patiently to hear his MUSE of FIRE so miserably murdered'. The next day, *The Times* revised its account to claim he dined quietly with Horne Tooke and Seward, afterwards joined by Paine. *Letters on the Present State of England and America*, 87, mentions a burst of applause at the rumour Paine had entered the dinner room. Godwin's diary entry for the dinner begins: 'Crown & Anchor: Rous & Merry: B. Hollis, Shore, Barbauld, Disney, Jennings, Rees, Morgan, Lindsey, Lewis. Fawcet sups'. Possibly both Merry and Paine appeared at the meeting, but did not stay to dine. Violence from a loyalist mob was widely feared. The presence of a crowd assembled outside Newgate planning to break out Lord Gordon was also generally reported. See, for instance, *Letters on the Present State of England and America*, 90–1, which reports both.

104 Guest, *Unbounded Attachment*, 45.

105 Merry, *Ode for the fourteenth of July*, 6–7. See Chapter 3 on the circulation of the ode in anthologies and elsewhere.

106 Guest, *Unbounded Attachment*, 46.

107 [William Fitzgerald], *The Sturdy Reformer*, 7. Fitzgerald seems to have been concerned that his poem was not being properly understood and reissued a second edition making his warnings against 'Wolves in Sheep's clothing' like Paine and Horne Tooke much more explicit. See Guest, *Unbounded Attachment*, 48.

108 Merry first attends a committee meeting of the Literary Fund on 18 May 1790. Fitzgerald first attends on 4 March 1791. Merry was not at Fitzgerald's

first meeting, but they are both in attendance at the next one (1 April 1791), when both were appointed to a committee to look at the staging of a benefit play at Covent Garden. Fitzgerald and Merry were both re-elected to the general committee (4 May 1792), but neither is listed as present at that meeting. For details, see BL, Royal Literary Fund, Loan 96 RLF 2/1/1. Fitzgerald later made a reputation – parodied by Byron – as a songwriter for Literary Fund events.

109 See the account of the dinner in Goodwin, *Friends of Liberty*, 329–31, and the brief excerpt from Groves, *Selections*, 153.

110 National Archive, TSP, TS 11/963, ff. 256–7. Wharton agree with the Privy Counsellors that it was 'dangerous' to 'give such toasts to such persons', implying that the latitude allowed to convivial political dinners among gentlemen could not be extended to other classes. Barrell notes, IKD, 207n, that Wharton's speech in Parliament in May 1793 on the erosion of the constitutional safeguards had become a canonical text of the reform movement, published by the LCS as *The Speech of John Wharton* (1793). The spy John Taylor claimed that Wharton gave the toasts: 'The Rights of Man' and 'May the Abettors of the present war be its victims'. *Ibid.*, 141–3.

111 National Archive, TSP, TS 11/963, f. 586.

112 See *The Toast Master* (1792), 'Advertisement' and viii; *Pocock's Everlasting Songster* (1800), ii. *The Toast Master* had been through at least two editions before 1792.

113 LT, 76 and 351, and 353–4.

114 See Clark, *Struggle for the Breeches*, especially Chapter 8, and Elaine Chalus's discussion of the more sharply drawn dividing lines towards the end of the century in *Elite Women in English Political Life*, 228–30.

115 Guest, *Unbounded Attachment*, 145.

116 Barbauld, *Civic sermons*, 22.

117 Thelwall, *Natural and Constitutional right*, 79.

118 Wagner, 'Domestic Invasions', 101.

119 Tribune, 2: xv.

120 Susan Thelwall's letter is at National Archive, TSP, TS 11/953. See TS 11/956 for Walsh's report. Thale describes it as 'the only first hand account of a debate between 1790 and 1795', 'London Debating Societies', 64–5. Susan Thelwall's letter provides a further source confirming most of the details provided by Walsh.

121 See 'London Debating Societies', 131 and 135.

122 See Thale, 'Women in London Debating Societies', n. 71, and Andrew, 'Popular Culture and Public Debate', for further information on women at the debating societies.

123 Susan Thelwall also complained that a successful play at Covent Garden had stolen from her husband's writing 'almost all the Characters, & many of the sentiments'. The play was Thomas Morton's *Columbus: or, a world discovered* (1792). Susan Thelwall noted that her husband had been served in this same way with *Incle and Yarico*. For a discussion of Thelwall's plays and doubts about the plagiarism claim, see *'Incle and Yarico' and 'The Incas'*, ed. Felsenstein and Scrivener, 14.

124 The second Susan Thelwall letter is at National Archive, TSP, TS 11/956. The letter must have been written soon after 6 March as it mentions the death of the Earl of Barrymore who died in a gun accident that day. The dinner of the Friends of the Press was held on 9 March. See Werkmeister, *Newspaper History of England, 1792–1793*, 237.

125 See Lee, *On the death of Mrs. Hardy* (1794), 3. When this poem came out, Lee was not yet a bookseller. The poem was sold by the radical partnership of Burks and Smith, both LCS members.

126 See Clark, *Battle for the Breeches*, 150, on 'plebeian men' defining themselves 'as husbands and citizens by depicting women as passive and helpless'.

127 *An account of the seizure of Thomas Hardy*, 1.

128 Jones, *Sketch of a political tour*, 28.

129 *An account of the seizure of Thomas Hardy*, 8

130 National Archive, TSP, TS 11/963, f. 288. Hillier was released from custody after Thelwall was acquitted. A former tallow-chandler, he had taken over Eaton's shop in Bishopsgate when he moved to Newgate Street in 1793. See Gosling's spy report, National Archive, TSP, TS 11/954.

131 Amelia Alderson to Mrs Taylor [1794], New York Public Library (NYPL). I owe my knowledge of this incident to Roxanne Eberle and Harriet Guest. Alderson's letter is partly reproduced in Brightwell, *Memorials*, 41–5. I am extremely grateful to Roxanne Eberle for generously sharing her transcription with me and to the NYPL for providing me with scans of the original.

132 According to Alderson's letter, Sinclair had 'rejoiced to learn from Merry, that Mrs. Merry, was so firm & a great deal more, that raised my curiosity to a most painful height'. Sinclair was suspected of informing after his trial was abandoned. See IKD, 157, for details.

133 That is not to imply that women did not run their own bookshops in the period. Martha Gurney, who published many of the editions of state trials, ran a bookshop at Holborn Hill. Gurney was a Baptist and an abolitionist. Her brother was Joseph Gurney, the leading court stenographer of the day. John Gurney, defence attorney for Eaton, who also advised Thelwall on his lectures, was her nephew. See Whelan, 'William Fox, Martha Gurney, and Radical Discourse'.

134 Alderson to William Godwin, 5 February [1796], MS Abinger c. 3, ff. 16–17, Bodleian Library. See the excellent discussion of this letter in Guest, *Unbounded Attachment*, 125–6. Confusion of the name MacDonnell and MacDonald is discussed in Haig, *The Gazetteer*, 232.

135 See Guest, *Unbounded Attachment*, especially, 126.

136 Chernock, *Men and the Making of Modern British Feminism*, 22, and Jones, *Sketch of a political tour*, 91. Chernock identifies William Hodgson, William Frend, and Spence as other LCS members who supported female suffrage.

137 See *Selections*, 80.

138 *Account of the proceedings of a meeting of the London Corresponding Society*, 4, 5 and 8.

139 *Ibid.*, 16
140 *Proposals for Publishing by Subscription ... the Female Citizen.* There is no sign that Hodgson's pamphlet was ever published.

Notes to Chapter 2

1 'An Essay on Man', AUM 2 (1797), 101–3. The essay is taken from the English translation of Mercier's *Fragments of Politics and History*, 1: 8–12.
2 Cotlar, *Tom Paine's America*, 8.
3 Paine, *Rights of Man*, 161.
4 See, especially, Scrivener, *Seditious Allegories*, Thompson, *John Thelwall in the Wordsworth Circle*, Solomonescu, *John Thelwall and the Materialist Imagination*, and the essays in Poole, ed., *John Thelwall.*
5 First published in *Past and Present* in 1994, Thompson's essay is now a chapter in his *The Romantics*, 156–203. Scrivener described Thelwall as 'an organic intellectual for the educated artisans and "middling classes"' in 'Rhetoric and Context', 115–16. See also Green, *Majesty of the People*, 56–7.
6 Place annotated Hardy's 'A History of the Origin and Progress of the London Corresponding Society', BL, Place Papers, Papers of the LCS, Add MS 27814 with the description, f. 8.
7 Thompson, *Making of the English Working Class*, 173. Thompson quotes Binns, 134.
8 Several 'Crispin' letters to the *Monthly Magazine* and other details mentioned in this sentence are to be found in Hardy's correspondence in BL, Place Papers, Draft Letters of Thomas Hardy, Add MS 27818. See also the discussion of Robert Thomson's return from France, on page 79. When Margarot returned from Botany Bay in 1810, he also turned to Hardy for help. Hardy had defended Margarot's reputation against those who thought he had acted as an informer against Muir and others on the voyage to Botany Bay. He attended Margarot's funeral on 19 November 1815 with Walne, Baxter and a few other old LCS associates. See BL, Place Papers, Papers of the LCS, Add MS 27816 for details and Roe, 'Maurice Margarot', 75–7. Hardy played an important role in disseminating Thelwall's literary works after they had both left the LCS. See, for instance, the communications with Hardy in BL, Place Papers, Papers of the LCS, Add MS 27817 ff. 87–8 and Draft Letters of Thomas Hardy, Add MS 27818 f. 15. See also Thelwall to Hardy, 28 February 1801, in the manuscript collection of the Wordsworth Trust asking for help with subscriptions for *Poems Written Chiefly in Retirement.*
9 Gagnier's *Subjectivities*, 160–1, discusses Hardy's *Memoir* as a template for nineteenth-century working-class autobiographies.
10 See the correspondence between Hardy and Collier, 8 September 1802, BL, Place Papers, Papers of the LCS, Add MS 27817 ff. 91–2, and 8 June 1807, Draft Letters of Thomas Hardy, Add MS 27818 f. 70. The first suggests Hardy had originally sent the manuscript to Collier as early as 1799. Thelwall asks Hardy to remember him to Collier in their correspondence. See Thelwall to Hardy,

25 October 1797, University of Notre Dame, MSE/MD 3811/4, f. 3. The idea of a history of the LCS itself passed as a project to Francis Place, whom it also defeated. There is still no history of the LCS.

11 Hardy to the Secretary, 27 August 1806, BL, Place Papers, Draft Letters of Thomas Hardy, Add MS 27818, f. 60.

12 The phrase 'public conversation' recurs in Turner's *Short History of the Westminster Forum*. See, for instance, 2: 131 and 216.

13 Clark, *British Clubs and Societies*, 119.

14 LT, 39–50. In February 1784 the Society debated the fate of the coalition and the Pitt ministry that succeeded it, including (19 February 1784): 'Does not a Minister, who keeps his place without the confidence of the House of Commons, deserve the public censure of the people?' See *London Debating Societies*, 158. Pitt had been defeated in the House, but refused to resign. When the election came on in March, he won by a massive majority.

15 'Harum Skarum', *Account of a Debate*, 2. For details of the petition, see Knights, 'The 1780 Protestant Petitions'. On Gordon's influence, see McCalman, 'Prophesying Revolution' and notes 17 and 72 below.

16 Hardy, *Memoir*, 8.

17 The central committee refused to accept Samuel Godfrey, Gordon's attorney, and his secretary, Robert Watson, as delegates. See *Selections*, 22–3 and 50–1n. Watson remained a member of the LCS. He was arrested for his involvement in the Crimp riots in the summer of 1794. See *Selections*, 211–12. Watson wrote a life of Gordon, published by Eaton and Symonds in 1795, which describes his employer's 'correspondence with societies and individuals, entertaining the same views, in the surrounding nations; and by mutual interchanges of publications, free thoughts, and essays upon the civil and religious settlements of various governments, and the general candour and inquiry after truth, which prevails among the people, he had been made acquainted with the sentiments of many virtuous Revolutionists of every denomination'. See Watson, *The Life of . . . Gordon*, 88. Charles Pigott also seems to have known Gordon, but joined the LCS only after the nobleman's death. See Chapter 4.

18 Hardy, *Memoir*, 8.

19 BL, Papers of the LCS, Add MS 27814, f. 24.

20 *Ibid.*, Add MS 27811, f. 3. For the published version of the paragraph, see *The London Corresponding Society. Addresses and Resolutions (reprinted)* (1792), 8.

21 Letter to T. Newell, 15 February 1792, BL, Papers of the LCS, Add MS 27811, f. 4.

22 Cotlar, *Tom Paine's America*, 8.

23 See Anderson, *Imagined Communities*, especially 35–6.

24 Barrell and Mee, 5: 222. The idea of radicalism as 'enthusiasm dangerous in the highest degree' was introduced by the Solicitor-General John Mitford, 221, and then mentioned again by Chief Justice James Eyre in his summing up, 441. Eyre was the son of a Church of England clergyman.

25 See Barrell and Mee 4: 43. Lynam mentions the attempt to exclude Watson because of the association with Gordon.

26 For the examination of Steven, see Barrell and Mee, 4: 349–51. Of the other character witnesses, Rev. Thomas Oliver was a dissenting minister, 336. The majority of the other witnesses were Scots: John Carr, 347, was sworn using the forms of the Church of Scotland, so too were William Henderson, a dealer in eggs, 349; the shoemaker Peter Macbean, 350, a former LCS member; and the carpenter John Bogue, 355. Matthew Dickey, 356, described himself as 'a Scotch factor'. Judging by their names, Alexander Gordon, a shoemaker, 354, James Hardy, no relation, and Alexander Gregg, 348, may also all have been part of the London Scots community and members of Steven's congregation.

27 See Hardy, *Memoir*, 4–5. For a brief account of Crown Court, see Wilson, *History and Antiquities of Dissenting Churches*, 4: 3–10.

28 Cruden, *Sermons on evangelical and practical subjects*, 85–6.

29 See Jones, '"In Favour of Popery"' and also Seed, '"The Fall of Romish Babylon anticipated"'.

30 See Durey, 'William Winterbotham's Trumpet of Sedition', 147. Durey suggests that Winterbotham had adopted a more tolerant position on religious difference by 1793–4 than he had in 1780. He seems to have turned to a literary career in Newgate, publishing a history of the Chinese empire with his fellow inmates Ridgway and Symonds. See Chapter 1, n. 37.

31 Often the petition was signed by congregation, see Seed, '"The Fall of Romish Babylon"', 77. The original petition is lost, but the name 'Thomas Hardy' appears on the copy at National Archive, TSP, TS 11/389, f. 175, next to 'William McMaster'. National Archive, Privy Council Papers, RG 4/4232 records the birth of a Janet McMaster to William and Janet McMaster of Bewick Street, Soho, baptised by Rev. James Steven, 11 June 1796. On the same page of the petition as Hardy and McMaster, there is also 'Alexander Gordon', who may be the character witness of that name who appeared at Hardy's trial.

32 BL, Thomas Hardy, Memoir Add MS 65153A, f. 7. Annotated 'leave this out' after the word 'kindle'.

33 See *Memoir*, 7. The incident presumably happened in the tense interlude between Cruden's death and the Steven's appointment.

34 *Divine Warrants, Ends, Advantages, and Rules*, 10. Among the other names given at the end of the pamphlet is John Stevenson of Little New-Street Shoe Lane, possibly the coal merchant who appeared as a character witness for Hardy at his trial.

35 For Daniel Turner's letter to Thompson see Essex County Records Office D/DQS 26. Thompson's response can be found in, 'A state of the Dissenting Interest in the several Counties of England & Wales', Dr, Williams Library, London, MS38.6. I am grateful to John Seed for these references.

36 See the accounts of these campaigns in Bradley, *Religion, Revolution, and English Radicalism.*

37 To John Evans, 14 March 1803, BL, Draft Letters of Thomas Hardy, Add MS 27818, ff. 47–8. Two Bogue pamphlets published by Dilly were *The Great Importance of having Right Sentiments in Religion* (1788) and *Reasons for Seeking a Repeal of the Corporation and Test Acts* (1790).

38 See ODNB and the records in the very helpful Dissenting Academy database: http://dissacad.english.qmul.ac.uk/new_dissacad/phpfiles/sample1.php?parameter=personretrieve&alpha=1749#tabs-6, accessed March 2014, although none of these sources mentions the association with Hardy.

39 Steven's portrait follows on closely after Bogue's in the second volume of the *Evangelical Magazine*, 2 (1794), 31–3. Steven held one of the Missionary Society's prayer meetings in Crown Court in early January 1799. See *Evangelical Magazine*, 7 (1799), 557. Steven's surname is sometimes spelt Stevens or Stephens in the magazine.

40 Hardy to Walter Wilson, 5 December 1809, BL, Draft Letters of Thomas Hardy, Add MS 27818, f. 106. Bogue ministered in London as assistant to Willliam Smith at the Independent Chapel in Silver Street from 1774 to 1777. See Wilson, *History*, 3: 114–15.

41 *The French Revolution foreseen, in 1639* (1796?) comprised extracts from the seventeenth-century divine Thomas Goodwin. See also *Thoughts on the Necessity and Means of a Reform in the Church of England* published by Johnson and Dilly in 1792.

42 On 5 November 1794, National Archive, TSP TS 11/966, Mr Arnaud wrote to the Treasury Solicitor alarmed to read in an account of Hardy's trial that there was a society called 'The Friends of the People' in Portsmouth. He called a meeting of his local loyalist association to consult on the best way to track it down. His postscript claims that Hardy had stayed at Bogue's house when they visited the ship.

43 Hardy, *Memoir*, 54.

44 Barrell and Mee, 4: 340. Oliver said that Hardy had mentioned Bogue's name but could not confirm anything about their visiting a 'convict ship'.

45 Hardy to Bogue, 2 June 1792, BL, Papers of the LCS, Add MS 27811, f. 13.

46 Hardy to Rev. Mr Mills, 24 July 1792. *Ibid.*, f. 15. Mills seems to have been associated with the Portsmouth Society for Reform, possibly the group mentioned in Arnaud's letter.

47 National Archive TSP, TS 24/12/1. Equiano lived in Hardy's house while he prepared the fifth edition of his interesting narrative. See Hardy's *Memoir*, 15; also Walvin, *An African's Life*, 162–3.

48 BL, Place Papers, Papers of the LCS, Add MS 27811, f. 4. Hardy's *Memoir*, 14–16, reproduces the letter to Bryant, describing it as 'the first correspondence of the society'.

49 Oldfield, *Popular Politics and British Anti-slavery* discusses Equiano in this context, 125–6, briefly mentioning Hardy's role.

50 See Linebaugh and Rediker. *The Many-Headed Hydra*, 339–40, and Bugg, 'The Other Interesting Narrative', 1433–4.

51 'Equiano to Thomas Hardy', 28 May 1792, National Archive, TSP, TS 24/12.

52 See, Weinstein's claim, 'Popular Constitutionalism', 46, that Hardy's attachment to the Duke of Richmond's plan 'did much to confine the LCS to a conservative and oddly aristocratic vision of reform', and Philp's reply, 294,

that this underestimates the ways 'in which constitutionalist language was repeatedly accompanied by more universalist claims'.

53 Lee, *Songs from the rock*, 107–12. See Chapter 5 for a fuller account of the collection.

54 Hardy to Bogue, 23 March 1793, BL, Place Papers, Papers of the LCS, Add MS 27811.

55 Warner, *Letters of the Republic*, 2–3.

56 BL, Place Papers, Papers of the LCS, Add MS 27814, f. 30v.

57 *Ibid.*, f. 31. James Bennett was David Bogue's student at Gosport from 1793. *Sacred Politics* was almost certainly written there. The two men later collaborated on the four-volume *History of the Dissenters* (1808–12). Bennett gave Bogue's funeral oration, published as *The Translation of Elijah* (1825)

58 See *Sacred Politics*, 2nd edn, 33.

59 Horne, *Three letters*, iii.

60 BL, Place Papers, Papers of the LCS, Add MS 27811, f. 9.

61 Hardy to Lord Daer, BL, Place Papers, Papers of the LCS, Add MS 27811, f. 15. Daer was educated at the Barbaulds' school in Suffolk, and later at Edinburgh University under Dugald Stewart. He travelled to Paris in 1789, and returned an enthusiast for the French Revolution. Though a strong critic of the union, Daer called for English and Scottish radical societies to work together: 'relieving you of that vermin from this country who infect your court, parliament and every establishment' (Daer to Charles Grey, 18 January 1793, quoted in Bewley, *Muir of Huntershill*, 55). Daer died of tuberculosis on 5 November 1794. See also Harris, 'Scottish-English Connections', 196–7.

62 Originally described as a meeting of Friends to a Parliamentary Reform, minutes and other details of the society are transcribed in BL, Place Papers, Papers of the LCS, Add MS 27817 ff. 22–6v. Several LCS and SCI members participated, including Cartwright, Daer, Hawes, and Thelwall.

63 BL, Place Papers, Papers of the LCS, Add MS, 27814, f. 36.

64 *Ibid.*, ff. 29–30. See also Gilmartin, *Print Politics*, 34, on the 'set of redefinitions of independence that severed its classical republican links with property, especially landed property, while preserving its empowering consequences for (male) political participation and public personality'.

65 See Hardy, *Memoir*, 17. A copy of the handbill is at 648 c. 26 (4) in the British Library, London; *London Corresponding Society, held at the Bell, Exeter Street* [Resolutions on the representation of the people in Parliament etc. Dated 2 April 1792.]

66 BL, Place Papers, Papers of the LCS, Add MS 27814 f. 30.

67 See Gagnier, *Subjectivities*, 161–2.

68 On the SCI and the dissemination of *Rights of Man*, and the rifts it caused within the SCI, see Keane, *Tom Paine*, 329–30.

69 BL, Place Papers, Papers of the LCS, Add MS 27814, f. 34.

70 *Ibid.*, f. 36.

71 See, for instance, the accounts given of both societies in Goodwin, *Friends of Liberty*.

72 In his evidence at Hardy's trial, Lynam discusses the central committee's rejection of Samuel Godfrey as delegate because of his association with Lord Gordon, who it was felt was using the attorney to exercise influence in the society. Godfrey signs *A Thing of Shreds and Patches*, dated March 1793, as Secretary of the Aldgate Society. Soon after his discussion of Godfrey, Lynam notes 'The Aldgate Society is now called the Bother'em Society – that Society is since broke up': Barrell and Mee, 4: 43–4. Later he notes it had been reported to the LCS that the society had thanked Mr Fox for his speech, 'saying that the People may alter the Constitution without giving their reasons for it – that is the Society that were got together, and called the Bother'em Society'. The thanks to Fox is recorded in *A Thing of Shreds and Patches*, 15–16. The same group protested at Godfrey's treatment in a letter to the general committee from the British Citizens, dated 13 March. Lynam's reported numbers increased to fifty attending the next day's general committee meeting at Godfrey's; see *Selections*, 56–7. Lynam noted on 14 February: 'the Friends of the People in the Borough yet exist; and it was determined to communicate to them and all other Societies, and enquire their intentions'. It appears the Borough Society refused to go as far politically as the LCS (*Selections*, 50). Lynam claimed that the Holborn Society were 'for republicanism', and later merged with the LCS. See Barrell and Mee, *Trials*, 4: 44.

73 See Dybikowski, *On Burning Ground*, 239. On Jardine, see Rendall, '"Political Reveries"'. See the first minute book of the society at BL, Royal Literary Fund, Loan 96 RLF 2/1/1. Merry and David Williams were given the task of preparing the constitution of the Fund on 1 June 1790, f. 4.

74 [John Gifford], 'The Literary Fund', *AntiJacobin Review and Magazine*, 3 (1799), 100–1. The society resolved to ask Merry to invite the Duke of Leeds at its meeting of 4 February 1791, BL, Royal Literary Fund, RLF 2/1/1, f. 9. At the same meeting, Merry and Captain Edward Topham were asked to approach the managements of Covent Garden and Drury Lane about staging a benefit. BL, Royal Literary Fund RLF 5/4/2 is a letter from Merry saying he had not been able to obtain an answer from Leeds about the presidency. Merry had excused the Duke, patron of the Philanthropic Society, from his general critique of the 'unmeaning Insects' of aristocratic privilege in *The Laurel of Liberty* (1790), 12.

75 See the SCI minutes at National Archive, TSP, TS 11/962. At this meeting, Horne Tooke proposed Joseph Gerrald as a member.

76 See Erdman, *Commerce des Lumières*, 242, and Rogers, 'Vectors of Revolution', 168–74.

77 Roland, 'Private Memoirs' in *An appeal to impartial posterity*, 42.

78 See Dybikowski, *On Burning Ground*, 161 and 208–9. On his visit to the National Assembly, Roland described Williams as 'uneasy at the disorder of the debates, afflicted at the influence exercised by the galleries'. See Roland, 'Private Memoirs', 42.

79 *Literary Fund* (1795), 29.

80 See the comparative discussion of their proposals in Rogers, 'Vectors of Revolution'.

81 *Literary Fund* (1795), 29. Williams was no mean satirist himself. See, for instance, his very popular *Royal Recollections on a Tour to Cheltenham* (1788). For a discussion of this aspect of Williams's writing, see Jones, *David Williams*, 67–9, 96–100, 111, and 191.

82 Williams to Brissot, 24 May 1792, quoted in Dybikowski, *On Burning Ground*, 210.

83 See the discussion, for instance, in *Letters on political liberty*, 3rd edn, 77–8. Gerrald acknowledges the influence of this volume in *A Convention the Only Means of Saving us*, 90. On Williams as a theorist of conventions, see Dybikowski, *On Burning Ground*, 175–9, largely drawing on his proposals for the French constitution, discussed more fully in context by Rogers, 'Vectors of Revolution', 278–93.

84 Williams, *Lessons to a young prince*, 82.

85 Dybikowski's appendix B provides a useful summary of the different circles in which Williams participated, including 'The Club of Thirteen'.

86 Lord Rawdon was invited to take the chair for the first dinner at the Crown and Anchor, but in the event Sir Joseph Andrews presided. See BL, Royal Literary Fund, RLF 4/1/1. The toast list for the 1795 dinner is at RLF 4/1/3. The list for 1800 is at 4/1/8.

87 *Selections*, 9, 19, and 20. A marginal note to the later copy of the minutes at BL, Place Papers, Papers of the LCS, Add MS 27814 f. 96 identifies 'God Save the Rights of Man' as the song and Thomson as its author. Thomson appeared in the place of Andrew Murray, who had deserted.

88 'History of the Society', MPM (1796)1: 221.

89 Hardy was still recommending Thomson's radical songs as late as 1826. He wrote to John Elstee of Chigwell: 'I hope you will have the goodness to excuse me for detaining for so long from you *The Tribute of Liberty*, that excellent collection of patriotic songs by the late *Robert Thomson*. It was not neglect, but for want of an opportunity to convey them to you. I often thought of it ... You then told me that you intended to publish a new edition of the songs. If you put your intention into execution, I hope you will not omit his excellent preface to the songs, and favour me with a copy, which by doing so you will much oblige.' See BL, Draft Letters of Thomas Hardy, Add MS 27818, f. 604.

90 See Thomson, *The Divine Authority of the Bible* (1801). Note that the book distinguishes Christianity from 'priestcraft', 11, and avoids repudiating Paine's political principles, 28. The pamphlet takes the view that 'the English government, I think, ought not to prosecute a work against religion, however forcible its arguments may appear – nay, the stronger the better for christianity will ever gain by discussion', 134. The tone and manner of Thomson's reply was regarded as just as rough as Paine's by the *Critical Review*, 33 (1802) 97–8. *Monthly Review*, 38 (1802), 435–6, noted that 'in their hatred of priests they are perfectly agreed', 436. Thomson noted that *Divine Authority* was positively reviewed in the *Church Orthodox Magazine* in his first application to the Literary Fund. Thomson's former LCS colleague, W. H. Reid, was editor of

the magazine at the time of the review, as Reid's own 1802 application to the Fund reveals. For Thomson's application see BL, Royal Literary Fund, RLF 1/35/1. Reid's first application to the Fund mentions the editorship at RLF 1/117/1.

91 Later applications garnered support from William Frend, Thomas Hardy and Robert Watson, who claimed to have suggested the idea of the epic poem on William Wallace that Thomson was working on at his death. See BL, Royal Literary Fund, RLF 1/351/3, 5 and 6.

92 *Selections*, 27–8.

93 Thomson, *Tribute to Liberty*, 52.

94 *Ibid.*

95 See the broadside copies in the British Library at 648.c.26.(58.) and 806.k.16 (119), respectively. The latter is ascribed to Spence, but it is the song printed by Thomson rather than the one of the same title printed in *Pig's Meat.*

96 See BL 648.c.26 (6 and 7). Hawes may later have become associated with the Moral and Political Society judging by the pamphlet *The Curses and Causes of War* (1795), which he printed for them.

97 See *Pig's Meat*, 3rd edn, 2: 91–3. The popularity of 'Burke's Address to the Swinish Multitude" is evinced by the variety of different places it appeared. Apart from the slip versions mentioned above, see *Pig's Meat* 1: 250 (there is a different song with the same title at 2: 39–41); *Five Excellent New Songs* (1792); and *An appeal to the inhabitants of Birmingham* (1792), 41–3. John Harrison wrote to Hardy from Coventry in October 1793 to acquire 'a few of the songs which begin with "God Save the Rights of Man &c"', 7 October 1793, National Archive, TSP, TS 1/953.

98 See *An abstract of the history and proceedings of the Revolution Society* (1789), 2. *The World*, 5 November 1790, disapprovingly commented of the toasts at the 1790 dinner: 'We have Heard before of the MAJESTY, but on this occasion, the toast was of the SOVEREIGNTY of the PEOPLE'.

99 Thomson, *Tribute to Liberty*, 87. He describes his toasts as 'Adapted to the Times'.

100 *The second report from the Committee of Secrecy*, 26.

101 Epstein and Karr, 'Playing at Revolution', 515.

102 Godwin, *Enquiry concerning political justice*, 1: 208. See also Vincent, *Literacy and Popular Culture*, 201: 'At every level, the sound of the human voice was magnified rather than quelled by the mass production and distribution of prose and verse', 201.

103 See the copies of 'News from Toulon', 'The Sheepsheering Song', 'Britons Glory' printed three to a sheet at National Archive, TSP, TS 11/953. For the interrogation of Goddard on these songs, see Barrell and Mee, 4: 312.

104 Place, *Autobiography*, 57. See Gatrell, *City of Laughter*, 583, for an account of Place as one of 'old laughter's enemies'. My discussion of Place and song is indebted to Newman's 'Civilizing Taste', which points out, 444, that Place's awareness of these songs comes from the 1780s when his father was landlord at the King's Arms, Arundel Street, off the Strand.

105 Place, *Autobiography*, 57–8.

106 See Place, 'Notes on grossness in publications and street songs', BL, Place Papers, Collections Relating to Manners and Morals, Add. MS 27825, f. 144r.
107 On the Association's relation to government, see Philp, *Reforming Ideas*, 45, n. 18.
108 See the account of these events in Keane, *Thomas Paine*, 324–48.
109 Paine, *Rights of Man*, 189 and 207.
110 Cotlar, *Tom Paine's America*, 166.
111 See the discussion of Erskine's attitude in Crosby, '"The Voice of Flattery vs Sober Truth"'.
112 Barrell and Mee, 1: 99, 51, 55, and 56.
113 *Ibid.*, 125, 126, 143, 149, 153, 162, and 179.
114 *Ibid.*, 183, 195, 197.
115 *Proceedings at the Meeting of the Friends of the Liberty of the Press* [1793?], 6–8.
116 *The Argus*, 16 November 1792. The SCI had ordered the secretary to transmit a copy to every member. See SCI minutes, 12 October 1792, National Archive, TSP, TS 11/962.
117 Both Perry and Thomson seem to have fled at the very end of 1792. The SCI minute book shows Perry attended its meetings in November. He was tried in absentia for a libel on the House of Commons from 6–8 December. See '*R.* v. *Sampson Perry*', National Archive, TSP, TS 11/41 and the coverage in the newspapers, for instance, *London Chronicle*, 8–11 December.
118 See accounts of the various prosecutions in Werkmeister, *Newspaper History of England 1792–1793* and the discussion of Pigott's *Jockey Club* in Chapter 4.
119 Thelwall, *The Natural and Constitutional right*, 39–40.
120 *An Explanation of the Word Equality*, 1 and 2–3.
121 *Selections*, 42. A later version at BL, Place Papers, Papers of the LCS, Add MS 27814, f. 101, puts the matter slightly differently: 'cautious of not running the Society into debt – it was negatived – but each of the delegates agreed to subscribe and have it printed and distributed at their own expense'.
122 For this older tradition, see Parssinen, 'Association, convention, and anti-parliament'.
123 See the account in IKD, 146–7 and 198–9, and *The second report*, Appendix D. Margarot's reply, 26 November, National Archive TSP, TS 11/958, was produced at Hardy's trial. See Barrell and Mee, 2: 234–5 and the prosecution's opinion at 5: 232. Shortly after receiving the second letter, Margarot wrote privately to John Cozens at Norwich to ask about the signatures on it. See *Selections*, 31.
124 United Societies at Norwich to LCS, in *Second report*, Appendix D.
125 See Knights, 'The 1780 Protestant Petitions' and the discussion at IKD, 138–9. Hardy and others also probably had experience of petitioning via the abolition movement, see page 31.
126 See Mark Knights, 'Participation and Representation'.
127 See Goodwin, *Friends of Liberty*, 280. Grey presented his petition on the same day he moved a motion for parliamentary reform.

128 See Barrell and Mee, 5: 229–30 and *Report of the Committee ... of the Constitution* (1794), 6.
129 *Report of the Committee ... of the Constitution,* 6.
130 Philp, *Reforming Ideas*, 299.
131 For Place's comment, see BL, Place Papers, Collections relating to Political Societies, Add MS 27808, f. 26.
132 Lottes, 'Radicalism, Revolution, and Political Culture', 88.
133 Powell's report on the executive committee meeting of 7 August 1795, for instance, mentions a letter from Herefordshire requesting advice on how to proceed in forming a society. See *Selections*, 284. John Ashley replied with a set of the LCS regulations. See *Correspondence of the LCS*, 48–9.
134 *Selections*, 78 and 82.
135 The society at Tewkesbury shared features with the many book societies of the time. See its letter to the LCS in July in response to a request for more information: 'As you wish'd to be inform'd respecting our society, shall give you a concise view of it. We call it the Society for Political & Moral Information – we have a sett of articles for the conducting of it – Monthly & Quarterly meetings for the proposing of Books & settling the Secretarys accounts – We take in a periodical work call'd the Patriot & a Town & country newspaper'. See their reply to the LCS in National Archive, TSP, TS 11/956.
136 Gerrald, *A Convention*, 80 and 85.
137 See Green, *Majesty of the People*, especially, 38–9.
138 Gerrald, *A Convention*, 87–8.
139 IKD, 144.
140 Gerrald, *A Convention*, 91 and 98.
141 John Barrell notes divisions within the association movement of the 1780s as to what they should do if their petitions to Parliament were rejected. Some believed that if their efforts were rejected then 'the association would be justified in establishing a convention which would act as an anti-parliament, disputing the right to govern with parliament itself'. IKD, 142. See the comparisons of Gerrald, Merry, and Williams's constitutional writings in Rogers, 'Vectors of Revolution'. On Paine's influence, see IKD, 143–4.
142 IKD, 147–8.
143 See *Selections*, 84–9 for the details of the general meeting. Breillat was arrested immediately after the meeting for seditious words spoken over a year earlier
144 BL, Place Papers, Papers of the LCS, Add MS 27814, f. 59. On Thelwall's disqualification from standing, see Chapter 6.
145 IKD, 151.
146 Goodwin, *Friends of Liberty*, 308–11. There were various published versions of the meeting at the Globe Tavern. The toasts began with 'THE RIGHTS OF MAN; and may Britons never want spirit to assert them.' See *At a general meeting ... 20th day of January*, 8.
147 Godwin to Gerrald, 23 January 1794, in *Letters*, 90. Brackets inserted in this edition.

148 See Epstein, 'Trial Defence and Radical Memory', 37, and *Selections*, 112, n. 37.
149 Epstein, "Our Real Constitution", 38, quoting Gerrald.
150 *At a general meeting of the London Corresponding Society, ... on Monday the 14th of April, 1794* (1794), 6–8.
151 Fairclough, *Romantic Crowd*, 10.
152 See title-page of *The Defence of Joseph Gerrald* (1794).
153 See, for instance, his lecture 'On Prosecutions for Pretended Treason' delivered on 13 May 1795, *Tribune*, 1: 279–81. The editors of Thelwall's *The Daughter of Adoption* have suggested that its hero, Henry Montfort, is modelled after Gerrald.
154 See *Politics for the People*, 2: 158–9, signed 'M. B.'
155 See *Lectures 1795*, and Coleridge to Thelwall, 13 May 1796, *Collected Letters*, 1: 214, and Thelwall, *Tribune*, 1: 274.
156 IKD, 293–5.
157 The LCS was revising its constitution anticipating that the law officers intended to move against them. Taylor reported that a proposal for entering the names of all those living in the same district in one book was being proposed so that that could be collected together in case of any emergency. He explained, 'the emergency I understand to mean in case the Society met with any opposition from legal authority'. He then reported that a member of another division had claimed that 'the Habeas Corpus Act would be suspended in the course of this or the ensuing week'. National Archive, TSP, TS 11/955.
158 See Taylor's notes on the lecture in National Archive, TSP, TS 11/956.
159 *Enquiry concerning political justice*, 2: 780.
160 *Selections*, 115–16. Appointed to serve on the new committee were Baxter, Pearce, and Thelwall.
161 *Selections*, 121.
162 See Loughlin, 'Constituent Power', 43, on the influence of Blackstone.
163 See *Selections*, 147 and 154. Moore, a member of division 2, had defended the rights of divisions when the question of the new constitution was raised in March. In the chair on 3 March, he observed that 'if the Committee wanted to *Cram a Constitution down their throats*, they were greatly mistaken', *ibid.*, 120. There was not the same dissension in every division. Division 2 passed 'every Clause . . . without a debate', *ibid.*, 155.
164 For the minutes of the first two conferences, see *ibid.*, 128 and 132. Sharp's account is at National Archive, TSP, TS 11/963. He claimed that at the weekly SCI meeting the day after the first conference Holcroft started a conversation 'on the Powers of the Human Mind which lasted an Hour and a half and the Meeting broke up without any business being done'.
165 *At a general meeting of the London Corresponding Society . . . on Monday the 14th April, 1794*, 4–5. For the debate on titles, see *Selections*, 138.
166 See IKD, 142–3
167 *Selections*, 189, 194, and 210. Although indicted in October with most of the other defendants at the trials, Hodgson never was arrested. He appeared openly at LCS meetings in September.

168 *An Account of the seizure of Citizen Thomas Hardy* (1794) acknowledged that the society had intended to call a convention, but only as a means of discovering the best means to attain reform. The pamphlet was published before 3 July, the date Smith was paid for printing costs. See *Selections*, 193.

169 *Ibid.*, 187. There is a copy of one, 'A Parody of Poor Jack', at National Archive TSP, TS 11/956.

170 *Selections*, 194

171 Parkinson admitted writing *Revolutions without Bloodshed* and *Vindication* when interviewed by the Privy Council in October. See *Assassination of the King*! (1795), 59–60. Parkinson also remembered the *Vindication* was printed by Hawes. He admitted having a hand in *Reformers no Rioters* at Thelwall's trial, Barrell and Mee, 8: 71, confirmed by the spy report on the meeting of 27 August, *Selections*, 215. *Reformers no Rioters* seems to have been published early in September, proofs being delivered to Burks for correction on 5 September. Parkinson's *Vindication* was in print by 7 October, but the original run was stopped because the pamphlet was deemed inappropriate with the trials so close.

172 *Selections*, 204, 207, 209, 212, and 214–15. Davis identifies Beaumont as John Thomas Baker Beaumont in his facsimile of *the publications of the LCS*. See his *London Corresponding Society*, 3: 1. See also Chapter 3.

173 Two days later, Parkinson reported that he had been unable to get the prospectus back from Bayley: *Selections*, 216. There are various candidates for this person. Given that he is given the title 'Mr.' in the minutes, this may be the 'Baily' who attended the SCI, for instance, on 15 March 1793. See Barrell and Mee, 6: 261. A Bailey attended the meetings between LCS members and Godwin discussed on pages 43–5. The LCS sometimes used a printer called Bailey, who was investigated as part of the 'Pop-gun plot'. A Citizen Bailey was a member of the Friends of Liberty in 1795. See his *The White Devils Un-Cased* and *Prince Brothers's Scarlet Devils Displayed* (1795).

174 See the account of the plot in IKD, 445–503.

175 *The Politician*, no. 2, 11–14, and no. 4, 26–7.

176 See Chapter 6, 182, for a further discussion of Thelwall's contributions.

177 *Selections*, 199.

178 *Death of Mrs Hardy*, 4. The poem is signed 'A FRIEND TO THE DISTRESSED PATRIOTS'. The profits were to go to the wives and families of those imprisoned by the suspension of Habeas Corpus. At this stage, Lee had not set up as a bookseller himself.

179 Barrell reproduces the series in *Exhibition Extraordinary!!*

180 *Pig's Meat*, 2: 57–8.

181 *John Horne Tooke Stripped Naked and Dissected*, 13. Tooke had compared Paine to Stephen Duck and equivocated in his testimony on Thelwall's character. The pamphlet reads as if written by someone from within the political elite, but its tendency is towards maximum self-determination for the members.

182 *Selections*, 249–50.

183 Cooper's letter is reproduced in *Selections*, 243–8. A print version is at Nuffield College Library, Oxford.
184 *Selections*, 312. The LCS committee discussed the letter 15 October. The United Friends of Religious and Civil Liberty issued an address to their Fellow Countrymen on 26 October, signed John Taylor as secretary. See the spy report on their debate on religion, 10 January 1796, National Archive Privy Council Papers, PC/1/23/A38.
185 See *United Friends of Religious and Civil Liberty* (1795), 4.
186 *Narrative of the Proceedings*, 2nd edn, 1, 3, and 5.
187 Iliff, *Duties of Citizenship*, 13–14.
188 He recommended not only forming new societies, but also using 'Parish, Town, and County Meetings'. See Baxter, *Resistance to Oppression*, 5.
189 See Bentham, *Fragment on Government*, 150–1, and the excellent discussion in Green, *Majesty of the People*, 26.
190 Gilmartin, *Print Politics*, 30.

Notes to Chapter 3

1 Boaden, *Memoirs of Kemble*, 2: 47.
2 See the *European Magazine*, 18 (1790), 388.
3 For a useful account of the Della Cruscan phenomenon, see Hargreaves-Mawdsley, *English Della Cruscans*.
4 *Thraliana*, 2: 714.
5 During this period, Merry kept up the flirtatious correspondence with Piozzi preserved in the John Rylands Library, ENG MS 614. On 21 April 1788, he told her of a quarto of poems that were to be dedicated to Sheridan. On 12 November, Merry looked to the death of the king and the 'glorious times we may now expect'. He was forced to admit later (23 April 1789) that the ode on the recovery of king 'was in part my composition … I was applied to on the occasion from a quarter [Sheridan] I could not refuse.' See Hargreaves-Mawdsley, *English Della Cruscans*, 195–7. Piozzi noted: 'The Ode Sheridan and he wrote together, is not liked' (*Thraliana*, 2: 743). The quarto Merry mentions is *The Poetry of the World,* dedicated to Sheridan and published by John Bell.
6 *The Laurel of Liberty* (1790), [title page] and [dedication].
7 See Topham to Wells, 4 October 1790, [Wells], *Memoirs of the Late Mrs Sumbel*, 2: 76.
8 Horace Walpole to Edward Jerningham, 10 November 1790, *Edward Jerningham and his Friends*, 50, and *Political Correspondence* (1793), 90. Others in the latter's list of able pens besides Merry and Priestley include James Mackintosh, Holcroft, Pigott, David Williams, Helen Maria Williams, and Wollstonecraft.
9 Taylor, *Records of My Life*, 2: 274. Merry attacked Taylor as 'the reptile oculist' in the *Telegraph* (4 November 1795) after a review in the *True Briton* condemned the democratic principles of Sheridan's revival of *Venice Preserved.* Merry wrongly supposed Taylor had written the review. Until then, Merry

and Taylor seem to have remained on friendly terms despite Taylor becoming a Treasury writer. They 'used to scribble verses in conjunction' for the *Morning Post*. See Taylor, *Records of My Life*, 2: 152 and 270–5. Merry was mocked in the *Tomahawk*, no. S1, 25 December 1795, 206, for trying to blame the epigram on drink.

10 *The Times*, 20 December 1790.

11 George Taylor, *The French Revolution and the London Stage*, 61–4.

12 Worrall, *Politics of Romantic Theatricality*, 52–3.

13 *Laurel of Liberty*, vi.

14 'Journal in 1792 of conversations with various persons', Rogers Notebook, Sharpe Papers MS 41, University College London, Special Collections.

15 'Written in 1794 – notes of conversation with Merry', MS Abinger c. 31, f. 101, Bodleian Library. Earlier in this document, Godwin lists people he has met by year. Merry appears in 1793 along with Frost, Gerrald, Pigott, and Thelwall.

16 'The *Separation* made between the Philosophical & satirical writers; the latter of which would have submitted to the former *under proper direction*', Williams traced to Fox's manipulation of the newspapers in the 1780s. Looking to the future, he believed once the peace was resolved 'then it is known, there are Phalanxes to attack Ministers instantly on the determination; not only by the fleeting arrows of Paragraphs, but by publications of another kind, & by solicitations to the country to petition & remonstrate'. See manuscript letter, signed 'D W' and entitled 'Observations on the Press' [1803?], BL, Pelham Papers, Add MS 33124, ff. 78–81. Without identifying Williams as the author, Barker, *Newspapers, Politics, and Public Opinion*, 43, notes its identification of 'paragraphs' with 'fleeting arrows'.

17 Clayden, *Early Life of Rogers*, 174. In terms of London's clubs, Bernard recalled that 'the members were all men of the world, and (London being a large cauldron, in which society is kept continually in a ferment, and something new is hourly rising to the surface,) they had well-stored heads to unburthen on coming together'. See his *Retrospections of the Stage*, 2: 116. He always found Sheridan cold compared to Merry. For further discussion of this group, see Mee, *Conversable Worlds*, 87–90.

18 *The World*, 14 July 1791.

19 Merry, *Ode for the fourteenth of July*, 5.

20 Nostalgic for a time when 'it was deemed not disloyal to celebrate the anniversary of the destruction of the *Bastille*', Perry reprinted the entire poem in *The Argus, or General Observer* (1796), 1: 13. Winterbotham published it in his *Selection of Poems Sacred and Moral*, 2: 135–8. The verses sung by Sedgwick are reproduced in the *Songster's Companion*, 77–8, *The whim of the day*, 89–90, and Paddock, *For 1794. The Apollo*. 86.

21 'Biographical Notice of Mr. Merry', *Monthly Magazine*, 7 (1799), 256.

22 See Guest, *Unbounded Attachment*, 70–1.

23 *The Baviad, and Mæviad*, 25.

24 Quoted in Ginter, 'The Financing of the Whig Party', 437, n. 51.

25 On 18 January 1792, Merry invited Rogers for 'a family mutton chop'. He also told him: 'My Opera will come out on Saturday … Jan. [y] 28th when I shall be much obliged to you to *lend me a hand*.' See Sharpe Papers 15/203–4.

26 Joseph Mazzinghi [and Robert Merry], *The Magician No Conjuror* (1792). The *Bon Ton Magazine* (February 17) believed the 'object of the satire was misapplied; and, besides, it was deficient in stage effect', 482, but reprinted some of the 'delightful' songs (489–90) and others in its March (33) and July issues (193). By July, the magazine was openly hostile to Merry's politics. Songs from the play were also reprinted in the *British Apollo*, 54 and 117. A manuscript of the play is at Larpent MSS, LA933, Huntington Library.

27 The *Gazeteer*, 3 February 1792. See the *Diary*, 3 February 1792, and the *London Chronicle*, 2–4 February 1792.

28 Werkmeister, *Newspaper History 1792–1793*, 92–3. Note the comment about the misapplication of the satire in the *Bon Ton Magazine* note 26 above. No further explanation is given. David Worrall reads the play in terms of the Birmingham Riots, with Priestley providing the obvious analogue to Talisman. I am not convinced by this specific identification, but agree with his comments about the oblique nature of the engagement with topical issues. See the *Politics of Romantic Theatricality*, 56–7.

29 *Political Miscellanies*, 91. The collection was ascribed to the authors of the *Rolliad*. Ridgeway kept the pamphlet in print in the 1790s. See my discussion on page 125 for its possible influence on Merry's *Pittachio* squib.

30 'Memorandum. Information obtained Last night and this day', 29 October, National Archive, TSP, TS 11/959 on a meeting in Compton Street. Alexander Stephens, who was present at the foundation of the *Argus*, thought it 'perhaps the boldest in its opposition of any publication in any age'. See 'Stephensiana, No. XIV', 427. Smith, 'English Radical Newspapers', 8, agrees it was the most radical London paper of the 1790s, but doubts that the LCS could have afforded any direct subsidy. John King was probably Perry's prime source of funds. Sheridan and Mackintosh finally suppressed the paper in Perry's absence, as deserving 'no more countenance from opposition than from ministry because it abused the leaders of the former, as much as it did the heads of the latter'. See 'Particulars of S. Perry's Case' in his *Historical Sketch of the French Revolution*, 2: np. Smith, 149, supplies the identities of Mackintosh and Sheridan.

31 'Stephensiana', No. XIV 427.

32 *Gentleman's Magazine*, 134 (1823) 280.

33 Titus, 'To the British Nation', *The Argus*, 11 July 1792. The paragraph was cut out and marked for attention by the law officers. See *Rex* v. *Perry* in National Archive, TSP, TS 11/41, which contains a copy of the indictment and various other cuttings from the *Argus*.

34 Minute book of the SCI at National Archive, TSP, TS 11/962, Friday 27 April.

35 'Biographical Notice of Merry', 256. The poems quoted here are all published in the obituary. Squibs from the *Argus* were also reproduced in 'Stephensiana',

427, which notes that Merry and Paine wrote two of them. They include another attack on Rose, unattributed.

36 *Ibid.* Merry's odes did also appear in the pages of the *Argus* too, at least in excerpt (3 and 5 March), when lines from his 'Ode to Freedom' (*Ode for the fourteenth of July*) served as epigraphs to articles 'On African Slavery' and 'Illustrious Depravity'.

37 *The World*, 10 December 1792. Perry had been back and forward to Paris in 1792, the paper being conducted in his absence by the lawyer Thomas Oldfield, who worked with the Friends of the People on their reports on the state of representation. Smith, 'English Radical Newspapers', 118.

38 Munro to Grenville, 17 December 1792, National Archive, Foreign Office Papers, FO 27/40, describes Merry as the president of those who gathered at White's.

39 Merry's name is listed in *Proceedings of the Society of Friends of the People*, 5.

40 Merry's name appears regularly in the SCI minute book at National Archive, TSP, TS 11/962 between March and early June 1792. He was an enthusiastic proposer of other members.

41 *The Oracle*, 15 June 1792.

42 See, for instance, the advertisement in *Lloyd's Evening Post,* 11 September. It gives the publishers as Ridgway and Symonds. I have found no advertisement in the newspapers using the title published by Littlejohn, Symonds, and Thomson dated 22 August. Littlejohn was present at the 12 October meeting of the SCI where Merry was elected to the committee to consult with the LCS over the addresses to the National Convention.

43 National Archive TSP, TS 11/951. The contract for the shoes was given to Thomas Hardy.

44 See 'Biographical Notice of Mr. Merry', 257. For a fuller discussion of the pamphlet, see Rogers, 'Vectors of Revolution', 245–62. Rogers notes that the pamphlet was discussed in J. G. Alger's *Englishmen in the French Revolution.* The copy in the Bibliothèque Nationale de France has the printed date 1792 crossed out and replaced with 1793. I am grateful to Rachel Rogers for this information.

45 'Some Account of Robert Merry, Esq.', *The European Magazine*, 24 (1793), 411.

46 See Rogers, 'Vectors of Revolution', 195–6.

47 Somewhat optimistically, Gerrald told Margarot that Merry would definitely honour the debt. Later Margarot wrote to John Williams from Port Jackson to ask him to enquire of Merry when he would pay the debt. See Margarot to Williams, [1795?], BL, Place Papers, Papers of the LCS, Add MS 27815, f. 107. Margarot had attended SCI meetings in 1792 with Merry present. The promissory note had been left with Hardy and was seized with other papers when the government arrested him in May 1794. Margarot came back from Australia in 1810 and sought the return of his bills from the government. See Roe, 'Radical in Two Hemispheres', 75, and the notes on the matter in National Archive, TSP, TS 11/959.

48 On 12 October, the *Oracle* reported, 'MERRY, the Poet, is in town'.

49 Sharpe Papers MS 15, ff. 211–14.

50 Thomas Amyot to William Pattison, 13 May 1794, in *Youth and Revolution*, ed. Corfield and Evans, 56–7. For a discussion of Godwin's relationship with Norwich, including the summer 1794 trip, see Grande, 'Roots of Godwinian Radicalism'. Godwin had been in the audience for the opening night of *The Magician No Conjuror* in 1792, despite 'Severe cold & fever'. The diary also records discussing Merry with Holcroft in June 1793, soon after the poet had returned from France.

51 Alderson to Mrs Taylor, NYPL, [1794], f. 4; Alderson to Godwin, 1 Nov. 1796, MS Abinger c. 3, f. 4; Godwin to Wollstonecraft [10 September 1796], *Letters of Godwin*, 1: 179.

52 Piozzi to Leonard Chappelow, 19 January 1796, *Piozzi Letters*, 2: 302: 'Poor Della Crusca begs Subscriptions – I'm sorry! But he should let his Wife act: what Nonsense it is to hinder her.' The *True Briton* commented that 'the stale trick of Subscriptions is now attempting by a sad poet but, from a variety of concurring circumstances, with very little prospect of success'. The *Oracle* (13 January 1796) added, 'Mr. Merry has a novel ready for the press; or has already been the subject of *premature sarcasm*'. Merry had asked Rogers about Cadell publishing a novel in December 1793.

53 Holcroft to Godwin, 7 July 1794, MS Abinger c. 2, f. 45v, Bodleian Library.

54 His name appeared on the record at Hardy and Horne Tooke's trials. See Barrell and Mee, 3: 7, 32, 52 and 6: 176, 185, and 193–205.

55 Merry to Rogers, 11 October 1794, Sharpe Papers MS 15, f. 216.

56 See Barrell, '"An Entire Change"', 21–2, on newspaper advertisements for conjurors in the period. Apart from those mentioned by Barrell, Monsieur Comus performed at the Great Exhibition Room, no. 28 Haymarket. Among his many 'operations' were 'magical looking glasses' and he concluded with 'The Grand Magical House' (both of which seem to have been picked up and developed by Merry and others who developed these pasquinades). See the advertisement in the *Morning Chronicle*, 18 December 1794.

57 'Robinson' is probably George Robinson the bookseller who published Godwin and Merry. On Godwin's relationship with Robinson, who was known for his convivial, often boozy dinners, see Fallon, 'Booksellers in the Godwin Diaries'. Charles Este had worked with Merry at the *World*. King is presumably John King. See Smith, 'English Radical Newspapers', 11. Beaumont is probably the person the LCS approached to write for *The Politician* towards the end of 1794.

58 'Biographical Notice', 257. This may include a return to his more sentimental strain, and perhaps even the Della Crusca pseudonym, if the anti-war 'Ode for the New Year' published in the *Telegraph* on 30 December 1794 is his.

59 D. E. MacDonnell was editor of the *Morning Post* (probably), the *Gazetteer*, and the *Telegraph*. He was among the founding members of the Society of the Friends of the People, April 1792, but seems to have followed something of Merry's trajectory thereafter, including involvement in the British Club in Paris in late 1792, if he is the MacDonald mentioned in Munro's reports. The minute books of the *Gazetteer* suggest he took a tour of the continent to gather information on the war in the summer of 1794. John Taylor gives an account

of his role as go-between with Merry after 'the reptile oculist' spat. See Haig, the *Gazetteer*, 232–9 and 250–3; Werkmeister, *The London Daily Press, 1772–1792*, 343 and 355, and *A Newspaper History of England, 1792–1793*, 37, 76, 168, 169, and Taylor, *Records of My Life*, 2: 272–8.

60 *Monthly Review*, 19 (1796), 274. The publisher of Merry's play was Parsons of Paternoster Row, purveyor of an eclectic mix of print from cheap editions of Paine in 1792 to sacred poetry, including Lee's *Songs from the rock* volume in 1794. Parsons also published anthologies of essays and a series of plays from the 'minor theatre'.

61 Hargreaves-Mawdsley, *English Della Cruscans*, 275, and Merry to Rogers, 3 December 1793, Sharpe Papers, MS 15/214.

62 Eaton, Spence, and Thelwall are among those advertised on the title-page of *The Wounded Soldier*. In addition to Ballard's edition, there is a penny edition published together with 'the Holy War. – A New Song', with no date or place of publication, in the collection of the National Library of Scotland at RB s. 445. Merry's poem was also included in the *Hive of Modern Literature*, 283–6, and in the *Cabinet of Curiosities*, no. 1, 150–3. Several of the Pittachio satires and other material associated with Lee and other radical booksellers were reprinted in the latter, which opens with the 'Ode for the New Year' from the *Telegraph*. For Ballard's associations, see Worrall, *Politics of Romantic Theatricality*, 59–61. Worrall suggests Ballard was involved with the Friends of Liberty after their split from the LCS. In Ballard's *Pitt's Ghost*, an extension of the *Death, Dissection of Pitt* satire that first appeared in the *Telegraph* in August, Merry's poem is advertised as selling for a penny under the title the *Horrors of War, or The Wounded Soldier*. 'The Horrors of War' was the title Merry used in his letter to Rogers in 1793.

63 See the title-page of *Pitti-Clout & Dun-Cuddy*. For the retraction, see the list 'SOLD BY CITIZEN LEE' inside the cover of *Mr. St. George, A True Story*. The same list has *The Wounded Soldier* for sale.

64 Merry may have socialised with the LCS member John Barnes during this period. When explaining his attack on Taylor, Merry claimed he had been drinking with the comedian Jack Bannister and someone called Barnes, who Taylor identified as involved in the pop-gun plot, *Records of My Life*, 2: 276–7. The *Telegraph* had been deeply involved in the dispute over whether the plot was an alarmist ruse to justify the repressive legislation. Under interrogation about his role in the plot, Le Maitre told Pitt he had come across a paper in Barnes's coffee room. See P. T. Lemaitre, *High treason!!*, 2nd edn (1795) 11.

65 Grande, 'Roots of Godwinian Dissent', 40.

66 See Godwin to Merry, 20 Sept. 1796, *Letters of Godwin*, 1: 181 and Alderson to Godwin, 14 Oct. 1796, MS Abinger c. 3, f. 38. For fuller accounts of Merry's America sojourn, see Adams, 'Della Cruscanism in America', Garnai, 'An Exile on the Coast', and Mee, 'Morals, Manners, and Liberty'.

67 Cooper, *Some Information respecting America*, 64.

68 See James Fennell, *An Apology*, 325. The success of the revolutionary armies under Dumouriez may have decided Merry to stay in France on the first

occasion. The acquittals at the treason trials may have caused a rethink the second time.

69 See Holcroft's letter of 1796 to William Dunlap in the latter's *A History of the American Theatre*, 1: 310.

70 AUM, 2 (1797), 189. The ode had originally been published in the *Baltimore Telegraph*, 16 November 1796.

71 Cobbett, *Works*, 9: 258.

72 Bernard, *Retrospections of America*, 124.

73 Robert Merry, *Pains of Memory. A New Edition*, 26. The poem is preceded by an address 'To the Public' (13 December 1796), announcing an edition of Merry's complete works. The works were also advertised in the AUM, but do not seem to have appeared. On Mathew Carey, publisher of the Philadelphia edition, see Durey, *Transatlantic Radicals*, especially 242 and 246–7.

74 See the advertisement in *Monthly Magazine*, 6 (1798), 129. Presumably it was the 'treatise on the justice of the *Agrarian system*' mentioned by Cobbett.

Notes to Chapter 4

1 Bernard, *Retrospections of the Stage*, 2: 146.

2 *An Answer to Three Scurrilous Pamphlets*, 11.

3 For biographical details, Charles Pigott, see *Notes and Queries*, 12 S. XI (1922), 347–8; (1922), 15–16 and (1922), 545, Robert Black, *The Jockey Club*, 226, 229–30, and [Harriet Pigott], *Private Correspondence*, 1: 55–6, 59, and 60. The exception to the general historiographical neglect is Rogers, 'Pigott's Private Eye'.

4 The letters appeared in the *Public Advertiser*, 8 and 18 March respectively. The first is dated 6 February 1785, but the second is undated.

5 On Fox and the newspapers, see Barker, *Newspapers, Politics, and Public Opinion*, 44–5.

6 *Morning Herald*, 16 March 1785. Ridgway later published the epigrams in *Political Miscellanies*, 105–6, but also published *The Jockey Club* in 1792.

7 See Robert Pigott, *Liberty of the Press* (1790). There is an ODNB entry on Robert Pigott, but see also Alger, *Englishmen in the French Revolution*, 39–45, Black, *The Jockey Club*, 126–7, 229–30, and Harriet Pigott, *Private Correspondence*, 1: 5–12. I have not seen the pamphlet on the commercial treaty, but the review is in the *Critical Review*, 63 (1787), 312.

8 Pigott, *Strictures on . . . Burke*, vi and vii.

9 *Ibid.*, v, 21, 65–6.

10 *Ibid.*, 32, 86 and 92.

11 *Ibid.*, 23 and 67.

12 *Treachery no Crime*, 141 and 128. See the advertisement by Ridgway in the *Morning Post*, 12 September 1793, days before Pigott set out to Harwich with Merry. The pamphlet itself is dated 31 July.

13 *Treachery no Crime*, 141 and 2. See also the references to Godwin, 39–40 and 149–50.

14 *Strictures*, vi–vii.
15 *The Jockey Club*. Part the First, 176
16 John Wilde, *An Address to the Lately Formed Society*, 68 note. Wilde describes Pigott as 'one of the brethren of Mr. Paine. This fellow (whoever he is) has not at the same time the full merit of the other, for he only copies (in general) and does not make the falsehoods. Being pretty much versant in that species of reading, I have found scarce any thing in the Jockey Club, unless where the characters are absolutely recent, which was new to me', 67n. Wilde described himself as 'a Rockingham Whig', vii, persuaded by Burke's arguments to support Pitt's government. He describes the principles of the Society of the Friends of the People as 'dangerous in the undertaking and pernicious in the effect; as of perilous example and unfounded theory; equally repugnant to the constitution of this country, and to the principles of the great Whig party, to which the associators (or most of them) had belonged', xvii.
17 Pigott, *The Jockey Club*, Part the First, [Preface].
18 *An Answer to Three Scurrilous Pamphlets*, 13.
19 *Analytical Review*, 12 (1792), 529, reviewing the fourth edition of Part I.
20 *British Constitution Invulnerable*, 16.
21 See the many stories gathered from Hanger's papers and elsewhere by William Combe writing as George Hanger in *Life, Adventures, and Opinions* (1801).
22 *The Jockey Club*, Part the First, 50.
23 *The Jockey Club*, Part the Second, 171.
24 Wilde, *An Address*, 67 note.
25 Selections from Ridgway's extortionary *Memoirs of Mrs. Billington* (1792) appeared over the January and February issues of the magazine. *The British Constitution Invulnerable*, viii, mentions the role of magazines in spreading scandal.
26 From September 1792, the magazine started to feature a section called 'Epitome of the Times' devoted to stories of mob violence in France.
27 *The Jockey Club*, Part the First, 1–2, 65, and 63.
28 *The Jockey Club*, Part the Second, np [Dedication] and 183. The *Morning Chronicle* announced the publication of Part II (and the fifth edition of Part I) on 11 May and of Part III on 12 September. For its shocked response to the opening section of Part III, see the *Analytical Review*, 14 (1792), 345.
29 *The Jockey Club*, Part the Third, 194, 195, and 197.
30 *Report of a Debate on Universal Suffrage* (1794), quoted in Hampsher-Monk, 'Civic Humanism and Parliamentary Reform', 79. The words are Sir Philip Francis's, a some time favourite of the LCS, castigating his fellow members of the Society for not making their own moderately reformist position clearer.
31 *The Jockey Club*, Part the First, 13.
32 *The Jockey Club*, Part the Third, 106–7 note. The indictment prepared for the Warwick assizes (see note 36 below) includes the whole quotation from Junius and the final paragraph where Pigott dissents from the praise of the constitution.
33 *The Jockey Club*, Part the Third, 44, 222–3, and 230 note.

34 Wilde, *An Address*, 67–8n. Rogers, 'Pigott's Private Eye' suggests that at 4s *The Jockey Club* must have been 'principally pitched at a genteel or middle-class rather than plebeian audience . . .[It is] only with the posthumous publication of his *Political Dictionary* in 1795 that Pigott's work really penetrated the world of the radical artisan', 248–9. Given his social background, it is no surprise that Pigott took time to recognise the possibility of a popular radical audience. When the first part of the *Jockey Club* was first issued, the LCS did not exist and Paine had not published the cheap editions of *Rights of Man*. Versions of the *Jockey Club* were made available for less than the 4s advertised in some newspapers. Symonds's fifth edition of the second part was available for 8d. J. S. Jordan was selling copies for 2s 6d in 1793, along with *An Answer to Three Scurrilous Pamphlets* at the same price. *The Female Jockey Club* (1794) was lent out by libraries. A letter from 'A Friend to Government' in Bath complained: 'I am sorry to say that the libraries in general do mischief. It is a practice here to lett out not sell the infamous Female Jockey Club.' See National Archive, Home Office Papers, HO 42/30/21, ff. 54–5.

35 George, Prince of Wales to Queen Charlotte, 24 September 1792, *Correspondence of George Prince of Wales*, 287 and 285. The date of the prince's response suggests that he had been reading Part III. The passages that the prince marked for his mother were almost certainly those comparing Louis XVI and George III that shocked the *Analytical Review*. Queen Charlotte described them as 'too strong & too personal as to be put into the hands of the Kg who so little deserves them': Queen Charlotte to George, Prince of Wales, 2 September 1792, *Correspondence of George Prince of Wales*, 291.

36 In early December, the Treasury Solicitor sent letters to provincial solicitors seeking their help in prosecuting seditious works. The named texts were the *Jockey Club*, and Paine's *Rights of Man* and *Letters Addressed to the Addressers* (1792). Advice was provided on how to obtain proof of publication, subject to clearance by the Treasury Solicitor. A series of prosecutions followed. On 13 December, the Attorney General claimed in Parliament to have had two hundred pieces of informations concerning seditious publications. See Smith, 'English Radical Newspapers' 227–8. Among them is *Rex v. James Belcher* at Warwick Assizes, July 1793. See the brief at National Archive, TSP, TS 11/578. I am grateful to Danielle MacDonnell for pointing this file out to me.

37 Henry Dundas to the Prince of Wales, 5 October 1792, *Correspondence of George Prince of Wales*, 298. Ridgway was taken up for the third part on 30 November. Details of the proceedings against Ridgway and Symonds are to be found in the *Morning Chronicle*, 9 May 1793. See *Rex* v. *H. D. Symonds*, National Archive, TSP, *TS* 11/944, and *Rex* v. *James Ridgway*, TS 11/141. Bills of indictment had been prepared on 28 November 1792. See also Manogue, 'The Plight of James Ridgway', 158. According to Richard Phillips, 'three Indictments were prepared in London, and presented, and found by the Grand Jury at the Borough Sessions on the 18th of January ensuing'. Phillips complained

at being charged with selling the *Jockey Club* when it had not yet been found to be a libel. See Phillips, *Original papers published at different times in the Leicester Herald*, 12–13.

38 Godwin's diary records that he read Pigott's Dumouriez pamphlet on 30 August.

39 See Alexander, *Richard Newton*, 37 and 121, and McCalman, 'Newgate in Revolution', 96. Pigott does not appear in *A Peep into the State Side of Newgate*, 12 July 1793, the earliest of the Newgate prints.

40 James Ridgway's affidavit, 1 May 1793, National Archive, King's Bench KB 1/27. See the report in the *London Chronicle*, 30 April – 2 May 1793. Judging by Newton's prints of August and October, Pigott kept Ridgway's company anyway.

41 See also *The whole proceedings on the King's commission*, 138–45. Hodgson, *The Case of William Hodgson* claimed they had earlier been drinking with William, Pigott's brother, who held the living at Chetwynd. See Black, *The Jockey Club*, 228–9. Epstein, '"Equality and no King"', 45–7 and Barrell, *Spirit of Despotism*, 86–92, provide further analysis.

42 The author of *Ethic epistles*, 23–4, suggests Pigott had previously been helped by the magistrate, perhaps when facing prison for debt, and charges him with ingratitude:

> P–, to thee and malice such as thine
> The *lev'lling Muse* I readily resign –
> And yet no lev'lling still, but partial Muse,
> That 'gainst the great and good you chiefly use.
> The bad still cautious never to offend,
> Of ev'ry Jacobin the constant friend.
> What joy to batten some benefactor to select!
> And where no crime of heart in A – t – n find,
> To mark or make some foible of his mind.
> Serpent to sting the hand that set thee free,
> To wound the breast that once had foster'd thee!

A note explains: 'This supposed author of the "Jockey Club" was with that good nature which he now abuses, relieved and protected from gaol in the house of Sir W. A.'

43 For details of the imprisonment and subsequent fates of Pigott and Hodgson, see the *Morning Chronicle*, 9 October and 2 November; *Public Advertizer*, 25 October; Pigott's, *Persecution* and Hodgson's the *Case of William Hodgson*. Hodgson could not pay his fine when his sentence was up in 1795 and was kept in prison. Over the course of 1794, Hodgson wrote several times to the LCS to complain about their lack of financial support for his family. His applications occasioned some dispute in the society because of his conduct. See *Selections*, 112, 128, 147, 154, 156 and *passim*.

44 *Persecution*, 6–7. The Frost case is mentioned, 49.

45 *Ibid.*, 37–8, 26., and [iii].

46 *Persecution!!!* is advertised in *The Times,* 6 December. For Thelwall's lectures in this period, see Chapter 6. His 26 March lecture was 'Historical Strictures on the Trials of Hampden, Russell, and Sidney.' See *Morning Post,* 10 February, and *Morning Chronicle,* 26 March 1794.
47 *Persecution!!!*, 15, 19, and 36–7.
48 See O'Shaughnessy, '*Caleb Williams* and the Philomaths', 444.
49 I have not found copies of the earlier Pigott pamphlets with Eaton's imprint. Possibly he was simply selling on Ridgway's stock. The December puffs for *Persecution* also mention Ridgway and Symonds. They were still in Newgate.
50 See the lists at National Archive, TSP, TS 11/966 and Privy Council Papers, PC 1/23/38 dated 26 February 1794.
51 Pigott to Rogers, 9 November 1793, University College London Special Collections, Sharpe Papers, MS 15/314. Pigott seems not to have had any direct contact with Rogers prior to this correspondence. Presumably he had relied on Merry.
52 See Priestman, *Romantic Atheism,* 14.
53 Reid, *The rise and dissolution,* 6.
54 Initially published by Crosby and Holt, the earliest of Richter's designs for Hodgson's translation is dated 20 March 1795. Symonds took over from Crosby for the later volumes. There are various advertisements for the translation in works published by congers of radical booksellers. *A Picture of the Times* (1795), 2nd edn, advertises the first volume of an eventual four-volume set at 5s in boards with weekly numbers available at 6d each. There were also a few numbers on 'super-fine paper' at a shilling each. I have found no edition or advertisement giving Pigott's name as translator of *The System of Nature,* but see note 57 below. Daniel Holt appears with Pigott in the two Newgate prints.
55 The 1795 edition says 'from the Manuscript of the late CHARLES PIGOTT' on the title page.
56 See the accounts in Young, *Revolutionary Ladies,* 142–71, and Knott, 'Female Liberty?', 435–7.
57 See *Memoirs of Mrs. Coghlan,* 2: 37. Advertisements for the book appeared in the *Whitehall Evening Post* (25 January) and in the *Morning Post* (29 January). Both described the *Memoirs* as 'written by HERSELF', but then seem to acknowledge another hand. Most of the 'well-known characters' mentioned on the title page are familiar from the *Jockey Club.* For the ascription to Pigott, see Young, *Revolutionary Ladies,* 168–70. Kearsley also published Godwin's *Cursory Strictures* (1794); John Fenwick's translation of *Memoirs of Dumouriez*; George Dyer's *Dissertation on the Theory and Practice of Benevolence*; and various works by Gilbert Wakefield. In 1797, he also brought out a four-volume translation of the *System of Nature* from a manuscript found in 'the library of a man celebrated for his learning'. Conceivably, this is the translation Pigott left behind at his death. Another single volume edition of Coghlan's *Memoirs* from 1794 exists under the imprint of Lane, but this seems a pirated version of Kearsley's.
58 *Memoirs of Mrs. Coghlan,* 71 and 78.

59 *British Critic*, 3 (1794), 346.
60 See *The Jockey Club*, Part the Second, 170, and *Memoirs of Mrs. Coghlan*, 1: 147–8.
61 *Persecution!!!*, 29–30 and 35. Pigott claimed that he told Hodgson he respected the Duke as son of the King, whatever his private character, a claim hardly borne out in his writing.
62 *Memoirs of Mrs. Coghlan*, 1: 143.
63 *Morning Chronicle*, 8 March.
64 *Female Jockey Club*, 144.
65 See the report of Erskine's speech at the trial of Eaton for publishing the book, *The Times*, 31 July.
66 *Female Jockey Club*, 98. In contrast, Pigott praised the Duchess of Devonshire for nursing her children herself: 'a maternal duty wholly neglected in the fashionable world'. He also tells the reader that 'the divine eloquence of Rousseau awakened her sensibility, and that no sooner was she inspired with a sense of her duty, than she had virtue and resolution to fulfil it', 16 note.
67 *Ibid.*, 1.
68 *Female Jockey Club*, 6, 2 and 7.
69 *Morning Chronicle*, 3 April, announced that 'uncommon sales' had induced Eaton to print five thousand more copies as a fourth edition.
70 *Female Jockey Club*, 176.
71 See the discussion in Davis, 'Behold the Man', 196–7.
72 *Morning Post*, 30 July.
73 *Politics for the People* becomes aware of Pigott only from the end of 1793, that is, after the incident with Hodgson. 'Verses on a Late Occasion' appeared on the front page of no. iv, 19 October (1: 37):

> When falling Britain wish'd to save her State,
> Mouchards came forth, t'avert th'impending Fate;
> *Leach*, *Vaughan*, and *Newman*, severally conjoin'd,
> To praise the King, and to enslave Mankind.
> *Pigott* and *Hodgson*, were to Dungeons sent,
> Because they dar'd to speak of discontent:
> Say then ye Britons, here's your boasted charter?
> *Freedom* you've resigned, and *Slavery* ta'en in barter.

A satirical 'Catalogue Raisonee' appeared on 14 December 1793 (1: 134), naming Pigott as author of 'Sketches from Nature in High Preservation'.
74 IKD, 1.
75 Pigott, *Political Dictionary* (1795), 170–1 and 40.
76 *Ibid.*, 69.
77 Burke, *Reflections*, 128.
78 *Political Dictionary* [i].
79 McCalman, 'Newgate in Revolution', 102.
80 See Watson, *The life of Gordon*, 83, 97, and 2 and Colson, *Strange History*, 237. Watson refers to Pigott's *Treachery no Crime* for a description of Newgate,

The life of Gordon, 83. On Watson's treatment of Marie Antoinette, see McCalman, 'Newgate Revolution', 102. There is a note on Gordon's death in *Persecution!!!*, 41. Robert Pigott's *Liberty of the Press* has a 'Supplement' discussing Gordon's case.

81 Dyer, *Complaints*, 17, compared Junius and Pigott as writers who 'aimed to show the errors of the English government, by exposing the vices of its ministers', 17. He thought Pigott had not made 'sufficient concessions in favour of those who have returned from the paths of folly: but the characters which the author draws are well known, in general to be accurately taken'. In his *Principles of the British Constitution Explained*, Flower answered the substantive points made in *Animadversions on the Jockey Club*, but dissociated himself from Pigott's method. Pigott was remembered more jovially in *The Festival of humour* (1800), 8, for repartee about the Crown always being 'surrounded by vermin'.

82 See his attack on 'Modern Patriotism' in *The Watchman*, 98–100. For Coleridge's attitude to Gerrald, see Chapter 2.

Notes to Chapter 5

1 See 69–70, Chapter 2.

2 *History of Two Acts*, 280, in a speech where Charles Sturt denies the claim.

3 See *Rex* v. *Richard Lee*, National Archive, TSP, TS 11/837.

4 Thompson, *Making of the English Working Class*, 155.

5 I am grateful to Tim Whelan for pointing out the presence of Lee's poems in the American editions of Maria de Fleury's *Divine Poems*.

6 On 10 September 1795, Reid was admitted to a general committee meeting in 'a deputation from the Moral and Political Society who bro't 70 Copies of their first production'. See *Selections*, 302, and McCalman, 'The Infidel as Prophet', 32–3. *The Curses and Causes of War* (1795), printed for the society by Hawes, has a distinctively millenarian flavour: 'these are the times of refreshment that have been spoken of by the mouths of all Prophets', 4. This may be the same group that was calling itself the United Friends of Religious and Civic Liberty a month later. See below, note 46. Reid later claimed to have been 'transported as a young man by the preaching of Calvinist Methodists Martin Madan and William Romaine'. See McCalman, 'Infidel as Prophet', 29.

7 'Preface', *Evangelical Magazine*, 1 (1793) 2.

8 *Flowers from Sharon*, 'Advertisement' [iii].

9 Wheeler, *The Rose of Sharon*, np.

10 *Evangelical Magazine*, 2 (1794) 82–3. The following poems from *Flowers from Sharon* had appeared in the magazine under the pseudonym 'Ebenezer': 'On the Heavenly Jerusalem', 1 (1793) 88, 'On the Ascension of Christ', 1 (1793) 132, 'The Afflicted Soul's Refuge', 1 (1793) 220, and 'The Christian's Attachment to the House of God', 2 (1794) 44. No poems appear under the names 'Ebenezer' or 'Richard Lee' after January 1794.

11 *Edinburgh Review*, 2 (1803), 197 and 200.

12 'Eternal Love', *Flowers from Sharon*, 1 and 14, Bennett and Bogue, *History of Dissenters*, 4: 392.

13 Reid, *Rise and dissolution*, 48. Interestingly, the second edition dropped this jibe, perhaps to save the blushes of some of Reid's evangelical sponsors.

14 See 'On the *Commencement of a* FRIDAY EVENING LECTURE, at the ADELPHI CHAPEL. . ..', *Flowers from Sharon*, 85–7, and Feltham, *The Picture of London for 1802*, 33. Grove stressed the importance of preaching 'a *free* and *full* salvation'. See Grove, *Substance of a sermon*, 11. His engraved portrait accompanies *Evangelical Magazine*, 3 (August 1795).

15 Terry had also collaborated with the hyper-Calvinist preacher William Huntington to reprint John Saltmarsh's tract *Free Grace* in 1792 (originally published in 1645). Huntington was to split with Terry, who had published his sermons, when he discovered him distributing Painite propaganda to the congregation. See Mee, 'Is there an Antinomian in the House?' For Reid's claim, see *Rise and dissolution*, 69. If nothing else, it shows that Reid himself was well versed in such literature and probably knew Jordan's edition. *Flowers from Sharon* was printed by E. Hodson, sometimes Hodgson, of 21 Bell Yard, Temple Bar, an LCS member who was interrogated by the Privy Council that summer and appeared as a witness at Hardy's trial. He claimed at the trial to have joined the society in February 1794. Barrell and Mee, 3: 120–4.

16 How, *Sufficiency*, 42.

17 See the advertisements for Terry's *Prophetic Vision, or Daniel's Great Image* in the *Morning Chronicle*, 15 February 1794, and for several days thereafter.

18 Barrell thinks Lee had joined the LCS by at least January 1794. See IKD, 609. Thelwall mentions being brought a letter by 'Citizen Lee' [possibly written 'Lea'] in the letter to Citizen Allum of 13 February 1794. See the detailed discussion of the letter in the next chapter. Interrogated by the Privy Council, Hodson claimed to have joined after Lee – transcribed as 'Legh' – in his interview before the Privy Council, National Archive, Privy Council Papers, PC 1/22/36A. Lee's poetry begins appearing in *Pig's Meat* before the arrest of Hardy in May as follows: 'The Triumph of Liberty' (2: 176–7); 'The Rights of God' (2: 204); and 'Sonnet to Freedom' (2: 284). The first is attributed to 'Richard Lee', author of 'a Volume of Poems lately Published'. 'The Rights of God' is described as 'an early production of RICHARD LEE'. The poem comes with an anti-monarchical epigraph combining a verse from Isaiah with three lines from Milton:

> *The Lord alone shall be exalted.*
> *Man over men, he made not LORD;*
> *Such title to himself reserving,*
> *Human left from human free.*

'Sonnet to Freedom' was issued after the treason trials, which may explain the topic.

19 For Powell's letters, see Chapter 1. Perchard and Brock are listed as merchants with premises in 13 Chatham Place, Blackfriars, in Boyle, *The general*

London guide (1793), 3. The *Evangelical Magazine*'s description of Lee as a 'laborious mechanic' suggests the haziness of class taxonomy in the period, especially to those, as it were, looking down.

20 The other poem in the *Death of Despotism* is 'The Crown a Bauble' that appears in *Songs from the rock* as 'The Baubles of Courts'.

21 Other versions of the title include *Songs for the Year 1795*, and *Songs and Odes Sacred to Truth, Liberty, and Peace. The Oracle*, 20 January 1795, carries an advertisement for William Belcher's *Account of a Late Circumstance* that lists Eaton and Lee as booksellers. Lee is described as 'a young man of genius, much, in Mr. Belcher's opinion, resembling Dr. Watts'. By this stage, Lee was selling books from St Ann's Court. His mother seems to have run a shop there. According to the advertisement, Lee was also selling 'his own Works, viz, Flowers from Sharon, price 3s. And Songs for the New Year, price 1s. 6d.' The copy of *Songs for the Year 1795* in the British Library at RB 23.a.10133 is a reissue of *Songs from the rock* with a new half title.

22 See, for instance, 'FREEDOM REIGNS', *Songs from the rock*, 52–3, which begins with what seems an ironic commentary on verdict at the treason trials:

> ******* thy Sentence just,
> Dooms thee to embrace the Dust.

23 See the note to the 'Tribute of Civic Gratitude', *Songs from the rock*, 111.

24 See *Songs from the rock*, 11–12, 3–35, 13–15, and 69–75.

25 Philp, *Reforming Ideas*, 35.

26 Barrell, 'Rus in Urbe'.

27 See *A Complete Library. Proposals for publishing by subscription, sacred to truth, liberty, and peace.*

28 Barrell's 'Rus in Urbe' mentions some of these poets in its account of the pastoral and elegiac verse sent to *Politics for the People* and elsewhere. For the specific place of James Thomson's memory in the radical societies of the 1790s, see Barrell and Guest, 'Thomson in the 1790s'.

29 See 'Justice and Equality', *Songs from the rock*, 31. I have not been able to trace the lines to any published Merry poem, nor the poem addressing 'Aminta', to any magazine from the period.

30 See the additional title-page in the British Library copy RB 23.a.10133 on the verso of which this dedication appears.

31 See *The Gospel of Reason*, 1–2. Once in Philadelphia, Lee reissued the translation with other of his pamphlets as *Political Curiosities*. The extract also appeared as an 'IMPORTANT AND CURIOUS EXTRACT FROM ROUSSEAU' in the AUM 2.14 (1797) 348–50. On the reception of Rousseau, see *Critical Review*, 15 (1763) 31 and Duffy, *Rousseau in England.*

32 See 'The Rights of God' in *Songs from the rock*, 17–18. For the phrase 'divine rights of republics', see *Monthly Review*, 16 (1795) 208, a review of John Cook's Civil War pamphlet *Monarchy no creature of God's making* (1651), reissued by Eaton in 1794. The *Monthly* comments: 'we see no end likely to be answered by this re-publication; except it be to show that fanaticism is a useful

instrument, which may be employed, at pleasure, in the service of either monarchy or democracy'.

33 See *Pig's Meat*, 2: 204. McCalman and Chase argue that Spence's use of biblical language and visions are fundamental to his outlook. Spence came from a Calvinist background. Chase suggests that his radicalism became overtly millenarian and visionary only when he submerged himself in London's metropolitan culture of enthusiasm. See McCalman, *Radical Underworld*, 66, and Chase, *People's Farm*, 48.

34 See note 13 above for the poems that appeared in *Pig's Meat*. Lee's poetry also appeared in various other places: *The Blessings of War*, 8, ends with the final stanza of 'The Horrors of War' (*Songs from the rock*, 40); *The Wrongs of Man*, 4, reprints 'Let us Hope to see Better Days' from *Songs from the rock*, 9–10; and *Warning to Tyrants* has on its title page an entry under 'Age, Golden' that is a poem 'By the author of "Songs, sacred to Truth, Liberty, and Peace"'. Lee does not name himself as *author* of any of these lines. *The Happy Reign of George the Last* ends with stanzas taken from James Kennedy's *Treason! Or Not Treason!*, 4, published by Eaton.

35 IKD, 546. Barrell, ed., *Exhibition Extraordinary!!*, 7, also notes that the playbill seems to have been found first in Yorkshire, from where it was sent to the Attorney General on 19 February 1794. Rev. Foley of Stourbridge also sent the law officers a copy, 24 February, National Archive, TSP, TS11/953. Barrell notes that it seems to have first appeared in London a few days later, reported by the spy John Taylor as read during an LCS meeting on 28 February. Thelwall also reportedly read it aloud at one of his lectures on the fast day itself. Apparently, it stayed in print throughout the year, appearing on Lee's advertisement pages as 'Nebuchadnezzar's decree for a Fast'. See IKD, 546.

36 Lee's compilations from Pigott and others can be dated fairly accurately because the date of the next is generally announced on the last page of the previous one. The sequence goes: *The Rights of Kings, No. 1 of a Political Dictionary*; *The Rights of Princes*; *The Rights of Nobles*; *The Rights of Priests*; *The Blessings of War*; *The Wrongs of Man*; *The Rights of Man*; *Warning to Tyrants*; *The Voice of the People*; *The Excellence of the British Constitution*. The final page of *The Rights of Kings* promises *The Rights of Princes* would be out on 20 July. They are all published from the Berwick Street address bar *The Excellence of the British Constitution,* which informs readers that the Tree of Liberty has been transplanted to the Strand. Its final page also advertises *Remedies for State Diseases*. I have not been able to trace a pamphlet with that title, but Barrell suggests it may be *King Killing*.

37 *Rights of Kings*, 4. The entry on 'Monarch' appears in *Political Dictionary*, 79.

38 *Admirable Satire on the Death, Dissection, and Funeral Procession, & Epitaph of Mr. Pitt!!!*, [3], 12, and 13.

39 The original satire was published in the *Telegraph*, 20, 21, and 24 August. Ballard published an edition as *Pitt's Ghost* for 2d. Lee's fifth edition was published as *A faithful narrative of the last illness, death, and interment* with the episodes on the dreadful apparition. It is advertised in *The*

Voice of the People. The sixth edition added extracts from the Prime Minister's will.

40 See *A faithful narrative of the last illness, death, and interment of the Rt. Hon. W. Pitt*, 6th edn, 21 and 24. A loyalist riposte to this series of satires appeared as *The decline and fall, death, dissection, and funeral procession of his most contemptible lowness the London Corresponding Society* (1796), where Lee appears 'with the Tree of Liberty tied to his back, wheeling a barrow full of seditious pamphlets', 20–1.

41 See IKD, especially 593.

42 *Account of the ... meeting of the inhabitants of Westminster*, 12. See IKD, 593 on the exchange between Fox and Sheridan.

43 *Happy Reign of George the Last*, title-page.

44 On Jekyll and Pittachio, see *Exhibition Extraordinary!!*, 13–15. Jekyll is routinely attacked as 'Jackal' in the *Tomahawk* later in 1795.

45 See 'On Tyrannicide' in *The Cabinet* (1795), 2: 67–80. See Corfield and Evans, *Youth and Revolution*, 188–90, on Pitchford.

46 *Rights of the Devil*, 7 and 14. The address of the United Friends of Religious and Civil Liberty uses similar language to argue against '*Arbitrary* and *Papal* Power', 3. Lee sold their tracts and may well have joined them after he left the LCS.

47 The information about the title was passed on to Parliament by Charles Sturt. See *History of Two Acts*, 369.

48 See the account in IKD, 613–22, on the discussions of Lee in Parliament.

49 See *History of Two Acts*, 275.

50 Barrell suggests that the Opposition had decided that Lee had to be sacrificed to the law officers if the campaign against the two bills was to succeed. Sheridan and Fox demanded to know why no prosecution of Lee had been brought on, IKD, 617.

51 *History of Two Acts*, 369.

52 Reid, *Rise and dissolution*, 6. The title-page of the British Library's copy of the *Rights of Princes* (1389 d. 27) has the following written on it: 'Sturt told the house that Lee had been twice turned out of the London Corresponding Society: Ballard (another bookseller involved in the radical movement) alledges [sic] that it was for disagree[ing] with some of the members in religious sentiments. Lee is a Methodist.' For the LCS's disclaimer of any association with Lee, see *History of Two Acts*, 330. Sturt's visit to Lee's mother caused much hilarity in the *Tomahawk*. See, for instance, nos. XXXVIII, 10 December 1795, 153, and XLIV, 17 December 1795, 177.

53 See Barrell's account of the ambivalent attitude of the LCS towards Lee during this period, IKD, 617–18.

54 *The True Briton*, 1 December 1795, announces: 'At the Westminster Quarter Sessions, held at Guildhall on Saturday, the Grand Jury found three Bills of Indictment against Citizen R. Lee for publishing Seditious Pamphlets.'

55 *The Times*, 19 December. 1795. The indictment against Lee, naming the three pamphlets, is at National Archive, TSP, TS 11/854.

56 See Durey, *Transatlantic Radicals*, 187.
57 Quoted *ibid.*, 682.
58 *Political Curiosities* comes with an ironic dedication to 'Peter Porcupine'. *Political Curiosities* may be the 'book' mentioned in Cobbett's account of Lee's fate, but more substantial was *Crimes of the Kings and Queens of England*, full of animus against the whole institution of the monarchy. Lee advertised this volume along with a new magazine to be called 'The American Library' by 'A SOCIETY OF LITERARY GENTLEMEN'. Subscriptions were accepted by Lee and another radical exile, William Y. Birch, an apprentice printer who fled Britain in 1794 after the *Manchester Herald* was suppressed. See Durey, *Transatlantic Radicals*, 32, on Birch.
59 Cobbett, *A Bone to Gnaw for the Democrats*, xxvi, and *Works*, 5: 75.
60 Cobbett, *Works*, 7: 59 and 9: 270 and 258.
61 Douglas, 'Citizen Lee and the Tree of Liberty', 11.
62 AUM, 1 (1797), 10. The magazine was launched as a weekly, but became bi-weekly after the first four numbers. It ceased publication in March 1798.
63 The *American senator* is announced as 'Publishing in Numbers' in the first number of the AUM, 1 (1797), 31, dated 2 January, and available at Lee's Chestnut Street shop. *Poems* by Della Crusca, Volney's *Ruins of Empire*, and Godwin's *Political justice* are advertised below this notice. 'Richard Lee, Philadelphia' appears on the unpaginated list 'Subscriber's Names' at the end of the third volume of the *American senator*.
64 AUM 1 (1797), 370.
65 *Ibid.*, 358–9.
66 Quoted from Rushton's letter to Washington, AUM, 2 (1797), 354. Lee is named as a committee member of the Pennsylvania Society Promoting the Abolition of Slavery, AUM, 2 (1797) 119. Rhees or Rhys was a Baptist minister who fled Wales to avoid arrest in 1794. See Davies, *Transatlantic Brethren*, 221–3, and Twomey, *Jacobins and Jeffersonians*, 102–3 on his disillusionment with American slavery and his letters to the AUM.
67 See Cotlar, *Tom Paine's America*, 65–6, and also Twomey, *Jacobins and Jeffersonians*, 104–5, on Lee and Rhees as exceptional in their opinions on slavery. Lee's name no longer appears in advertisements for the AUM after August 1797. Cobbett's claim that he tried travelling and ended up in gaol in New York is given some credence by a subscription bill for an edition of Vicesimus Knox's *Elegant Extracts* from New York (mentioning a reduced price for subscriptions received before 1 November 1798). See *A Complete Library* (1798). If Cobbett's 'travelling' implies some sort of salesmanship, then he may be the Richard Lee who turns up selling medicine in Baltimore and then New York in various newspaper advertisements in the American press from 1803. Some maintain a connection with William Y. Birch in Philadelphia and others refer to the street in New York from which the 1798 subscription was issued. Some also claim Lee had been involved in selling medicine for 'upwards of six years'. Lee had founded the AUM six years previously and may have been selling medicines – as many booksellers did – from his shop.

Twomey briefly mentions Birch and Lee going into partnership as apothecaries in *Jacobins and Jeffersonians*, 67. What really matters about this uncertain final narrative, as Lee vanishes almost to nothing, is that he seems to have been squeezed out of the public sphere by a new generation of American editors who identified themselves as Democrats in terms of a political party rather than the utopian aspirations of the earlier 1790s.

Notes to Chapter 6

1 The phrase 'erect and independent' appears in Godwin, *Caleb Williams*, 230.
2 See Green's excellent discussion of this idea in *Majesty of the People*, 41–61.
3 See Fairclough, *Romantic Crowd*, especially 69–70.
4 The phrase appears in Thelwall's notes for the lecture on 'abuses in the profession and practices of the law', f. 4 in National Archive, TSP, TS 11/956. Seized at his arrest, the Privy Council showed the notes to Henry Eaton, supposedly for him to confirm Thelwall's handwriting. Taylor's notes on the 21 February lecture are also at TS 11/956. Henry Eaton took tickets at the door and also sold copies of Gilbert Wakefield's *The Spirit of Christianity compared with the Spirit of the Times in Great Britain* (1794). Two songs, 'The Rights of Britons' and 'Johnny Frost', were also sold. Copies of both are in the same file.
5 LT, 18 and 22.
6 Thelwall to Coleridge, 10 May 1796, in Gibbs 'An Unpublished Letter', 88.
7 LT, 33
8 *Ibid.*, 33–4. He also produced a long poem *Orlando and Almeyda* (1787). *Ibid.*, 27.
9 Thelwall submitted the first play to George Colman the Elder at the Haymarket, who brought his own *Incle and Yorico* (1787) on to the stage instead. As Susan Thelwall's letter shows, see page 56. Thelwall suspected Thomas Harris had passed the manuscript of the *Incas* on to Thomas Morton to use for his *Columbus* (1792).
10 LT describes Coachmakers' Hall as a 'mock senate and synod', 45, but also gives a sense of how important it was to Thelwall's intellectual development, not least in relation to the efforts he took to keeping it open, corroborated by Susan Thelwall's letters of December. LT sometimes affects a literary condescension to the popular print sociability of the 1780s and 1790s.
11 See Thompson, 'From Forum to Repository'.
12 LT, 49.
13 On the archaeology of this idea, see Mee, *Conversable Worlds*, 24–5, 68–74, and 147–8.
14 LT, 51.
15 Godwin and Thelwall met often in the period 1793–5, as Godwin's diary shows, but there is no evidence of contact before 1793. Thelwall was a member of the Philomaths before Godwin began to attend in 1793. See his *Ode to science* (1791).
16 Thale, *London Debating Societies*, 321.
17 *Rights of Nature*, 21.

18 Solomonescu, *Materialist Imagination*, 3. See also Fairclough, *Romantic Crowd*, especially 107–21.
19 Solomonescu, *Materialist Imagination*, 16.
20 *Ibid.*, 15. When called as a witness at his trial, Parkinson said he had been 'pretty intimate with Thelwall over the last seven years'. See Barrell and Mee, 8: 72.
21 LT, 145.
22 *The Peripatetic* (1793), 1: 83 and viii.
23 See the discussion of this context for the allegory in Solomonescu, *Materialist Imagination*, 29–30. On Eaton's trial for using the allegory, see Chapter 1.
24 *Tribune*, 3: 200.
25 On Thelwall's use of the electricity trope, see Fairclough, *Romantic Crowd*, especially, 116.
26 Thelwall, *Natural and Constitutional Right*, 68. See the discussion in Green, *Majesty of the People*, 49–56.The same passage is discussed from the perspective of Thelwall's materialism, in Solomonescu, *Materialist Imagination*, 23–4.
27 LT, 69–70.
28 See BL, Place Papers, Papers of the LCS, Add MS 27817 f. 23. The Society agreed that the 'number of Members shall be unlimited, and each subscribe not less than 1s 6d per quarter' (f. 24). At their next meeting, a week later, they confirmed their name as the 'London Society of the Friends of the People'. They also resolved to appoint a committee to confer with the Southwark society and adopt its rules. See Chapter 2, note 62.
29 *Whole of the Proceedings at the Meeting of the Friends of the Liberty of the Press*, 6–7.
30 Susan Thelwall to Jack Vellum, [9 March 1793], National Archive, TSP, TS 11/956. Her letter takes the problems with *The Peripatetic* as a sign that the liberty of the press 'is already gone': 'Mr. Thelwall after some trouble pr[ocur]'d a printer to print the publication I before spoke to you of, but this printer after getting the first volume almost ready to come out declin'd printing any more [unless] T. would strike out all the political matter or turn it on the Aristocratical side this [T.] certainly refus'd to do.' Thelwall made a short speech at the dinner. See *Morning Chronicle*, 11 March 1793, which notes the Edwards letter explaining his absence and Sheridan's drollery on it.
31 LT, 115. Thelwall joined around 17 October and was elected delegate for division 25 four days later. See *Selections*, 88n. For the high opinion of Gerrald that Thelwall shared with many others see Chapter 2.
32 Thelwall made his offer to the general committee on 14 November. See *Selections*, 93 and note. Thelwall was proposed and disqualified as a delegate to the Edinburgh Convention at the general meeting of 24 October, *ibid.*, 88. The article of disqualification had caused some debate before being passed, *ibid.*, 87.
33 Divisions of the LCS seems to have begun to use the Compton Street address from May 1793. The central committee met there from January 1794. See *Selections*, 66, 103n, and 109.

34 He gave only a single performance in the Minories; 'to a thronged audience who received it with enthusiasm', LT, 130.

35 The early 'Memoir of Mr. John Thelwall, the Celebrated Political Lecturer', describes Allum and Thelwall as closely involved in rallying the Southwark 'Friends of the People' after the November 1792 proclamation. See the *New, General, and Complete Weekly Magazine* 1 (1796), 29. Allum's letter is at National Archive, TSP, TS 11/953. The Allum letter is reproduced in one of the versions of Hardy's trial, *The proceedings in cases of high treason, under a special commission of oyer and terminer*, 682–4, published by Ridgway and Symonds from Ramsey's shorthand notes. Ramsey was the shorthand writer that Thelwall used for his lectures. See page 181 for Gurney's advice on this precaution.

36 Barrell and Mee, 8: 22 and 24.

37 Gurney described him as 'a man liable in the warmth of speaking to be hurried away by his passion' (Barrell and Mee, 8: 34). See Mee, *Romanticism, Enthusiasm, and Regulation*, 115–27.

38 *Political Lectures* (1795), 4.

39 See Hazlitt, 'On the Difference between Writing and Speaking', 264–5.

40 *Political Lectures* (1795), 17.

41 The various reports from Taylor are in the file at National Archive, TSP, TS 11/953. See IKD, 567. Eaton drew on Otway's play for the epigraph to Pigott's *Persecution* a few weeks before. Eaton, Pigott, and Thelwall were all members of division 25 in February 1794. *Political Lectures* (1795) mentions the arrest of Hodgson and Pigott briefly (13).

42 See IKD, 395. Printed slips with the title *The Speeches of Pierre and Jaffeir* are in the BL, Place Papers, Draft of Letters of Thomas Hardy, Add MS 27818 f. 4. Both are inscribed 'in 1793', but they may date from the time of Thelwall's lecture early in 1794. In a later incident, the ministerial press blamed the Kemble and Sheridan revival of the play in October 1795 for inciting the attack on the king's coach. See IKD, 567–8. Note also Piozzi's comparison of Merry and Pierre above 114.

43 Apart from the British Library copy (Figure 11), copies of the handbill are in National Archive, TSP, TS 11/953 (with the covering note from Reeves).

44 See the discussion of Lee's reissue of the bill in 1795 in the previous chapter.

45 These letters and reports are in National Archive, TSP, TS 11/953 with other material gathered for Thelwall's prosecution. The anonymous letter to Banks is dated '19 April'. The letter from Banks to the law officers is dated 22 April. See Taylor's evidence at Thelwall's trial (Barrell and Mee, 8: 37–43). The prosecution's claim that it possessed new material that would succeed against Thelwall, where they had failed with Hardy and Tooke, largely depended upon Taylor's evidence, but this strategy collapsed when Erskine revealed him to be a bigamist and perjurer. See IKD, 395–6.

46 See Thelwall's account in the dedication to the two juries affixed to *Political lectures, (no. II.) Sketches of the history of prosecutions for political opinion*, iii–iv, published immediately after the events.

47 The note is at National Archive, TSP, TS 11/953. It was produced in court, where Gurney's behaviour was animadverted upon. See Barrell and Mee, 8: 22, 30, and 33–5.

48 Ritson's role is acknowledged in LT, 141. He and Thelwall appear together several times in Godwin's diary. In the middle of Reeves's attempts to prosecute Thelwall, Ritson joined Godwin and Thelwall on 4 May, when they dined at Holcroft's. On 12 June 1795, Godwin supped at Thelwall's with the Richters and Ritson after attending his last lecture before the summer break.

49 LT, 164.

50 In his lecture on the abuses of the law, f. 2, Thelwall suggested that 'A National Convention may some time or other, perhaps, take this subject into consideration in its fullest extent', National Archive, TSP, TS 11/956.

51 *Natural and Constitutional Right*, 37.

52 The poems published in the *Politician* were 'Stanzas written by J. Thelwall in the Tower upon Hearing that the Commission was Sealed, for Trying the State Prisoners for High Treason', dated 28 September, and 'The Cell' dated October 24. He had also promised 'The Crisis' and 'The Farewell'. See the *Politician*, no. 3, 20–1, and no. 4, 28. 'The Cell' was originally published in the *Morning Post* the day after it was written. See Chapter 2 for a discussion of the *Politician*'s genesis.

53 *The Politician*, no. 3, 26.

54 Coleridge to Thelwall, 13 May 1796, Coleridge's *Collected Letters*, 1: 213, where he told him 'on your *heart* I should rest for my safety'. The exchange was part of their ongoing discussion of whether morality had to be underpinned by religion.

55 *Tribune*, 2: xv.

56 McCann, *Cultural Politics*, 86.

57 The third volume of the *Tribune* did print 'Lines written by a Female Citizen', 3: 105–6.

58 See the account in LT, 76, and 53.

59 *Political Lectures* (1795), 3–4.

60 McCann, *Cultural Politics*, 90.

61 *Political Lectures* (1795), 58.

62 'Advertisement', *Poems written in Close Confinement* [i]. The lectures recommenced in February. Thelwall used the proceeds to try and repair his domestic finances. While he had been in prison, Susan Thelwall had relied on support from the LCS.

63 *Tribune*, 2: 363, using the authority of Blackstone.

64 Godwin, *Considerations*, 14, 16, and 20.

65 The diary also records Godwin's appearance at the lecture on 4 February 1794. Apart from these two visits, Godwin and Thelwall regularly met and dined from late 1793.

66 Alderson to Godwin, 5 February [1796], MS Abinger c. 3, Bodleian Library. Alderson playfully imagines Godwin being accused of accepting a government pension, a joke one doubts he enjoyed.

67 See Thelwall, *Sober Reflections*, 105.
68 See the discussion in Fairclough, *Romantic Crowd*, 118–21.
69 Thelwall, *Sober Reflections*, 16–17.
70 Thelwall, *Tribune*, 3: 188. See also Michael Scrivener, 'John Thelwall and the Revolution of 1649'.
71 *Natural and Constitutional Right*, 39–40.
72 See Thompson, *The Romantics*, 156–203.
73 See above 38–9.
74 See Thelwall to Hardy, 28 Feb. 1801, Wordsworth Trust and *Poems Written Chiefly in Retirement;* BL, Place Papers, Papers of the LCS, Add MS 27817, ff. 87–8 has a subscription sheet for the volume, with a note dated 19 April 1801 for Hardy to pass on. The name of the addressee is scribbled out, 88v, but seems to be Geddes, possibly Alexander Geddes, Thelwall's former ally in the Friends of the Liberty of the Press. Hardy was also involved in circulating *The Daughters of Adoption* to a circle of Thelwall's friends in Nottingham. See Hardy to Thomas Oldham, 14 November 1800, BL, Place Papers, Draft Letters of Thomas Hardy, Add MS 27818, f. 15.
75 A rich scholarly literature on Thelwall's elocutionary practices has emerged lately. See, for instance, Duchan, 'Conceptual Underpinnings', Fleming, 'Tracing the Textual Reverberation', and Solomonescu, *Materialist Imagination*, 93–109 and 117–19. On the dispute between Jeffrey and Thelwall, see *Mr Thelwall's Letter to Francis Jeffray* (1804) and *Mr. Thelwall's reply to the calumnies* (1804) and the discussion in Mee, 'Policing Enthusiasm in the Romantic Period', especially 188–90.
76 See McCann, *Cultural Politics*, 104–5.
77 The fullest account is Judith Thompson, *John Thelwall in the Wordsworth Circle*, but see also Mee, '"The Dungeon and the Cell"'.

Bibliography

Primary works

Manuscript collections

Bodleian Library

William Godwin, Original Correspondence [1780]–1835, MS Abinger c. 1–3, Abinger Collection

British Library (BL)

Thomas Hardy, Memoir, *c.* 1798–1832, Add MS 65153 A–B

Thomas Pelham, Earl of Chichester, Papers of Thomas Pelham, Earl of Chichester, Add MS 33124

Place Papers

Collections relating to Manners and Morals, Add MSS 27825–27830

Collections relating to Political Societies, Add MSS 27808–27810

Papers of the London Corresponding Society, 1791–1847, Add MSS 27811–27817

Draft of Letters of Thomas Hardy to editors of periodicals etc., Add MS 27818

Royal Literary Fund (RLF), 'Archive of the Royal Literary Fund', Loan 96 RLF 1–5

Dr Williams Library, London

Josiah Thompson, 'Dissenting Interest in England & Wales 1715–1773'. 2 vols, MSS 38, 5–6

Essex County Records Office

Collection of John Avery, D/DQs 26

Henry E. Huntington Library

John Larpent papers, 1737–1824, LA 933

John Rylands Library, Manchester

Piozzi Merry Correspondence, GB 133 ENG MS 614

National Archive Kew, London
Books and Correspondence of the *Gazetteer*, C 104/67 and C 104/68

Foreign Office Papers
Letters from Captain George Monro to Lord Grenville, December 1792, FO 27/40

Home Office Papers
Domestic Correspondence, George III, May 1794, HO 42/30
Cases and Reports, 1793, HO 48/3

King's Bench
Court of King's Bench, Affidavits, KB 1/27

Privy Council Papers
London Corresponding Society: lists of members of several branches, etc. PC 1/23
Draft Minutes chiefly including examinations of those accused of revolutionary designs, 1794, PC 1/22/36 A–C 1794
Privy Council Minutes, 1 1 May–31 July, PC 2/140

Registers of Births, Marriages and Deaths surrendered to the Non-parochial Registers Commissions of 1837 and 1857
Crown Court, Russell Street, RG4/4232

Treasury Solicitor's Papers (TSP)
Miscellaneous Libel Cases, TS 11/41
Miscellaneous Correspondence, TS 24/12
Papers Relating to the London Corresponding Society and the Constitutional Society, TS 11/ 952–66
Rex v. *Lord George Gordon* for high treason, TS 11/389
Rex v. *James Belcher*, 1793, TS 11/578
Rex v. *Richard Lee*, TS 11/837
Rex v. *H. D. Symonds*, 1793, TS 11/944

New York Public Library (NYPL)
Amelia Alderson Opie to Susannah Cook Taylor [1794–12, August 1797], Alderson-Opie Papers, Berg Collection New York Public Library

University College London Special Collections
'Samuel Rogers (1763–1855)', Sharpe Papers (1715–1935), MSS 14–60

University of Notre Dame, Special Collections
John Thelwall Letters, MSE/MD 3811

Wordsworth Trust
Manuscript Collection, Jerwood Centre

Printed materials

Place of publication is London unless otherwise stated.

Account of the proceedings of a meeting of the inhabitants of Westminster, in Palace-Yard, Monday, Nov. 26, 1795. Including the substance of the speeches of the Duke of Bedford, Mr. Sheridan, Mr. Fox ... [1795].

Account of the proceedings of a meeting of the London Corresponding Society, held in a Field near Copenhagen House, Monday, Oct. 26... 1795.

Admirable Satire on the Death, Dissection, and Funeral Procession, & Epitaph of Mr. Pitt!!! [copied from the TELEGRAPH *of the 20th, 21st, and 22d of August, 1795.].* 1795.

Aldgate Society of the Friends of the People. *A Thing of Shreds and Patches by an Association against Levellers.* 1793.

An Answer to Three Scurrilous Pamphlets, entitled the Jockey Club. By a member of the Jockey Club, 2nd edn. 1793.

'Antitype' [Daniel Isaac Eaton?]. *The Pernicious Effects of the Art of Printing, exposed. A short essay. Addressed to the friends of social order.* 1794.

Assassination of the King! The conspirators exposed, or, an account of the apprehension, treatment in prison, and repeated examinations before the Privy Council, of John Smith and George Higgins, on a charge of high Treason etc ... 1795.

Bailey, 'Citizen'. *Prince Brothers's Scarlet Devils Displayed, being the First Discourse on the Origin of Nobility.* 1795.

The White Devils Un-Cased, Being the first discourse upon Ecclesiastical Tyranny, and Superstition. 1795.

Barbauld, Anna Laetitia. *Civic sermons to the people. Number II. From mutual Wants springs mutual Happiness.* 1792.

Barker, E. H. *Parriana, or Notices of the Rev. Samuel Parr.* Vol. I, 1828.

Baxter, John. *A new and impartial history of England, from the most early period of genuine historical evidence to the present important and alarming crisis.* 1796.

Resistance to Oppression, The Constitutional Rights of Britons asserted in a Lecture delivered before a section of the Friends of Liberty. 1795.

Belcher, William. *Holcroft's Folly:, or, A Word on the Monstrous Doctrine that Crimes are but Mistakes.* [1795?].

Bennett, James. [A Lover of Truth]. *Sacred Politics, or, an impartial inquiry into the doctrine of the Sacred Scriptures and especially of the New Testament, respecting Civil Government,* 2nd edn. [1795?].

The Translation of Elijah; A Funeral Sermon for the Late Rev David Bogue preached at the Poultry Chapel before the Directors of the London Missionary Society. 1825.

Bennett, James and David Bogue. *History of the Dissenters, from the Revolution in 1688, to the year 1808.* 4 vols. 1808–12.

Bentham, Jeremy. *A Fragment on Government; being an examination of what is delivered on the subject of government in general, in the introduction to Sir William Blackstone's Commentaries.* 1776.

Bernard, John, *Retrospections of America 1797–1811*, ed. Mrs Bayle Bernard. New York: Benjamin Blom, 1887.

Retrospections of the Stage. 2 vols. 1830.

Billington, Mrs. *Memoirs of Mrs. Billington, from her birth: ... - with copies of several original letters, now in the possession of the publisher, written by Mrs. Billington, to her mother*. 1792.

The Blessings of War. consisting of extracts from Pigott's Political Dictionary, and others. 1795.

Boaden, James. *Memoirs of the Life of John Philip Kemble Esq.* 2 vols. 1825.

Bogue, David. *The Great Importance of having Right Sentiments in Religion*. 1788.

Reasons for Seeking a Repeal of the Corporation and Test Acts. 1790.

Thoughts on the Necessity and Means of a Reform in the Church of England. By a Friend to Religion and his Country. 1792.

Bonner, Charles, and Robert Merry. *Airs, duetts, and chorusses, arrangement of scenery, and sketch of the pantomime, entitled The Picture of Paris. Taken in the year 1790. As performed at the Theatre-Royal, Covent-Garden*. 1790.

Boyle, Patrick. *The general London guide; or, tradesman's directory for the year 1794. With a general index to trades. Containing a separate arrangement of all* ... 1793.

Brightwell, Cecilia. *Memorials of the Life of Amelia Opie, selected and arranged from her Letters, Diaries, and other Manuscripts*. Norwich, 1854.

The British Constitution Invulnerable. Animadversions on a Late Publication, entitled The Jockey club. 1792.

The British Constitution Invulnerable. Animadversions on a Late Publication, 2nd edn [1792?].

Bull, John [pseud]. *Mr. St George: A True Story*. [1795].

Burke, Edmund. *Letters on a Regicide Peace* (1796), in *The Writings and Speeches of Edmund Burke*, gen. ed. Paul Langford. Vol. IX: *The Revolutionary War 1794–7*, ed. R. B. McDowell. Oxford University Press, 1991.

Reflections on the Revolution in France, in *The Writings and Speeches of Edmund Burke*, gen. ed. Paul Langford. Vol. VIII: *The French Revolution 1790–94*, ed. L. G. Mitchell. Oxford University Press, 1989.

The Cabinet of Curiosities. 1795.

Carpenter, Thomas. *The American senator, or a copious and impartial report of the debates in the Congress of the United States*. 3 vols. Philadelphia, PA: 1796–7.

Chalmers, George. *The Life of Thomas Pain, the author of the seditious writings, entitled Rights of Man. By Francis Oldys, A.M. of the University of Pensylvania*, 10th edn. 1793.

Charnock, John. *Rights of a Free People. An Essay on the Origin, Progress, and Perfection of the British constitution*. 1792.

A Circumstantial History of the Transactions at Paris on the Tenth of August, plainly showing the Perfidy of Louis XVI and the General Unanimity of the People in Defence of their Rights. 1792.

Cobbett, William. *A Bone to Gnaw for the Democrats*. 1797.

Porcupine's Works containing various writings and selections, exhibiting a faithful picture of the United States of America. 12 vols. 1801.

Coghlan, Margaret. *Memoirs of Mrs. Coghlan (Daughter of the late Major Moncrieffe,) written by herself, and dedicated to the British nation; being interspersed with anecdotes of the late American and present French war, with remarks moral and political.* 2 vols. 1794.

Coleridge, Samuel Taylor, *The Collected Letters of Samuel Taylor Coleridge*, ed. E. L. Griggs. 6 vols. Oxford University Press, 1956–71.

The Friend, ed. Barbara E. Rooke. 2 vols. Princeton University Press, 1969.

Lectures 1795 on Politics and Religion, ed. Lewis Patten and Peter Mann. Princeton University Press, 1971.

The Watchman, ed. Lewis Patton. Princeton University Press, 1970.

A Complete Library. Proposals for Publishing by Subscription, Extracts, Elegant, Instructive, and Entertaining, in Prose and Verse...BY THE CELEBRATED DOCT. KNOX. New York, NY. [1798].

Cook, John. *Monarchy no creature of God's making. wherein is proved, by Scripture and reason, that monarchial government is against the mind of God*, new ed. 1794.

Cooper, Thomas. *Some Information respecting America*... 1794.

Cruden, William. *Sermons on evangelical and practical subjects*... 1787.

The decline and fall, death, dissection, and funeral procession of his most contemptible lowness the London Corresponding Society; ... Interspersed with correct copies of all the solemn dirges, hymns, anthems, chorusses and Psalms, sung and chaunted at the dissection and in the funeral procession as it moved from palace-Yard to Copenhagen-House. To which is added, the funeral oration delivered on this melancholy occasion by the Reverend John Horne Tooke ... 1796.

De Fleury, Maria. *Divine Poems and Essays on Various Subjects*. 1791.

Divine Poems and Essays on Various Subjects. Philadelphia. 1803.

[Dinmore, Jr, Richard] *A Brief account of the Moral and Political Acts of the Kings and Queens of England from William the Conqueror to the Revolution in 1688*. 1793.

Divine Warrants, Ends, Advantages, and Rules of the Fellowship Society, held at the Meeting House in Crown-Court, Russell-street, Covent Garden, London, for Prayer, Spiritual Conversation, &c. 1791.

Dunlap, William. *A History of the American Theatre*. 2 vols. 1833.

Dyer, George. *Complaints of the Poor People of England: Containing remarks I. On government. II. On the defects in the English government*. 1793.

Eaton, Daniel Isaac. *Eager to abolish the* ARISTOCRACY *of the Press, and so Liberate the Republic of Letters* ... 1793.

Equiano, Olaudah. *The interesting narrative of the life of Olaudah Equiano, or Gustavus Vassa, the African. Written by himself*, 6th edn. [1793].

Ethic epistles to the Earl of Carnarvon, on the mind and its operations, as bearing generally on the events of the world, particularly on those of France... 1794.

Erskine, David Steuart, Earl of Buchan. *Essays on the Lives and Writings of Fletcher of Saltoun and the Poet Thomson*. 1792.

Evans, John. *A Sketch of all the Denominations of the Christian World: to which is prefixed an outline of Atheism, Deism, and Theophilanthropism, Judaism, and Mahometism*. 1808.

The Excellence of the British Constitution, &c &c. Consisting of Extracts from Pigott, Barlow, &c. 1795.

Exhibition Extraordinary!! Radical Broadsides of the 1790s, ed. and introduced John Barrell. Nottingham: Trent Editions, 2001.

Explanation of the Word Equality. [1793].

Extermination, or an appeal to the People of England on the Present War with France. 1793.

A Faithful narrative of the last illness, death, and interment of the Rt. Hon. William Pitt . . . with an account of the dreadful apparition in Downing Street, 5th ed. 1795.

A faithful narrative of the last illness, death, and interment of the Rt. Hon. W. Pitt . . . with an account of the dreadful apparition in Downing Street . . . to which is added . . . important extracts from the Premier's . . . Will, 6th ed. 1795.

Feltham, John, *The Picture of London for 1802*. 1802.

Fennell, James. *An Apology for the Life of James Fennell*. Philadelphia, PA: 1814.

The Festival of humour; or, banquet of wit. Being a collection of the best anecdotes, repartees, Bon Mots, Epigrams, Whimsical and Laughable Adventures, . . . 1800.

Field, William. *Memoirs of the Life, Writings, and Opinions of the Rev. Samuel Parr, LL.D.: With Biographical Notices of Many of His Friends, Pupils, and Contemporaries*. 2 vols. 1828.

[Fitzgerald, William T.] *The Sturdy Reformer, A New Song, exemplifying to the Good People of England, the Doctrines of the Rights of Man*. 1792.

The Second Edition (with Additions) of The Sturdy Reformer, A New Song, exemplifying to the Good People of England, the Doctrines of the Rights of Man, 2nd edn. 1792.

Five Excellent New Songs. I. The Lady's Love for a Sailor. II. The True Lover's Farewell. III. The Greenwich Pensioner. IV. Burke's Address to the Swinish Multitude. V. The Rose Tree. 1792.

Flower, Benjamin. *The Principles of the British Constitution Explained; and the right, necessity, and expediency of reform, asserted*. . . 1793.

Fox, Charles James. *The speech of the Right Hon. Charles James Fox: containing the declaration of his principles, respecting the present crisis of public affairs*. 1792.

The speech of the Right Hon. Charles James Fox: containing the declaration of his principles, respecting the present crisis of public affairs, 3rd edn. 1792.

George, Prince of Wales, *The Correspondence of George Prince of Wales 1770–1812*, Vol. II (1789–94), ed. Arthur Aspinall. Cassell, 1963.

Gerrald, Joseph, *Authentic biographical anecdotes of Joseph Gerrald, a delegate to the British Convention in Scotland from the London Corresponding Society*. 1795.

Authentic biographical anecdotes of Joseph Gerrald, a delegate to the British Convention in Scotland from the London Corresponding Society, 2nd edn. 1795.

A Convention the Only Means of Saving us from Ruin. 1793.

The Defence of Joseph Gerrald on a Charge of Sedition. . . to which is Prefixed a Sketch of his Character. 1794.

Gerrald. A Fragment; containing some Account of the Life of this Devoted Citizen. . .. [1795].

[Gifford, John], 'The Literary Fund', *AntiJacobin Review and Magazine*, 3 (1799), 100–1.

Gifford, William. *The Baviad, and Mæviad*, new edn rev. 1797.

Godwin, William. *Caleb Williams*, Ed. with introduction by Pamela Clemit. Oxford University Press, 2009.

Considerations on Lord Grenville's and Mr. Pitt's bills, concerning treasonable and seditious practices, and unlawful assemblies. 1795.

Cursory Strictures on the Charge Delivered by Lord Chief Justice Eyre to the Grand Jury. October 2, 1794. 1794.

Enquiry concerning political justice, and its influence on morals and happiness. 2 vols. 1793.

The Letters of William Godwin. Vol. 1: *1778–1797*, ed. Pamela Clemit. Oxford University Press, 2011.

Goodwin, Thomas. *The French Revolution foreseen, in 1639. Extracts from an Exposition of the Revelation, by an eminent divine of both universities*. [1796?].

Grove, Thomas. *The Substance of a sermon preached August the 26th, 1787, at the chapel in Tottenham-Court-Road, and the tabernacle near Moorfields, ...* 2nd edn. 1787.

Hanger, George [William Combe]. *Life, Adventures, and Opinions, written by Himself*. 2 vols. 1801.

A Hanoverian, [pseud.] *John Bull Starving to Pay the Debts of the Royal Prodigal: A letter to the House of Peers*. [1795].

Hardy, Thomas. *Memoir of Thomas Hardy, Founder of and Secretary to, the London Corresponding Society, for the Diffusing Useful Political Knowledge among the People of Great Britain and Ireland, and for Promoting Parliamentary Reform*. 1832.

'Harum Skarum', *Account of a Debate in Coachmakers' Hall*. 1780.

Hawles, Sir John. *The Englishman's Right: A Dialogue between a Barrister at Law and a Juryman, ...* new edn. 1793.

Hazlitt, William. 'On the Difference between Writing and Speaking,' in *Complete Works*. Vol. 12, ed. P. P. Howe, 262–79. J. M. Dent, 1930.

The History of Two Acts, entitled an act for the safety and preservation of His Majesty's person and government against treasonable and seditious practices and attempts, and an act for the more effectually preventing seditious meetings and assemblies ... 1796.

The Hive of Modern Literature: A Collection of Essays, narratives, Allegories, and Instructive Compositions. Newcastle upon Tyne. [1795?].

Hodgson, William. *The Case of William Hodgson, now confined in Newgate, for the payment of two hundred pounds, after having suffered two years' imprisonment on a charge of sedition ...* 1796.

The Commonwealth of Reason. 1795.

Proposals for Publishing by Subscription, a Treatise Called the Female Citizen ... 1796.

[d'Holbach, Baron] *The System of Nature; or the Laws of the Moral and Physical World*, trans William Hodgson. 4 vols. 1795–6.

Holcroft, Thomas. *A narrative of facts, relating to a prosecution for high treason; including the address to the jury, ... and the defence the author had prepared, if he had been brought to trial...* 1795.

Horne, Melvill. *Three letters to a lover of truth: or, an answer to sacred politics*. 1795.

How, Samuel. *The Sufficiency of the Spirit's Teaching, without human learning. or, a treatise tending to prove human learning to be no help to the spiritual*, 8th edn. 1792.

Iliff, Edward Henry. *Angelo, a novel, founded on melancholy facts*. 2 vols. 1796.

A summary of the duties of citizenship! Written expressly for the members of the London Corresponding Society; including observations on the contemptuous neglect of the Secretary of State, with regard to their late address to the king! 1795.

Jebb, John. *An Address to the Freeholders of Middlesex assembled at the Freemasons Tavern*. 1780.

Jerningham, Edward. *Edward Jerningham and his Friends: A Series of Eighteenth-Century Letters*, ed. Lewis Bettany. Chatto and Windus, 1919.

John Horne Tooke Stripped Naked and Dissected, and his Political Anatomy Exposed to the Electors of Westminster. 1795.

'Johnny Frost'. [1794?] Single sheet.

Jones, John Gale. *Sketch of a political tour through Rochester, Chatham, Maidstone, Gravesend, &c... Part the First*. 1796.

Joyce, Jeremiah. *Mr. Joyce's arrest for "treasonable practices:" his examination before His Majesty's ... privy council; his commitment to the tower, and subsequent treatment...*, 2nd edn 1795.

Kennedy, James. *Treason! Or Not Treason! Alias the Weaver's Budget*. 1795.

Lee, Richard. *Death of Despotism and the Doom of Tyrants*. [1794?].

On the death of Mrs. Hardy, wife of Mr. Thomas Hardy, of Piccadilly; imprisoned in the tower for high treason. 1794.

Flowers from Sharon: or, Original Poems on Divine Subjects. 1794.

King Killing. [1795] Single sheet.

Proposals for publishing by subscription, sacred to truth, liberty, and peace, songs from the rock, to hail the approaching day, ... by Richard Lee. [1794?].

Songs from the rock, to hail the approaching day, sacred to truth, liberty and peace. To which is added, the tribute of civic gratitude; a congratulatory address to Thomas Hardy. 1795.

Songs for the year 1795, sacred to truth, liberty and peace inscribed to the sovereign people. With a congratulatory address to Thomas Hardy. 1795.

Lemaitre, Paul Thomas. *High treason!! Narrative of the arrest, examinations before the Privy Council, and imprisonment of P.T. Lemaitre, accused of being a party in the pop-gun plot, or, a pretended plot to kill the King! ...*, 2nd edn. 1795.

Letters on the Present State of England and America: containing a Review of Several Interesting Particulars etc. 1794.

Literary Fund. *An account of the Institution of the Society for the Establishment of a Literary Fund: the transactions of the committee for the application of the subscriptions: poems on anniversaries, &c*. 1795.

An account of the institution of the Society for the establishment of a Literary fund: constitutions of the Society: transactions of the committee in the application of subscriptions: list of subscribers: cash accompt of the fund: and poems on anniversaries, &c. from 1794 to 1798. 1799.

London Corresponding Society. *An account of the seizure of citizen Thomas Hardy, secretary to the London Corresponding Society; with some remarks on the suspension of The Habeas Corpus Act*. [1794].

Address of the London Corresponding Society to the other societies of Great Britain, united for obtaining a reform in Parliament. 1792.

Address to the Nation from the London Corresponding Society. On the Subject of Parliamentary Reform. 1793.

Correspondence of the London Corresponding Society ... for the Use of its Members. 1795.

At a general meeting of the London Corresponding Society, held at the Globe Tavern Strand; on Monday the 20th day of January, 1794 Citizen John Martin, in the Chair. [1794]

London Corresponding Society, held at the Bell, Exeter Street [Resolutions on the representation of the people in parliament, etc. Dated 2 April 1792.]

The London Corresponding Society. Addresses and Resolutions (reprinted). 1792.

London Corresponding Society, 1792–1799, ed. Michael T. Davis. 6 vols. Pickering and Chatto, 2002.

Narrative of the proceedings at a general meeting of the London Corresponding Society...., on Monday the 29th of June, 1795, 2nd edn. [1795].

Reformers no Rioters. Printed by Order of the London Corresponding Society. 1794.

Report of the Committee, appointed to revise and abridge a former report of the constitution, of the London Corresponding Society. 1794.

Selections from the Papers of the London Corresponding Society 1792–1799, ed. Mary Thale. Cambridge University Press, 1983.

London Debating Societies, 1776–1799, compiled and introduced by Donna T. Andrew. London Record Society, 1994.

London Reforming Society, *Report of the Committee to the London Reforming Society, containing a Statement of its Numbers, Connexions, and the Progress it has made in the Cause of Reform*. 1795.

Mazzinghi, Joseph [and Robert Merry]. *The Magician No Conjuror, A Comic Opera in 3 Acts*. [1792].

Mercier, Louis Sébastien. *Fragments of Politics and History*, trans. from the French, 2 vols. 1795.

Merry, Robert. *Fenelon: or, the nuns of Cambray. A serious drama, in three acts. (Altered from the French.)*. 1795.

The Laurel of Liberty. A Poem. 1790.

Lorenzo. A Tragedy in Five Acts. 1791

Ode for the fourteenth of July, 1791, the day consecrated to Freedom: being the anniversary of the revolution in France. 1791.

The Pains of Memory. 1796.

The Pains of Memory. A New Edition. Philadelphia, PA: 1796.

Réflexions politiques sur la nouvelle constitution qui se prépare en France, adressées à la république. Paris. 1792 [1793].

Wonderful Exhibition!!! Signor Gulielmo Pittachio. 1794. Single sheet.

The Wounded Soldier. A Poem by Mr. M—Y. [1795].

Moral and Political Society. *The Curses and Causes of War, Pointed out; and the approaching cessation of both determined*. 1795.

A New Song. Sung by Mr. Dignum. At the Anniversary of the Revolution of 1688. Held at the London Tavern, Nov. 1792. Single sheet.

Nott, John. *An appeal to the inhabitants of Birmingham: designed as an answer to Job Nott, buckle-maker* . . . 1792.
Paddock, R. *For 1794. The Apollo: being an elegant selection of approved modern songs, by the most esteemed writers; . . . To which is prefixed, Loyalty and masonry, a new song*. Bath: 1794.
Paine, Thomas. *The Complete Writings of Thomas Paine*, ed. Philip S. Foner. 2 vols. New York, NY: Citadel Press, 1945.
Rights of Man, edit. with an introduction by Eric Foner. Harmondsworth: Penguin Classics rpt. 1985.
[Parkinson, James]. Old Hubert, *Pearls Cast before Swine by Edmund Burke*. 1793.
Revolutions without Bloodshed; or, Reformation preferable to Revolt. 1794
Vindication of the London Corresponding Society. 1794.
Perry, Sampson. *The Argus, or General Observer, A Political Miscellany*. 1796.
A Disquisition of the Stone and Gravel; with Strictures on the Gout, When combined with those Disorders, 7th edn. 1785.
Historical Sketch of the French Revolution. Commencing with its Predisposition, causes, and carried on to the acceptation of the constitution, in 1795. 2 vols. 1796.
A Picture of the Times in a Letter Addressed to the People of England by a Lover of Peace, 2nd ed. 1795.
Phillips, Richard. *Original papers published at different times in the Leicester Herald*. Leicester: 1793.
Pigott, Charles. *The Female Jockey Club, or A Sketch of the Manners of the Age*, 6th edn., 1794.
The Jockey Club, or A Sketch of the Manners of the Age, Part the First, 13th edn. 1792.
The Jockey Club, or A Sketch of the Manners of the Age, Part the Second, 7th edn. 1792.
The Jockey Club, or A Sketch of the Manners of the Age, Part the Third, 3rd edn. 1792.
New Hoyle, or the general repository of games; containing rules and instructions for playing whist, Cribbage, Piquet, Quinzf, Goff, Draughts, Faro, Hazard, Quaerille &c . . . 1795.
Persecution!!! The case of Charles Pigott: contained in the defence he had prepared, and which would have been delivered by him on his trial, if the grand jury had not thrown out the bill preferred against him. 1793.
A Political Dictionary: Explaining the True Meaning of Words. 1795.
Strictures on the New Political Tenets of the Rt. Hon. Edmund Burke, 1791.
Treachery no Crime, or the system of courts. Exemplified in the life, character, and late desertion of General Dumourier, in the virtue of implicit confidence in kings and ministers, and in the present concert of princes, against the French republic. 1793.
Pigott, Harriet. *Private Correspondence of A Woman of Fashion*. 2 vols. 1832.
Pigott, Robert. *Liberty of the Press. A letter addressed to the National Assembly of France, . . . with notes and supplement afterwards added; and offered to the consideration of every Englishman*. Paris: 1790.

Piozzi, Hester Lynch. *The Piozzi Letters: Correspondence of Hester Lynch Piozzi, 1784–1821 (formerly Mrs. Thrale)* Vol. 2. *1792–97*. ed. Edward A. Bloom and Lillian D. Bloom. Newark, NJ: University of Delaware Press, 1991.

Thraliana: The Diary of Mrs. Hester Lynch Thrale (later Mrs. Piozzi) 1776–1809, ed. Katherine C. Balderston. 2nd edn. Oxford University Press, 1951.

Pitt's Ghost. Being An Account of the Death, Dissection, Funeral Procession, Epitaph, an Horrible apparition, of the Much Lamented Late Minister of State. 1795.

Pitti-Clout & Dun-Cuddy: A pastoral Eclogue, wherein is expressed in Courtly Lays, the Inviolable Attachment and Constant Loves of the Treasury Shepheards, and their Firm Resolutions to Sacrifice Everything that Opposes the Possession of their Respective Sweethearts, Polly Power and Sally Plunder. [1795].

Place, Francis. *The Autobiography of Francis Place (1771–1854)*, ed. Mary Thale. Cambridge University Press, 1972.

Pocock's Everlasting Songster, containing a selection of the most approved songs, ... Also a collection of toasts & sentiments, upon a plan perfectly new, to which is added, original rules for behaviour. Gravesend: 1800.

Political Correspondence, or, Letters to a Country Gentleman retired from Parliament on the Subject of some of the Leading Characters and Events of the Present Day. 1793.

Political curiosities, including an account of the state of political affairs in Europe. Philadelphia, PA: 1796.

Political Miscellanies, Part the First by the Authors of the Rolliad and the Probationary odes. 1787.

The political martyrs, Thomas Muir, Thomas Fyshe Palmer, William Skirving, Joseph Gerrald, and Maurice Margarot, who were persecuted in the year 1793–4, for advocating the cause of reform in parliament. [1837].

Powell, James. *The Narcotic and Private Theatricals two Dramatic Pieces*. 1793.

Preston, Thomas. *The Life and Opinions of Thomas Preston*. 1817.

The proceedings in cases of high treason, under a special commission of oyer and terminer, which was first opened at Hicks's Hall, Oct. 2, 1794, and afterwards continued at the Sessions House, in the Old Bailey. Taken in short hand, by William Ramsey. 1794.

Prophetic Vision, or Daniel's Great Image. 1794.

Reid, W. H. 'Hum! Hum! A New Song' [1793]. Single sheet.

The rise and dissolution of the infidel societies in this metropolis: including, the origin of modern deism and atheism; the genius and conduct of those associations; their lecture-rooms, field-meetings, and deputations; from the Publication of Paine's Age of Reason till the present Period... 1800.

The rise and dissolution of the infidel societies in this metropolis ..., 2nd edn. 1800.

A Republican [pseud]. *The Happy Reign of George the Last, An Address to the Little Tradesmen and Labouring poor in England*. 1795.

Revolution Society. *An abstract of the history and proceedings of the Revolution Society, in London. To which is annexed a copy of the bill of rights*. 1789.

'Rights of Britons' [1794?]. Single sheet.

The Rights of the Devil; or, Consolation for the Democrats, dedicated to the King, Lords, and Commons; likewise humbly submitted to the devout consideration of the Bench of Bishops and the Prince of Wales, 2nd edn. 1795.

The Rights of Kings, No. 1 of a Political Dictionary. 1795.

The Rights of Man. Consisting of Extracts from PIGOTT's Political Dictionary, &c. 1795.

The Rights of Nobles. Consisting of Extracts from Pigott's Political Dictionary, 1795

The Rights of Priests. Consisting of Extracts from Pigott's Political Dictionary. 1795.

The Rights of Princes. Consisting of Extracts from Pigott's Political Dictionary, containing a Definition of the following Words, relative to the above NON-NATURALS. 1795.

The Rights of Swine. An Address to the Poor. 1795.

Roland, Manon. *An appeal to impartial posterity, by Citizenness Roland, . . .: or, a collection of pieces written by her during her confinement in the prisons of the Abbey, and St. Pélagie*. 1795.

Rousseau, Jean Jacques. *The Gospel of Reason. By J. J. Rousseau, citizen of Gerova*. [1795].

A Treatise of the Social Compact. Or, The Principles of Political Law. Political Classics. 1795

The second report from the Committee of Secrecy of the House of Commons, To whom the several papers referred to in His Majesty's message of the 12th day of May 1794, and which were presented (sealed up) to the House, by Mr. Secretary Dundas, upon the 12th and 13th days of the said month, by His Majesty's command, were referred: to which is added The first and second reports of the secret committee of the House of Lords . . . 1794.

Sheffield Society for Constitutional Information, *Proceedings of the Public Meeting, held at Sheffield in the Open Air, on 7 April 1794*. Sheffield: 1794.

Society of the Friends of the People. *At a General Meeting of the Society established on the 11th instant, under the Title of the Friends of the People , associated for the Purpose of obtaining a Parliamentary Reform*. 1792.

Proceedings of the Society of Friends of the People; associated for the purpose of obtaining a Parliamentary reform. 1792.

A Song sung at the Anniversary of the Revolution of 1688, held at the London Tavern, Nov. 5., 1792. Tune, "How imperfect is expression". Single sheet.

The Songster's Companion. A choice collection of more than two hundred songs, . . . To which is added, a selection of toasts and sentiments, 5th edn. Coventry: [1791?].

A Speech at the Whig Club; or, A Great Statesman's Own Exposition of his Political Principles. 1793.

Stanhope, Charles, Earl, *Substance of Earl Stanhope's speech, delivered from the chair, at a meeting of citizens, at the Crown and Anchor, on the 4th of February 1795*. 1795.

Stephens, Alexander. *Memoirs of John Horne Tooke: Interspersed with Original Documents*. 2 vols. 1813.

'Stephensiana. No. VI.' *Monthly Magazine*, 53 (1822): 138–42.

'Stephensiana. No. XIV.' *Monthly Magazine*, 54 (1822): 425–8.

Taylor, John. *Records of My Life*. 2 vols. 1832.

Thelwall, John. *The Daughter of Adoption: A Tale of Modern Times*. Ed. Michael Scrivener, Yasmin Solomonescu, and Judith Thompson. Peterborough, ON: Broadview Press, 2013.

'Incle and Yarico' and 'The Incas', ed. Frank Felsenstein and Michael Scrivener. Madison. Farleigh Dickinson University Press. 2006.

The Natural and Constitutional Right of Britons to annual Parliaments, Universal Suffrage, and the freedom of popular Association. 1795.

Ode to science. Recited at the anniversary meeting of the Philomathian Society, June 20, 1791. 1791.

The Peripatetic; or, sketches of the heart, of nature and society; in a series of politico-sentimental journals, in verse and prose, of the eccentric excursions of Sylvanus Theophrastus... 3 vols. 1793.

The Peripatetic, ed. Judith Thompson. Detroit: Wayne State University Press, 2001.

Political lectures (no. I.) On the moral tendency of a system of spies and informers, and the conduct to be observed by the friends of liberty ... 1794

Political lectures. Volume the first - part the first: containing the lecture on spies and informers, and the first lecture on prosecutions for political opinion. To which is prefixed a narrative of facts relative to the recent attempts to wrest from the people the palladium of their natural and constitutional rights. liberty of speech [??]

Political lectures, (no. II.) Sketches of the history of prosecutions for political opinion; with strictures on the late proceedings of the court ... 1794.

Poems written Chiefly in Retirement, 2nd edn. Hereford, 1802.

Poems written in Close Confinement in the Tower and Newgate, under a charge of high treason. 1795.

The Rights of Nature, against the Usurpations of Establishments. A Series of Letters to the People of Britain, on ... Public Affairs, and the Recent Effusions of the Right Honourable Edmund Burke, 2nd edn. 1796.

Sober Reflections on the Seditious and Inflammatory Letter of the Right Hon. Edmund Burke, to a Noble Lord, 2nd edn. 1796.

The Speeches of Pierre and Jaeleir, extracted from VENICE PRESERVED [1793?].

Mr Thelwall's Letter to Francis Jeffray, Esq. on Certain calumnies and misrepresentations in the Edinburgh Review. Edinburgh: 1804.

Mr. Thelwall's reply to the calumnies, misrepresentations, and literary forgeries, contained in the anonymous observations on his Letter to the Editor of the Edinburgh Review. Glasgow: 1804.

The Tribune. 3 vols. 1795–6.

Thelwall, Mrs [Henrietta Cecil], *The Life of John Thelwall, by his Widow*, Vol. I [Volume 2 was never published]. 1837.

Thomson, Robert. *Burke's Address to the Swinish Multitude*. [1792?]. Single sheet.

The Divine Authority of the Bible, in Answer to Paine's Age of Reason. 1801.

A New song, to an old tune,-viz. "God save the king." [1792]. Single sheet.

A Tribute to Liberty: or, A New Collection of Patriotic Songs; entirely Original to which are added the Most Select Songs which have lately appeared in Public; ... together with a Collection of Toasts and Sentiments sacred to the Rights of Man. 1793 [1792?].

Whitehall Alarm'd! and a Council Called! [1792?]. Single sheet.

The Toast Master, being a Genteel Collection of Sentiments and Toasts, calculated for the most Polite Circles to heighten Social Mirth and to add fresh Charms to the cheerful Glass, new edn. 1792.

Trials for Treason and Sedition, 1792–1794, ed. John Barrell and Jon Mee. 8 vols. Pickering & Chatto, 2006–7.

[Turner, David]. *A Short History of the Westminster Forum: containing some Remarks upon the Laws; where in the Nature of such Societies is Examined.* 2 vols. 1781.

United Friends of Religious and Civil Liberty. *The united friends of religious and civil liberty, associated for the purpose of obtaining universal suffrage and annual parliaments.* 1795.

The Voice of the People, &c Consisting of Extracts from Pigott, Gerrald, &c. 1795.

Wakefield, Gilbert. *The Spirit of Christianity compared with the Spirit of the Times in Great Britain.* 1794

A warning to judges and jurors on state trials; being an abstract from an ancient Lilliputian chronicle; which shews how a chief justice was executed . . ., and how the Grand Vizir afterwards hanged himself in despair. [1795]

Warning to Tyrants, Consisting of Extracts from Pigott, Gerrald, &c. 1795.

Watson, Robert. *The life of Lord George Gordon: with a philosophical review of his political conduct.* 1795.

[Wells, Becky.] *Memoirs of the Late Mrs Sumbel, Late Wells, Written by Herself.* 2 vols. 1811.

Wharton, John. *The Speech of John Wharton, Esq. M.P. . . . on his Motion on the Constitution.* 1793.

Wheeler, James. *The Rose of Sharon: A Poem.* 1790.

The whim of the day, (for 1792.) Containing an entertaining selection of the choicest and most approved songs, now singing at the Theatres-Royal, the Anacreontic Society, the Beef-Steak Club . . . 1792.

The whole proceedings on the King's commission of the peace, Oyer and Terminer, and Gaol Delivery for the City of London; and also the gaol delivery for the county of Middlesex; held at Justice Hall in the Old Bailey, on Wednesday the 4th of December 1793 . . . 1793–4.

The Whole of The Proceedings at the Meeting of the Friends of the Liberty of the Press, at Free Masons' Tavern, on Saturday, December 22, 1792. [1793?].

Wilde, John. *An Address to the Lately Formed Society of the Friends of the People,* Edinburgh: 1793.

Williams, David. *Lessons to a young prince, by an old statesman, On the present disposition in Europe to a general revolution . . .*, 5th edn. 1790.

Letters on political liberty, and the principles of the English and Irish projects of reform . . ., 3rd edn. 1789.

Royal Recollections of a Tour to Cheltenham, Gloucester, Worcester, and Places Adjacent . . . 1788.

Observations sur la dernière constitution de la France, avec des vues sur la formation de la nouvelle constitution.

Wilson, Walter. *The History and Antiquities of Dissenting Churches and Meeting Houses in London, Westminster, and Southwark.* 4 vols. 1808–14.

Winterbotham, William. *An historical, geographical and philosophical view of the Chinese Empire; comprehending a description of the fifteen provinces of China* ... 2 vols. Philadelphia, PA: 1796.

A Selection of Poems Sacred and Moral. 2 vols. 1797.

The Wrongs of Man, &c Consisting of Extracts from PIGOTT's Political Dictionary, &c. 1795.

Yorke, Henry Redhead. *Thoughts on Civil Government addressed to the disenfranchised Citizens of Sheffield.* 1794.

The Trial of Henry Yorke, for a Conspiracy, &c. before the Hon. Mr. Justice Rooke, at the assizes held for the county of York, on Saturday, July 10, 1795. York: [1796].

Secondary works

Adams, M. Ray. 'Della Cruscanism in America'. *PMLA*, 79 (1964): 259–65.

Alexander, David. *Richard Newton and English Caricature in the 1790s.* Manchester University Press, 1998.

Alger, J. G. *Englishmen in the French Revolutions.* Low, Marston, Searle & Rivington, 1889.

Paris in 1789–94: Farewell Letters of Victims of the Guillotine. George Allen, 1902.

Allan, David. *A Nation of Readers: The Lending Library in Georgian England.* London: British Library, 2008.

Anderson, Benedict. *Imagined Communities: Reflections on the Origins and Spread of Nationalism*, rev. edn. Verso, 1991.

Andrew, Donna T. 'Popular Culture and Public Debate: London 1780', *Historical Journal*, 39 (1996): 405–23.

Arnold, Walter. *The Life and Death of the Sublime Society of the Beefsteaks*, Bradbury and Evans, 1871.

Aspinall, Arthur. *Politics and the Press c. 1780–1850.* Home and Van Tal, 1949.

Barker, Hannah. *Newspapers, Politics, and Public Opinion in Late Eighteenth Century England.* Oxford University Press, 1998.

Barrell, John. '"An Entire Change of Performances?" The Politicisation of Theatre and the Theatricalisation of Politics in the mid 1790s,' *Lumen*, 17 (1998): 11–50.

Imagining the King's Death: Figurative Treason, Fantasies of Regicide 1793–1796. Oxford University Press, 2000.

'Rus in urbe', in *Romanticism and Popular Culture in Britain and Ireland*, ed. Philip Connell and Nigel Leask, 109–127. Cambridge University Press, 2009.

The Spirit of Despotism: Invasions of Privacy in the 1790s. Oxford University Press, 2006.

Barrell, John, and Harriet Guest. 'Thomson in the 1790s', in *James Thomson: Essays for the Tercentenary*, ed. Richard Terry, 217–46. Liverpool University Press, 2000.

Bewley, Christina. *Muir of Huntershill.* Oxford University Press, 1981.

Bewley, Christina and David Bewley. *Gentleman Radical: The Life of John Horne Tooke, 1736–1812*. Tauris, 1998.

Black, Robert. *The Jockey Club and its Founders*. 1896.

Bradley, James E. *Religion, Revolution, and English Radicalism: Nonconformity In Eighteenth-century Politics and Society*. Cambridge University Press, 1990.

Bonnett, Alastair, and Keith Armstrong, eds. *Thomas Spence: The Poor Man's Revolutionary*. Breviary Stuff Publication, 2014.

Brewer, John. 'Commercialization and Politics', in *The Birth of a Consumer Society: The Commercialization of Eighteenth-Century England*, ed. N. McKendrick *et al.*, 197–262. Bloomington, IN: Indiana University Press, 1982.

Bugg, John. *Five Long Winters: The Trials of British Romanticism*. Stanford University Press, 2013.

'The Other Interesting Narrative: Olaudah Equiano's Public Book Tour,' *PMLA*, 121 (2006): 1422–42.

Cannon, John. *Parliamentary Reform, 1640–1832*. Cambridge University Press, 1973.

de Certeau, Michel. *The Practice of Everyday Life*. Berkeley, CA: University of California Press, 1984.

Chalus, Elaine. *Elite Women in English Political Life c. 1754–1790*. Oxford University Press, 2005.

Chase, Malcolm. *The People's Farm: English Radical Agrarianism 1775–1840*. Oxford University Press, 1988.

Chernock, Arianne. *Men and the Making of Modern British Feminism*. Stanford University Press, 2010.

Clark, Anna. *The Struggle for the Breeches: Gender and the Making of the British Working Class*. Berkeley, CA: University of California Press, 1995.

Clark, Peter. *British Clubs and Societies 1580–1800: The Origins of an Associational World*. Oxford University Press, 2000.

Clayden, P. W. *The Early Life of Samuel Rogers*. Smith, Elder and Co., 1887.

Colson, Percy. *The Strange History of Lord George Gordon*. R. Hale, 1937.

Corfield, Penelope J. 'Class by Name and Number in Eighteenth–century Britain', in *Language, History and Class*, ed. Penelope J. Corfield, 101–30. Oxford: Basil Blackwell, 1991.

Corfield, Penelope J. and Chris Evans. *Youth and Revolution in the 1790s: Letters of William Pattison, Thomas Amyot and Henry Crabb Robinson*. Stroud: Alan Sutton, 1996.

Cotlar, Seth. *Tom Paine's America: The Rise and Fall of Transatlantic Radicalism in the Early Republic*. Charlottesville VA: University of Virginia Press, 2011.

Crosby, 'The Voice of Flattery vs Sober Truth: William Godwin, Thomas Erskine and the 1792 Trial of Thomas Paine for Sedition', *Review of English Studies*, 62 (2010): 90–112.

Critchley, Macdonald, ed. *James Parkinson (1755–1824): A Bicentenary Volume of Papers dealing with Parkinson's Disease*. Macmillan, 1955.

Dart, Gregory. *Rousseau, Robespierre, and English Romanticism*. Cambridge University Press, 1999.

Davis, Michael T. 'Behold the Man: The Life, Times and Circle of Daniel Isaac Eaton, 1753 – 1814', PhD dissertation, University of Queensland, 1995.

'"An Evening of Pleasure Rather than Business": Songs, Subversion and Radical Sub-Culture in the 1790s', *Journal for the Study of British Cultures*, 12 (2005): 115–26.

'"The Mob Club?" The London Corresponding Society and the Politics of Civility in the 1790s', in *Unrespectable Radicals? Popular Politics in the Age of Reform*, ed. Davis and Paul A. Pickering, 21–40. Ashgate: Aldershot, 2008.

'"That Odious Class of Men Called Democrats": Daniel Isaac Eaton and the Romantics 1794–1795', *History*, 84 (1999): 73–92.

Davies, Hywel M. *Transatlantic Brethren: Rev. Samuel Jones (1735–1814) and his Friends: Baptists in Wales, Pennsylvannia, and Beyond.* Bethlehem, PA: Lehigh University Press, 1995.

Dickinson, H. T. *Liberty and Property: Political Ideology in Eighteenth Century Britain.* Taylor and Francis, 1977.

Douglas, Jane. 'Citizen Lee and the Tree of Liberty', *Factotum*, 7 (1979), 8–11.

Duchan, Judith. 'The Conceptual Underpinnings of John Thelwall's Elocutionary Practices', in *John Thelwall: Radical Romantic and Acquitted Felon*, ed. Poole, 139–45.

Duffy, Edward. *Rousseau in England: The Context for Shelley's Critique of Enlightenment.* Berkeley, CA: University of California Press, 1979.

Durey, Michael. *Transatlantic Radicals and the Early American Republic.* Lawrence, KS: University Press of Kansas, 1997.

'William Winterbotham's Trumpet of Sedition: Religious Dissent and Political Radicalism in the 1790s', *Journal of Religious History*, 19 (1995): 141–57.

Dybikowski, J. *On Burning Ground: An Examination of the Ideas, Projects and Life of David Williams.* Oxford: Voltaire Foundation, 1993.

Eagleton, Terry. *The Function of Criticism, from The Spectator to Post-Structuralism.* Verso, 1984.

Eley, Geoff. *A Crooked Line: From Cultural History to the History of Society.* Ann Arbor, MI: University of Michigan Press, 2005.

'Nations, Publics, and Political Cultures: Placing Habermas in the Nineteenth Century', in *Habermas and the Public Sphere*, ed. Craig Calhoun, 289–339, Cambridge, MA: MIT Press, 1996.

Emsley, Clive. 'An Aspect of Pitt's "terror": Prosecutions for Sedition during the 1790s', *Social History*, 6 (1981): 155–84.

'Repression, Terror and the Rule of Law in England during the Decade of Revolution', *English Historical Review*, 100 (1985): 801–25.

Epstein, James '"Equality and No King": Sociability and Sedition: The Case of John Frost', in *Romantic Sociability: Social Networks and Literary Culture in Britain, 1770–1840*, ed. Gillian Russell and Clara Tuite, 43–61. Cambridge University Press, 2006.

'"Our Real Constitution": Trial Defence and Radical Memory in the Age of Revolution', in *Re-reading the Constitution: New Narratives in the Political History of England's Long Nineteenth Century*, ed. James Vernon, 22–51. Cambridge University Press, 1996.

Radical Expression: Political Language, Ritual, and Symbol in England, 1790–1850. Oxford University Press, 1994.
'Spatial Practices/Democratic Vistas', *Social History*, 24 (1999): 294–310.
Epstein, James and David Karr. 'Playing at Revolution: British "Jacobin" Performance', *Journal of Modern History*, 79 (2007): 495–530.
Erdman, David V. *Commerce des Lumières: John Oswald and the British in Paris, 1790–1793*. Columbia, MO: University of Missouri Press, 1986.
Fallon, David. 'Booksellers in the Godwin Diaries', *Bodleian Library Record*, 24 (2011): 25–34.
Fairclough, Mary. *The Romantic Crowd: Sympathy, Controversy and Print Culture*. Cambridge University Press, 2013.
Featherstone, David. 'The Spaces of Politics of the London Corresponding Society', *Journal of Historical Geography*, 30 (2004): 783–91.
Fleming, Tara-Lyn. 'Tracing the Textual Reverberation: The Role of Thelwall's Elocutionary Selections in the British Lyceum', in *John Thelwall: Radical Romantic and Acquitted Felon*, ed. Poole, 147–60.
Fraser, Nancy. 'Rethinking the Public Sphere: A Contribution to the Critique of Actually Existing Democracy', in *Habermas and the Public Sphere*, ed. Craig Calhoun, 109–42. Cambridge, MA: MIT Press, 1996.
Gatrell, Vic. *City of Laughter: Sex and Satire in Eighteenth-century London*. Atlantic Books, 2006.
Gagnier, Regenia. *Subjectivities: A History of Self-Representation in Britain, 1832–1920*. Oxford University Press, 1991.
Garnai, Amy. 'An Exile on the Coast: Robert Merry's Transatlantic Journey, 1796–1798', *Review of English Studies*, 64 (2013): 87–104.
Gibbs, Warren E. 'An Unpublished Letter from John Thelwall to S. T. Coleridge', *Modern Language Review*, 25 (1930): 85–90.
Gilmartin, Kevin. *Print Politics: The Press and Radical Opposition in Early Nineteenth-Century England*. Cambridge University Press, 1996.
Writing against Revolution: Literary Conservatism in Britain, 1790–1832 Cambridge University Press, 2007.
Ginter, Donald E. 'The Financing of the Whig Party Organization', *American Historical Review*, 71 (1966): 433–9.
Goodrich, Amanda. 'Radical "Citizens of the World," 1790–95: The Early Career of Henry Redhead Yorke', *Journal of British Studies*, 53 (2014): 611–35.
Goodwin, Albert. *The Friends of Liberty: The English Democratic Movement in the Age of the French Revolution*. Hutchinson, 1979.
Grande, James. 'The Roots of Godwinian Radicalism: Norfolk Dissent in the Diary', *Bodleian Library Record*, 24 (2011): 35–43.
Green, Georgina. *The Majesty of the People: Popular Sovereignty and the Role of the Writer in the 1790s*. Oxford University Press, 2014.
Griswold, Rufus W. *The Poets and Poetry of America*, 7th edn. Philadelphia, PA: Carey and Hart, 1856.
Guest, Harriet. *Unbounded Attachment: Sentiment and Politics in the Age of the French Revolution*. Oxford University Press, 2013.

Habermas, Jürgen. *The Structural Transformation of the Public Sphere: An Inquiry Into a Category of Bourgeois Society*, transl. Thomas Burger with the assistance of Frederick Lawrence. Cambridge MA: MIT Press, 1991.

Haig, Robert L. *The Gazetteer 1735–1797*. Carbondale, IL: Sth Illinois University Press, 1960.

Hammersley, Rachel. 'Spence's *Property in Land Every One's Right*: Problems and Solutions', in *Thomas Spence: The Poor Man's Revolutionary*, ed. Bonnett and Armstrong, 35–52.

Hampsher-Monk, Iain. 'Civic Humanism and Parliamentary Reform: The Case of the Society of the Friends of the People', *Journal of British Studies*, 18 (1979): 70–89.

'On Not Inventing the English Revolution: The Radical Failure of the 1790s as Linguistic Non-Performance', in *English Radicalism, 1550–1850*, ed. Glenn Burgess and Matthew Festenstein, 135–56. Cambridge University Press, 2007.

Hargreaves-Mawdsley, W. N. *The English Della Cruscans and their Time, 1783–1828*. The Hague: Martinus Nijhoff, 1967.

Harling, Philip. 'The Law of Libel and the Limits of Repression, 1790–1832', *Historical Journal*, 44 (2001): 107–34.

Harris, Bob. 'Scottish-English Connections in British Radicalism in the 1790s', in *Anglo-Scottish Relations from 1603 to 1900*, ed. T. C. Smout, 189–212. Oxford University Press for the British Academy, 2005.

Hatfield, E. F. *The Poets of the Church*. Randolph, 1884.

Honeyman Valerie. 'That ye may judge for yourselves: The Contribution of Scottish Presbyterianism towards the Emergence of Political or Awareness amongst Ordinary People in Scotland between 1746 and 1792'. PhD thesis, University of Stirling, 2012.

Horgan, Kate. *The Politics of Songs in Eighteenth-Century Britain, 1723–1795*. Pickering & Chatto, 2014.

Huzzey, Richard. 'The Moral Geography of British Anti-slavery Responsibilities', *Transactions of the Royal Historical Society*, 22 (2012): 111–39.

Inston, Kevin. 'Representing the Unrepresentable: Rousseau's Legislator and the Impossible Object of the People', *Contemporary Political Theory*, 9 (2010): 393–413.

Johnston, Kenneth R. *Unusual Suspects: Pitt's Reign of Alarm and the Lost Generation of the 1790s*. Oxford University Press, 2013.

Jones, Brad. '"In Favour of Popery": Patriotism, Protestantism, and the Gordon Riots in the Revolutionary British Atlantic', *Journal of British Studies*, 52 (2013): 79–102.

Jones, Whitney R. D. *David Williams: The Anvil & the Hammer*. Tuscaloosa, AL: University of Alabama Press, 1986.

Keen, Paul. *The Crisis of Literature in the 1790s: Print Culture and the Public Sphere*. Cambridge University Press, 1999.

Keane, John: *Tom Paine: A Political Life*. Bloomsbury, 1995.

Knights, Mark. 'The 1780 Protestant Petitions and the Culture of Petitioning', in *The Gordon Riots: Politics, Culture and Insurrection in Late Eighteenth-century Britain*, ed. Ian Haywood and John Seed, 46–68. Cambridge University Press, 2012.

'Participation and Representation before Democracy: Petitions and Addresses in Premodern Britain', in *Political Representation*, ed. Ian Shapiro *et al.*, 15–57. Cambridge University Press 2009.

Knott, Sarah. 'Female Liberty? Sentimental Gallantry, Republican Womanhood, and Rights Feminism in the Age of Revolutions', *William and Mary Quarterly*, 7 (2014): 425–56.

Kropf, C. R. 'Libel and Satire in the Eighteenth Century', *Eighteenth-Century Studies*, 8 (1974–5):153–68.

Laclau, Ernesto. *On Populist Reason*. Verso, 2005.

Lefebvre, Henri. *The Production of Space*, trans. D. Nicholson-Smith. Oxford: Blackwell, 1996.

Lévy-Bruhl, Lucien. *How Natives Think*, trans. Lilian A. Clare. New York, NY: Washington Square Press, 1966 rpt.

Linebaugh, Peter and Marcus Rediker. *The Many-Headed Hydra: Sailors, Slaves, Commoners and the Hidden History of the Revolutionary Atlantic*. Boston, MA: Beacon Press, 2000.

Lottes, Günther. 'Radicalism, Revolution, and Political Culture: An Anglo-French Comparison', in *The French Revolution and British Popular Politics*, ed. Mark Philp, 78–98. Cambridge University Press, 1991.

Loughlin, Martin. 'Constituent Power Subverted: From English Constitutional Argument to British Constitutional Practice', in *The Paradox of Constitutionalism: Constituent Power and Constitutional Form*, ed. Loughlin and Walker, 27–49. Oxford University Press, 2008.

McCalman, Iain. 'The Infidel as Prophet: William Hamilton Reid and Blakean Radicalism', in *Historicizing Blake*, ed. Steve Clark and David Worrall, 24–42. Macmillan, 1994.

'Newgate in Revolution: Radical Enthusiasm and Romantic Counterculture', *Eighteenth Century Life*, 22 (1998): 95–110.

'Prophesying Revolution: Lord George Gordon, Edmund Burke and Madame la Motte', in *Learning and Living: Essays in Honour of John Harrison*, ed. Ian Dyck and Malcom Chase. Aldershot: 1996.

Radical Underworld: Prophets, Revolutionaries and Pornographers in London, 1795–1840. Cambridge University Press, 1988.

McCann, Andrew. *Cultural Politics in the 1790s: Literature, Radicalism and the Public Sphere*. Basingstoke: Macmillan, 1999.

Macdonald, Simon. 'English-Language Newspapers in Revolutionary France', *Journal for Eighteenth-Century Studies*, 36 (2013): 17–33.

McCue, Daniel. 'Daniel Isaac Eaton and Politics for the People'. PhD dissertation, Columbia University, 1974.

McKenzie, D. F. 'Printers of the Mind: Some Notes on Bibliographical Theories and Printing-House Practices', *Studies in Bibliography*, 22 (1969): 1–76.

Makdisi, Saree. *Making England Western: Occidentalism, Race and Imperial Culture*. University of Chicago Press, 2014.

Malinowski, Bronisław. *Magic, Science and Religion and other Essays*. Garden City, NY: Doubleday Anchor Books, 1954.

Manogue, Ralph A. 'The Plight of James Ridgway, London Bookseller and Publisher, and the Newgate Radicals, 1792–1797', *Wordsworth Circle*, 27 (1996): 158–66.

Mee, Jon. '"A Bold and Outspoken Man": The Strange Career of Charles Pigott II'. In *Cultures of Whiggism: New Essays on English Literature and Culture in the Long Eighteenth Century*, ed. David Womersley, 330–50. Newark, DE: University of Delaware Press, 2005.

Conversable Worlds: Literature, Contention, and Community 1762–1830. Oxford University Press, 2011.

"'The Dungeon and the Cell' in *John Thelwall: Radical Romantic and Acquitted Felon*, ed. Poole, 95–106.

'"Examples of Safe Printing": Censorship and Popular Radical Literature in the 1790s', in *Literature and Censorship*, ed. Nigel Smith, 81–95. D. S. Brewer, 1993.

'Is there an Antinomian in the House? William Blake and the After-Life of a Heresy', in *Historicizing Blake*, ed. Steve Clark and David Worrall, 43–58. Houndmills: Palgrave Macmillan, 1994.

'Libertines and Radicals in the 1790s: The Strange Case of Charles Pigott I', in *Libertine Enlightenment: Sex, Liberty and Licence in the Eighteenth Century*, ed. Peter Cryle and Lisa O'Connell, 183–203. Houndmills: Palgrave, 2004.

'Morals, Manners, and Liberty: British Radicals and Perceptions of America in the 1790s', in *The American Experiment and the Idea of Democracy in British Culture, 1776–1914*, ed. Ella Dzelainis and Ruth Livesey, 31–43. Farnham: Ashgate, 2013.

'Policing Enthusiasm in the Romantic Period: Literary Periodicals and the "Rational" Public Sphere', in *Spheres of Influence: Intellectual and Cultural Publics from Shakespeare to Habermas*, ed. Alex Benichimol and Willy Maley, 175–95. Peter Lang, 2007.

'"The Press and Danger of the Crowd": Godwin, Thelwall and the Counter-Public Sphere', in *Godwinian Moments: From Enlightenment to Romanticism*, ed. Robert Maniquis and Victoria Myers, 83–102. University of Toronto Press, 2011.

'Popular Radical Culture', in *The Cambridge Companion to British Literature of the French Revolution in the 1790s*, ed. Pamela Clemit, 117–28. Cambridge University Press, 2011.

'"Reciprocal Expressions of Kindness": Robert Merry at the Limits of Sociability', in *Romantic Sociability: Social Networks and Literary Culture in Britain, 1770–1840*, ed. Gillian Russell and Clara Tuite, 104–122. Cambridge University Press, 2002.

Romanticism, Enthusiasm, and Regulation: Poetics and the Policing of Culture in the Romantic Period. Oxford University Press, 2003.

'The Strange Career of Richard "Citizen" Lee', in *British Literary Radicalism, 1650–1830: From Revolution to Revolution*, ed. Timothy Morton and Nigel Smith, 151–66. Cambridge University Press, 2002.

Moran, James. *Printing Presses: History and Development from the Fifteenth Century to Modern Times*. Berkeley, CA: University of California Press, 1978.

Mosley, James. 'The Technologies of Print', in *The Cambridge History of the Book in Britain*, Vol. 5, *1695–1830*, ed. Michael F. Suarez and Michael L. Turner, 163–69. Cambridge University Press, 2009.

Mulvihill, James. *Notorious Facts: Publicity in Romantic England, 1780–1830*. Newark, DE: University of Delaware Press, 2011.

Negri, Antonio. *Insurgencies: Constituent Power and the Modern State*, trans. M. Boscagli, ed. S. Buckley *et al.* Minneapolis, MN: University of Minnesota Press, 1999.

Negt, Oskar and Alexander Kluge. *Public Sphere and Experience: Towards an Analysis of the Bourgeois and Proletarian Public Sphere*, trans. Peter Labanyi *et al.* Minneapolis, MN: University of Minnesota Press, 1993.

Newman, Ian. 'Civilizing Taste: "Sandman Joe", the Bawdy Ballad, and Metropolitan Improvement.' *Eighteenth-Century Studies*, 48 (215): 437–56.

'Edmund Burke in the Tavern', *European Romantic Review*, 24 (2013): 125–48.

O'Gorman, Frank. *Voters, Patrons and Parties: The Unreformed Electorate of Hanoverian England, 1734–1832*. Oxford University Press, 1989.

Oldfield, J. R. *Popular Politics and British Anti-slavery: The Mobilisation of Public Opinion against the Slave Trade, 1787–1807*. Manchester University Press, 1995.

O'Shaughnessy, David. '*Caleb Williams* and the Philomaths: Recalibrating Political Justice for the Nineteenth Century', *Nineteenth-Century Literature*, 66 (2012): 423–48.

Parolin, Christina. *Radical Spaces: Venues of Popular Politics in London 1790-c. 1845*. Canberra: Australian National University Press, 2010.

Parssinen, T. M. 'Association, Convention, and Anti-parliament in British Radical Politics, 1771–1848', *English Historical Review*, 88 (1973): 504–33.

Philp, Mark. 'Paine, Rights of Man, 1791–2', in *The Cambridge Companion to British Literature of the French Revolution in the 1790s*, ed. Pamela Clemit, 31–46.

Reforming Ideas in Britain: Politics and Language in the Shadow of the French Revolution, 1789–1815. Cambridge University Press, 2014.

Pole, J. R. *Political Representation in England and the Origins of the American Republic*. Macmillan, 1960.

Poole, Steve. 'Pitt's Terror Reconsidered: Jacobinism and the Law in Two South-western Counties, 1791–1803', *Southern History*, 17 (1995): 65–87.

Ed. *John Thelwall: Radical Romantic and Acquitted Felon*. Pickering and Chatto, 2009.

Price, Leah. *How to Do Things with Books in Victorian Britain*. Princeton University Press, 2012.

Priestman, Martin. *Romantic Atheism: Poetry and Freethought, 1780–1830*. Cambridge University Press, 2006.

Rancière, Jacques. *Nights of Labour: The Workers' Dream in Nineteenth-Century France*, trans. John Drury. Philadelphia PA: Temple University Press, 1989.

Raven, James. *The Business of Books: Booksellers and the English Book Trade*. Oxford University Press, 2007.

Rendall, Jane. 'The "Political Reveries" of Alexander Jardine (1739?-1799)', in *Enlightenment and Revolution: Essays in Honour of Norman Hampson*, ed. Malcolm Crook *et al.*, 90–113. Farnham: Ashgate, 2004.

Roe, Michael. 'Maurice Margarot: Radical in Two Hemispheres, 1792–1815', *Historical Research*, 31 (1958): 68–78.

Rogers, Nicholas. 'Pigott's Private Eye: Radicalism and Scandal in Eighteenth-Century England', *Journal of the Canadian Historical Association*, 4 (1993): 247–63.

Rogers, Rachel. '*Vectors of Revolution: The British Radical Community in Early Republican Paris, 1792–1794*'. PhD dissertation, Université Toulouse Le Mirail, 2012.

Rose, Jonathan. *The Intellectual Life of the British Working Classes*. New Haven CT: Yale University Press, 2001.

St Clair, William. *The Reading Nation in the Romantic Period*. Cambridge University Press, 2004.

Scrivener, Michael. 'John Thelwall and the Revolution of 1649', in *Radicalism in British Literary Culture: From Revolution to Revolution*, ed. Nigel Smith and Timothy Morton, 119–32. Cambridge University Press, 2002.

'The Philosopher and the Moneylender: The Relationship between William Godwin and John King', in *Godwinian Moments: From the Enlightenment to Romanticism*, ed. Robert M. Maniquis and Victoria Myers, 241–60. University of Toronto Press, 2011.

'The Rhetoric and Context of Thelwall's Memoir', in *Spirits Of Fire: English Romantic Writers and Historical Methods*, ed. G. A. Rosso and D. P. Watkins, 112–30. Madison NJ: Farleigh Dickinson University Press, 1990.

Seditious Allegories: John Thelwall and Jacobin Writing. University Park PA: Pennsylvania University Press, 2001.

Seed, John. '"The Fall of Romish Babylon Anticipated": Plebean Dissenters and anti-popery in the Gordon Riots', in *The Gordon Riots: Politics, Culture and Insurrection in Late Eighteenth-century Britain*, ed. Ian Haywood and John Seed, 69–92. Cambridge University Press, 2012.

Sennet, Richard. *The Fall of Public Man: On the Social Psychology of Capitalism*. Cambridge University Press, 1978.

Siskin, Clifford, and William Warner. 'This is Enlightenment: An Invitation in the Form of an Argument', in *This is Enlightenment*, ed. Siskin and Warner. University of Chicago Press, 2009.

Smith, Martin John. 'English Radical Newspapers in the French Revolution Era 1790–1803'. PhD dissertation, University of London, 1979.

Smith, Olivia, *The Politics of Language 1791–1819*. Oxford University Press, 1984.

Solomonescu, Yasmin. *John Thelwall and the Materialist Imagination.* Houndmills: Palgrave Macmillan, 2014.

Steedman, Carolyn. *Dust: The Archive and Cultural History.* Manchester University Press, 2001.

An Everyday Life of the English Working Class: Work, Self, and Sociability in the Early Nineteenth Century. Cambridge University Press, 2013.

Suarez, Michael F. S. J. 'Towards a bibliometric analysis of the surviving record, 1701–1800', in *The Cambridge History of the Book.* Vol. 5, *1695–1830*, ed. Suarez and Michael L. Turner, 39–65. Cambridge University Press, 2009.

Swindells, Julia. *Glorious Causes: The Grand Theatre of Political Change, 1789 to 1833.* Oxford University Press, 2001.

Taylor, George. *The French Revolution and the London Stage.* Cambridge University Press, 2000.

Thale, Mary. 'London Debating Societies in the 1790s', *Historical Journal*, 32 (1989): 57–86.

'Women in London Debating Societies in 1780', *Gender & History*, 7 (1995): 5–24.

Thompson, E. P. *The Making of the English Working Class*, rev. edn. Harmondsworth: Penguin, 1968.

The Romantics: England in a Revolutionary Age. New York, NY: The New Press, 1997.

Thompson, Judith. 'From Forum to Repository: A Case Study in Romantic Cultural Geography', *European Romantic Review*, 15 (2004): 177–91.

John Thelwall in the Wordsworth Circle: The Silenced Partner. Houndmills: Palgrave Macmillan, 2012.

Twomey, Richard J. *Jacobins and Jeffersonians: Anglo-American Radicalism in the United States 1790–1820.* New York, NY: Garland Publishing, 1989.

Vincent, David. *Literacy and Popular Culture: England 1750–1914.* Cambridge University Press, 1989

Wagner, Corinna. 'Domestic Invasions: John Thelwall and the Exploitation of Privacy', in *John Thelwall: Radical Romantic and Acquitted Felon*, ed. Poole, 95–106.

Wahrman, Dror. *Imagining the Middle Class: The Political Representation of Class in Britain, c. 1780–1840.* Cambridge University Press, 1995.

Walsh, John. '"Methodism" and the Origins of English Speaking Evangelicalism', in *Evangelicalism: Comparative Studies of Popular Protestantism in N. America, the British Isles, and Beyond, 1700–1900*, ed. Mark A. Noll, David W. Bebbington, and George A. Rawlyk, 19–37. Oxford University Press, 1994.

Walvin, James. *An African's Life: The Life and Times of Olaudah Equiano, 1745–1797.* Continuum, 1998.

'The Impact of Slavery on British Radical Politics: 1787–1838', *Annals of the New York Academy of Sciences*, 292 (1977): 343–55.

Making the Black Atlantic. Cassell, 2000.

Warner, Michael. *The Letters of the Republic: Publication and the Public Sphere in Eighteenth-century America.* Cambridge, MA: Harvard University Press, 1990.

Publics and Counterpublics. New York, NY: Zone Books, 2002.

Warner, William. 'Transmitting Liberty: The Boston Committee of Correspondence's Revolutionary Experiments in Enlightenment Mediation', in *This is Enlightenment*, ed. Siskin and Warner, 102–19.

Weinstein, Benjamin. 'Popular Constitutionalism and the London Corresponding Society', *Albion*, 34 (2002): 37–57.

Werkmeister, Lucyle. *The London Daily Press, 1772–1792*. Lincoln, NB: University of Nebraska Press, 1963.

A Newspaper History of England 1792–1793. Lincoln NB: University of Nebraska Press, 1967.

Whelan, Timothy. '"For the Hand of a Woman, has Levell'd the Blow": Maria de Fleury's Pamphlet War with William Huntington, 1787–1791', *Women's Studies*, 36 (2007): 431–54.

'William Fox, Martha Gurney, and Radical Discourse in the 1790s', *Eighteenth-century Studies*, 42 (2009): 397–411.

Whyman, Susan E. *The Pen and the People: English Letter Writers 1660–1800*. Oxford University Press, 2009.

Williams, Raymond. *Culture and Society, 1780–1950*. Harmondsworth: Penguin, 1958, 1984 rpt.

The Long Revolution. Harmondsworth: Penguin, 1961, 1984 rpt.

Keywords: A Vocabulary of Culture and Society, revised and expanded. Flamingo, 1983.

Marxism and Literature. Oxford University Press, 1977, 1985 rpt.

Wilson, Kathleen. *The Sense of the People: Politics, Culture, and Imperialism in England, 1715–1785*. Cambridge University Press, 1995.

Worrall, David. *The Politics of Romantic Theatricality, 1787–1832: The Road to the Stage*. Houndmills: Palgrave Macmillan, 2007.

Radical Culture: Discourse, Resistance and Surveillance, 1790–1820. Detroit, MI: Wayne State University Press, 1992.

Theatric Revolution: Drama, Censorship and Romantic Period Subcultures 1773–1832. Oxford University Press, 2009.

Young, Philip. *Revolutionary Ladies*. New York, NY: Knopf, 1977.

Yuval, Amnon. 'Between Heroism and Acquittal: Henry Redhead Yorke and the Inherent Instability of Political Trials in Britain during the 1790s', *Journal of British Studies*, 50 (2011): 612–38.

Online resoures

Dissenting Academies Online, Database and Encyclopedia at http://dissacad.english.qmul.ac.uk/

'William Godwin's Diary' at http://godwindiary.bodleian.ox.ac.uk/index2.html (all references to the diary are given by date in the main text)

Index

CAMBRIDGE STUDIES IN ROMANTICISM

General Editor
JAMES CHANDLER, *University of Chicago*

1. *Romantic Correspondence: Women, Politics and the Fiction of Letters*
MARY A. FAVRET

2. *British Romantic Writers and the East: Anxieties of Empire*
NIGEL LEASK

3. *Poetry as an Occupation and an Art in Britain, 1760–1830*
PETER MURPHY

4. *Edmund Burke's Aesthetic Ideology: Language, Gender and Political Economy in Revolution*
TOM FURNISS

5. *In the Theatre of Romanticism: Coleridge, Nationalism, Women*
JULIE A. CARLSON

6. *Keats, Narrative and Audience*
ANDREW BENNETT

7. *Romance and Revolution: Shelley and the Politics of a Genre*
DAVID DUFF

8. *Literature, Education, and Romanticism: Reading as Social Practice, 1780–1832*
ALAN RICHARDSON

9. *Women Writing about Money: Women's Fiction in England, 1790–1820*
EDWARD COPELAND

10. *Shelley and the Revolution in Taste: The Body and the Natural World*
TIMOTHY MORTON

11. *William Cobbett: The Politics of Style*
LEONORA NATTRASS

12. *The Rise of Supernatural Fiction, 1762–1800*
E. J. CLERY

13. *Women Travel Writers and the Language of Aesthetics, 1716–1818*
ELIZABETH A. BOHLS

14. *Napoleon and English Romanticism*
SIMON BAINBRIDGE

15. *Romantic Vagrancy: Wordsworth and the Simulation of Freedom*
CELESTE LANGAN

16. *Wordsworth and the Geologists*
JOHN WYATT

17. *Wordsworth's Pope: A Study in Literary Historiography*
ROBERT J. GRIFFIN

18. *The Politics of Sensibility: Race, Gender and Commerce in the Sentimental Novel*
MARKMAN ELLIS

19. *Reading Daughters' Fictions, 1709–1834: Novels and Society from Manley to Edgeworth*
CAROLINE GONDA

20. *Romantic Identities: Varieties of Subjectivity, 1774–1830*
ANDREA K. HENDERSON

21. *Print Politics: The Press and Radical Opposition: in Early Nineteenth-Century England*
KEVIN GILMARTIN

22. *Reinventing Allegory*
THERESA M. KELLEY

23. *British Satire and the Politics of Style, 1789–1832*
GARY DYER

24. *The Romantic Reformation: Religious Politics in English Literature, 1789–1824*
ROBERT M. RYAN

25. *De Quincey's Romanticism: Canonical Minority and the Forms of Transmission*
MARGARET RUSSETT

26. *Coleridge on Dreaming: Romanticism, Dreams and the Medical Imagination*
JENNIFER FORD

27. *Romantic Imperialism: Universal Empire and the Culture of Modernity*
SAREE MAKDISI

28. *Ideology and Utopia in the Poetry of William Blake*
NICHOLAS M. WILLIAMS

29. *Sexual Politics and the Romantic Author*
SONIA HOFKOSH

30. *Lyric and Labour in the Romantic Tradition*
ANNE JANOWITZ

31. *Poetry and Politics in the Cockney School: Keats, Shelley, Hunt and their Circle*
JEFFREY N. COX

32. *Rousseau, Robespierre and English Romanticism*
GREGORY DART

33. *Contesting the Gothic: Fiction, Genre and Cultural Conflict, 1764–1832*
JAMES WATT

34. *Romanticism, Aesthetics, and Nationalism*
DAVID ARAM KAISER

35. *Romantic Poets and the Culture of Posterity*
ANDREW BENNETT

36. *The Crisis of Literature in the 1790s: Print Culture and the Public Sphere*
PAUL KEEN

37. *Romantic Atheism: Poetry and Freethought, 1780–1830*
MARTIN PRIESTMAN

38. *Romanticism and Slave Narratives: Transatlantic Testimonies*
HELEN THOMAS

39. *Imagination under Pressure, 1789–1832: Aesthetics, Politics, and Utility*
JOHN WHALE

40. *Romanticism and the Gothic: Genre, Reception, and Canon Formation, 1790–1820*
MICHAEL GAMER

41. *Romanticism and the Human Sciences: Poetry, Population, and the Discourse of the Species*
MAUREEN N. MCLANE

42. *The Poetics of Spice: Romantic Consumerism and the Exotic*
TIMOTHY MORTON

43. *British Fiction and the Production of Social Order, 1740–1830*
MIRANDA J. BURGESS

44. *Women Writers and the English Nation in the 1790s*
ANGELA KEANE

45. *Literary Magazines and British Romanticism*
MARK PARKER

46. *Women, Nationalism and the Romantic Stage: Theatre and Politics in Britain, 1780–1800*
BETSY BOLTON

47. *British Romanticism and the Science of the Mind*
ALAN RICHARDSON

48. *The Anti-Jacobin Novel: British Conservatism and the French Revolution*
M. O. GRENBY

49. *Romantic Austen: Sexual Politics and the Literary Canon*
CLARA TUITE

50. *Byron and Romanticism*
JEROME MCGANN AND JAMES SODERHOLM

51. *The Romantic National Tale and the Question of Ireland*
INA FERRIS

52. *Byron, Poetics and History*
JANE STABLER

53. *Religion, Toleration, and British Writing, 1790–1830*
MARK CANUEL

54. *Fatal Women of Romanticism*
ADRIANA CRACIUN

55. *Knowledge and Indifference in English Romantic Prose*
TIM MILNES

56. *Mary Wollstonecraft and the Feminist Imagination*
BARBARA TAYLOR

57. *Romanticism, Maternity and the Body Politic*
JULIE KIPP

58. *Romanticism and Animal Rights*
DAVID PERKINS

59. *Georgic Modernity and British Romanticism: Poetry and the Mediation of History*
KEVIS GOODMAN

60. *Literature, Science and Exploration in the Romantic Era: Bodies of Knowledge*
TIMOTHY FULFORD, DEBBIE LEE, AND PETER J. KITSON

61. *Romantic Colonization and British Anti-Slavery*
DEIRDRE COLEMAN

62. *Anger, Revolution, and Romanticism*
ANDREW M. STAUFFER

63. *Shelley and the Revolutionary Sublime*
CIAN DUFFY

64. *Fictions and Fakes: Forging Romantic Authenticity, 1760–1845*
MARGARET RUSSETT

65. *Early Romanticism and Religious Dissent*
DANIEL E. WHITE

66. *The Invention of Evening: Perception and Time in Romantic Poetry*
CHRISTOPHER R. MILLER

67. *Wordsworth's Philosophic Song*
SIMON JARVIS

68. *Romanticism and the Rise of the Mass Public*
ANDREW FRANTA

69. *Writing against Revolution: Literary Conservatism in Britain, 1790–1832*
KEVIN GILMARTIN

70. *Women, Sociability and Theatre in Georgian London*
GILLIAN RUSSELL

71. *The Lake Poets and Professional Identity*
BRIAN GOLDBERG

72. *Wordsworth Writing*
ANDREW BENNETT

73. *Science and Sensation in Romantic Poetry*
NOEL JACKSON

74. *Advertising and Satirical Culture in the Romantic Period*
JOHN STRACHAN

75. *Romanticism and the Painful Pleasures of Modern Life*
ANDREA K. HENDERSON

76. *Balladeering, Minstrelsy, and the Making of British Romantic Poetry*
MAUREEN N. MCLANE

77. *Romanticism and Improvisation, 1750–1850*
ANGELA ESTERHAMMER

78. *Scotland and the Fictions of Geography: North Britain, 1760–1830*
PENNY FIELDING

79. *Wordsworth, Commodification and Social Concern: The Poetics of Modernity*
DAVID SIMPSON

80. *Sentimental Masculinity and the Rise of History, 1790–1890*
MIKE GOODE

81. *Fracture and Fragmentation in British Romanticism*
ALEXANDER REGIER

82. *Romanticism and Music Culture in Britain, 1770–1840: Virtue and Virtuosity*
GILLEN D'ARCY WOOD

83. *The Truth about Romanticism: Pragmatism and Idealism in Keats, Shelley, Coleridge*
TIM MILNES

84. *Blake's Gifts: Poetry and the Politics of Exchange*
SARAH HAGGARTY

85. *Real Money and Romanticism*
MATTHEW ROWLINSON

86. *Sentimental Literature and Anglo-Scottish Identity, 1745–1820*
JULIET SHIELDS

87. *Romantic Tragedies: The Dark Employments of Wordsworth, Coleridge, and Shelley*
REEVE PARKER

88. *Blake, Sexuality and Bourgeois Politeness*
SUSAN MATTHEWS

89. *Idleness, Contemplation and the Aesthetic*
RICHARD ADELMAN

90. *Shelley's Visual Imagination*
NANCY MOORE GOSLEE

91. *A Cultural History of the Irish Novel, 1790–1829*
CLAIRE CONNOLLY

92. *Literature, Commerce, and the Spectacle of Modernity, 1750–1800*
PAUL KEEN

93. *Romanticism and Childhood: The Infantilization of British Literary Culture*
ANN WEIRDA ROWLAND

94. *Metropolitan Art and Literature, 1810–1840: Cockney Adventures*
GREGORY DART

95. *Wordsworth and the Enlightenment Idea of Pleasure*
ROWAN BOYSON

96. *John Clare and Community*
JOHN GOODRIDGE

97. *The Romantic Crowd*
MARY FAIRCLOUGH

98. *Romantic Women Writers, Revolution and Prophecy*
ORIANNE SMITH

99. *Britain, France and the Gothic, 1764–1820*
ANGELA WRIGHT

100. *Transfiguring the Arts and Sciences*
JON KLANCHER

101. *Shelley and the Apprehension of Life*
ROSS WILSON

102. *Poetics of Character: Transatlantic Encounters 1700–1900*
SUSAN MANNING

103. *Romanticism and Caricature*
IAN HAYWOOD

104. *The Late Poetry of the Lake Poets: Romanticism Revised*
TIM FULFORD

105. *Forging Romantic China: Sino-British Cultural Exchange 1760–1840*
PETER J. KITSON

106. *Coleridge and the Philosophy of Poetic Form*
EWAN JAMES JONES

107. *Romanticism in the Shadow of War: Literary Culture in the Napoleonic War Years*
JEFFREY N. COX

108. *Slavery and the Politics of Place: Representing the Colonial Caribbean, 1770–1833*
ELIZABETH A. BOHLS

109. *The Orient and the Young Romantics*
ANDREW WARREN

110. *Lord Byron and Scandalous Celebrity*
CLARA TUITE

111. *Radical Orientalism: Rights, Reform, and Romanticism*
GERARD COHEN-VRIGNAUD

112. *Print, Publicity, and Popular Radicalism in the 1790s*
JON MEE

Lightning Source UK Ltd.
Milton Keynes UK
UKHW022107031119
352854UK00021B/452/P

9 781107 590083